Buffalo Soldiers in the West
A Black Soldiers Anthology

edited by
BRUCE A. GLASRUD
and
MICHAEL N. SEARLES

Texas A&M University Press

College Station, Texas

The paper used in this book meets the minimum requirements
of the American National Standard for Permanence
of Paper for Printed Library Materials, Z39.48-1984.
Binding materials have been chosen for durability.
∞ ♻

Library of Congress Cataloging-in-Publication Data

Buffalo soldiers in the West : a Black soldiers anthology / edited by Bruce A.
Glasrud and Michael N. Searles. — 1st ed.
    p. cm.
    Includes bibliographical references and index.
    ISBN-13: 978-1-58544-612-4 (cloth : alk. paper)
    ISBN-10: 1-58544-612-2 (cloth : alk. paper)
    ISBN-13: 978-1-58544-620-9 (pbk. : alk. paper)
    ISBN-10: 1-58544-620-3 (pbk. : alk. paper)
    1. African Americans—West (U.S.)—History—19th century. 2. African
Americans—West (U.S.)—History—20th century. 3. African American
soldiers—West (U.S.)—History—19th century. 4. African American
soldiers—West (U.S.)—History—20th century. 5. African American
soldiers—West (U.S.)—Biography. 6. United States. Army—African
American troops—History. 7. Frontier and pioneer life—West (U.S.) 8. West
(U.S.)—Race relations. 9. West (U.S.)—History—1860-1890. 10. West
(U.S.)—History—1890-1945. I. Glasrud, Bruce A. II. Searles, Michael N.,
1942-
    E185.925.B84 2007
    973.8—dc22

                                                              2007003202

TABLE OF CONTENTS

Buffalo Soldiers in the West

This anthology—*Buffalo Soldiers in the West: A Black Soldiers Anthology*—is the result of a collaborative effort by two historians, Bruce A. Glasrud and Michael N. Searles, colleagues who became acquainted with each other while attending western history meetings over the years. During that time they discussed various aspects of African American western history such as black cowboys, white violence and intimidation, black soldiers, and the history of African Americans in the Lone Star State. Both Searles and Glasrud have been interested in the black soldiers in the West, Searles as a result of conversations with Frank N. Schubert as well as Searles' involvement with re-enactment groups on the campus of Augusta State University, and Glasrud as a result of friendship and initial encouragement on studying the buffalo soldiers from William H. Leckie, subsequent conversations with James N. Leiker and Paul H. Carlson, and Glasrud's eight-year residence near Fort Davis.

With that foundation, this book focuses on the buffalo soldiers, the African Americans in the latter years of the nineteenth and early twentieth century who were primarily engaged in soldiering in the western United States. They compiled a proud and honorable, albeit difficult and rigorous, record on the racial and military frontier of the United States. They reckoned with racism, they spent much of their military service on a violent and often lawless frontier, and they struggled to make a better, more equitable life for themselves in the U.S. West. As Frank "Mickey" Schubert put it in his essay, "Buffalo Soldiers: Myths and Realities:"

> of primary importance is the fact that buffalo soldiers participated in major mainstream American processes, the expansion of the United States and its populations and the displacement of native peoples. At the same time, because of white racism and the discrimination that it spawned, they performed their duties and lived the lives of soldiers under conditions that were peculiarly trying (p. 4).

The name buffalo soldiers was first applied to the black western soldiers as a descriptive phrase to the black cavalry, in particular the Tenth Cavalry (which eventually led to a patch of honor that the Tenth Cavalrymen wore on their sleeves), then to the Ninth, and then to the infantrymen as well. Black soldiers served in most previous military conflicts in U.S. history: the American Revolution, the War of 1812, and the Civil War. However, not until the end of the Civil War were black troops able to enlist in the peacetime regular army. They served well, and by the end of the nineteenth century they engaged in the Spanish-American War, early in the twentieth century in the Filipino-American War, and prior to World War I they went with Gen. "Black Jack" Pershing on his campaign into Mexico. Racism once more reared its ugly head during World War I: Those black soldiers who actually fought served not under U.S. command and flag, but under the French, while nearly ninety percent of black soldiers were placed in non-fighting labor battalions.

Despite an unfortunate popular and scholarly assumption that little is known or written about the buffalo soldiers, they have indeed received considerable attention from scholars of the military, and of social and cultural movements alike. Through such efforts as William Leckie's *The Buffalo Soldiers*, re-enactment groups, the superb publications of Frank Schubert, ceremonies at Fort Leavenworth, the career of Gen. Colin Powell, movies, and a host of additional articles and books published over the past forty years, information on the buffalo soldiers has been well distributed. Most of the latter books and articles are discussed in Bruce Glasrud's essay introducing this collection as well as included in the chapter (with William H. Leckie), "Buffalo Soldiers," in Glasrud's bibliography, *The African American West*. So, one might ask, what does this anthology add to the existing body of work? Our purpose is to make available in one easily located collection the results of scholarly investigation into the lives, activities, and responsibilities of the black soldiers in the western United States. We also developed this collection to offer readers the variety and depth of historical studies published about these soldiers. The anthology provides readers with an awareness of the interesting experiences of the black military in the West following the Civil War. Moreover, although much has been written about the military exploits of these African American soldiers, coverage of their non-fighting roles in the American West is less readily available.

This anthology is a compendium of scholarly articles published by historians in professional journals. The journals are sometimes difficult to locate. More difficult was the selection by the editors of which articles to include out of the myriad published over the past forty years in order to give the reader a richer understanding of the fascinating position of these men. We selected seventeen articles that focus on the buffalo soldier in the western United States, hoping to provide individuals interested in learning more about the buffalo soldiers with a deeper knowledge. We chose these articles out of the many that have been written because we found them to be thought-provoking, well-written, readable, well-researched, and perceptive. Though tempted to do otherwise, we determined to use only one article per author. In sum, these articles, all published since 1971, are among the best journal selections on the buffalo soldiers in the American West.

We begin the collection with an introductory, historiographical article, and then divide the work into four distinct sections—The Officers and the Troops, The Black Soldier, Discrimination and Violence, and the Community of Soldiers. The four chapters/sections investigate the lives and accomplishments of the soldiers both individually and collectively (not primarily their military battles and fighting), the lives they developed for themselves as black troops in white, red, and brown regions of the West, their relationships to their officers (most of whom were white) and to their respective roles, and to the discrimination black soldiers faced from citizens, generally white, frequently those whom they were charged to protect. In each section, we have included four articles examining the black soldiers and their relationships within and without the military structure. Each of the articles is well documented (read their notes for further information) and we have included a bibliography at the end of the book as well. Introductions for each chapter/section include the relationship of the articles within to each other and to the general topic.

It is important to note that the selections in this anthology are written by prominent scholars who have delved into the history of black soldiers in the West. They do not always agree; some approach their topic from a military history point of view, some from the point of view of either western or national history, and others from the point of view of black history. All are interested in presenting carefully, with solid research and evidence, the significance and place of the African American soldiers—the buffalo soldiers—in United States western history. The authors frequently point to discriminatory treatment of the buffalo soldiers, sometimes by white civilians, sometimes by white officers, sometimes by the army. They also point out that these soldiers developed a re-spected and well-earned life of their own as black soldiers. This book, we trust, will help fill a significant gap in the minds of both scholars and general readers about the lives and responsibilities of black soldiers in the American West. Overall, this anthology includes writings that empha-size the social, cultural, and communal lives of the black soldiers as lived within the U.S. military during the late nineteenth and early twentieth centuries.

As in any such study, we have incurred many debts. The library staffs at Sul Ross State University and at Augusta State University helped in numerous ways; we appreciate their professionalism and kindness. "Spe-cial thanks" are extended to Leza F. Witherington and Kathy Newton of Augusta State University for their assistance in scanning and proofing the articles; their diligence and knowledge was greatly needed and ap-preciated. We thank the sixteen scholars, and their publishers, who al-lowed us to use their work in this study of the black western soldiers; obviously, without them there would have been no book. Two readers conscientiously read and commented upon this manuscript; they cer-tainly deserve our thanks, and we know that the book is much better for their support and recommendations. We must also give thanks to our encouraging colleagues, the late William H. Leckie, and to Frank N. Schubert, known affectionately at his website as "Captain Buffalo." Finally, and probably most importantly, we thank the editor-in-chief at Texas A&M University Press, Mary Lenn Dixon, for her encourage-ment and unflagging zeal in getting our ideas and then manuscript made into a book.

Bruce A. Glasrud
Michael N. Searles

BRUCE A. GLASRUD

Western Black Soldiers since The Buffalo Soldiers
A REVIEW OF THE LITERATURE

As recently freed black Americans moved westward in the decades after the Civil War, they sought employment opportunities and to escape from an oppressive racial environment. Some men became U.S. soldiers, named the buffalo soldiers by plains Indians, serving in the West. They were neglected by the white public and scholars for years, until William H. Leckie's now-classic book, *The Buffalo Soldiers,* was published in 1967. Since then, a flood of scholarly and more general works investigating the life, careers, and roles of these black western soldiers has been produced. This study serves as an interpretive review of that literature. Even so, more research and writing is left to be accomplished. What is important to remember is that these soldiers served with distinction and valor, offered a source of pride to black Americans, and both faced and fought racial injustice in the West—even though the discrimination was not usually as virulent as that on the other side of the Mississippi River.

During the late nineteenth century, beginning in the years immediately following the Civil War, free black Americans moved west in search of new, and better, opportunities. Among options open to black males was that of joining the regular army. That opportunity arose when in 1866 Congress authorized six regiments of the regular U.S. Army staffed by blacks—two cavalry and four infantry.[1] By 1869, in an overall troop reduction, Congress cut the number of black infantry units to two, and potential black soldiers enlisted in either the Ninth or Tenth Cavalry, or the Twenty-fourth or Twenty-fifth Infantry. Dubbed the buffalo soldiers by plains Indians impressed with the black soldiers' courage and valor as well as their visage and attire, the buffalo soldiers performed a crucial role in protecting settlers, in paving the way for peace, and in countering discrimination on the western frontier, in the process enabling a multicultural society in the West. Their contributions were significant, their challenges great, and their experiences varied but always tempered by the fact that they were black soldiers in "white" and "red" and "brown" territory.

The earliest significant scholarly treatment of these black western soldiers arrived in 1967 with the University of Oklahoma Press publication of William H. Leckie's *The Buffalo Soldiers: A Narrative of the Negro Cavalry in the West.* This now-classic study of the black cavalry in the late nineteenth century West, as the author put it, told "the story of the Ninth and Tenth Cavalry, in the conviction that they deserve recognition for what they were—first rate regiments by any standards one wishes to apply and major spearheads in the settlement of the West."[2] Leckie obviously used this approach and responded in part to rebut comments such as those of Paul T. Arnold, who, in the midst of an otherwise valuable and thorough six-part series (1910) on "Negro Soldiers in the United States Army," remarked that "it is unnecessary to go into details in regard to the services of the negro troops in the West. The infantry was mainly engaged in garrison duty, the cavalry in Indian fights, none of which were very important."[3] However, subsequent writers and scholars recognized the import of what Leckie contended, and for the past forty years a growing and sophisticated study of black soldiers in the West continued to emerge. It is the purpose of this essay to delineate these works and to note the comments of Bruce Dinges in the *New Mexico Historical Review* who asserted:

> nor has the story of blacks in the frontier army been fully or adequately told. Until now [1991], historians have focused on narrative histories of the black infantry and cavalry, and these studies are two decades old. Students need to dig deeper into military records, the diaries and correspondences of white officers, contemporary newspapers, and other sources to explore the relationship between whites, blacks, and Indians in the West.[4]

Students and more advanced scholars accepted the challenge and have conducted and published numerous investigations during the past quarter century, which utilized those very sources for developing the story of the black soldier in the West.

Leckie's emphasis on the need for recognition of the black troops precipitated comments from a few authors such as Jack Forbes in his short study, *Afro-Americans in the Far West*, who pointed to the white *use* of black troops in subjugating Native Americans. Leckie's approach also led to his being considered as part of the "recognition" school of black western history by Lawrence B. de Graaf in his first-rate historiographical essay "Recognition, Racism, and Reflections on the Writing of Western Black History."[5] De Graaf argued that Forbes represented the "racism" school of western historians—that is, historians who emphasized the difficulties encountered by the soldiers rather than their contributions. What is important to note is that as valuable as these historiographical terms were in 1970, the passage of a quarter century of scholarship has led to the emergence of a new school of black western historians, and by extension, historians of the buffalo soldiers—those who point out the overall contributions of black westerners; their presence in the West amid race-restricted activities, inequitable laws, discriminatory treatment, and segregation; and their creative responses to these indignities.

Leckie still stands at the forefront—every serious scholar of black soldiers in the West must refer to his book. Leckie has been criticized and in retrospect, sometimes deservedly. However, C. M. Hurtt's negative assertion that Leckie knew the infantry existed but "failed to highlight their accomplishments with the necessary detailed documentation" ignored the fact that in his book Leckie purposefully focused on the cavalry.[6] Roger Hardaway, on the other hand, offered some constructive comments. He noted that not enough time and space was spent on the role of the buffalo soldiers when they were not engaged in fighting the Indians, that derogatory terms occasionally were used to depict the Indians, and that the photographs are predominantly of whites. These items will be corrected in a revised version. Monroe Lee Billington, with some exaggeration, noted that "Leckie limits his subject matter to the cavalry and the Indian Wars, and his work is more a military organizational history than a focus on the common troops. In addition, he chooses not to include the non-Indian-related activities of the black cavalrymen."[7] Most reviewers agreed with William Barrow, who in a *Negro Digest* essay referred to "this carefully researched report." "It is more than a little appropriate," Barrow noted, "that their [buffalo soldiers'] role in the development of the West be told—at last—in detail and with fairness."[8]

However, a question emerged: "fairness" to whom? Quintard Taylor pointed to the soldiers' and subsequent historians' moral dilemma when

he asserted that "no debate in black western history has been more con-
tentious than that surrounding the 'buffalo soldiers.'" He recognized Jack
Forbes's suggestion that black soldiers were instruments in the subjugation of native peoples in order to "erect thriving *white* cities, grow fertile
white fields and leave no real monuments to the memory of brave, but
denigrated-in-their-lifetime soldiers." With this critical exception, no
additional controversy has been noted by the author of this essay.[9] Rather,
although differing approaches and perspectives have been developed,
authors over the past forty years principally have filled in gaps left by
Leckie and in this process have developed a new approach to, and understanding of, the role and relationships of blacks in the western military.

    This is not to say that Leckie started the study of the black military
in the West or that he wrote from a vacuum; in fact, a few scholarly contributions could be found by 1967. The two pioneering historians of
blacks in the West included the black military in their efforts. W. Sherman Savage, in an article entitled "Role of Negro Troops in Protecting
the Indian Territory from Intruders," noted that black soldiers serving
in the Indian Territory faced varied pressures. In "Negroes and Indians
on the Texas Frontier," an exploratory essay in the *Southwestern Historical Quarterly,* Kenneth W. Porter explained the role of black soldiers in
patrolling the Indian borders in Texas; he further developed those ideas
in an extensive two-article study published in the *Journal of Negro History,* and also explored the unique position of the black Seminole Indian
scouts in another investigation. Two articles by Edward S. Wallace described the relationship of the U.S. commander, John Lapham Bullis,
with the black Seminole Indian scouts. Two even earlier accounts of
these intrepid scouts can be located in *Frontier Times.* The plight of the
troops led by Capt. Nicholas Nolan when they became lost without
water for a substantial length of time on the Texas plains had been an
item of research.[10]

    The leadership capabilities of white officers—Colonels Buell,
Shafter, and Grierson—as they led their troops in Mexico, West Texas,
and New Mexico, also was explored.[11] As interest in the career and difficulties of a black officer evolved, the writings of Lt. Henry O. Flipper,
the first black graduate of West Point, were edited and published by
Theodore Harris and Sara Jackson respectively. A current edition of
Harris's version recently has been published as *Black Frontiersman;* Harris also wrote a dissertation at the University of Minnesota on "Henry
Ossian Flipper." Quintard Taylor recently introduced and edited Flip-

per's autobiography, *The Colored Cadet at WestPoint* (for more on Flipper see nn. 35–37). Robert A. Murray considered "The United States Army in the Aftermath of the Johnson County Invasion" in a volatile Wyoming incident affecting the buffalo soldiers.[12]

By 1967, a few regimental histories also were available to the diligent scholar. Short histories of the four black regiments could be found in *The Army of the United States*, which was edited by Theodore F. Rodenbaugh and William L. Haskin. Additional efforts included Herschel V. Cashin, *Under Fire with the Tenth U.S. Cavalry;* Edward L. N. Glass, *The History of the Tenth Cavalry;* William G. Muller, *The Twenty-fourth Infantry;* Frank M. Temple, "The Tenth United States Cavalry in Texas"; L. Albert Scipio II, *Last of the Black Regulars: A History of the Twenty-fourth Infantry Regiment;* and John Henry Nankivell, *History of the Twenty-fifth Regiment.*[13] Although these works were more popular studies, and generally written by participants, they provided valuable information.

What Leckie accomplished was to inspire a host of other studies of the role of black soldiers in the American West, their venture overseas during the Spanish-American and Filipino-American wars, and the ugly racial violence that erupted early in the twentieth century. Quickly, scholars joined Leckie in pursuing the legacy of the black soldiers in the western military. In fact, as Leckie worked on the cavalry, others delved into the role and status of the black infantry together with that of the black cavalry. Four historians in particular warrant mention: Erwin Thompson wrote a master's thesis at the University of California at Davis in which he explored the black military in the West, and followed that up with three articles particularly describing the complex duties of the black soldiers while near or at Fort Davis, in West Texas.[14]

The other three followed suit. Frank Schubert, in a 1970 thesis written at the University of Wyoming, portrayed the life of the black army regulars in Wyoming and paid especial attention to the problems and discrimination that the troopers faced, as well as to their reactions to this unwanted and ill-warranted treatment in two articles published in 1971 and 1973, respectively. One article was entitled "Black Soldiers on the White Frontier: Some Factors Influencing Race Relations" and the other was called "The Suggs Affray: The Black Cavalry in the Johnson County War." Perhaps most importantly, Arlen L. Fowler published his convincing and engaging study of *The Black Infantry in the West, 1869–1891.* Fowler's monograph, still the principal study of the black infantry, depicted the "service, hardships, and contributions" of these soldiers, who received neither the glory nor the recognition of their compatriots in the cavalry, nor certainly the esteem of the white infantry in the West. The fourth early scholar of the black military in the West, Thomas Phillips, wrote a comprehensive doctoral dissertation at the University of Wisconsin and continued his effort in a notable article that he published on "The Black Regulars." In his article, Phillips noted the multifaceted experiences of the black soldiers in the West.[15]

Phillips was not alone in developing a broad, multiple approach to the study of black western troops, and by the mid-1970s, a few studies had been concluded. John M. Carroll issued *Buffalo Soldiers West* and published his compendium on *The Black Military Experience in the American West,* in which he used previously published sources to describe the officers, soldiers, infantry, cavalry, forts, contributions, and problems of black troops in the West. The aforementioned W. Sherman Savage, in *Blacks in the West,* summarized the black military experience, as did Fairfax Downey in his book written for the popular juvenile audience, *The Buffalo Soldiers in the Indian Wars.* Jack D. Foner, using chapters in two books, produced a valuable summation of the status and careers of black soldiers in the West. He observed that "despite numerous problems, many of which reflected prejudice and discrimination both within and outside the army, the experiment launched in 1866 can be counted a success."[16] More recently, a number of general overviews that explain the status of black soldiers in the West have been added to this body of knowledge; these include works by Ira Berlin, Meg Chorlian, Lenwood G. Davis and George Hill, Sarah Erwin, Donnie D. Good, Robert Ewell Greene, William Loren Katz, John P. Langellier, Bernard C. Nalty, Jo Ann Pospicil, and Don Rickey.[17]

One of the obvious gaps in the works of Leckie and Fowler concerned the paucity of stories of individual black soldiers. This was not surprising since, at the time they wrote, those stories remained buried. As Leckie noted in his recent forward to Fowler's book, "the principle criticism, and a legitimate one, . . . is the lack of attention to individual 'buffalo soldiers.'"[18] Recent studies, however, have done much to rectify that neglect. Black congressional Medal of Honor recipients have been recognized beginning with the 1967 publication of Irvin H. Lee's *Negro Medal of Honor Men,* a book for juveniles (with some errors), an article by William L. Katz on "Six 'New' Medal of Honor Men," and the more systematic study by Preston Amos of black Medal of Honor winners in the West from 1870 to 1890. The recent publication of Frank N. Schubert's *Black Valor: Buffalo Soldiers and the Medal of Honor, 1870–1898,* provides scholars and the general public with helpful and informative materials on twenty-three honored black soldiers. They, Schubert judiciously noted, "kept alive a tradition of courage under fire."[19]

To grasp and appreciate the lives and activities of the non-decorated black western soldiers, however, one must consult other works. Begin with the comprehensive effort of Frank N. Schubert's *On the Trail of the Buffalo Soldier: Biographies of African-Americans in the U.S. Army, 1866–1917;* his book is essential for anyone interested in studying, learning, or writing about black soldiers. Harold Ray Sayre used pension petition records and other government sources to uncover much about the lives of a group of soldiers who resided at Fort Davis in the 1880s in *Warriors of Color.* Three articles show what diligent and imaginative research can uncover: Frank Schubert discussed the life and difficulties faced by Medal of Honor winner Emanuel Stance; Thomas R. Buecker covered the three-decade career of Caleb Benson, who, when he retired, needed his friends to support him; and John Allen Johnson devoted his attention to two Medal of Honor recipients from Arkansas. In another imaginative search, William A. Dobak used the *Slave Narratives* collected by the Federal Writer's Project and added to our understanding of the roles of black soldiers in "Black Regulars Speak." For a shorter vignette, see Erwin Thompson's "Private Bentley's Buzzard."[20] These writers and their efforts mean that one can better include and discuss the role of individual black soldiers on the western plains.

Both William Leckie and Arlen Fowler concentrated on the role of black soldiers on the plains of Texas and the remainder of the nation's interior where the buffalo soldiers performed much of their duties. But, the black soldiers also served widely and in other regions of the West. Monroe Lee Billington, for example, staked out the territory of New Mexico as his special contribution. In his book, *New Mexico's Buffalo Soldiers, 1866–1900* and three exploratory articles, Billington pointed out the role of black soldiers in New Mexico. He discovered that despite their enumerable contributions to the safety of the region, whites still resented the presence of the black troopers. They were content to watch blacks play in a baseball game or perform in the company band, but that was the extent of the socializing. Billington's studies ended in 1900. Horace Daniel Nash, in an eminently publishable dissertation, "Town and Sword: Black Soldiers in Columbus, New Mexico, in the Early Twentieth Century," imaginatively and thoroughly fulfilled the expectations of his title.[21]

Scholars also moved beyond the Southwest. In a seminal study,

Buffalo Soldiers, Braves, and the Brass: The Story of Fort Robinson, Nebraska,
Frank Schubert examined the roles of black soldiers stationed in Fort
Robinson, Nebraska. Not to be outdone, Michael J. Clark constructed
an impressive dissertation detailing the stationing of black troops in
Utah in the late 1890s.[22] Other authors covered black soldiers in Washington, Wyoming,[23] Arizona, New Mexico,[24] Nebraska, Montana,
Dakotas,[25] Kansas, Texas,[26] Utah, Iowa,[27] and the Indian Territory. Although not much has yet been produced on the role of the buffalo soldiers in the Indian Territory, an interpretive overview of red/black
relations in that territory can be found in Donald A. Grinde Jr. and
Quintard Taylor, "Red v. Black: Conflict and Accommodation in the
Post Civil War Indian Territory." Bruce A. Glasrud contributed a suc-
cinct assessment, "Buffalo Soldiers in Oklahoma," to the 2007 publication, *Encyclopedia of Oklahoma History and Culture.*[28] These investigations extended the knowledge of areas of the nation (always in the West)
in which the black troops served, allowed for comparisons, and enabled
investigators to complete the picture of the duties of the buffalo soldiers
after the close of the Indian wars.

Since the only officers who could be appointed to command the
black troops were white, studies of the relationships between the white
officers and the black troops are important. A number have been completed, although most studies of those who commanded the black troops
diminish that aspect of their career and quickly leave the black troops
and move to a more "glamorous" time in their military careers. One exemplary work that explored the relationship of black troops and white
officers during the Civil War was Joseph T. Glatthar, *Forged in Battle:
The Civil War Alliance of Black Soldiers and White Officers.*[29] In a post-war
study based on one of the black cavalry regiments, Charles L. Kenner
depicted the relationships of white officers and black soldiers in *Buffalo
Soldiers and Officers of the Ninth Cavalry.* His subtitle, "black and white
together," indicates the direction of his approach. Col. Benjamin H.
Grierson, commander of the Tenth Cavalry, has been studied from a
number of differing perspectives. The definitive work on Grierson and
his family by William H. Leckie and Shirley Leckie successfully discussed the Griersons' relations with the black troops. Grierson has also
been portrayed in three articles, one by Douglas McChristian, one by
Bruce J. Dinges, and the other by Mary L. Williams. Col. William R.
Shafter has also been written about. Paul H. Carlson remarkably made
this ornery individual come alive in *"Pecos Bill": A Military Biography of*

William R. Shafter, and in three first-rate articles Carlson detailed the experiences of Shafter and the black troops in Texas. Robert Utley set the stage for the study of Shafter in a readable essay entitled " 'Pecos Bill' on the Texas Frontier."[30]

Other studies of white officers raised some additional issues. The complications and machinations at boring posts apparently also crept into black white relations; Bruce J. Dinges in articles "Scandal in the Tenth Cavalry: A Fort Sill Case History" and "The Irrepressible Captain Armes: Politics and Justice in the Indian-Fighting Army" indicated that squabbles could affect officer behavior and treatment of the black troops. Armes's tribulations also fascinated Wayne Daniel, who wrote "The Many Trials of Captain Armes." Frank M. Temple's article noted "Discipline and Turmoil in the Tenth U.S. Cavalry." John Bigelow, a lieutenant in the Tenth Cavalry, left reminiscences of his own, one of which was edited by Douglas C. McChristian and entitled *Garrison Tangles in the Friendless Tenth.* Marcos E. Kinevan has written a book entitled *Frontier Cavalryman: Lieutenant John Bigelow and the Buffalo Soldiers in Texas.* Kinevan answered some of the questions concerning Bigelow and his relationship with the black troops—at times Bigelow seemed as if he did not want to be with the buffalo soldiers, at other times as if he admired them. Capt. Louis Carpenter of the Tenth Cavalry, "considered the best company commander in the regiment," served as the focus for James T. Matthews' articles. For an interesting aspect of officer-soldier relations, E. G. Longacre's "Philadelphia Aristocrat with the Buffalo Soldiers" has some telling insights. Despite these labors, more needs to be completed on this important subject. In one impressive article on a related topic, "'Dress on the Colors, Boys!' Black Noncommissioned Officers in the Regular Army, 1866–1898," Douglas C. McChristian showed the way for one other group that merits inclusion in the history of black western soldiers. [31]

Some topics recently seemed to enthrall investigators, and deservedly so. The black Seminole Indian scouts are one such group. Their ancestors escaped from U.S. slavery to Florida, fought the U.S. Army in three or more wars in a search for freedom, were finally forcefully moved to the Indian Territory, and when able fled that area for freedom in Mexico. They served with distinction in the Mexican army and desired to return to the United States once slavery was abolished. The means they worked out for recrossing the border was service in the U.S. Army as Indian scouts. An author who has uncovered some or most of their story is Thomas Britten, author of two enlightening articles and a published thesis, *A Brief History of the Seminole-Negro Indian Scouts*. Other black Seminole Indian studies include William G. Gwaltney's brief account in *Lest We Forget*; Kevin Mulroy, whose book, *Freedom on the Border: The Seminole Maroons in Florida, the Indian Territory, Coahuila, and Texas*, is the most complete study; Doug Sivad's *The Black Seminole Indians of Texas*; C. Kevin Swisher, "Frontier Heroes"; and Scott Thybony, "Against All Odds Black Seminoles Won Their Freedom." Kenneth W. Porter, who first began writing a book on the Seminoles in 1947, also has written exhaustively on the subject. His manuscript, posthumously revised and edited by Alcione M. Amos and Thomas P. Senter, has recently been published as *The Black Seminoles: History of a Freedom-Seeking People*. Ultimately, according to Seminole tradition, these black scouts agreed to settle in Texas in return for land near present-day Bracketville. As Eric Emmerson Strong discovered in "The Lost Treaty of the Black Seminoles," the treaty cannot be located; the land was never received. [32]

One buffalo soldier topic recently fascinated scholars and readers alike. During the Civil War, a black woman slave (Cathay Williams) in Missouri was taken as contraband and pressed into service as a cook for the Union Army. Her experience during the war apparently was satisfactory, and in 1866 she disguised herself as a man with the name William Cathay, and enlisted as a soldier in the regular army. Williams served well and without discovery during her two-year period of enlistment. Cathay Williams' story was first mentioned in a newspaper article in the *St. Louis Daily Times* (January 2, 1876); William Cathay/Cathay Williams also is included in Frank Schubert, *Voices of the Buffalo Soldier*, the subject of an interesting article, "Cathey Williams: Black Woman Soldier, 1866–1868," by De Anne Blanton, and featured in a book (though filled with conjecture), Philip Thomas Tucker's *Cathy Williams: From Slave to Female Soldier*. [33]

Another topic related to the buffalo soldiers that occupied the attention of recent scholarship was the story of the first black graduate of West Point, Lt. Henry O. Flipper. Ostracized and shunned while at West Point, Flipper nonetheless graduated and was given a post with the buffalo soldiers and eventually stationed at Fort Davis, Texas. There he performed valiantly, but in an illuminating set of circumstances was accused of theft and conduct unbecoming an officer, found guilty of the latter, and summarily dismissed from the army. Flipper was not alone in receiving such treatment; John F. Marszalek Jr. pointed out that other black cadets also faced discrimination and harassment. [34]

Flipper consistently maintained his innocence, and claimed that his dismissal was plotted by white officers at the fort, including Colonel Shafter. At least five books have covered Flipper's story: Lowell D. Black and Sara H. Black, *An Officer and a Gentleman: The Military Career of Lieutenant Henry O. Flipper,* who decried Flipper's "unjust court-martial"; James C. Cage and James M. Day, *The Court Martial of Henry Ossian Flipper: West Point's First Black Graduate,* who covered Flipper's background as well as the trial; Charles M. Robinson III, *The Court-Martial of Lieutenant Henry Flipper,* a thorough investigation of the actual trial; Jane Eppinga, *Henry Ossian Flipper: West Point's First Black Graduate,* which asserted that "there can be no doubt that racial prejudice played a part in his court-martial;" and Barry C. Johnson, *Flipper's Dismissal: The Ruin of Lt. Henry O. Flipper,* who concluded that race was not a key factor in Flipper's dismissal. In fact, Johnson lays much of the blame on Flipper.[35]

Other studies have also been produced, which usually exonerate Lieutenant Flipper, though leaning toward faulty bookkeeping and institutional racism. These include a master's thesis and at least five articles, the titles of which are instructive. A thesis and one article were written by Donald R. McClung—the thesis entitled "Henry O. Flipper: The First Negro Officer in the United States Army, 1878–1882," and the article on "Second Lieutenant Henry O. Flipper: A Negro Officer on the West Texas Frontier." Other articles include Bruce J. Dinges's "The Court-Martial of Lieutenant Henry O. Flipper: An Example of Black-White Relationships in the Army"; Brenda East, "Henry Ossian Flipper: Lieutenant of the Buffalo Soldiers"; Ezra J. Warner, "A Black Man in the Long Gray Line"; and Steve Wilson, "A Black Lieutenant in the Ranks." Intriguing episodes in Flipper's later career include Jane Eppinga, "Henry O. Flipper in the Court of Private Land Claims: The Arizona Career of West Point's First Black Graduate," and Theodore D. Harris, "Henry Flipper and Pancho Villa."[36] Recently, following a lengthy congressional hearing, the U.S. Army cleansed Flipper's record.

Black soldiers such as Flipper spent many hours on pursuits not always recognized as part of military life, and scholars have been delving into these activities. Even Flipper might not have been so summarily treated if he had not gone on horseback rides with a white woman, thus incurring the jealousy of a white officer. Other activities of black soldiers, beyond fighting, building, guarding, and watching, included playing baseball and other sports, establishing bands, participating in the great bicycle experiment, developing an effective means of using machine guns, going to town, fighting fires, and attending classes.[37] The latter were usually provided by the army chaplains, with one assigned to each black regiment. Ultimately, five black chaplains were enlisted in the service; their story has been illuminated by Alan K. Lamm in his book *Five Black Preachers in Army Blue,* among other studies. The chaplains' wives also provided valuable service to the enlisted soldiers.[38]

Discrimination befell black soldiers, and their means of support were sometimes limited. Blacks occasionally retaliated when all was not well on the frontier posts, and a number of nineteenth-century mutinies—such as those at Fort Cummings, San Pedro Springs, Fort Concho, and Fort Stockton—presaged the more violent outbreaks of the early twentieth century.[39]

Although much of the information regarding the role of black soldiers in the West derives from government documents, diaries and letters of officers, newspaper and magazine articles, and occasionally enlisted men's comments,[40] some fictional accounts make an effort to give artistic vent to the feelings and behavior of buffalo soldiers. Most of these accounts, however, fail at being more than romantic dramatizations that neglect the history of the period. Imagine Bill Leckie's excitement, for example, when researching for his book he discovered John Prebble's 1959 novel entitled *The Buffalo Soldiers,* and his immediate disappointment when the written-for-juveniles account provided a white-biased depiction of the relations among white, red, and black. A similar reaction occurred after perusing the 1996 novel by Tom Willard, *Buffalo Soldiers,* where one learns that the buffalo soldiers served with General Custer (obviously ignoring the fact that General Custer turned down an opportunity to command a black regiment because he did not want to be associated with an inferior race). On the other hand, for an accurate and readable rendition of buffalo soldiers from a literary perspective, read Elmer Kelton, *The Wolf and the Buffalo.* His characters are real, his history first-rate, and his writing superb.[41] Hopefully, other novelists will begin to explore the lives, duties, and responsibilities of black soldiers in the West.

The period from the end of the Indian Wars to World War I[42] also has been covered by historians. In addition to the works mentioned throughout the earlier pages of this article, other studies include Marvin E. Fletcher, *The Black Soldier and Officer in the United States Army, 1891–1917,* in which he carried forward the chronicle begun by Leckie and Fowler; Willard B. Gatewood Jr., "Black Americans and the Quest for

Empire," and his book *Black Americans and the White Man's Burden, 1893–1903,* an analysis of blacks in both the Spanish- and Filipino- American wars;[43] and several investigations that reviewed U.S.-Mexico border troubles as well as Gen. "Black Jack" Pershing's "punitive expedition" against Mexico.[44] The infamous 1906 Brownsville incident has been approached in two books—Ann J. Lane, *The Brownsville Affair: National Crisis and Black Reaction;* and John D. Weaver, *The Brownsville Raid*—and articles by Lewis N. Wynne, Richard Young, and Thomas R. Buecker. Buecker noted that a cause of the Brownsville incident was that the troops had been treated with respect at their previous locale in Nebraska, and the racism in Texas was a severe blow.[45] Even this animosity had been foretold by violence and virulent prejudice in other Texas communities in the early twentieth century. In a thoroughly researched book, *Black Soldiers in Jim Crow Texas, 1899–1917,* and an impressive array of articles, Garna L. Christian clearly portrayed the hostility and tense feelings that existed between Texas communities and the black soldiers. As a result, racial violence too often broke out.[46] This period ended in violence as well when black infantrymen in Houston no longer tolerated vicious white attacks. As Robert V. Haynes noted in *A Night of Violence: The Houston Riot of 1917,* no justice was served the soldiers; some were quickly executed after being found "guilty."[47]

To summarize the state of historical research regarding the role of black soldiers in the West is both easy and hard, fraught with shadows yet remarkably transparent. There are some exciting portents for the future. Scholarly studies, such as Paul H. Carlson's *The Buffalo Soldier Tragedy of 1877;* William A. Dobak and Thomas Phillips, *The Black Regulars;* James Leiker's *Racial Borders: Black Soldiers along the Rio Grande;* plus two books from the dean of buffalo soldiers' studies, Frank N. Schubert—*Voices of the Buffalo Soldier* and, with Irene Schubert, volume II of *On the Trail of the Buffalo Soldiers*—continue to reach the market. Leiker in particular points a path to a broader consideration; he emphasizes multiracial rather than a standard black-white dichotomy.[48]

Additional examples of exciting developments regarding the buffalo soldiers abound. A statue honoring the buffalo soldiers' heroic contributions was unveiled in 1990 at Fort Leavenworth after a lengthy effort by Colin Powell and others. Two investigations portrayed the buffalo soldiers in the 1920s and 1930s, and Robert F. Jefferson completed a dissertation on black servicemen during the Depression and World War II. Also, John F. Marszalek and Horace D. Nash published an historiographical essay about blacks in the military. The International Museum of the Horse made available on the World Wide Web a section on "The Buffalo Soldiers on the Western Frontier."[49] Furthermore, a revision of William H. Leckie's book has been completed; buffalo soldier's organizations and reenactments are developing around the country; Bruce A. Glasrud and William H. Leckie compiled an extensive bibliography of the western black soldiers; and Quintard Taylor created a skillful synthesis of those "Comrades of Color: Buffalo Soldiers in the West, 1866–1917," which ought to serve as a beacon for future investigators.[50]

Some topics still beg for research and publication: The original commander of the Ninth Cavalry, Col. Edward Hatch, deserves a biography, as does Maj. Guy Henry; the lives of black soldiers after they leave the military merit careful investigation; black soldiers in the Indian Territory/Oklahoma invite additional research; the nearby communities around the forts where the soldiers were stationed could be further explicated; the role of family and friends of the soldiers has little information available at this time; and information on leisure time activities of the black soldiers is incomplete. Two additional avenues of potential investigation include black soldiers in the West between World War I and World War II, and the attitudes and relations among police (such as the Texas Rangers), the state militias, and the black soldiers. Very definitely, the relationship of soldiers and women needs to be opened up for study. The role of the black troops in other non-fighting military exploits such as guarding stages, stringing telegraph wires, fire fighting, building roads, providing escort services, strikebreaking, and aiding in calamities warrant further attention as well.

The advanced status of buffalo soldiers' scholarship may be measured by developing historiographical arguments of present-day historians. As Bill Leckie and Shirley Leckie assert in the preface to their revised edition of *The Buffalo Soldiers*, "historians have identified new historical concerns and have questioned some longstanding beliefs (xi)." James Leiker, *Racial Borders*, for instance, pointed out that discussion of issues of race conflict in the West was not limited to black-white relationships, but also included brown and red interactions. Vernon Bellecourt argued that acknowledging the importance of black soldiers in the Indian wars also focuses attention on their warfare against and treatment of the Indians. Charles L. Kenner, *Buffalo Soldiers and Officers of the Ninth Cavalry;* and William A. Dobak and Thomas Phillips, *The Black Regulars;* asserted that the U.S. Army treated white and black soldiers equally and that the situation of black soldiers was neither better nor worse than that of white soldiers. Dobak and Phillips also posited that the black soldiers, in the few letters and instances known, rarely used the term *buffalo soldiers*.[51] Historians of the western army have noted the multipurpose nature of the army in the West, and its "nation-building" role in developing the region. One can assume that sophisticated, hardworking scholars of the future will critically examine our current assumptions.

However, as Quintard Taylor so aptly stated, "The buffalo soldiers served fifty years in western states and territories. During that period they created a legacy of courage, cunning, and skill that forced even their detractors to respect them and black people across the country to view them with pride." This pride was evident in Rayford Logan's comment in his exceptional study of blacks at the turn of the twentieth century, *The Betrayal of the Negro*, where he reported:

> Negroes had little at the turn of the century to help sustain our faith in ourselves except the pride that we took in the Ninth and Tenth Cavalry, the Twenty-fourth and Twenty-fifth Infantry. . . . They were our Ralph Bunche, Marian Anderson, Joe Louis, and Jackie Robinson.[52]

Thanks to the contributions of the many historians and scholars discussed in this article, the role of the black troops in the West is much better known and can now be an even greater source of pride for all Americans, but especially for black Americans. The history of black soldiers allows everyone to note that black westerners fulfilled their obligations, shaped their destiny, survived the varied stumbling blocks, battled racial discrimination, and created a new and multicultural society. The West was not, as Richard White has vividly pointed out, New Jersey with mountains and deserts.[53]

Notes

1. Blacks also pursued "the lure of the west" for political and physical freedom, less rigid racial barriers, adventure, acquiring an education, a "better life," and escape. For background on the black regiments' formation, see Harry Johnson, "Buffalo Soldiers: The Formation of the Ninth Cavalry Regiment: July, 1866–March, 1867" (Master's thesis, U.S. Army Command and General Staff College, 1991); Anita Williams McMiller, "Buffalo Soldiers: The Formation of the Tenth Cavalry Regiment from September 1866 to August 1867" (Master's

thesis, U.S. Army Command and General Staff College, 1990). One early black infantry unit served in Texas, see Wayne Randolph Austerman, "Black Regulars: The 41st Infantry in Texas, 1867–1869" (Master's thesis, Louisiana State University, 1971).

2. William H. Leckie, *The Buffalo Soldiers: A Narrative of the Negro Cavalry in the West* (Norman: University of Oklahoma Press, 1967), viii. Leckie, after a distinguished career that culminated as Professor of History and Vice President for Academic Affairs at the University of Toledo, resided in Winter Springs, Florida until his death in 2005.

3. Paul T. Arnold, "Negro Soldiers in the United States Army," *Magazine of History* 10 (August 1909): 61–70; 10 (September 1909): 123–29; 10 (October 1909): 185–93; 10 (November 1909): 247–55; 11 (January 1910): 1–12 [quote from 12]; 11 (March 1910): 119–25. Arnold also inexplicably noted that "there is no prejudice within the army against them."

4. Bruce J. Dinges, "New Directions in Frontier Military History: A Review Essay," *New Mexico Historical Review* 66 (January 1991): 103–16.

5. Jack D. Forbes, *Afro-Americans in the Far West* (Berkeley: Far West Laboratory for Research and Development, 1967); Lawrence B. de Graaf, "Recognition, Racism, and Reflections on the Writing of Western Black History," *Pacific Historical Review* 44 (February 1975): 22–51.

6. C. M. Hurtt, "The Role of Black Infantry in the Expansion of the West," *West Virginia History* 40 (1979): 123–57, quote from 125. Hurtt borrowed extensively from Arlen Fowler's dissertation, but did not reference publication of Fowler's book, *The Black Infantry in the West*, even though it had been published for more than five years by the time of Hurtt's essay.

7. Roger D. Hardaway, "Buffalo Soldiers," in *A Narrative Bibliography of the African-American Frontier: Blacks in the Rocky Mountain West, 1535–1912* (Lewiston, N.Y.: Mellen Press, 1995): 127–28; Monroe Lee Billington, *New Mexico's Buffalo Soldiers, 1866–1900* (Niwot, Colo.: University Press of Colorado, 1991), xii.

8. William Barrow, "The Buffalo Soldiers: The Negro Cavalry in the West, 1866–1891," *Negro Digest* 16 (July 1967): 34–37, 89.

9. Quintard Taylor, "From Esteban to Rodney King: Five Centuries of African American History in the West," *Montana: The Journal of Western History* 46 (Winter 1996): 9; Forbes, *Afro-Americans in the Far West,* 33. What Taylor's point also reflects is the essentially early stage of western black history; much is left to be uncovered, and much is left to be interpreted.

10. W. Sherman Savage, "The Role of Negro Soldiers in Protecting the Indian Territory from Intruders," *Journal of Negro History* 36 (1951): 25–34; Kenneth W. Porter, "Negroes and Indians on the Texas Frontier, 1831–1876," *Journal of Negro History* 41 (July 1956): 185–214; 41 (October 1956): 285–310; "The Seminole-Negro Indian Scouts, 1870–1881," *Southwestern Historical Quarterly* 55 (1952): 358–77; Edward S. Wallace, "General John Lapham Bullis: The Thunderbolt of the Texas Frontier," *Southwestern Historical Quarterly* 54 (April 1951): 452–61; 55 (July 1951): 77–85; H. Conger Jones, "Old Seminole Scouts Still

Thrive on Border," *Frontier Times* 11 (1934): 327–32; Frost Woodhull, "The Seminole Indian Scouts on the Border," *Frontier Times* 15 (1937): 118–27; Col. Martin L. Crimmins, "Captain Nolan's Lost Troop on the Staked Plains," *West Texas Historical Association Year Book* 10 (October 1934): 68–73; W. Curtis Nunn, "Eighty-six Hours without Water on the Texas Plains," *Southwestern Historical Quarterly* 43 (January 1940): 356–64; Elvis Eugene Fleming, "Captain Nicholas Nolan: Lost on the Staked Plains," *Texana* 4 (Spring 1966): 1–13.

11. Col. Martin L. Crimmins, "Colonel Buell's Expedition into Mexico," *New Mexico Historical Review* 10 (April 1935): 133–42; "Shafter's Exploration in Western Texas, 1875," *West Texas Historical Association Yearbook* 9 (October 1933): 82–96; Frank M. Temple, "Colonel B. H. Grierson's Victorio Campaign," *West Texas Historical Association Year Book* 35 (October 1959): 99–111.

12. Theodore D. Harris, ed., *Negro Frontiersman: The Western Memoirs of Henry O. Flipper, First Negro Graduate of West Point* (El Paso: Texas Western College Press, 1963); Sara Dunlap Jackson, ed., *Henry O. Flipper, The Colored Cadet at West Point* (New York: Arno Press Reprint, 1968); Theodore D. Harris, ed., *Black Frontiersman: The Western Memoirs of Henry O. Flipper* (Fort Worth: Texas Christian University Press, 1997); Theodore D. Harris, "Henry Ossian Flipper: The First Negro Graduate of West Point" (Ph.D. diss., University of Minnesota, 1971); Quintard Taylor, ed., *The Colored Cadet at West Point: Autobiography of Lieutenant Henry Ossian Flipper, U.S.A.* (Lincoln: University of Nebraska Press, 1998); Robert A. Murray, "The United States Army in the Aftermath of the Johnson County Invasion: April Through November 1892," *Annals of Wyoming* 38 (April 1966): 59–75.

13. George Andrews, "The Twenty-fifth Regiment of Infantry," in *The Army of the United States: Historical Sketches of Staff and Line with Portraits of Generals-in-Chief,* edited by Theo. F. Rodenbaugh and William L. Haskin, 697–99 (New York: Argonaut Press, 1966). See also John Bigelow Jr., "The Tenth Regiment of Cavalry," 288–97; H. W. Hovey, "The Twenty-fourth Regiment of Infantry," 695–96; Grote Hutchison, "The Ninth Regiment of Cavalry," 280–87. Herschel V. Cashin, *Under Fire with the Tenth U.S. Cavalry* (New York: F. Tennyson Neely, 1899); Edward L. N. Glass, *The History of the Tenth Cavalry, 1866–1921* (Tucson: Acme Printing, 1921); William G. Muller, *The Twenty-fourth Infantry: Past and Present* (Ft. Collins, Colo.: Old Army Press, 1972); Frank M. Temple, "The Tenth United States Cavalry in Texas," *Fort Concho Report* 17 (Winter 1985): 11–17; L. Albert Scipio II, *Last of the Black Regulars: A History of the Twenty-fourth Infantry Regiment (1869–1951)* (Silver Springs, Md.: Roman Publications, 1983); John Henry Nankivell, *History of the Twenty-fifth Regiment, United States Infantry, 1869–1926* (Denver: Smith-Brooks Printing, 1926).

14. Erwin N. Thompson, "The Negro Regiments of the U.S. Army, 1866–1900," (Master's thesis, University of California at Davis, 1966); "The Negro Soldier and His Officers," in *The Black Military Experience in the American West,* edited by John M. Carroll, 258–80 (New York: Liveright, 1971); "The Negro Soldiers on the Frontier: A Fort Davis Case Study," *Journal of the West* 7 (1968):

217–35; "Private Bentley's Buzzard," in *The Black Military Experience in the American West* edited by John M. Carroll, 437–40 (New York: Liveright, 1971).

15. Frank N. Schubert, "The Black Regular Army Regiments in Wyoming, 1885–1912" (Master's thesis, University of Wyoming, 1970); "Black Soldiers on the White Frontier: Some Factors Influencing Race Relations," *Phylon* 32 no. 4 (Winter 1971): 410–15; "The Suggs Affray: The Black Cavalry in the Johnson County War," *Western Historical Quarterly* 4 (1973): 57–68; Arlen L. Fowler, *The Black Infantry in the West, 1869–1891* (Westport, Conn.: Greenwich Publishing, 1971); Thomas D. Phillips, "The Black Regulars: Negro Soldiers in the United States Army, 1866–1891" (Ph.D. diss., University of Wisconsin, 1970); "The Black Regulars," in *The West of the American People,* edited by Allan G. Bogue, Thomas D. Phillips, and James E. Wright, 138–43 (Itasca, Ill.: Peacock Publishers, 1970).

16. John M. Carroll, *Buffalo Soldiers West* (Fort Collins: Old Army Press, 1971); Carroll, ed., *Black Military Experience in the American West;* W. Sherman Savage, "Blacks in the Military," in *Blacks in the West,* 48–64 (Westport, Conn.: Greenwood Press, 1976); Fairfax Downey, *The Buffalo Soldiers in the Indian Wars* (New York: McGraw Hill, 1969); Jack D. Foner, "The Negro in the Post-Civil War Army," in *The United States Soldier between Two Wars: Army Life and Reforms, 1865–1898,* 127–47, 195–201 (New York: Humanities Press, 1970); "Blacks in the Post-Civil War Army," in *Blacks and the Military in American History: A Perspective,* 52–71, 266–67 (New York: Praeger Publishers, 1974). See also William Loren Katz, "The Black Infantry and Cavalry," in *The Black West: A Documentary and Pictorial History of the African American in the Westward Expansion of the United States,* 199–244 (New York: Simon and Schuster, 1996).

17. Ira Berlin, ed., "The Black Military Experience, 1861–1867," in *The Black Military Experience,* 1–34 (Cambridge: Cambridge University Press, 1982); Meg Chorlian, ed., "Buffalo Soldiers," *Cobblestone* (February 1995): 1–49; Lenwood G. Davis and George Hill, comps., "Blacks in the American West," in *Blacks in the American Armed Forces, 1776–1983: A Bibliography,* 34–46 (Westport, Conn.: Greenwood Press, 1985); Sarah Erwin, ed., *The Buffalo Soldier on the American Frontier* (Tulsa: Thomas Gilcrease Museum Association, 1996); Donnie D. Good, "Buffalo Soldiers," *American Scene Magazine* 10 no. 4 (April 1970); Robert Ewell Greene, "The Indian Campaigns, 1866–1890," in *Black Defenders of America, 1775–1973,* 109–22 (Chicago: Johnson Publishing, 1974); John P. Langellier, *Men A-Marching: The African American Soldier in the West, 1866–1896* (Springfield, Penn.: Steven Wright Publishing, 1995); Bernard C. Nalty, "Reaction in the South, Action in the West," in *Strength for the Fight: A History of Black Americans in the Military,* 47–62, 364–66 (New York: Free Press, 1986); JoAnn Pospicil, "Black Defenders in the American West, 1865–1890," *West Texas Historical Association Year Book* 76 (2000): 106–25; Don Rickey Jr., "An Indian Wars Combat Record," *By Valor and Arms* 2 (Fall 1975): 4–11.

18. William H. Leckie, forward to *The Black Infantry in the West,* rev. ed., by Arlen L. Fowler, xvi (Norman: University of Oklahoma Press, 1996).

19. Irvin H. Lee, *Negro Medal of Honor Men* (New York: Dodd, Mead, 1967), chap. 13; Preston E. Amos, *Above and Beyond in the West: Black Medal of*

Honor Winners, 1870–1890 (Washington, D.C.: Potomac Corral, The Western-ers, 1974); William Loren Katz, "Six 'New' Medal of Honor Men," *Journal of Negro History* 53 (January 1968): 77–81; Frank N. Schubert, *Black Valor: Buffalo Soldiers and the Medal of Honor, 1870–1898* (Wilmington, Del.: Scholarly Re-sources, 1997).

20. Frank N. Schubert, *On the Trail of the Buffalo Soldier: Biographies of African-Americans in the U.S. Army, 1866–1917* (Wilmington, Del.: Scholarly Resources, 1994); Harold Ray Sayre, *Warriors of Color* (Fort Davis, Tex.: pri-vately printed, 1995); Frank N. Schubert, "The Violent World of Emanuel Stance, Fort Robinson, 1887," *Nebraska History* 55 (Summer 1974): 203–19; Thomas R. Buecker, "One Soldier's Service: Caleb Benson in the Ninth and Tenth Cavalry, 1875–1908," *Nebraska History* 74 (Summer 1993): 54–62; John Allen Johnson, "The Medal of Honor and Sergeant John Ward and Private Pompey Factor," *Arkansas Historical Quarterly* 29 (Winter 1970): 361–75; Wil-liam A. Dobak, "Black Regulars Speak," *Panhandle-Plains Historical Review* 47 (1974): 19–27; Erwin N. Thompson, "Private Bentley's Buzzard," in *The Black Military Experience in the American West,* edited by John M. Carroll, 437–40 (New York: Liveright, 1971).

21. Monroe Lee Billington, *New Mexico's Buffalo Soldiers, 1866–1900* (Ni-wot, Col.: University Press of Colorado, 1991); "Black Soldiers at Fort Selden, New Mexico, 1868–1891," *New Mexico Historical Review* 62 (January 1987): 65–80; "Civilians and Black Soldiers in New Mexico Territory, 1866–1900: A Cross-Cultural Experience," *Military History of the Southwest* 19 (Spring 1989): 71–82; "Black Cavalrymen and Apache Indians in New Mexico Territory," *Fort Concho and the South Plains Journal* 22 (Summer 1990): 55–75; Horace Daniel Nash, "Town and Sword: Black Soldiers in Columbus, New Mexico, in the Early Twentieth Century" (Ph.D. diss., Mississippi State University, 1996). For additional information on black military life in New Mexico see Horace D. Nash, "Blacks on the Border: Columbus, New Mexico, 1916–1922" (Master's thesis, New Mexico State University, 1988).

22. Frank N. Schubert, *Buffalo Soldiers, Braves, and the Brass: The Story of Fort Robinson, Nebraska* (Shippensburg: White Mane Publishing, 1993); Michael J. Clark, "U.S. Army Pioneers: Black Soldiers in Nineteenth Century Utah" (Ph.D. diss., University of Utah, 1981).

23. Mary Ellen Rowe, "The Early History of Fort George Wright: Black Infantrymen and Theodore Roosevelt in Spokane," *Pacific Northwest Quarterly* 80 (July 1989): 91–100; Richard P. Zollo, "General Francis P. Dodge and His Brave Black Soldiers [1879, Wyoming]," *Essex Institute Historical Collection* 122 (July 1986): 181–206; Frank N. Schubert, "The Black Regular Army Regiments in Wyoming, 1885–1912" (Master's thesis, University of Wyoming, 1970).

24. Mark F. Baumler and Richard V. N. Ahlstrom, "The Garfield Monu-ment: An 1886 Memorial of the Buffalo Soldiers in Arizona," *Cochise County Quarterly* 18 (Spring 1988): 3–34; Col. H. B. Wharfield, *With Scouts and Cavalry at Fort Apache* (Tucson: Arizona Pioneers' Historical Society, 1965); Lee Scott Thiesen, ed., "The Fight in Lincoln, N.M., 1878: The Testimony of Two Negro Participants," *Arizona and the West* 12 (Summer 1970): 173–78; Robert M. Utley,

"The Buffalo Soldiers and Victorio," *New Mexico Magazine* 62 (March 1984): 47–50, 53–54.

25. Frank N. Schubert, "Troopers, Taverns, and Taxes: Fort Robinson, NE, and Its Municipal Parasite, 1886–1911," in *Soldiers and Civilians: The U.S. Army and the American People,* edited by Garry D. Ryan and Timothy K. Nenninger, 91–103 (Washington, D.C.: National Archives and Records Administration, 1987); Thomas R. Buecker, "The Tenth Cavalry at Fort Robinson, 1902–1907," *Military Images* 7 (May-June, 1991): 6–10; Frank N. Schubert, "The Fort Robinson Y.M.C.A., 1902–1907: A Social Organization in a Black Regiment," *Nebraska History* 55 (Summer 1974): 165–79; Nicholas P. Hardeman, "Brick Stronghold of the Border: Fort Assinniboine, 1879–1911," *Montana: The Magazine of Western History* 29 (Spring 1979): 54–67; Thomas R. Buecker, "Confrontation at Sturgis: An Episode in Civil-Military Race Relations, 1885," *South Dakota History* 14 (Fall 1984): 238–61.

26. James N. Leiker, "Black Soldiers at Fort Hays, Kansas, 1867–1869: A Study in Civilian and Military Violence," *Great Plains Quarterly* 17 (Winter 1996): 3–17; William H. Leckie, "Black Regulars on the Texas Frontier, 1866–1885," in *The Texas Military Experience,* edited by Joseph G. Dawson, 86–96, 219–21 (College Station: Texas A&M University Press, 1995); Patricia E. Lamkin, "Blacks in San Angelo: Relations between Fort Concho and the City, 1875–1889," *West Texas Historical Association Year Book* 66 (1990): 26–37; Mary L. Williams, "Fort Davis, Texas: Key Defense Post on the San Antonio-El Paso Road," *Password* 31 (Winter 1986): 205–10; Garna L. Christian, "Adding on Fort Bliss to Black Military Historiography," *West Texas Historical Association Year Book* 54 (1978): 41–54; Wayne Daniel, "The 10th at Fort Concho, 1875–1882," *Fort Concho Report* 14 (Spring 1982): 7–14.

27. Michael J. Clark, "Improbable Ambassadors: Black Soldiers at Fort Douglas, 1896–1899," *Utah Historical Quarterly* 46 (1978): 282–301; Ronald G. Coleman, "The Buffalo Soldiers: Guardians of the Utah Frontier, 1886–1901," *Utah Historical Quarterly* 47 (1979): 421–39; Douglas Kachel, "Fort Des Moines and Its African-American Troops in 1903/1904," *Palimpsest* 74 (Spring 1993): 42–48.

28. Donald A. Grinde Jr. and Quintard Taylor, "Red v. Black: Conflict and Accommodation in the Post Civil War Indian Territory, 1865–1907," *American Indian Quarterly* 8 (1984): 211–25; Bruce A. Glasrud, "Buffalo Soldiers in Oklahoma," in *Encyclopedia of Oklahoma History and Culture* (Oklahoma City: Oklahoma Historical Society, 2007).

29. Joseph T. Glatthar, *Forged in Battle: The Civil War Alliance of Black Soldiers and White Officers* (New York: Free Press, 1990). Other studies of black soldiers in the Civil War that consider the West include Dudley T. Cornish, *The Sable Arm: Negro Troops in the Union Army, 1861–1865* (New York: W. W. Norton, 1966); Dudley T. Cornish, "Kansas Negro Regiments in the Civil War," *Kansas Historical Quarterly* 20 (1953): 417–29; Keith Philip Wilson, "White Officers in Black Units in the Civil War" (Ph.D. diss., La Trobe University, 1985); John W. Blassingame, "The Recruitment of Negro Troops in Missouri

During the Civil War," *Missouri Historical Review* 58 (April 1964): 326–38; Albert Castel, "Civil War Kansas and the Negro," *Journal of Negro History* 51 (April 1966): 125–38; Noah Andre Trudeau, *Like Men of War: Black Troops in the Civil War, 1862–1865* (Boston: Little, Brown, 1998).

30. Charles L. Kenner, *Buffalo Soldiers and Officers of the Ninth Cavalry, 1867–1898: Black and White Together* (Norman: University of Oklahoma Press, 1999; William H. Leckie and Shirley Leckie, *Unlikely Warriors: General Benjamin Grierson and His Family* (Norman: University of Oklahoma Press, 1984); Douglas C. McChristian, "Grierson's Fight at Tinajade las Palmas: An Episode in the Victorio Campaign," *Red River Valley Historical Review* 71 (Winter 1982): 45–63; Mary L. Williams, "Empire Building: Colonel Benjamin H. Grierson at Fort Davis, 1882–1885," *West Texas Historical Association Year Book* 61 (1985): 58–73; Paul H. Carlson, *"Pecos Bill": A Military Biography of William R. Shafter* (College Station: Texas A&M University Press, 1989); "William R. Shafter, Black Troops, and the Finale to the Red River War," *Red River Valley Historical Review* 3 (Spring 1978): 247–58; "William R. Shafter, Black Troops, and the Opening of the Llano Estacado, 1870–1875," *Panhandle-Plains Historical Review* 47 (1974): 1–18; "William R. Shafter Commanding Black Troops in West Texas," *West Texas Historical Association Year Book* 50 (1974): 104–16; Robert M. Utley, "'Pecos Bill' on the Texas Frontier," *American West* 6 (January 1969): 4–13, 61–62.

31. Bruce J. Dinges, "Scandal in the Tenth Cavalry: A Fort Sill Case History," *Arizona and the West* 28 (Summer 1986): 125–40; "The Irrepressible Captain Armes: Politics and Justice in the Indian-Fighting Army," *Journal of the West* 32 (April 1993): 38–52; Frank M. Temple, "Discipline and Turmoil in the Tenth U.S. Cavalry," *West Texas Historical Association Year Book* 58 (1982): 103–18; Douglas C. McChristian, ed., *Garrison Tangles in the Friendless Tenth: The Journal of First Lieutenant John Bigelow, Jr., Fort Davis, Texas* (Bryan, Tex.: J. M. Carroll, 1985); Marcos E. Kinevan, *Frontier Cavalryman: Lieutenant John Bigelow with the Buffalo Soldiers in Texas* (El Paso: Texas Western Press, 1997); James T. Matthews, "Always in the Vanguard: Patrolling the Texas Frontier with Captain Louis Carpenter and Company H of the Tenth Cavalry," *West Texas Historical Association Year Book* 75 (1999): 110–19; E. G. Longacre, "Philadelphia Aristocrat with the Buffalo Soldiers," *Journal of the West* 18 (April 1979): 79–84; Douglas C. McChristian, "'Dress on the Colors, Boys!' Black Noncommissioned Officers in the Regular Army, 1866–1898," *Colorado Heritage* (Spring 1996): 38–44. On Armes, see also Wayne Daniel, "The Many Trials of Captain Armes," *Fort Concho Report* 13 (Fall 1981): 5–16.

32. Thomas A. Britten, *A Brief History of the Seminole-Negro Indian Scouts* (Lewiston, New York: Edward Mellen Press, 1993); Thomas A. Britten, "The Seminole-Negro Indian Scouts in the Big Bend," *Journal of Big Bend Studies* 5 (1993): 67–77; "The Dismissal of the Seminole-Negro Indian Scouts, 1880–1914," *Fort Concho and the South Plains Journal* 24 (Fall 1992): 54–77; Bill Gwaltney, "The Story of the Seminole-Negro Indian Scouts," *Lest We Forget* 4 (October 1996): 9, 12, 14; Kevin Mulroy, "the Seminole Negro Indian Scouts," in *Freedom on the Border: The Seminole Maroons in Florida, the Indian Territory,*

Coahuila, and Texas, 107–32 (Lubbock: Texas Tech University Press, 1993); Doug Sivad, *The Black Seminole Indians of Texas* (Boston: American Press, 1984); C. Kevin Swisher, "Frontier Heroes [Seminole-Negro-Indian Scouts]," *Texas Highways* 39 (July 1992): 48–51; Scott Thybony, "Against All Odds, Black Seminoles Won Their Freedom," *Smithsonian* 22 (1991): 90–101; Kenneth W. Porter, "The Seminole Negro Indian Scouts, Texas, 1870–1914," in *The Black Seminoles: History of a Freedom-Seeking People,* edited by Alcione M. Amos and Thomas P. Senter, 173–214 (Gainesville, Fla.: University of Florida Press, 1996); Eric Emmerson Strong, "The Lost Treaty of the Black Seminoles," *West Texas Historical Association Year Book* 75 (1999): 120–30.

33. "Cathy Williams' Story," *St. Louis Daily Times* (January 2, 1876); Frank N. Schubert, "William Cathay/Cathay Williams," *Voices of the Buffalo Soldier,* 33–35 (Albuquerque: University of New Mexico Press, 2003); DeAnne Blanton, "Cathey Williams: Black Woman Soldier, 1866–1868," *Minerva: Quarterly Report of Women and the Military* 10 (1992): 1–12; Philip Thomas Tucker, *Cathy Williams: From Slave to Female Buffalo Soldier* (Mechanicsburg, Penn.: Stackpole Books, 2002).

34. John F. Marszalek Jr., "A Black Cadet at West Point," *American Heritage* 12 (August, 1971): 30–37, 104–6; John F. Marszalek Jr., *Assault at West Point: The Court-Martial of Johnson Whittaker* (New York: Collier Books, 1994).

35. Lowell D. Black and Sara H. Black, *An Officer and a Gentleman: The Military Career of Lieutenant Henry O. Flipper* (Dayton, Ohio: Lora, 1985); James C. Cage and James M. Day, *The Court Martial of Henry Ossian Flipper: West Point's First Black Graduate* (El Paso: El Paso Corral of Westerners, 1981); Charles M. Robinson III, *The Court-Martial of Lieutenant Henry Flipper* (El Paso: Texas Western Press, 1994); Jane Eppinga, *Henry Ossian Flipper: West Point's First Black Graduate* (Plano, Tex.: Republic of Texas Press, 1996); Barry C. Johnson, *Flipper's Dismissal: The Ruin of Lt. Henry O. Flipper, U.S.A. First Coloured Graduate of West Point* (London: Privately printed, 1980).

36. Donald R. McClung, "Henry O. Flipper: The First Negro Officer in the United States Army, 1878–1882" (Master's thesis, East Texas State University, 1970); "Second Lieutenant Henry O. Flipper: A Negro Officer on the West Texas Frontier," *West Texas Historical Association Year Book* 47 (1971): 20–31; Bruce J. Dinges, "The Court-Martial of Lieutenant Henry O. Flipper: An Example of Black-White Relationships in the Army," *American West* 9 (January 1972): 12–17, 59–61; Brenda K. East, "Henry Ossian Flipper: Lieutenant of the Buffalo Soldiers," *Persimmon Hill* 23 (Summer 1995): 68–69; Ezra J. Warner, "A Black Man in the Long Gray Line," *American History Illustrated* 4 (January 1970): 30–38; Steve Wilson, "A Black Lieutenant in the Ranks," *American History Illustrated* 18 (December 1983): 31–39; Jane Eppinga, "Henry O. Flipper in the Court of Private Land Claims: The Arizona Career of West Point's First Black Graduate," *Journal of Arizona History* 36 (Spring 1995): 33–54; Theodore D. Harris, "Henry Flipper and Pancho Villa," *Password* 6 (Spring 1961): 39–46.

37. Marvin E. Fletcher, "The Black Soldier Athlete in the United States Army, 1890–1916," *Canadian Journal of History of Sport and Physical Education* 3

(December 1972): 16–26; Monroe Lee Billington, "Civilians and Black Soldiers in New Mexico Territory, 1866–1900: A Cross-Cultural Experience," *Military History of the Southwest* 19 (Spring 1989): 71–82; Horace Daniel Nash, "Community Building on the Border: The Role of the 24th Infantry Band at Columbus, New Mexico, 1916–1922," *Fort Concho and the South Plains Journal* 22 (Summer 1990): 77–86; Charles M. Dollar, "Putting the Army on Wheels: The Story of the Twenty-fifth Infantry Bicycle Corps," *Prologue* 17 (Spring 1985): 7–24; Marvin E. Fletcher, "The Black Bicycle Corps," *Arizona and the West* 16 (1974): 219–32; William Loren Katz, "The Black Infantry and Cavalry," in *The Black West,* 199–244 (New York: Simon and Schuster, 1996); Frank N. Schubert, "Troopers, Taverns, and Taxes: Fort Robinson, NE, and Its Municipal Parasite, 1886–1911," in *Soldiers and Civilians: The U.S. Army and the American People,* edited by Garry D. Ryan and Timothy K. Nenninger, 80–130 (Washington, D.C.: National Archives and Records Administration, 1987); John Henry Nankivell, *History of the Twenty-fifth Regiment, United States Infantry, 1869–1926* (Denver: Smith-Brooks Printing, 1926); Marvin E. Fletcher, "Army Fire Fighters," *Idaho Yesterdays* 16 (Summer 1972): 12–15.

38. Alan K. Lamm, *Five Black Preachers in Army Blue, 1884–1901* (Lewiston, N.Y.: Edwin Mellen Press, 1998); John P. Langellier and Alan M. Osur, "Chaplain Allen Allensworth and the 24th Infantry, 1886–1906," *The Smoke Signal* no. 40 (Fall 1980): 189–208; Earl F. Stover, "Black Chaplains," in *Up from Handymen: The United States Army Chaplaincy, 1865–1920,* 88–92, 98–99 (Washington, D.C.: Department of the Army, 1977); Earl F. Stover, "Chaplain Henry V. Plummer: His Ministry and His Court Martial," *Nebraska History* 56 (Spring 1971): 20–50; William Seraille, "Theophilus G. Steward, Intellectual Chaplain, 25th U.S. Colored Infantry," *Nebraska History* 66 (Fall 1985): 272–93; Alan K. Lamm, "Buffalo Soldiers Chaplains: A Case Study of the Five Black United States Army Chaplains, 1884–1901" (Ph.D. diss., University of South Carolina, 1995); Frank Schubert, "Allen Allensworth," *Dictionary of American Negro Biography,* edited by Rayford W. Logan and Michael R. Winston, 13–14 (New York: W. W. Norton, 1982); "Henry Vinton Plummer," in *DANB,* edited by Rayford W. Logan and Michael R. Winston, 498–99 (New York: W. W. Norton, 1982);; "Theophilus Gould Steward, in *DANB,* edited by Rayford W. Logan and Michael R. Winston, 570–71 (New York: W. W. Norton, 1982); Bruce A. Glasrud, "Josephine Leavell Allensworth," in *African American Women: A Biographical Dictionary,* edited by Dorothy C. Salem, 9–10 (New York: Garland Publishing, 1993).

39. Lee Myers, "Mutiny at Fort Cummings," *New Mexico Historical Review* 46 (1971): 337–50; Byron Price, "Mutiny at San Pedro Springs," *By Valor and Arms* 1 (Spring 1975): 31–34; John Warren Hunter, "Mutiny of Negro Soldiers at Fort Concho, 1882," *Hunter's Magazine* (December 1911): 4–5, 13; Susan Miles, "The Soldiers' Riot," *Fort Concho Report* 13 (Spring 1981): 1–20; Clayton W. Williams, "A Threatened Mutiny of Soldiers at Fort Stockton in 1873 Resulted in Penitentiary Sentences of Five to Fifteen Years," *West Texas Historical Association Year Book* 52 (1976): 78–83.

40. The type of sources available at the National Archives, and their possible use, has imaginatively been depicted in Elaine Everly, "Red, Black, and White: The U.S. Army at Columbus, GA," in *Soldiers and Civilians: The U.S. Army and the American People,* edited by Garry D. Ryan and Timothy K. Nenninger, 104–13 (Washington, D.C.: National Archives and Records Administration, 1987). Other examples of the available sources can be viewed in Bernard C. Nalty and Morris J. MacGregor, eds., "Freedom and Jim Crow, 1865–1917," in *Blacks in the Military: Essential Documents,* 43–71 (Wilmington, Del.: Scholarly Resources, 1981). See also Preston E. Amos, "Military Records for Nonmilitary History," *Afro-American History: Sources for Research,* edited by Robert L. Clarke, 65–73 (Washington, D.C.: Howard University Press, 1981).

41. John Prebble, *The Buffalo Soldiers* (New York: Harcourt, Brace, 1959); Tom Willard, *Buffalo Soldiers* (New York: Tom Doherty Associates, 1996); Elmer Kelton, *The Wolf and the Buffalo* (Fort Worth: Texas Christian University Press, 1986). See also William Heuman, *Buffalo Soldier* (New York: Dodd, Mead, 1969).

42. On black soldiers in World War I see Arthur E. Barbeau and Florette Henri, *The Unknown Soldiers: Black American Troops in World War I* (Philadelphia: Temple University Press, 1974); Florette Henri and Richard Stillman, *Bitter Victory: A History of Black Soldiers in World War I* (New York: Doubleday, 1970); Hal J. Chase, "Struggle for Equality: Fort Des Moines Training Camp for Colored Officers, 1917," *Phylon* 39 (Winter 1978): 297–310; James W. Jackson, "The Black Man and Military Mobilization in the United States, 1916–1919" (Master's thesis, California State University, Hayward, 1970).

43. Marvin E. Fletcher, *The Black Soldier and Officer in the United States Army, 1891–1917* (Columbia: University of Missouri Press, 1974); Willard B. Gatewood Jr., *Black Americans and the White Man's Burden, 1893–1903* (Urbana: University of Illinois Press, 1975); Willard B. Gatewood Jr., *"Smoked Yankees" and the Struggle for Empire: Letters from Negro Soldiers, 1898–1902* (Urbana: University of Illinois Press, 1971); Willard B. Gatewood Jr., "Black Americans and the Quest for Empire, 1898–1903," *Journal of Southern History* 38 (1972): 545–66.

44. Clarence C. Clendenen, *Blood on the Border: The United States Army and the Mexican Irregulars* (New York: Macmillan, 1969); Clarence C. Clendenen, "The Punitive Expedition of 1916: Reevaluation," *Arizona and the West* 3 (Winter 1961): 311–20; Linda B. Hall and Don M. Coerver, *Revolution on the Border: The United States and Mexico, 1910–1920* (Albuquerque: University of New Mexico Press, 1988); Glenn Justice, *Revolution on the Rio Grande: Mexican Raids and Army Pursuits, 1916–1919* (El Paso: Texas Western Press, 1992); James P. Finley, "Buffalo Soldiers at Fort Huachuca: Military Events in the American Southwest from 1910–1916," *Huachuca Illustrated* 1 (1993); Robert B. Johnson, "The Punitive Expedition: A Military, Diplomatic, and Political History of Pershing's Chase after Pancho Villa, 1916–1917" (Ph.D. diss., University of Southern California, 1964); Richard Meltzer, "On Villa's Trail in Mexico: The Experience of a Black Cavalryman and a White Infantry Officer, 1916–1917," *Military History of the Southwest* 21 (Fall 1991): 173–90; Andrew Wallace, "The Sabre Retires:

Pershing's Cavalry Campaign in Mexico, 1916," *Smoke Signal* no. 9 (Spring 1964): 1–24; Richard O'Connor, "Black Jack of the 10th," *American Heritage* 18 (February, 1967): 14–17, 102–7; Donald Smyth, "John Pershing at Fort Assiniboine," *Montana* 18 (January, 1968): 19–23; Orlando C. Troxel, "The Tenth Cavalry in Mexico," *Journal of the United States Cavalry Association* 18 (October, 1917): 197–205; Col. H. B. Wharfield, *Tenth Cavalry and Border Fights* (El Cajon, CA: Privately printed, 1964); Col. H. B. Wharfield, "The Affair at Carrizal: Pershing's Punitive Expedition," *Montana* 18 (October 1968): 24–39.

45. Ann J. Lane, *The Brownsville Affair: National Crisis and Black Reaction* (Port Washington: Kennikat Press, 1971); John D. Weaver, *The Brownsville Raid* (New York: W. W. Norton, 1970); Lewis N. Wynne, "Brownsville: The Reaction of the Negro Press," *Phylon* 33 (Summer 1972): 153–60; Richard Young, "The Brownsville Affray," *American History Illustrated* 21 (October 1986): 10–17; Thomas R. Buecker, "Prelude to Brownsville: The Twenty-fifth Infantry at Fort Niobrara, Nebraska, 1902–06," *Great Plains Quarterly* 16 (Spring 1996): 95–106.

46. Bruce A. Glasrud, "Enforcing White Supremacy in Texas, 1900–1910," *Red River Valley Historical Review* 4 (Fall 1979): 65–74; Garna L. Christian, *Black Soldiers in Jim Crow Texas, 1899–1917* (College Station: Texas A&M University Press, 1995); "The El Paso Racial Crisis of 1900," *Red River Valley Historical Review* 6 (Spring 1981): 28–41; "The Violent Possibility: The Tenth Cavalry at Texarkana," *East Texas Historical Journal* 23 (Spring 1985): 3–15; "Rio Grande City: Prelude to the Brownsville Raid," *West Texas Historical Association Year Book* 57 (1981): 118–32; "The Brownsville Raid's 168th Man: The Court-Martial of Corporal Knowles," *Southwestern Historical Quarterly* 93 (1989): 45–59; "The Twenty-fifth Regiment at Fort McIntosh: Precursor to Retaliatory Racial Violence," *West Texas Historical Association Year Book* 55 (1979): 149–61.

47. Robert V. Haynes, *A Night of Violence: The Houston Riot of 1917* (Baton Rouge: Louisiana State University Press, 1976); Robert V. Haynes, "The Houston Mutiny and Riot of 1917," *Southwestern Historical Quarterly* 76 (1973): 418–39. Also on the Houston conflagration, see Thomas Richard Adams, "The Houston Riot of 1917" (Master's thesis, Texas A&M University, 1972); Phocion Samuel Park Jr., "The Twenty-fourth Infantry Regiment and the Houston Riot of 1917" (Master's thesis, University of Houston, 1971); and especially two recent articles by C. Calvin Smith, "The Houston Riot of 1917, Revisited," *Houston Review* 13 (1991): 84–102, and "On the Edge: The Houston Riot of 1917 Revisited," *Griot* 10 (Spring 1991): 3–12. Shortly before the Houston episode an incendiary moment involving white citizens and black soldiers transpired in Waco, but the tense situation ebbed; see Garna L. Christian, "The Ordeal and the Prize: The 24th Infantry and Camp MacArthur," *Military Affairs* 50 (April 1986): 65–70.

48. Paul H. Carlson, *The Buffalo Soldier Tragedy of 1877* (College Station: Texas A&M University Press, 2003); William A. Dobak and Thomas D. Phillips, *The Black Regulars, 1866–1898* (Norman: University of Oklahoma Press, 2001); James N. Leiker, *Racial Borders: Black Soldiers along the Rio Grande* (College Station: Texas A&M University Press, 2002); Frank N. Schubert, *Voices of the Buffalo Soldier: Records, Reports, and Recollections of Military Life and Service*

in the West (Albuquerque: University of New Mexico Press, 2003); Frank N. Schubert and Irene Schubert, *On the Trail of the Buffalo Soldiers*, vol. II (Wilmington, Del.: Scholarly Resources, 2003).

49. Colin L. Powell and Joseph E. Persico, *My American Journey* (New York: Random House, 1995); James P. Finley, *The Buffalo Soldiers at Fort Huachuca*, 3 issues (Fort Huachuca, Ariz.: Huachuca Museum Society, 1993–96); George E. Knapp, *Buffalo Soldiers at Fort Leavenworth in the 1930s and Early 1940s* (Fort Leavenworth: Combat Studies Institute, 1991); International Museum of the Horse, "The Buffalo Soldiers on the Western Frontier." [http:/www.horseworld.com/imh/buf/buftoc.htm].

50. William H. Leckie and Shirley Leckie, *The Buffalo Soldiers: A Narrative of the Black Cavalry in the West*, rev. ed. (Norman: University of Oklahoma Press, 2003; Bruce A. Glasrud and William H. Leckie, "Buffalo Soldiers," in *African Americans in the West: A Bibliography of Secondary Sources*, edited by Bruce A. Glasrud, 32–53 (Alpine, Tex.: SRSU Center for Big Bend Studies, 1998); Quintard Taylor, "Comrades of Color: Buffalo Soldiers in the West, 1866–1917," *Colorado Heritage* (Spring 1996): 3–27.

51. Leckie and Leckie, *Buffalo Soldiers*, xi; Leiker, *Racial Borders;* Vernon Bellecourt, "The Glorification of Buffalo Soldiers Raises Racial Divisions between Black, Indians," *Indian Country Today* (May 4, 1994); Kenner, *Buffalo Soldiers and Officers of the Ninth Cavalry;* Dobak and Phillips, *Black Regulars.*

52. Quintard Taylor, "Blacks in the American West: An Overview," *Western Journal of Black Studies* 1 (March 1977): 7; Rayford W. Logan, *The Betrayal of the Negro from Rutherford B. Hayes to Woodrow Wilson* (New York: Collier Books, 1965), 335.

53. Richard White, "Race Relations in the American West," *American Quarterly* 38 (1986): 394–416.

PART I

The Officers and the Troops

During the late nineteenth century, as previously noted, the regularly enlisted black soldiers served in four regiments—the Ninth and Tenth Cavalry, and the Twenty-fourth and Twenty-fifth Infantry. Their military experiences have been well detailed, the cavalry in William Leckie's *The Buffalo Soldiers,* the infantry in Arlen Fowler's *The Black Infantry in the West,* and an inclusive assessment in William A. Dobak and Thomas D. Phillip's *The Black Regulars.* Black soldiers of necessity needed to come to grips with three military related factors: (1) their position and responsibilities in the changing military presence in the West; (2) their behavior and duties at the garrisons in which they were stationed; and (3) their interrelationships with their officers, most of whom were white. Since the interrelationships of officers and soldiers were so important, solid professional contributions, including the above mentioned studies, have delved into that relationship. Scholars, such as Marvin E. Fletcher, *The Black Soldier and Officer in the United States Army;* Paul H. Carlson, *"Pecos Bill": A Military Biography of William R. Shafter;* Charles L. Kenner, *Soldiers and Officers of the Ninth Cavalry;* Marcos E. Kinevan, *Frontier Cavalryman: Lieutenant John Bigelow with the Buffalo Soldiers in Texas;* and William Leckie and Shirley Leckie, *Unlikely Warriors: General Benjamin Grierson and His Family;* have furthered our understanding of the respective positions of white officer and black soldier. Charles Kenner argued that both sought honor, and though his subtitle declaimed "black and white together," not always was the togetherness noticeable.

The enlistment of black soldiers into the regular army in the years after the Civil War coincided with another critical development for the

U.S. Army, that of its emergent role in protecting and promoting the national move across the West. Using Fort Riley, Kansas, and black soldiers as examples, William A. Dobak in "Fort Riley's Black Soldiers and the Army's Changing Role in the West," shows how the two developments interacted with each other. When black soldiers in the Tenth Cavalry arrived at Fort Riley for their base of operations, their assignment, in addition to garrison duty itself, was to protect transportation routes then being constructed. In the spring they were sent west to guard construction crews and to ensure safe travel, but they wintered back at Fort Riley. Years later, when the Ninth Cavalry arrived at Fort Riley, the railroads moved them quickly to various spots in demonstrations of federal authority such as the southern border of Kansas, to keep "Boomers" from illegally entering Indian Territory. Soldiers at Fort Riley, and the U.S. Army, moved from protecting railroad construction to utilization of the railroads for troop deployment quickly and efficiently. In the intervening years the Native Americans in the West had been subdued, the bison virtually eliminated, and the remaining Indians placed on reservations, all results that could be attributed in part to the black soldiers.

Fort Riley was one of many posts that housed black troops in the late nineteenth century. Though they engaged in fighting, building roads, or protecting stage lines or people, back at the fort, the life of the black soldier offered little relief to isolation and monotony; the black soldier sought to improve his education, attended endless drills, parades, and inspections, struggled with the absence of families, and suffered boring and tedious garrison duty.

The assignment of black troops to posts distant from populated areas naturally affected their lives as soldiers in the U.S. West after the Civil War, but on and off duty black soldiers were commanded by officers, almost all of whom were white. White officers, in general, believed blacks to be inferior, preferred not to be attached to a black regiment, and considered such an assignment as belittling; a few, such as George A. Custer, refused outright such an assignment. Those officers who were successful leaders, and who treated black soldiers equitably, appreciated the bravery and dedication of the black soldiers. Such officers often tried to protect the black troops from racial antagonisms, and in most matters supported their troops. Paul H. Carlson's article, "William R. Shafter, Black Troops, and the Opening of the Llano Estacado," examines the attitude and behavior of a white officer who demanded much from his troops, but who supported them and considered them to be good soldiers. Carlson also pointed out the professional response of Shafter's black troops to the demands made on them.

From the end of the Civil War to 1900, only eight officers—three line and five chaplains—were black. The three commissioned officers were graduates of West Point, and upon receiving their commissions were assigned to lead the black troops. One of these officers (as will be noted in chapter two), Lt. Henry O. Flipper, was dishonorably discharged from the army, almost certainly on the basis of racism. The other two, John Alexander and Charles Young, remained in service with the Ninth Cavalry. The other black officers were army chaplains, and in the late nineteenth century five African Americans received assignment as chaplains in black units. As Alan K. Lamm points out in his article "Buffalo Soldier Chaplains of the Old West," the five had varied backgrounds, and varied success in their assignments. As with Lieutenant Flipper, the chaplains faced racism from white leaders and peers. Chaplain Charles V. Plummer was dismissed from the army for what could only be called "conduct unbecoming a black man." But against long odds the chaplains managed to meet the needs of the black serviceman. A key reason for the appointment of black chaplains was to assist the black soldiers with their education. Chaplain Allen Allensworth, for example, especially was successful in developing an educational plan that worked for the black soldier, thereby benefiting the army and society as well as the soldier.

The officers who had the most contact with black soldiers, of course, were the black noncommissioned officers. Douglas C. McChristian's informative and path-breaking article, "'Dress on the Colors, Boys!' Black Noncommissioned Officers in the Regular Army," notes that these officers needed to be professional soldiers, preferably veterans, who had to be tough, able to enforce discipline, have an ability to manage men, and, as a plus, would be educated with administrative skills. The noncommissioned officers truly were the backbone of the western army in the late nineteenth century. Overall, black troops were commanded by white officers, but followed the direct orders in training and duty details of tough, wise, black noncommissioned officers. This was the case whether on a well-established post such as Fort Riley or on a frontier post. The overall success of the black cavalry and the black infantry during the late nineteenth century can be attributed to the ability of black soldiers, white officers, and black noncommissioned officers to work together on behalf of their common goals while at the same time adapting to changing roles and changing traditions within the western U.S. military.

WILLIAM A. DOBAK

Fort Riley's Black Soldiers and the Army's Changing Role in the West, 1867–85

At the end of the Civil War, the U.S. Army faced three major strategic challenges. The states of the former Confederacy required a military occupation force. South of the Rio Grande, Mexican nationalist forces were fighting a French army of occupation, which created turmoil along the border. Transportation routes westward to the Pacific Coast, and to recently developed goldfields in Montana and Colorado, also required protection. To meet these needs, the regular army mustered a force that numbered, by law, fewer than forty thousand men.

Part of the solution to these new problems was to enlarge the army and increase available manpower by enlisting black soldiers in the regular army for the first time. Before the Civil War the regular army had accepted no black recruits, but Republicans in Congress noticed the satisfactory performance of the black volunteers—more than 175,000 of them—who had served in the U.S. colored troops during the war. When the appropriation act of 1866 provided for an expanded army, it specified that four regiments of infantry and two of cavalry would be "composed of colored men."[1]

As it turned out, both of the black cavalry regiments passed through Kansas and furnished part of Fort Riley's garrison during the next two decades. The years they spent at the fort—the Tenth Cavalry in 1867 and 1868 and the Ninth from 1881 to 1885—bracketed an epoch in the military history of the American West. The army's duties in the West changed during these years, and the black regiments' service at Fort Riley exemplified that change.

Although Fort Riley had been the westernmost fort on the central route to Colorado during the gold rush of 1859, by the mid-1860s it no longer was an isolated frontier post. The fort and its twenty-thousand-acre military reservation lay close to major transportation routes, a few days' march from the Platte River to the north and to the Arkansas River to the south. The Kansas state census of 1865 counted 3,002 residents in adjacent Davis (now Geary) and Riley counties. Gen. William Tecumseh Sherman, on a tour of inspection in the summer of 1866, remarked that "the country out as far as Fort Riley is as much a settled country as Illinois and Missouri." What, then, justified keeping the post open?[2]

A few weeks before Sherman's visit; the commanding officer, Maj. John W. Davidson, had pondered the fort's future:

> As a station of troops . . . in [the] event of Indian hostilities Fort Riley has lost its importance, settlements being well in advance of it on both the Smokey [sic] Hill and Republican Rivers. But as a Depot for the supply of the posts in our western Territories . . . is of great importance to the Government. This should be, in my opinion, the Cavalry Depot of the West. The Government owns a large reserve here; the facilities for grazing are unsurpassed in the West. . . . The remount horses of all the cavalry Posts . . . should be kept here. The broken down stock, instead of being condemned or sold at the posts, should be conducted here for recuperation.[3]

It would be eighteen years before the army's high command followed Davidson's recommendation and ten beyond that before the Mounted Branch School—for cavalry and horse-drawn field artillery—opened. In the meantime, cost-conscious military leaders used Fort Riley as a winter dormitory for troops whose summer campaigns took them far to the west and south, often by rail. Railroads enabled the troops to travel farther and faster than ever before.[4]

To keep open the central transportation corridor between the Arkansas and Platte rivers, the federal government negotiated new treaties with the Plains tribes. When the Cheyennes and Arapahos signed the Treaty of Medicine Lodge in October 1867, they "reserve[d] the right to hunt on any lands south of the Arkansas as long as the buffalo may range thereon in such numbers as to justify the chase." The following spring the Sioux reserved the right to hunt buffalo on the Republican River, in an identically worded clause of the treaty they signed at Fort Laramie. The Medicine Lodge and Fort Laramie treaties were intended to assure the whites of a central region, free of Indians, through which railroads could pass to California, Colorado, and New Mexico. Within a few years these railroads made possible the commercial slaughter of the buffalo, eliminating the hunting rights guaranteed in the treaties. Meanwhile, the railroads afforded the army a cheap way to move supplies and troops—always a paramount concern of a government agency with a fixed annual budgets.[5]

The new black regiments knew well the army's concern with transportation costs. The Ninth Cavalry and the Forty-first Infantry organized in Louisiana and moved to Texas by sea in 1867, marching inland from the coast. The Tenth Cavalry and the Thirty-eighth Infantry followed the line of the Kansas Pacific Railway west through Fort Riley and dispersed from there. Half of the Thirty-eighth Infantry stayed in Kansas, guarding the railroad, while the other half marched overland to New Mexico. By 1869 the Tenth Cavalry had gathered in Indian Territory, where it built Fort Sill, the regiment's main station for the next five years. From the fall of 1867 to the spring of 1868, however, the Tenth became the first cavalry regiment to take advantage of Fort Riley's position on the railroad, using the barracks as winter quarters for the troops and the spacious reservation as pasture for the horses.

Beginning in April 1867 companies of the Tenth had been heading west, as fast as they could be organized, to guard construction crews on the Kansas Pacific. A common dateline on the bimonthly company muster rolls that summer and fall was "Near end of track Pacific Railroad." The Tenth's commanding officer, Col. Benjamin H. Grierson, asked that companies of his regiment be sent to winter at Fort Riley, to receive recruits, fresh horses, and weapons, and to drill "as nearly as possible in the order in which they marched to the field." Six companies arrived in November and December. Company K, marching in from Fort Harker, near Ellsworth, "was caught in a severe snow storm . . . and the men suffered severely from frozen feet."[6]

At Fort Riley, the companies spent the winter taking in recruits and horses and replenishing their clothing, arms, and equipment. They left in April 1868 and passed the rest of the year on the Plains, looking for Indians who were living in the valleys of the Republican and Smoky Hill rivers, off their reservations, and raiding both white homesteads and other Indians as far east as the Kansas tribe's agency at Council Grove. In September, Company H of the Tenth rode hurriedly to relieve a beleaguered company of fifty-two civilian scouts at Beecher Island in the Arikaree Fork of the Republican River. The scouts were Kansas residents for the most part, auxiliaries recruited for their knowledge of the Plains, but a force of about six hundred Cheyennes and Sioux from nearby camps had cornered them for eight days before the soldiers arrived.[7]

The year 1868 ended for the Tenth Cavalry with four companies taking part in a winter campaign out of Fort Lyon, Colorado, that kept them in the field from November to February. "The weather was so very cold that our horses froze to death on the picket line," Pvt. James H. Massey recalled years later. "Every man who lost his horse had to march with his saddle on his back. We run short of rations, was without anything to eat except quarter rations for some three or four days." Meanwhile, four other companies of the regiment wintered at posts along the line of the Kansas Pacific. The Tenth Cavalry did not return to Fort Riley, but the army's practice of using the post as winter quarters and leaving in the spring to campaign on the Plains continued whenever cavalry served there. Raids had not halted railroad construction in 1868 as they had the year before, and trains loaded with supplies rolled past Fort Riley to forts Hays, Wallace and, by 1872, Dodge, and kept the troops in the field armed, fed, and clad.[8]

Soldiers guarded construction of the railroads, which in turn helped supply the army and, within a few years, changed the face of the West and the army's role in it. An unforeseen result of the railroads' presence was the trade in raw buffalo hides, which destroyed the Plains Indians' chief source of food, clothing, and shelter. About 1870 a new tanning technique made possible the use of buffalo hides for shoe leather and industrial drive belts. The new railroads were the only profitable means of shipping the high-bulk, low-value hides. By the late 1870s the buffalo had been nearly exterminated in the Central and Southern Plains. Their disappearance annulled those treaty provisions that allowed Plains Indians to leave their reservations to hunt. For the army, this meant that instead of camping out in the summer to keep an eye on buffalo-hunting Indians in sparsely settled western Kansas, troops would be called on at any time of year to frustrate schemes for white occupation of tribal lands in Indian Territory, just to the south.[9]

By the end of the 1870s new railroad lines were able to carry troops from Fort Riley to several campaigns that historians seldom mention. Military historians do not write much about the army's activities in the 1880s because little shooting occurred. Nor does the army appear frequently in tribal histories of the early reservation period unless there was a fort adjacent to the agency, such as Fort Sill on the Comanche and

Kiowa reservation or Fort Reno on the Cheyenne and Arapaho. Yet the army spent a large part of its time, manpower, and budget during the 1880s in quiet demonstrations of federal authority. Those in which troops from Fort Riley took part are worth examining, since they were more typical of the army's activities during the last two decades of the century than were the more violent incidents that usually receive historians' attention.[10]

Late in the fall of 1881 four companies of the Ninth Cavalry arrived at Fort Riley, hoping for a rest from years of rigorous campaigning in New Mexico, where the regiment had been scattered at a dozen small posts. A quotation from one company's "Record of Events" (part of the bimonthly muster and payroll) offers a sample of the regiment's activities during the previous six years.

> About 8 o'clock found trail of hostile Chiricahua Apache Indians going south and followed it along the eastern slope of the Dragoon Mountains Struck hostiles about 2 o'clock P.M. a running fight took place which lasted for 15 miles when the Indians took to the rocks in the main range and made a stand about sunset a sharp fight ensued continuing until Dark Pvts James Goodlow, Henry Harrison and Wm H Carroll were wounded one horse slightly wounded Indians escaped during the night and crossed into Mexico.[11]

Many brief narratives like this appear in company records of the Ninth Cavalry, especially in the years from 1879 to 1881, when the men of the regiment exchanged shots with Indians on thirty-seven occasions. The regiment, Gen. John Pope reported, had been "almost continuously in the field, the greater part of the time in harassing and wearisome pursuit of small bands of Indians" and was "much run down in every way." Pope hoped to give the Ninth a rest, stationing regimental headquarters and four of the regiment's companies at Fort Riley, with its good rail connections, and the other eight companies at posts in the western part of Indian Territory.[12]

Dispersed as they had been throughout New Mexico, companies of the Ninth arrived piecemeal at Fort Riley in December 1881. They soon made themselves at home at the fort and in nearby Junction City, adopting a more tranquil routine than they had known for years past. "About a dozen" singers from the regiment came to town on Christmas Eve "for our colored folks Christmas tree entertainment," the *Junction City Union* reported, and two days later enlisted men invited their black civilian neighbors to a ball at the post. In January members of the regimental band played at a meeting of Junction City's black Masons.[13]

When orders came for the Ninth to go to Colorado the following June, the *Union's* editor wrote: "Our whole community sincerely regrets this, because the entire command, officers and men, are very popular with our people, in social and business circles." During the Ninth's six months' residence at Fort Riley, the newspaper had only once reported drunken soldiers in the streets of town, and a soldier's cap left at the site of an attempted burglary. The men of the Ninth Cavalry seem to have been good neighbors.[14]

The errand that took the Ninth from Kansas to Colorado in June 1882 was the removal of the Ute Indians from their old reservation, which had taken up the western third of Colorado. After statehood in 1876, Coloradans set about opening up the mineral-rich Ute reservation, which they accomplished with only a brief shooting war in 1879 and a treaty the next year that removed the northern Utes to a reservation in Utah, and confined the southern Utes to a much smaller reservation in southwestern Colorado. (Gen. John Pope, supervising operations from Fort Leavenworth, remarked that the "whites were so eager and so unrestrained by common decency that it was absolutely necessary to use military force to keep them off the reservation until the Indians were fairly gone.") In 1881 the Fourth Cavalry had traveled by rail from Fort Riley to attend the Utes' removal. The year after it was the Ninth Cavalry's turn to spend a summer in the mountains.[15]

The cars of the Atchison, Topeka, and Santa Fe Railroad took them as far as Pueblo, Colorado, where men and horses transferred to the narrow-gauge Denver and Rio Grande. They chugged on west through Royal Gorge and beyond the town of Gunnison, until the train dropped them at the end of track, a spot named Kezar. It was "a counterpart of all terminal points," M Troop's Lt. John F. McBlain, who signed his letters VERITAS, wrote to the *Junction City Union:* the businesses comprised one butcher, one blacksmith, and "some fifteen" saloons. The companies of the Ninth moved five days' march west, which put them five weeks' distance ahead of the track-laying crews. Officers and men spent their time fishing and wondering why they were there. "The Indians are, at present, perfectly quiet," McBlain wrote, "and my idea is that we will move through the country in order to pacify the settlers and prevent conflict between them and the Indians. There is scarcely any possibility of trouble with the Utes unless the policy of disarming them is insisted upon by Secretary of the Interior Henry M. Teller." Vehement reaction to camp rumors about a move to Wyoming showed that the troops really had no idea what lay in store for them. "After five years hard campaigning in New Mexico, having been sent there for a rest after hard service in Texas, only to get into another hornet's nest. We came to Kansas with a hope that we were to have at least a couple of years of rest," only to be told "that having done nothing for almost five months we must pick up, and take ourselves to another department." But the men of the Ninth stayed put until Denver and Rio Grande construction crews caught up with them, and when the troops left Colorado early in October, the railroad carried them back to Fort Riley.[16]

There they resumed garrison life. A few weeks after their return, a group of enlisted men who called themselves the Social Dancing Club sponsored a ball. "The music was furnished by the orchestra of the Ninth Cavalry Band. Supper was served at midnight, then dancing continued until three in the morning," the *Union* reported. Late in the winter, Pvt. Nicholas Dunlap of the band married Nancy Johnson, daughter of a Junction City farmer. In the spring of 1883 men of the regiment strung the first telephone line between Junction City and Fort Riley. The band took part in Decoration Day ceremonies at the post and in town. Throughout the years of the Ninth Cavalry's stay at Fort Riley, only an occasional announcement in the *Union*, advertising the sale of condemned cavalry horses, hinted at the rigors of summer campaigns in which no shots were fired. [17]

With rail transportation available, however, even smaller disturbances could evoke responses that would not have been possible ten, or even five, years earlier. In June 1883, when Navajo herdsmen were reported to be grazing sheep off their reservation, two companies of the Ninth Cavalry from Fort Riley again went by rail to southwestern Colorado. This time the "narrow but comfortable cars" of the Denver and Rio Grande dropped them at Fort Lewis, near Durango, about a hundred miles farther along than the tracks had run the previous year.[18]

The Navajos were a large tribe, numbering about sixteen thousand, with an estimated eight hundred thousand sheep. The reservation that they had been assigned in 1869 had been enlarged substantially in 1880, and soon would be again, although it remained inadequate for a large pastoral population. With few white settlements nearby to bother them, the Navajos did not pay much attention to the reservation boundaries. Their flocks had "clear[ed] the country of every blade of grass," the commanding officer at Fort Lewis reported, and reinforcements from Fort Riley would have to bring a grain ration for their horses. When word of the cavalry's arrival reached them, the Navajos withdrew to their reservation. Ninth Cavalry patrols "saw no Indians with herds" and "found no trouble."[19]

In August, M Troop accompanied about seven hundred Jicarilla Apaches during their removal from northern New Mexico to another reservation in the southeastern part of the territory. They parted company with the Apaches near Santa Fe, where a company from another regiment took over the escort duty. The men "went to bed full of anticipations," Lieutenant McBlain wrote,

> for we had been informed that we were to leave Santa Fe for Fort Riley. . . . About 10 o'clock, Capt. Lawton, of the Fourth cavalry, rode into camp with an order . . . to immediately draw rations and forage, and return to Fort Lewis as rapidly as practicable as a man had been killed by the Navajoes . . . and that the Indians were threatening. . . . The wagons which had been sent to Santa Fe after supplies returned to camp and we at once broke camp and started on our return, the most dejected looking lot of mortals the sun ever shone on.[20]

Soon after M Troop reached Fort Lewis, a scouting party of the Ninth learned that a few Utes or Navajos had shot and killed a white farmer ("a violent man," who "on former occasions had pointed his gun at Indians," according to the commanding officer at Fort Lewis) when he accused them of stealing his corn and melons. The incident did not foreshadow a general rising.[21]

McBlain was disgusted. "What few settlers there are" near Fort Lewis "will keep up their cry of wolf, fooling the troops, until . . . when they may possibly require assistance it will be denied them under the impression that it is the old cry. The quartering of troops in that locality is asked for without the shadow of a necessity, but solely with a view of getting the trade and what little money the soldiers may have to dispose of." This was a common attitude among civilians throughout the West. General Sherman had noted it soon after the Civil War; it was the prevalent view in the neighborhood of Fort Riley, and the men of the Ninth Cavalry would encounter it again soon, for their next field of operations lay in Indian Territory, where they struggled with white trespassers on tribal lands.[22]

Just south of Kansas, in present Oklahoma, Indian Territory was home to five tribes that had been removed there from the Southeast before the Civil War. Most of these people had sided with the Confederacy, and in 1866 the federal government imposed a series of punitive treaties by which the tribes forfeited about one-third of their lands. Some of the ceded area was assigned as reservations to southern Plains tribes—Arapaho, Cheyenne, Comanche, and Kiowa—and some to tribes who were moving south from Kansas, where their old, pre-war reservations were being opened to white settlement. In the middle of Indian Territory lay the Oklahoma District, nearly two million acres that had not been assigned to any tribe.[23]

During the 1870s settlement in Kansas approached the ninety-eighth meridian (approximately the twenty-inch rainfall line), beyond which farmers found it increasingly difficult to make a crop using traditional methods. At the same time, new military posts in Indian Territory promised stricter control of potentially hostile Plains Indians. The commercial slaughter of buffalo increased the urgency of government efforts to teach tribesmen to farm, which, reformers contended, would enable them to survive on a greatly reduced land base. All these developments led railroad promoters, land speculators, and farmers to cast covetous eyes on the Oklahoma District.[24]

The Boomers (named for the land boom they hoped to create) argued that in not assigning the Oklahoma District to any tribe, Congress had implicitly added it to the part of the public domain that was open to settlement. Carl Schurz, the secretary of the interior, expressed a different view in a letter to the secretary of war, in which he requested the army's help to forestall the Boomers' colonization scheme and, if necessary, to arrest their leaders. Not only had Congress failed to authorize settlement in the Oklahoma District at any time since the treaties of 1866, Schurz pointed out, but recent legislation had explicitly placed the district, along with the rest of Indian Territory, within the jurisdiction of the federal court at Fort Smith, Arkansas. He asked the secretary of war to send troops to Coffeyville, Wichita, and Arkansas City, Kansas, three towns where the Boomers were assembling.[25]

Beginning in the summer of 1879, troops from Fort Riley and other posts paid frequent visits to towns along the southern state line of Kansas, sometimes staying for months at a time, sometimes pursuing the Boomers into Indian Territory. The only penalty for trespass on Indian lands, however, was a fine for the second offense. Since the Boomers who were convicted owned no property and could not pay a fine, federal authorities released them each time, and each time the Boomers prepared another invasion. The Ninth Cavalry's Col. Edward Hatch, who in 1884 commanded the army's newly created District of Oklahoma, thought that the Boomers' leaders were confidence men who sought to "obtain money from the ignorant people deluded into the purchase of claims and town lots, and from the fees paid on joining what they term the 'Oklahoma Colony.'" They had already collected, Hatch reckoned, in "the neighborhood of $100,000. . . . Should the country be open to settlers there would be an end to their profits." The Boomers' leaders, Hatch said, grew fat on their annual circuit from the assembly points on the Kansas state line, to a campsite in the Indian Territory where troops arrested them, to the federal court in Fort Smith, and back to Kansas again.[26]

Officials of the War Department and the Office of Indian Affairs urged imprisonment as punishment for trespass, and bills were introduced in session after session of Congress, but none passed. Finally, the death of the Boomers' leader in 1884 deprived them of their guiding spirit, and the question of the Oklahoma District merged with the larger one of the allotment of Indian lands in severalty-individual ownership of land, a step toward eventual assimilation and citizenship—and the opening of reservations throughout the Plains, which led in 1887 to the General Allotment Act. The federal government allowed white settlement in the Oklahoma District in 1889, and in 1907, after federal efforts to wreck tribal governments in Indian Territory had succeeded, Oklahoma attained statehood.[27]

Companies of the Ninth Cavalry at Fort Sill and other posts in Indian Territory had been chasing the Boomers since early 1882. In the summer of 1884 two companies from Fort Riley marched south to Indian Territory to help make the last arrest of the Boomers' leader, David L. Payne. The troops returned to Fort Riley in October.[28]

Payne died a month later in Wellington, Kansas, while preparing yet another assault on the Oklahoma District, and his followers soon crossed the line again. This time the soldiers from Fort Riley took the railroad—four coaches for the men and sixteen freight cars for their horses and equipment. It was the coldest winter in nine years. From the Ninth Cavalry's camp at Caldwell, Colonel Hatch telegraphed repeatedly to Fort Riley's post quartermaster, requesting arctic overshoes and baled hay. Before January was over, twenty railroad carloads of hay would travel from Fort Riley to the Ninth Cavalry's camps at Arkansas City and Caldwell.[29]

The railroad, however, could not comfort the men once they were ahorse in the field. 1st Lt. Patrick Cusack, who had served with the Ninth for sixteen years, marched seventy-three miles in two days during February 1883. "[T]his was one of the worst marches I Ever Experienced in the Service," he wrote, and "although the Command Suffered Sever[e]ly I never heard a man Grumble or make any Complaints." Pvt. Benjamin Bolt's horse went through the ice crossing one stream, leaving him in wet clothes, fifteen miles from camp; he mentioned the incident twenty years later, when he filed for a military pension because of his rheumatism. In another pension case, Pvt. Frank Marshall recalled that "nearly all of the company were frozen, some more and some less."[30]

The men of the Ninth rounded up the Boomers, escorted them across the Kansas line, and camped on Chilocco Creek, a few miles south of Arkansas City, to head off occasional small groups still trying to steal across the line. The *Arkansas City Republican*'s editor indulged in some gloating that Lieutenant McBlain, author of the VERITAS letters, would have recognized at once. "This is another luscious plum for Arkansas City," the editor crowed.

> Poor old Caldwell. This will be a bitter pill for her to swallow. The [Caldwell] *Journal* has boasted that that city was the headquarters for the soldiers while Arkansas City was for the boomers. We are headquarters for both now. Gen. Hatch pronounced this city the natural gateway to Oklahoma and accordingly moved the troops here. . . . They will be stationed here for quite a while, and as the companies will draw their pay here lots of shining shekels will find their way into the coffers of our merchants. [31]

By early March it was time for officers to detail a couple of men from each company to go back to Fort Riley and start the company gardens. Some of the companies had been called into the field the previous summer and had missed the fresh vegetables that they had planted in the spring. Just a month later, however, came orders that put the Ninth Cavalry on the road for Nebraska and Wyoming.[32]

This routine change of station ended chapters in the histories of the regiment and of Fort Riley. The Ninth Cavalry would patrol the Pine Ridge Reservation during the Ghost Dance winter of 1891, and the year after that they would occupy Johnson County, Wyoming, to prevent a range war there. The collapse of the Boomer movement meant that Fort Riley would not serve as a staging ground for field operations again until companies of the Seventh Cavalry traveled to Nebraska by train during the Ghost Dance disturbance. After that, the founding of training schools for cavalry and field artillery would further change the nature of service at Fort Riley.

General Sherman had written about all of this a few years earlier, on the eve of his retirement, when the Boomer movement was at its height. He foresaw no more large Indian outbreaks, he told the secretary of war in the fall of 1883. "The Army has been a large factor in producing this result, but it is not the only one," Sherman wrote. "Immigration and the occupation by industrious farmers and miners of lands vacated by the aborigines have been largely instrumental to that end, but the railroad which used to follow in the rear now goes forward in the picket-line in the great battle of civilization with barbarism, and has become the greater cause." The year before, Sherman had outlined plans for concentrating the army's troops in large garrisons, at strategic points along the railroads. Fort Riley, on the Kansas Pacific and with short-line connections to the Union Pacific, the Santa Fe, and the Missouri, Kansas & Texas, was on Sherman's list of permanent posts, to be repaired and augmented.[33]

As it happened, the cavalry regiments whose service marked two periods in Fort Riley's history were both, as the army appropriation act of 1866 put it, "composed of colored men." The Tenth Cavalry, guarding construction crews of the Kansas Pacific railroad against possible Indian attack during the late 1860s, was the first regiment to be ordered into winter quarters at the fort, to rest its horses and graze them on the twenty-thousand-acre military reservation. Some fifteen years later, the Ninth Cavalry was the last regiment to use Fort Riley as a base for seasonal operations to which the troops traveled each year by rail—by the 1880s these operations were mostly to protect Indian lands from white invaders. That the Tenth and the Ninth passed through Fort Riley was purely chance, for the army assigned stations to black troops as it did to whites and expected the same service of them. To this end, the army paid, fed, clothed, housed, armed and, in the cavalry, mounted them just as it did whites. As long as the army needed men to keep order in the West—whether to guard railroad construction or, later, to assure the orderly opening of Indian lands to white settlement—a sort of parity between black soldiers and white prevailed. A change became apparent by the end of the century, and increasingly restrictive Jim Crow laws in civilian life were reflected in the army's thirty-three-thousand-man expansion of 1901, which provided for no new black regiments. During the First World War the army assigned nearly 90 percent of its black soldiers to labor battalions and other service organizations.[34] However, throughout the post–Civil War era black soldiers, despite having to serve in segregated regiments, enjoyed a more equal footing with white soldiers than they would see again for decades. Black soldiers' military ability assured their regiments' survival within the army, and the continued presence of black soldiers in the army was itself as important for the country's future as were the regiments' particular services in the army's changing strategic schemes in the late nineteenth century.

Notes

1. *U.S. Statutes at Large* 14 (1866): 332.

2. William T. Sherman to John A. Rawlins, August 17, 1866, in *Protection of Routes Across the Continent,* 39th Cong., 2d sess., H. Doc. 23, 3; Kansas State Census, 1865, Davis and Riley Counties.

3. John W. Davidson to Roger Jones, May 16, 1866, Letters Sent, Fort Riley, RG 393, National Archives, Washington, D.C. Major Davidson of the Second Cavalry would be promoted to lieutenant colonel of the Tenth Cavalry in December 1866 and serve with the Tenth for more than twelve years. See Francis B. Heitman, *Historical Register and Dictionary of the United States Army,* 2 vols. (Washington, D.C.: Government Printing Office, 1903), 1:355.

4. Sherman regarded the Kansas Pacific as "the most important element now in progress to facilitate the military interests of our Frontier. . . . Fort Riley is a well built post with ample quarters stables and storehouses, . . . and the Govt will save a vast amount in money, and will increase the efficiency of the Army on the Frontier by facilitating . . . the Construction of the Pacific Railroad to that point." William T. Sherman to John A. Rawlins, October 23, 1865, in *The Papers of Ulysses S. Grant,* ed. John Y. Simon, vol. 15 (Carbondale: Southern Illinois University Press, 1988), 381–82.

5. Charles J. Kappler, *Indian Affairs: Laws and Treaties,* vol. 2 (Washington, D.C.: Government Printing Office, 1904), 988, 1002.

6. John N. Craig to Chauncey McKeever, April 15, 1867, Letters Sent, Fort Riley; Muster Roll, H Company, Tenth Cavalry, August 31, 1867, RG 94, National Archives; Benjamin H. Grierson to McKeever, October 1, 1867, Letters Sent, Tenth Cavalry, RG 391, National Archives; Muster Roll, K Company, Tenth Cavalry, December 31, 1867.

7. Donald J. Berthrong, *The Southern Cheyennes* (Norman: University of Oklahoma Press, 1963), 299–314, and John H. Moore, *The Cheyenne Nation: A Social and Demographic History* (Lincoln: University of Nebraska II: Press, 1987), 198–201, are recent accounts that include Indian evidence. William H. Leckie, *The Buffalo Soldiers: A Narrative of the Negro Cavalry in the West* (Norman: Uni-

versity of Oklahoma Press, 1967), 19–44, sketches the Tenth Cavalry's activities from 1867 through 1868. John H. Monnett, *The Battle of Beecher Island and the Indian War of 1867–1869* (Niwot: University Press of Colorado, 1992), includes Indian evidence about the fight. David Dixon, *Hero of Beecher Island: The Life and Military Career of George A. Forsyth* (Lincoln: University of Nebraska Press, 1994), is the biography of a major in the Ninth Cavalry whose duties on Gen. Philip H. Sheridan's staff kept him away from the regiment during most of the years when his name appeared on its rolls.

8. James H. Massey, Pension File, IWSC 7902, RG 15, National Archives.

9. David A. Dary, *The Buffalo Book* (Chicago: Swallow Press, 1974), 94–95, lists several attempts to make leather of buffalo hides. Before the 1870s the only commercial demand was for robes (tanned buffalo skins with the hair).

10. Fort Sill figures in William T. Hagan, *United States-Comanche Relations: The Reservation Years* (New Haven: Yale University Press, 1976), and Fort Reno in Donald J. Berthrong, *The Cheyenne and Arapaho Ordeal* (Norman: University of Oklahoma Press, 1976). For the cost of these operations, see William T. Sherman's remarks in *Annual Report of the Secretary of War*, 1879, 46th Cong., 2d sess., H. Doc. 1, pt. 2, 6; John Pope's remarks in ibid., 1882, 47th Cong., 2d sess., H. Doc. 1, pt. 2, 99; Pope's remarks in ibid., 1883, 48th Cong., 1st sess., H. Doc. 1, pt. 2, 130; Christopher C. Augur's remarks in ibid., 1884, 48th Cong., 2d sess., H. Doc. 1, pt. 2, 118–19.

11. Muster Roll, F Company, Ninth Cavalry, October 31, 1881. For other examples, see Muster Rolls, B Company, October 31, 1879, February 28, 1881; C Company, February 28, 1877, June 30, October 31, 1879, February 29, 1880; F Company, October 31, 1876, August 31, 1878; I Company, August 31, 1881; K Company, October 31, 1878.

12. *Annual Report of the Secretary of War*, 1881, 47th Cong., 1st sess., H. Doc. 1, pt. 2, 124. Heitman, *Historical Register*, 2:444–47, lists the Ninth Cavalry's Indian fights. The number of fights conveys no idea of the weeks spent in the saddle or the thousands of miles marched. Muster rolls from these years show that companies of the Ninth rode more than 350 miles a month, on average. Leckie, *The Buffalo Soldiers*, 172–229, covers the regiment's service in New Mexico, including the Lincoln County War. Dan L. Thrapp, *Victorio and the Mimbres Apaches* (Norman: University of Oklahoma Press, 1974), 175–274, concentrates on Indian affairs in New Mexico, particularly military campaigns from 1876 to 1880.

13. *Junction City Union*, December 17, 31, 1881; January 14, 1882.

14. Ibid., February 4, April 15, June 24, 1882.

15. Robert M. Utley, *Frontier Regulars: The United States Army and the Indian, 1866–1891* (New York: MacMillan, 1973), 332–44; Francis P. Prucha, *The Great Father: The United States Government and the American Indians* (Lincoln: University of Nebraska Press, 1984), 542–44; *Annual Report of the Secretary of War*, 1881, 116.

16. *Junction City Union*, July 8, 22, August 26, 1882. Later references to McBlain make his identity quite clear. He was the only officer in the Ninth to

have served as an enlisted man in the Second Cavalry, see ibid., May 12, 1883; he did not send letters about the Ninth's operations while he was "on a leave of absence in California," see ibid., October 11, 1884; and the editor sometimes mentioned McBlain's letters or visits to the Union office, see ibid., January 17, April 4, 1885.

17. Ibid., November 25, 1882, March 17, June 2, 1883. Sales of condemned horses are in ibid., December 1, 1883, May 31, December 20, 1884.

18. Ibid., June 23, 1883.

19. Estimates of Navajo population and sheep are in agents' reports in *Annual Report of the Commissioner of Indian Affairs*, 1881, 47th Cong., 1st sess., H. Doc. 1, pt. 5, 195; ibid., 1883, 48th Cong., 1st sess., H. Doc. 1, pt 5, 180. Edward H. Spicer, *Cycles of Conquest: The Impact of Spain, Mexico, and the United States on the Indians of the Southwest, 1533–1960* (Tucson University of Arizona Press, 1961), 222, calls the "original land arrangement simply . . . not sufficient to support the increasing numbers of Navajos and livestock." Richard White, *The Roots of Dependency: Subsistence, Environment, and Social Change among the Choctaws, Pawnees, and Navajos* (Lincoln: University of Nebraska Press, 1983), 216, comments: "Reservation boundaries had little immediate impact on Navajo life." Commanding Officer to Adjutant General, District of New Mexico, April 17, 1883, Letters Sent, Fort Lewis, RG 393; Adjutant to Adjutant General, District of New Mexico, June 28, 1883, ibid.; Commanding Officer to Adjutant General, District of New Mexico, August 11, 1883, ibid. The results of the cavalry patrols are in *Annual Report of the Secretary of War*, 1883, 139. Population figures for the Jicarilla Apaches are in *Annual Report of the Commission of Indian Affairs*, 1883, 176. Veronica E. Velarde Tiller, *The Jicarilla Apache Tribe: A History*, rev. ed. (Lincoln: University of Nebraska Press, 1992), 89–90, describes the removal.

20. *Junction City Union*, September 22, 1883.

21. Commanding Officer to Warren Patten, September 1, 1883, Letters Sent, Fort Lewis.

22. *Junction City Union*, September 22, 1883; *Army and Navy Journal*, December 4, 1880. Years earlier Sherman had complained that "people west of the Mississippi River look to the army as their legitimate field of profit and support and the quicker they are undeceived the better for all." See William T. Sherman to John A. Rawlins, September 30, 1866, in *Protection of Routes Across the Continent*, 18–19.

23. Prucha, *The Great Father*, 434–36, 743–44.

24. By 1880 the army had stationed fifteen companies of cavalry—one-eighth of its mounted force—and seventeen companies of infantry at posts in or close to Indian Territory. See *Army and Navy Journal*, December 13, 1879. For early efforts to teach Plains Indians to farm, see Berthrong *The Cheyenne and Arapaho Ordeal*, 48–71.

25. Carl Schurz to George W. McCrary, May 1, 1879, in *Occupation of Indian Territory by White Settlers*, 46th Cong., 1st sess., S. Doc. 20, 16–18.

26. *Certain Lands in the Indian Territory*, 1884, 48th Cong., 2d sess., S. Doc. 50, 5.

27. *Annual Report of the Commission of Indian Affairs,* 1880, 46th Cong., 2d sess., H. Doc. 1, pt. 5.93; ibid., 1881, 55; ibid., 1883, 147; ibid., 1884, 48th Cong., 2nd sess., H. Doc. 1, pt. 5, 33–34. *Annual Report of the Secretary of War,* 1883, 70; ibid., 1884, 118–19, which are the annual reports of John Pope and Christopher C. Augur, respectively. Augur was Pope's successor in command of the Department of the Missouri, whose troops were responsible for restraining and removing the Boomers. See also *Prevention of Trespass on Indian Lands,* 1881, 47th Cong., 1st sess., H. Doc. 145, 2; *Trespass on Indian Lands,* 1883, 48th Cong., 1st sess., H. Doc. 17, 2; Prucha, *The Great Father,* 737–57.

28. Muster Rolls, H and L Troops, Ninth Cavalry, August 31, October 31, 1884.

29. Edward Hatch to John F. Guilfoyle, December 31, 1884, January 1, 1885, Letters and Telegrams Sent, District of Oklahoma, RG 393; Hatch to James Gilliss, January 5, 7, 1885, ibid.; *Junction City Union,* January 10, 31, 1885.

30. Muster Roll, G Troop, Ninth Cavalry, February 28, 1883; Benjamin Bolt's affidavit, March 21, 1906, in Bolt, Pension File, IWSO 10602, RG 15; Frank Marshall's affidavit, June 18, 1895, in Elias Hayes, Pension File, SC 902778, RG 15.

31. *Arkansas City Republican,* February 28, 1885.

32. Eugene D. Dimmick, John S. Loud, and Jerauld A. Olmsted to Assistant Adjutant General, Department of the Missouri, March 9, 1885, Letters Received, District of Oklahoma; General Orders 44, Headquarters of the Army, April 9, 1885, RG 94.

33. *Annual Report of the Secretary of War,* 1883, 45–46.

34. Bernard C. Nalty, *Strength for the Fight: A History of Black Americans in the Military* (New York: Free Press, 1986), 112.

PAUL H. CARLSON

William R. Shafter, Black Troops, and the Opening of the Llano Estacado, 1870–75

From the time the first white men reached the region with Coronado in the sixteenth century until well into the second half of the nineteenth century, the Great Plains were referred to as the "Great American Desert." The description was applied particularly to the Llano Estacado portion of the southern plains which, it was commonly believed, would be uninhabited for hundreds of years if, indeed, it would ever be suitable for civilization.

Because it was void of timber, had only scattered water holes, lacked adequate landmarks, and presented an almost limitless "ocean" of waving grass, white men tended to stay clear of the Llano Estacado. Even Indians frequented the Staked Plains only to hunt buffalo or to cross it. The Texan–Santa Fe Expedition, designed to establish the jurisdiction of Texas over Santa Fe, crossed it in 1841, Capt. Randolph B. Marcy crossed and recrossed it by different routes in 1849 and explored the headstreams of the Red River in 1852. Capt. John Pope of the U.S. Army visited the region three years later, and in 1868 the Butterfield Overland Mail route touched the southern portions as it wound its dusty way to Fort Davis and beyond. As late as 1870, however, travelers still looked upon the plains with trepidation. Those bound for California through Texas usually followed the Old Butterfield Trail. Even the cattlemen avoided the region. By 1870 they had spread westward on the Texas Plains almost to the Caprock escarpment and were well established along the slopes of the Rockies farther west. Not for almost another decade, however, did they drive their longhorns to graze on the Llano Estacado.

The existence and location of the High Plains was well known. The

Great American Desert myth for decades had been perpetuated by school histories, geographies, and popular atlases.[1] Moreover, descriptions of the Great Plains made by men who traveled through it, including Coronado, Lewis and Clark, Stephen H. Long, and others, were widely circulated. Captain Marcy, whose report was published by Congress, vividly portrayed the plains as a "natural barrier between civilized man and the savage, as, upon the east side are numerous spring-brooks, flowing over a highly prolific soil . . . while on the other side commence those barren and desolate wastes, where but few small streams greet the eye of the traveller, and these are soon swallowed up by the thirsty sands over which they flow. . . ."[2] As late as 1859, Horace Greeley, editor of the *New York Tribune,* described the plains as "a desert indeed."[3]

No one, it now seems clear, did more to dispel the desert myth attached to the mysterious Llano Estacado than Lt. Col. William R. Shafter, Twenty-fourth U.S. Infantry Regiment, and black soldiers of the Twenty-fourth and Twenty-fifth infantries and the Ninth and Tenth cavalries. Between 1870 and 1875 the black troops under Shafter crisscrossed the region exploring it or pursuing Indians from the Red River south to the Rio Grande and from the eastern Caprock west to the Pecos River. Shafter personally led black troops on several extensive expeditions across the plains and served as second in command on others. Moreover, he directed additional scouts from such isolated frontier posts as Forts McKavett, Concho, and Davis onto the plains and along its southern, eastern, and western fringes.

William R. Shafter, who led U.S. troops to Cuba in the Spanish-American War, was corpulent, but considered the most energetic man of his rank in the Department of Texas.[4] A Civil War veteran from Michigan, he had led an African American outfit in the war and afterward with the colorful Ranald S. Mackenzie trained and organized one of the army's first all black regiments. Weighing over 220 pounds in the 1870s and standing five feet eleven inches tall, his huge frame was set upon very short legs. Something of an anomaly, he enjoyed the respect, but rarely the affection of his men. To many he was a coarse, profane martinet, the "terror of his subordinates."[5] But to those who knew him well, he was a "splendid, handsome, jovial, helpful man . . . ," regarded with "admiration and love."[6]

The segregated African American regiments of the regular army were established in 1866. Reorganization of the army three years later created the four units that played such a vital part in the opening of the

Llano Estacado. The cavalry regiments were known to the Indians as "buffalo soldiers." But, since Indians seldom distinguished between infantry and cavalry units (in fact the infantry was often mounted), all the black troops came to be called by the storied sobriquet.

Closely teamed with Shafter and the buffalo soldiers was a special unit of black Seminole Indian scouts headed by Lt. John L. Bullis of the Twenty-fourth Infantry. The remarkable scouts were descendants of Seminole Indians and runaway slaves of the Florida swamps who, during the 1840s, were removed from the Everglades state. Many of them had been transported to Indian Territory, but one band, under the leadership of Chief Wild Cat, fled to the Mexican side of the Rio Grande in the neighborhood of Piedras Negras. In subsequent years others had joined the band in northern Mexico. In 1870 the black Seminole Indians below the Rio Grande were invited to enlist as scouts in the U.S. Army. Many of them agreed, bringing their families and settling on the 3,900-acre government military reservation near Fort Clark at Bracketville. For the next eleven years they were attached to various commands in the Southwest.[7]

Late in 1869 the first of a series of military campaigns, which led to the opening of the Llano Estacado, began. In that year Col. Edward Hatch, Ninth Cavalry, ordered two expeditions to the Brazos River country near the eastern Caprock. For forty-two days in September and October Capt. Henry Carroll and Edward M. Heyl, Ninth Cavalry, with ninety-five men, pursued a war party of Kiowas and Comanches who had committed depredations in the vicinity of Fort McKavett, near San Saba. The trail led to the headwaters of the Salt Fork (Main Fork) of the Brazos and an Indian camp of two hundred lodges. In the fighting that followed more than twenty Indians were killed or wounded, and their entire camp and all its equipage was captured or destroyed.[8]

Meanwhile, Capt. John Bacon, Ninth Cavalry, with his Company G and detachments from five other companies of his regiment, in all 199 officers and enlisted men, marched from Fort Concho, at present San Angelo, to the site of old Fort Phantom Hill on the Brazos River. From here, he moved up river near the headwaters and went into camp. At sunrise on October 28, Bacon and his black troops were attacked by an estimated five hundred Kiowa and Comanche warriors. In a bitter and at times hand-to-hand struggle, the bluecoats forced the Indians to flee. After making necessary preparations, the soldiers pursued and near midafternoon of the following day overtook the demoralized Indians. In the subsequent attack the Indians scattered in all directions. About forty braves were killed, seven women and fifty-one horses captured. The soldiers' casualties were eight wounded.[9]

Although both climbed the Caprock onto the Staked Plains, neither expedition brought back important information about the Llano Estacado. In fact, officers of both scouts chose not to pursue the Indians across the flat, perplexing country and, instead, returned to their respective posts along the outward trails. Nevertheless, the campaigns, by marking the beginning of operations against Indians there, paved the way for major expeditions on the plains that were soon to follow. Indeed, three months later, in February 1870, Bacon with his buffalo soldiers struck a small Mescalaro Apache camp seventy-five miles southwest of Fort McKavett. He captured eighty horses and mules and destroyed the Indian lodges, camp equipment, and six hundred hides. Having touched portions of the High Plains he brought back some useful information about the little known Llano Estacado.[10]

But it was William R. Shafter who, with his black troops, provided most of the reliable knowledge of the dreaded and barren Llano Estacado and led the final assault against hostile Indians there. Two months after arriving at Fort McKavett in mid-June, he received word of Indian horse thieves camping on the southern reaches of the plains and immediately planned a major scouting expedition to the Pecos River to give chase. Then, on August 28, with four officers and 128 enlisted men of companies F and M, Ninth Cavalry, lieutenants Samuel E. Armstrong and B. M. Custer, Twenty-fourth Infantry, and two surgeons, he left on what for military purposes became the most important crossing of the West Texas Plains to that time.

After moving nearly due south to the South Llano River, the expedition turned right and headed toward Beaver Lake, near present-day Juno, where it was to meet a detachment of troops, including some guides, and a wagon load of corn from Fort Clark. Pushing westward, the command, misreading a compass, veered too far southward and marched through a canyon that led to Devil's River, twelve miles below Fort Hudson. From here, to correct its error, the expedition proceeded northward along the Fort Hudson road, finally reaching the rendezvous several days late.

Since the small detachment from Fort Clark had already left Beaver Lake in an easterly direction, apparently planning to return to its post, Shafter, believing he needed the guides, rushed off a small party with orders for it to return. The messengers returned with the detachment and four days later, with the expedition fully organized, the lieutenant colonel struck for the Pecos. Gaining the river about twenty miles below present Sheffield, he descended it a "considerable" distance.[11]

To expedite his operations in the largely unexplored country, Shafter divided his African American command. Leaving most of it at the Pecos, he and Captain Heyl with fifteen men of the Ninth Cavalry crossed to the west bank of the river, climbed up onto the tablelands, and marched due south for twenty miles, keeping all the time within four miles of the river. Using his field glasses to examine each ravine, Shafter, while noting the topography, discovered no indications of Indians. Here, he left the river and rode southwestward for six or seven miles to Painted Rock Arroyo, only ten miles from the Rio Grande, before returning to the main camp.

For more than a week the command continued to scout in the vicinity of the lower Pecos. Although a few patrols probed beyond the river, the expedition concentrated its efforts in the region to the east where in February Captain Bacon had sighted some Apaches. Still, no Indians were seen; neither were there trails nor other indications of Indians having passed through the country since Bacon's scout. Eight Indian ponies, which Shafter believed had been near the Pecos for six months, were caught.

Unable to locate either Indians or recent signs of them, Shafter, on September 18 decided to return to Fort McKavett. Sending the detachment from Fort Clark to its post, he ordered his troops into their saddles. On the return march two days later his scouts reported the location of several large trails, running in a north-south direction and from two to six months old, about thirty-five miles west of the headwaters of the North and South Llano and the San Saba rivers. While examining them, the scouts discovered some abandoned Indian villages. One, about thirty miles west of the head of the South Llano, had been deserted only three or four months earlier and had contained possibly as many as 150 Indians. Shafter believed that this camp was a rendezvous for Indians who committed depredations in the country near the headwaters of the Nueces.

One mile southwest of this site Lt. George W. Budd, Ninth Cavalry, and one of the surgeons found a large, permanent pond of water about two hundred yards long and deep enough to swim horses. For years the army had heard reports of the water pond, but its location had been known only to Indians. Since there were no cattle west of the head of the South Llano, neither the cattlemen nor the army frequented the region, and Captain Bacon had missed it in February. As Shafter indicated, it was also a convenient rendezvous for raiders to strike the ranches and settlements southeast of the water hole as well as in the vicinity of Fort McKavett.[12]

The scout, which returned to its post on September 26, after thirty-five days in the field, was significant. Having marched 473 miles, it showed that no Indians were lurking south of the plains in the vicinity of the Pecos and the headwaters of the Llano rivers. Eight horses had been captured. A strategic and favorite camping place had been located, and no longer would the Indians be able to use the water hole as a safe rendezvous.

Anxious to follow up the scout, Shafter, on November 1, ordered Captain Carroll with thirty buffalo soldiers to the vicinity of the recently discovered water hole. During two weeks of search Carroll discovered neither Indians nor fresh signs of them. Disappointed with Carroll's results, but undeterred, Shafter throughout December sent small scouting and exploring patrols southwestward. Because of the cold weather in January 1871, however, very little scouting was undertaken, and early the following month, as Shafter was to be transferred, scouting activity was halted completely.[13]

At the end of April, Shafter, having been ordered to the trans-Pecos region, left with a small escort for Fort Davis. Less than sixty days after assuming command at the post, he with his diligent black troops, prompted by a daring Comanche attack at Barrilla Springs, northeast of Fort Davis, resulting in the theft of forty-four horses and mules, was again probing the untamed Llano Estacado.

With a command totaling eighty-six officers and men, Shafter and the hard-driving bluecoats turned a routine pursuit of Indian horse thieves into a major exploration of the Monahans Sandhills and the southwestern Staked Plains. For twenty-two days they followed Indian trails which led through the torrid Sand Hills and onto the Llano Estacado to a point southwest of present Hobbs, New Mexico, and thence southwestward to the Pecos River. In all they covered some 417 grueling miles, suffering enroute from thirst, dust, sand, heat, and other maladies of the region. During one stretch of seventy miles they marched almost two days without water.[14]

The immediate results of the scout proved revealing. Shafter and his black troops discovered and destroyed an abandoned Indian village, two dozen buffalo robes, skins, and a large supply of provisions. They captured about twenty horses and mules and an old squaw who informed them that the Comanches and the Lipan and Mescalero Apaches, longtime enemies, had concluded a peace in the Monahans Sandhills. Lead they found at the Indian camp, stamped with the trademark of a St. Louis, Missouri firm, provided important evidence that the sand hills were a place of barter for the Comancheros. Of far more significance, the long range results lay in the successful penetration into the sand hills where it was generally believed that soldiers could not operate. The expedition not only destroyed another Indian sanctuary, but it brought back geographical knowledge necessary for future operations.[15]

Shafter believed that extensive scouting, such as in the sand hills, even though no engagements with the Indians were fought produced valuable results. "My experience has been that Indians will not stay where they consider themselves liable to attacks," he informed his superiors, "and I believe the best way to rid the country of them . . . is to thoroughly scour the country with cavalry." Since his scout in 1870 to the Pecos and his recent one to the sand hills seemed to support his thesis, he applied the technique to the Big Bend region of Texas where, it had been reported by at least one military patrol, Apaches were camping.

Accordingly, on October 5, 1871, leading twenty-two men of Company D, seventeen men of Company K, Ninth Cavalry, thirty men of Company G, Twenty-fifth Infantry and several commissioned officers, Shafter rode southeastward to the Chisos Mountains and beyond to the Rio Grande. He struck the river below San Vincente, a village on the Mexican side of the Rio Grande about twenty-five miles above its Great Bend. Here, near the lower end of Mariscal Canyon, he reported that because its banks were several hundred feet high, it was impossible to get down to the river with animals. Shafter, Lt. Isaiah McDonald, and four buffalo soldiers, however, by climbing down a ravine which ran to it, succeeded with difficulty in getting to the Rio Grande.[16] Since signs indicated that Indians were almost constantly in the Big Bend, Shafter and the black troops reconnoitered the country, crossing and recrossing trails, noting important water holes and marking the sites of old Indian camps. At San Vincente they discovered an important Apache crossing on the river. They reported abandoned Indian encampments twenty-five miles southwest of Pena Blanca. The grass along their line of march was excellent, but the only wood they found was a few large cottonwood trees along the streams. Where they struck the Rio Grande, there was no timber.[17]

When it returned to Fort Davis on November 5, the expedition had covered nearly five hundred miles. Although it had seen no Indians, it had found abundant evidence that Apaches used the Big Bend as a sanctuary. Perhaps more important, it added considerably to the geographical knowledge of the extreme southern plains and the Big Bend mountains. Indeed, the information it gained about the territory and its resources enabled the army later to maneuver more confidently in the region. In addition, it smoothed the way for later settlement.[18]

Having tested his theory by scouting the Big Bend, Shafter, at the end of December, led black troops on another expedition in pursuit of Indians, this time into the mountainous region to the west of the Llano Estacado. Taking seventeen enlisted men from Company K, Ninth Cavalry, two enlisted men, Twenty-fourth Infantry, and three commissioned officers, he marched on December 28 into the heart of the Davis Mountains, hoping to overtake a small band of raiders who had been committing depredations in the vicinity. After riding only two days, however, bad weather caused him to turn back. The expedition, which returned on December 31, covered over 120 miles in the mountains where travel was difficult and checked several well-known water holes. Forty miles northwest of Fort Davis, it noted the location of an old Indian rendezvous, but no Indians were sighted.[19]

Early in 1872 Shafter laid plans to continue his scouting of isolated areas bordering the Llano Estacado. He intended, on condition that he would receive the proper authority from his superiors in the Department of Texas, during the spring to spend a month combing the Guadalupe Mountains and another two months exploring the long stretch of broken country west of the Staked Plains.[20] Through March and April a number of small detachments and scouts combed the region west of the Plains, but Shafter was ordered back to Fort McKavett before he could lead the extended expedition. To the east Ranald S. Mackenzie was organizing a campaign against hostile Indians believed to be on the Llano Estacado, and he wanted his former lieutenant colonel and the black troops, already conditioned to the awesome region, to form one arm of the scout.[21]

Accordingly, Shafter returned to Fort McKavett and assumed command on June 12. Barely a week later, leaving the post in charge of Capt. Henry C. Corbin, with companies E, H, and I, Twenty-fourth Infantry, comprising five officers and 177 enlisted men, and five six-mule wagons, he left to join Mackenzie on July 1 on the Freshwater Fork of the

Brazos.[22] Rain, swollen streams, and general bad weather slowed his march. He reached the rendezvous on July 6, too late to aid in trapping a band of Comanches in Blanco Canyon from which the waters of the Freshwater Fork gushed.[23]

Three days later, when he left camp for the Palo Duro country, Mackenzie instructed Shafter to lead his buffalo soldiers on a short scout in the vicinity of the headwaters of the Salt Fork of the Brazos. A week afterward, taking a command consisting of forty enlisted men of Company H, Twenty-fourth Infantry, and fifteen others, Shafter galloped south. After retracing his inbound route down the Freshwater Fork during the first day and a half, he turned off the trail slightly and headed southwestward for the Salt Fork, reaching it at a point ten miles above the mouth of the Freshwater Fork. Heavy rains during the evening of July 17 slowed the command considerably. It covered only eight miles on the eighteenth, and a little less than eleven miles the following day. At the end of the fourth day's march, the command reached the headwaters of the Brazos. From there, it returned along the Caprock before it descended into Blanco Canyon to follow the Freshwater Fork to supply camp, which it reached on July 21, after a march of sixty miles. [24]

During the scout, Shafter and the black troops made certain that there were no Indians lurking south of the supply camp at the foot of the Staked Plains. Along the Salt Fork of the Brazos, they found abundant evidence of old Indian camps near all the springs they visited, but discovered only one small, two-days-old trail made by a party of six Indians. While exploring the eastern edge of the Llano Estacado, they located water and fuel supplies and made a map of the country they observed.[25]

One week after Shafter's return, Mackenzie, who arrived back at supply camp on July 19, left again. Taking along Capt. John W. Clouse, Company E, Twenty-fourth Infantry, with sixty-two enlisted men of Company E, and five companies of cavalry, he departed on July 28 on a daring venture across the Staked Plains, which took him and the African American troops to Fort Sumner, New Mexico, and beyond. For more than a month the command explored the northern Llano Estacado. It mapped the region, marking water holes and fuel supplies. Returning by way of the Red River, Mackenzie noted that there was good water and grass along both routes.[26] Shafter, meanwhile, was left to guard the supply camp. For a month the lieutenant colonel ordered his men to prowl the Caprock north and south of the rendezvous camp.

After returning on September 2 from New Mexico, Mackenzie laid plans for another expedition north to the Red River. Again he took some black soldiers, including sixty enlisted men, Company I, Twenty-fourth Infantry. They rode with six companies of the Fourth Cavalry, two surgeons, and nine Tonkawa Indian scouts, nearly three hundred officers and men in all. The bluecoats proceeded north, splashed across the Prairie Dog Town Fork (Main Fork) of the Red River, and rode to the Salt Fork at a point in present Donley County. On September 29, they moved northward to McClellan Creek and followed it. After marching two miles they found the fresh trail of a mule leading northwestward. Guessing it would lead to a hostile Indian camp, they gave chase. They guessed correctly. At 4:00 P.M. they came upon a large Comanche village containing an estimated 262 lodges on the North Fork of the Red River about seven miles above the mouth of McClellan Creek. Quickly Mackenzie outlined attack plans and then ordered a charge. After a brisk and at times hand to hand fight, the troops took the village, killing about thirty warriors, capturing more than 120 women and children, and driving off the rest. The soldiers, who suffered four casualties, burned the lodges, destroyed the camp equipment and rounded up several horses and mules, which had been stolen the year previous in a sanguinary attack at Howard's Wells. After the engagement, Mackenzie headed his men south to the camp on the Freshwater Fork.[27]

Meanwhile, Shafter supervised the scouting and mapping of the country to the south of the supply camp along the Double Mountain Fork of the Brazos. First, he detached Lt. William Hoffman, Eleventh Infantry, with a half dozen troops of his regiment to perform the task. Then, he led Company H, Twenty-fourth Infantry, on several exploratory scouts up the Double Mountain Fork. On one he climbed the Caprock near present Posey to inspect an old Indian trail and hunt buffalo, which he encountered in enormous herds, riding southwestward on the Llano Estacado about twenty miles before returning to the supply camp. In all, Shafter and the buffalo soldiers traveled during September over 330 miles.[28]

When he returned from his successful expedition to the North Fork of the Red River, Mackenzie broke camp and sent his troops to their respective posts. As they rode southward, Shafter and the black troops could point with pride to several important consequences of the recent campaign. They had aided in sweeping for a time the northern rim of the Llano Estacado clear of Indians, mapped the region westward to Fort Sumner, noted sources of water, explored thoroughly the Double Mountain Fork of the Brazos River, and gained valuable knowledge needed for further operations on the Staked Plains. Their operations against Comanches along tributaries of the Brazos and Red rivers had scattered the Indians.

Results of the Shafter-Mackenzie expedition changed for a time military operations in Texas. Driven from their camps along the canyons and ravines, which cut deep into the Llano Estacado, the Indians returned to their reservations or moved farther west into New Mexico. Consequently, the attention of Texas military commanders was turned to the Rio Grande border. Accordingly, for the next twenty months, Shafter and many of the black troops campaigned along the Mexican border.

The Llano Estacado was hardly neglected. Comancheros entered the region. Buffalo hunters set up camps along the Red River. Bootleggers and arms runners plied their trades west of Indian Territory. Comanches, Kiowa, Cheyennes and other Indians again pitched their tepees in the Palo Duro and other canyons; sometimes they battled the tough and smelly buffalo hunters. In addition, Indians swarmed over the North Texas and southwest Kansas frontiers, raiding settlements, running off livestock, and killing pioneers. These factors plus the failure in 1874 of the unworkable Quaker Peace Policy—inaugurated in 1869 by President Ulysses S. Grant, it provided that churchmen should serve as Indian agents, that military personnel must stay away from reservations, and that a general humanitarian approach to Indian problems would be followed—caused the Red River War.

The Red River War was short. Beginning in August 1874, it was to all practical purposes over by January 1875. During the conflict the army dispatched five strong columns into the Texas Panhandle from all directions to strike the Indians in a continuing operation. Black troops of the Ninth and Tenth cavalries formed the backbone of the two columns that moved westward from forts Griffin and Sill. The buffalo soldiers performed admirably. During the fall fighting they captured nearly four hundred Indians and over two thousand animals. They destroyed more than seven hundred lodges, tons of supplies, and much camp equipment. Their operations along with those of Mackenzie, Nelson A. Miles, Sixth Cavalry, and Maj. William R. Price, Eighth Cavalry, who led the other commands, produced remarkable success. More than most campaigns the Red River War made the immense northern border of the Llano Estacado safe for an advancing civilization.[29]

Meanwhile, Shafter, who had been in New York testing infantry field equipment, in February, 1875, returned to Texas. He found that most, but not all hostile Indians on the Llano Estacado had returned to their reservations. As the finale to the Red River War, Shafter with his black troops was to scout the Staked Plains pursuing holdouts. The resulting expedition was the most thorough exploration of that region to that time. For six months, June to December, the African American soldiers of his command crisscrossed the Llano Estacado over a veritable maze of trails, covering more than 2,500 miles of the High Plains between the Caprock and the Pecos River. Not only did it pursue Indians, but the command explored the region thoroughly, marking water holes, mapping the country, and noting fuel supplies, resources, and flora and fauna.

All enlisted men of the expedition were buffalo soldiers. The troops included companies A, C, F, I, G, and L of the Tenth Cavalry, Company A of the Twenty-fifth Infantry, and Companies D and F of the Twenty-fourth Infantry. Supporting the regular troops was a company of black Seminole Indian scouts led by the indestructible Lieutenant Bullis.

After rendezvousing in June at Fort Concho, the crack command marched northward to establish a supply camp on the Freshwater Fork of the Brazos. From there, taking a single wagon to carry medical supplies and the sick and with rations on pack mules, Shafter and 220 officers and men made, perhaps, the most remarkable march in the history of the Llano Estacado. After climbing the Caprock near present Mount Blanco, they headed northwest. Then, making a large horseshoe bend, in the vicinity of present Petersburg, they proceeded due south.

On August 7, near present Lorenzo, Shafter with his men overtook nine Comancheros, mounted, armed, and with several pack mules. Although the traders would say nothing as to the whereabouts of Indians, Shafter took them into his service as guides.[30] From here, he continued south, waded the Double Mountain Fork of the Brazos near present Slaton, turned and marched northwest to Punta del Agua on the Yellowhouse stream and within the present city of Lubbock, reaching it late the next day. Thence following the Yellowhouse Canyon, he moved forty-two miles farther west to Casas Amarillas Lake, an old Comanchero campground and prominent watering place. From this prominent landmark, he headed toward the southwest into a region absolutely unknown to Anglo and African Americans.

Upon leaving Casas Amarillas, the command had hoped to find sufficient water in the large circular depressions characteristic of the Llano Estacado. During the first two days it was successful, but having found no water by the expiration of the third day. Shafter concluded that his troops must either strike for the Pecos or turn back. Characteristically, the resolute officer ordered his buffalo soldiers to make for the Pecos some eighty miles distant. During the following two days and one night of marching, the men suffered desperately from heat, dust, and thirst. Exhausted bluecoats were tied in their saddles; slackers were forced to keep up. On the last night out, many of the officers and men, having lost all hope of reaching the river, wrote messages to be taken home by those fortunate enough to survive.[31] After great hardship and privation the advance troops reached the Pecos about 9:00 P.M. By midnight everyone was encamped along the river near present Carlsbad, New Mexico.

Upon gaining the refreshing waters of the Pecos without a casualty, the expedition proceeded down river toward Horsehead Crossing, approximately 160 miles distant. To avoid following several wide bends of the river, Shafter moved his troops in as straight a line as possible, thus forcing the command to make several dry camps along the way.

At Horsehead Crossing, where he arrived on the twenty-third, Shafter rested his force a few days before he backtracked up the river forty miles to Pecos Falls. Here he remained five days. Then, with the command sufficiently rested, he rode northeast around the southern end of the Monahans Sandhills, which he had visited in 1871. From here, he marched northeast, climbed the Caprock in the vicinity of present Penwell, and, once again on the High Plains, struck a northward course. When his troops began to suffer from lack of water, he made a forced march due west about thirty miles to water holes at the upper end of the Sand Hills, near present Kermit, reaching them on September 13.

On this march the buffalo soldiers found signs of an old Indian trail that bore northwest. Although they had only six days rations and the animals were suffering from the heat, dust, and sand, a party of an estimated thirty Apache warriors struck the camp but scattered when the guards returned the fire. There were no casualties. At dawn, Shafter and forty-five picked troops went after the Apaches. Twenty miles to the northwest, near present Hobbs, New Mexico, they found a hastily abandoned camp near a large prominent spring. After burning the lodges and other camp equipage, they built a rock monument on a hill a mile and a quarter to the southwest. The marker, of white stone, eight feet at the base, four at the top, and seven and a half feet high, could be seen for several miles in every direction. This important watering place subsequently became known as Monument Spring.[32]

Here Shafter decided to give up the chase. The Indians had scattered in all directions, his rations were very low, his animals were badly worn, and his supply camp was two hundred miles away. Consequently, he headed north, struck his inbound trail, and followed it back to the supply camp, which he reached on September 25 after an absence of fifty-two days and a march of some 860 miles, nearly the whole distance through country heretofore unknown to troops.[33]

It was an arduous march. Not only did the men lose twenty-nine horses, but much of their clothes. Boots, leggings, and blouses were worn thin or, in some cases, completely missing. The men were exhausted. Although the scout had captured no Indians, it had destroyed camp equipment and located several previously unknown water holes. Moreover, Shafter and his black troops again had shown that bluecoats could penetrate successfully an area previously known only to the Indians.

Twice more during the campaign, Shafter led his men on expeditions across the Plains. On one he trailed them southward from Punto del Agua some fifty miles into the heart of the Llano Estacado before turning southwestward toward present Andrews and thence to Monument Springs, discovering enroute Double Lake, Cedar Lake, and Shafter Lake among other South Plains landmarks. On the other, the expeditions' third major crossing, he pushed westward from Big Spring to the Pecos River and beyond, mapping the country, marking trails, and looking for Indians. Meanwhile, he directed captains Nicholas Nolan, Theodore A. Baldwin, and Charles Viele and Lt. Thomas Lebo, Tenth Cavalry, and Lt. Andrew Geddes, Twenty-fourth Infantry, to lead additional explorations. Geddes pursued a party of Apaches to the Rio Grande. Lebo prowled the Casas Amarillas country. Viele rode west toward Fort Sumner and north to Tule Canyon. Baldwin probed the area south of Big Spring. Nolan chased Apaches along a trail that took him to the vicinity of present Midland before bad weather forced him to return to the supply camp. In addition, Bullis and Lt. C. R. Ward, Tenth Cavalry, with the Indian scouts examined several draws and water holes in the vicinity of Seminole. Upon returning to Fort Concho on December 9, 1875, Shafter broke up the expedition by sending the troops to their respective stations.

Unquestionably, it was a remarkable scout. The command dramatically fulfilled its orders to sweep the plains of Indians. It found only a few traces of them on the plains, killed one warrior, and captured five Indians. Scouts from one patrol showed that no aboriginals were, or recently had been, along the Staked Plains. Scouts of another, other than the trail it followed to beyond the Rio Grande, found no recent signs of Indians in the south. The Indians who had been on the plains had scattered, most of them to reservations in Indian Territory or to New Mexico. Although an occasional malcontent from time to time would lead a few of his followers from the reservations to the vast reaches of the Llano Estacado, the magnificent horse and buffalo days of the proud Southern Plains Indians were gone forever. Indeed, the next year, 1876, Charles Goodnight trailed a large cattle herd from Colorado southwestward into the Palo Duro Canyon, thus marking the opening of the Staked Plains and the beginning of the colorful and romantic West Texas cattle industry.

Clearly, William R. Shafter and black troops of the Twenty-fourth and Twenty-fifth infantries and the Ninth and Tenth cavalries played no small role in opening the Llano Estacado. Between 1870 and 1875 they had prowled the mountains and deserts bordering the region and thoroughly explored, mapped, and recorded topographical features of the Staked Plains from the Caprock on the east, through the sand hills to the Pecos River on the west, and from below Fort McKavett and Horsehead Crossing on the south to above Palo Duro Canyon on the north. They had connected by wagon roads previously unknown water holes on the plains with well-known trails. They had observed the extreme western range of the buffalo and noted the region's excellent potential for ranching and farming. Perhaps most important for an advancing civilization, they had been the major force in sweeping the Llano Estacado clear of Indians.

Notes

1. Walter Prescott Webb, *The Great Plains* (New York: Grosset & Dunlop, 1931), 152–60.

2. Randolph E. Marcy, "Exploration of the Red River of Louisiana in 1852," 32 Cong., 2 Sess., *Senate Exec. Doc.* 54, 84–85.

3. Horace Greeley, *An Overland Journey, from New York to San Francisco in the Summer of 1859* (New York: C. M. Saxton, Barbar, 1860), 128–30.

4. James Parker, *The Old Army: Memories* (Philadelphia: Dorrance, 1929), 100.

5. Robert M. Utley. "Pecos Bill on the Texas Frontier," *American West* 6 (January 1969), 4–6.

6. William A. Newcome, Clerk, Dept. of State, to Mary McKittrict (Shafter's daughter), August 11, ca. 1912, in Shafter Collection, Michigan Historical Collection, University of Michigan, Ann Arbor; see also Frank D.

Reeve, ed., "Frederick E. Phelps: A Soldier's Memoirs," *New Mexico Historical Review* 25 (1950), 217.

7. Kenneth W. Porter, "The Seminole-Negro Scouts, 1870–1881," *Southwestern Historical Quarterly* 55 (1951), 358–77; also see, Frost Woodhull, "Seminole Indian Scouts on the Border," *Frontier Times* 15 (December 1937), 118–21.

8. Post Returns, Fort Concho, November 1869, Microcopy No. 617, Roll 336, National Archives (NA); Post Returns, Fort McKavett, November 1869, Microcopy No. 617, Roll 689, NA.

9. Post Returns, Fort Concho, November 1869, Microcopy No. 617, Roll 336, NA; William H. Leckie, *The Buffalo Soldiers: A Narrative of the Negro Cavalry in the West* (Norman: University of Oklahoma Press, 1967), 88, 90.

10. Post Returns, Fort McKavett, January–February 1870, Microcopy No. 617, Roll 689, NA; Leckie. *The Buffalo Soldiers*, 91.

11. Shafter to H. Clay Wood, Assistant Adjutant General, Department of Texas, October 10, 1870, Post Records, Fort McKavett, Record Group (RG) 393, NA, in Jerry Sullivan, ed., "Lieutenant Colonel W. R. Shafter's Pecos River Expedition of 1870," *West Texas Historical Association Yearbook* 47 (1971), 146–52; Post Returns, Fort McKavett, August 1870, Microcopy No, 617, Roll 689, NA.

12. Shafter to Wood, October 10, 1870, Post Records Fort McKavett, RG 393, NA, in Sullivan, ed., "Lieutenant Colonel W. R. Shafter's Pecos River Expedition of 1870," 149–52.

13. Post Returns, Fort McKavett, November 1870–February 1871, Microcopy No. 617, Roll 689, NA; Post Returns Fort Davis, May–June 1871, Microcopy No. 617, Roll 297, NA.

14 Shafter to Wood, July 15, 1871, Letters Sent (LS), Fort Davis, United States Army Commands (USAC), RG 78, NA; Post Returns, Fort Davis, June–July 1871, Microcopy No. 617, Roll 297, NA; Post Medical Reports, Fort Davis, June–July, 1871, Book No, 7–9–12, Old Records Division (ORD), Adjutant General's Office (AGO), NA; see also J. Evetts Haley, *Fort Concho and the Texas Frontier* (San Angelo, Texas: San Angelo Standard-Times, 1952), 163–67.

15. Shafter to Wood, July 15, 1871, LS, Fort Davis, USAC, RG 98, NA.

16. Shafter to Wood, February 12, 1872, LS, Fort Davis, USAC, RG 98, NA.

17. Shafter to Wood. February 1, 1872, LS, Fort Davis, USAC, RG 98, NA.

18. Ibid.; Post Returns, Fort Davis, October 1871, Microcopy No. 617, Roll 297, NA; Post Medical Reports, Fort Davis, October–November 1871, Book No. 7–9–12, ORD, AGO, NA.

19. Post Returns, Fort Davis, December 1871, Microcopy No. 617, Roll 297, NA.

20. Shafter to Wood, February 12, 1872, LS, Fort Davis, USAC, RG 98, NA.

21. Ernest Wallace, *Ranald S. Mackenzie on the Texas Frontier* (Lubbock: West Texas Museum Association, 1964), 64–65.

22. Special Orders No. 102, Department of Texas, May 31,187, Shafter Papers, Stanford University (microfilm copies in Southwest Collection, Texas Tech University, Lubbock); Post Returns, Fort McKavett, June 1872, Microcopy No. 617, Roll 689, NA.

23. Brig. Gen. C. C. Augur, Commanding, Department of Texas, to Shafter, June 12, 1872, Shafter Papers; Ranald S. Mackenzie to Wood, July 6, 1872, in Ernest Wallace, ed., *Ranald S. Mackenzie's Official Correspondence Relating to Texas, 1871–1873* (Lubbock: West Texas Museum Association, 1967), 101 (hereafter cited as Wallace, *Mackenzie's Correspondence, 1871–1873*).

24. Shafter, "Report of Scout," July 22, 1872, and Lt. Wentz C. Miller, Fourth Cavalry, "Report of Scout," September 2, 1872, in Wallace, *Mackenzie's Correspondence, 1871–1873*, 120–23.

25. Shafter "Report of Scout," July 22, 1872, in Wallace, *Mackenzie's Correspondence, 1871–1873*, 120–23.

26. Mackenzie to Wood, August 7, August 15, and September 19, 1872, in Wallace, *Mackenzie's Correspondence, 1871–1873*, 127–35.

27. Mackenzie to Wood, October 12, 1872, in Wallace, *Mackenzie's Correspondence, 1871–1873*, 141–45.

28. Regimental Returns, Twenty-fourth Infantry, September 1872, Microcopy No. 665, Roll 245, NA.

29. Leckie, *Buffalo Soldiers*, 113–40.

30. Capt. Theodore A. Baldwin, Tenth Cavalry, to his wife, August 1875, in L. F. Sheffy, ed., "Letters and Reminiscences of Gen. Theodore A. Baldwin: Scouting after Indians on the Plains of Texas," *Panhandle Plains Historical Review* 11 (1938), 7–30 (hereafter cited as Baldwin, "Letters and Reminiscences").

31 William G. Muller, *The Twenty-fourth Infantry, Past and Present* (n.p., 1928), 1–8.

32. Shafter to J. H. Taylor, Assistant Adjutant General, Department of Texas, January 4, 1876, 4688 AGO 1876, Letters Received, RG 94, NA.

33. Ibid.; Leckie, *The Buffalo Soldiers*, 143–47; Haley, *Fort Concho and the Texas Frontier*, 230–45; Baldwin to his wife.

ALAN K. LAMM

Buffalo Soldier Chaplains of the Old West

African American soldiers made up one-fifth of the U.S. Army's cavalry force and one-tenth of its infantry in the Old West during the last quarter of the nineteenth century. The men served in the Ninth and Tenth Cavalry Regiments, and Twenty-fourth and Twenty-fifth Infantry Regiments. They faced two primary challenges in the performance of their duty: hostile Native Americans and racism. Their bravery, valor, and unique appearance led their Native American foes to honor them with the name "buffalo soldiers," a nickname the black troops accepted with pride. The buffalo soldiers faced the second challenge of racism from white troops and local citizens as courageously as the one presented by fierce Native American warriors.[1]

Unlike the all-white units, a chaplain was assigned to each buffalo soldier regiment primarily to serve as teacher to the largely illiterate black troops, and to minister to the unique religious needs of these men because of their distinct African American Christianity. The first chaplains to serve were white, but ultimately five black men answered the call to serve as buffalo soldier chaplains between 1884 and 1901.

African American Christianity

The story of the buffalo soldier chaplains must begin with the formation of their religious heritage in the antebellum South. The oppressed slaves merged elements from their African heritage, slave experience, and evangelical Christianity to form a new, African American Christianity. That end product possessed the same external form as their white masters' Christian faith, but was also much different thanks to a strong and persistent black folk religious element. For instance, both whites and blacks worshiped on Sunday all across the South, but unlike whites, blacks "shouted" during worship services, sang a new type of song called the "spiritual," believed in spirit possession, and were generally much more vocal, lively, and enthusiastic than whites. Even black funerals were different, for African Americans broke up the possessions of the dead and placed them on top of the grave to help release the spirit of the deceased, just as they had in Africa. Whites tried to suppress this new African American Christianity by restricting blacks and telling them that it was God's will that they were slaves. But blacks resisted by quietly slipping away at night to secret "hush harbors" in the woods where they could practice their faith in peace in what scholars call the "Invisible Institution."

African American Christianity helped blacks deal with American slavery. Slavery severely damaged the African religious and cultural heritage of blacks, but African American Christianity helped them to survive by developing a new coherent worldview in which they felt worthy of love, respect, and dignity. The slaves' religion stressed the biblical message of suffering, resistance, and liberation from oppression through preaching on such favorite texts as the Israelite's exodus from Egyptian slavery, the prophet Amos's call for justice, and Jesus' identification with the poor and oppressed. The message, then, was one of hope, salvation, and ultimately liberation from bondage and racism. That was the message preached by the Civil War era black chaplains, and their successors, the buffalo soldier chaplains of the Old West.

The Forerunners: Black Chaplains of the Civil War

At the start of the Civil War, only whites could serve as chaplains. As the army rapidly expanded, many of the new chaplains were rogues and rascals. Their incompetent behavior resulted in numerous complaints by disgusted soldiers and the handful of good clergymen. These protests finally motivated Congress to revamp the entire system so that by 1863 the chaplain's branch was a thoroughly professional outfit.

Fourteen African American clergymen entered this improved chaplaincy in 1863 after the Emancipation Proclamation was issued. The two-year delay from the start of the war to their official entry into the army proved fortuitous for it meant that these first black chaplains entered a

professional organization and were spared the days when miscreant clergymen in uniform were far too plentiful. The higher educational and ec-
clesiastical standards of the revised chaplaincy meant that fewer black
clergymen qualified, yet those who did were some of the best leaders in
the African American community.[2] The example of the fourteen black
chaplains of the Civil War is important because they set a precedent for
the later buffalo soldier chaplains of the Old West.

All fourteen of the black chaplains resigned at the end of the Civil
War to concentrate their efforts on helping the freed slaves during Reconstruction. By 1884, the African American community was ready to
look beyond the South to the possibilities presented by the opening of the
American West. Some young black men had already taken advantage of
these opportunities by joining the army. These were the buffalo soldiers
who had earned a respectable reputation for themselves in the Ninth and
Tenth Cavalry, and Twenty-fourth and Twenty-fifth Infantry.

The Buffalo Soldier Chaplains

Five black ministers answered the call to serve as buffalo soldier chaplains
from 1884 to 1901. They were all different men with diverse backgrounds,
abilities, styles, and experiences. Four of the five were southerners born
into slavery; one was a freeborn northerner. Three of the five were African Methodist Episcopal (AME) pastors; two were Baptists. All five
men were highly successful civilian pastors who had played a major role
in helping the freedman in the Reconstruction South. All five were
active supporters of the Republican Party, which helped them obtain
their commissions. Each man's experience was unique, but three themes
emerge. First and foremost, they did their duty as chaplains serving the
religious and morale needs of the troops. Second, they were major participants in the promoting of education for their soldiers. Finally, each
man had to confront racism.

CHAPLAIN HENRY V. PLUMMER (1834–1905)

was a former slave from Maryland who had escaped bondage during the
Civil War and served in the U.S. Navy. After the war, he became a Baptist minister and, by the early 1880s, he felt a calling to serve as an army
chaplain. Frederick Douglass and several other notable nineteenth century leaders wrote letters to President Chester Arthur on Plummer's behalf, and in 1884, he became the first buffalo soldier chaplain, replacing

the Ninth Cavalry's white chaplain, Charles Pierce. The Ninth Cavalry was assigned to Fort Robinson, Nebraska and Chaplain Plummer's first ten years in service were positive ones. His typical chaplain duties included teaching Sunday school, leading Sunday worship, counseling with soldiers, visiting men on sick call and in the stockade, and so forth. In addition, he served as post school superintendent and post bakery manager. In 1890, the army began issuing monthly efficiency reports and Chaplain Plummer consistently scored "good," "very good," and "excellent" in every category. But all that changed once Chaplain Plummer moved beyond his routine duties and actively promoted temperance, sought decent quarters, wrote antiracist articles and called for Africa's colonization.

Those were issues that some other white chaplains addressed, but none was rebuked as was Plummer. Plummer's real crime, it seems, was that he was too outspoken for a black man in the Jim Crow era. For example, he was not the first and certainly not the only chaplain involved in the temperance movement. Temperance was the biggest reform movement in Protestant America in the late nineteenth and early twentieth century, ultimately leading to Prohibition in 1918 with the passage of the Eighteenth Amendment to the U.S. Constitution. Chaplain Orville J. Nave, a white minister, had been a key advocate and organizer of temperance among army chaplains beginning in 1887 at Fort Omaha, Nebraska. Many chaplains, including Chaplain Plummer, attended Nave's temperance meetings and went back to their posts dedicated to promoting temperance in their regiment and ending the army's policy of selling alcoholic beverages at army forts. Plummer addressed the alcohol abuse problem with the leadership of the regiment as well as in his monthly chaplain's report to the Adjutant General's Office in Washington, D.C. His efforts to curb alcohol abuse might not have been popular with the command of Plummer's regiment, but even they had to admit that there was a serious drinking problem among their soldiers. Indeed, the vast majority of disciplinary problems in all army regiments stemmed from alcohol abuse.

Plummer also raised eyebrows among the command of the Ninth Cavalry with his objections to being assigned inferior quarters at Fort Robinson. Better living facilities were one of the few "perks" awarded officers on military bases. But Plummer was not even permitted housing with the other officers of the Ninth who were white; instead, he, his wife, sister, and four of his six children living with him were forced to reside on the "lower line" with the officers' servants and enlisted men. Further, his quarters were damp, moldy, and in serious need of repairs. Plummer's request for better housing was denied, and to add insult to injury, the denial came in the form of an official order read aloud before the entire regiment with great pomp and ceremony.

Plummer also alienated many in the command with both real and alleged antiracist writings in the *Fort Robinson Weekly Bulletin* and *Omaha Progress* newspapers. The letters of protest came in response to both physical and verbal abuse suffered by some black troopers at the hands of white civilians in the nearby town of Crawford, Nebraska. Strong language was used in the articles, but not threatening anything worse than what had been perpetrated against the buffalo soldiers of the Ninth Cavalry. The tragedy was that the law would not protect the black soldiers, the same soldiers sent to defend the very lives of the people of Crawford. Yet, when the soldiers tried to defend themselves from lynch mobs, they were denounced as criminals.

Chaplain Plummer's unsuccessful call to lead a volunteer force to explore and possibly colonize Africa was another point that put him at odds with the senior officers of his unit. Admittedly, such a goal was unusual for a chaplain, but it did not violate any army regulations. And in fact, Plummer's quest was one shared by many black leaders of his day such as Henry McNeal Turner, and later, Marcus Garvey.

These incidents, as bad as they seemed to the command, were not enough to bring Plummer up on any specific charges. That problem was finally resolved when he was caught taking a drink with some enlisted men while off-duty. This led to charges of conduct unbecoming an officer and a gentleman and fraternization. Plummer's having a drink was not unlawful in and of itself, though it was hypocritical after his temperance efforts. Moreover, line officers had to keep a proper distance between themselves and the rank and file, but chaplains were unique in the fact that they were supposed to have free access to soldiers of all ranks. Nevertheless, Plummer was found guilty and dismissed from the army in 1894. He left the service a bitter and broken man and worked for the rest of his life to reverse the military' court's decision, but to no avail. Plummer's main crime, it seems, was "conduct unbecoming a black man" in the 1890s.

CHAPLAIN GEORGE W. PRIOLEAU (1856–1927)

Plummer's replacement in the Ninth, had a much better experience. Prioleau was a former slave from Charleston, South Carolina. After the

Civil War, he went on to earn degrees from the AME's elite flagship college, Wilberforce University in Ohio. He served as an AME pastor, denominational leader, and eventually religion professor at Wilberforce. In 1895, he was commissioned as an army chaplain and assigned to the Ninth Cavalry to take Chaplain Plummer's place. Unlike Plummer, Chaplain Prioleau avoided controversial areas like temperance and confined his work to more traditional chaplain duties and to running the post school at Fort Robinson.

In 1898, the Ninth Cavalry left the West to fight in the Spanish-American War. The buffalo soldiers had faced racist incidents in the West as noted in the story of Chaplain Plummer. For the most part, though, the people in that region recognized that the buffalo soldiers were essential for protection against hostile Native Americans, bandits, and so forth. Therefore, they appreciated, if grudgingly, the black troopers. But when the buffalo soldiers traveled south to the training and deployment bases at Chickamauga Park, Georgia and Tampa, Florida, they were shocked to find the cold reception they received by whites in the Jim Crow South.

Because of the wretched conditions in the training camps, Prioleau fell victim to malaria and was not deployed to Cuba with his regiment. Instead, upon his recovery, he was assigned recruiting duty in the South to help fill the regiment's ranks. He wrote about his experiences in letters to the *Cleveland Gazette* newspaper. In one article he protested that blacks were not able to purchase goods at the same counter as whites in the South and that local blacks obeyed these and other Jim Crow laws without question. Then he criticized the hypocrisy of American racism while in the midst of fighting a war to free the Cubans, noting:

> You talk about freedom, liberty, etc. Why sir, the Negro of [America] is a freeman and yet a slave. Talk of fighting and freeing poor Cuba and Spain's brutality of Cubans murdered by the thousands, and starving reconcentradoes. Is America any better than Spain? Has she not subjects in her midst who are murdered daily without trial, judge or jury? Has she not subjects in her own borders whose children are half-fed and half-clothed, because their father's skin is black?

In an angry tone Prioleau continued:

> Yet the Negro is loyal to his country's flag. O! He is a noble creature, loyal and true. Forgetting that he is ostracized, his race considered

as dumb as driven cattle, yet, as loyal and true men, he answers the call to arms and with blinding tears in eyes and sobs he goes forth: he sings "My Country 'tis of Thee, Sweet Land of Liberty," and though the word "liberty" chokes him, he swallows it and finishes the stanza "of Thee I sing."[3]

While in Tuskegee, Alabama, Prioleau complained to the white citizenry that their behavior toward him was "heinous, uncivilized, unchristian, and un-American." Responding to his complaints the day after, the good Christians of Tuskegee

informed [him] that niggers [sic] have been lynched in Alabama for saying less than that. We replied that only cowards and assassins would overpower a man at midnight and take him from his bed and lynch him, but the night you dirty cowards come to my quarters for that purpose there will be a hot time in Tuskegee that hour; that we were only three who would die but not alone. We stayed there ten days, enlisted 34 men.[4]

Even after the war ended and word of the buffalo soldiers' bravery at San Juan Hill and El Caney became public knowledge, Prioleau found that prejudice against the black troops remained in many parts of the country. In a letter that appeared in the *Cleveland Gazette* on October 22, 1898, the chaplain described the reception the Ninth received, first at Long Island, New York, and then at Kansas City, Missouri. At Long Island, the black soldiers were treated as returning heroes. But by the time the Ninth reached Kansas City, the mood had changed dramatically. Both the all-black Ninth and all-white First Cavalry appeared together in that city, but whereas the First Cavalry was received as conquering heroes praised for their exploits in Cuba, the Ninth was "unkindly and sneeringly received." Prioleau noted that of the two units:

both were under the same flag, both wore blue, and yet these black boys, heroes of our country, were not allowed to stand at the counters of restaurants and eat a sandwich and drink a cup of coffee, while the white soldiers were welcomed and invited to sit at the tables and eat free of charge. You call this American "prejudice." I call it American "hatred" conceived only in hellish minds.[5]

Sadly, Prioleau concluded that patriotic service and military duty would not erase the color line in the minds of many white Americans. Nevertheless, Prioleau continued to believe that the U.S. Army provided one of the best opportunities for young black men of his day, and he remained in the army until he retired in 1920.

CHAPLAIN WILLIAM T. ANDERSON (1859–1934)

served with the Tenth Cavalry. He was born into slavery in Texas and like Chaplain Prioleau was educated at Wilberforce University. He also obtained a theological degree from Howard University in Washington, D.C., and a medical degree from Cleveland University School of Medicine and Surgery. Thus, Anderson was the best educated buffalo soldier chaplain in the Old West era.

In 1897, Anderson sought and received an army commission when the Tenth Cavalry's white chaplain, Francis H. Weaver, retired. Booker T. Washington and other notables wrote glowing letters of endorsement for Anderson, and he was quickly approved. The Tenth Cavalry was then stationed at Fort Assiniboine, Montana. Anderson was less vocal than the chaplains of the Ninth Cavalry in reacting to racism. He concentrated his efforts on trying to save the bodies as well as souls of his men through the use of his training as a physician and ministerial skills.

When the regiment was sent to Chickamauga in preparation for deploying to Cuba, Anderson was left behind at Fort Assiniboine temporarily to serve as post commander, quartermaster, commissary officer, and post exchange officer. Thus, Anderson goes down in history as the first African American to command a U.S. Army fort. He also made history as the only buffalo soldier chaplain sent to Cuba during the Spanish-American War. In Cuba, he carried out his normal chaplain duties, but he also set up a library for the men, gave a "Stereopticon Exhibition" (or early slide show) that was much appreciated by the troops, and worked with the Young Men's Christian Association (YMCA), a group dedicated to helping provide wholesome diversions for the men in their off-duty hours.

But Anderson did more and used his skills and training as a physician to treat his soldiers and local Cuban citizens suffering from a deadly outbreak of yellow fever. Lt. Col. T. A. Baldwin of the Tenth later described Anderson's services:

> He at once applied himself to assisting in the relief in [yellow] fever patients then in the regiment by visiting and nursing the sick and cheering them by his Christian example and fortitude even after he

was sick and suffering himself and effected much good. While Chaplain Anderson is not an applicant for promotion or brevet, I think that his services should be recognized and I believe that all of the officers of the regiment that served in Cuba will bear me out to that end. I would request that this communication be made a matter of record and that it be forwarded to the War Department to be placed upon file.[6]

Maj. Charles H. Grierson, son of Civil War hero Gen. Benjamin Grierson, the Tenth's first commander, added more praise and said that while Anderson was in Cuba he inspected every house and school personally, and twice a month checked houses in the nearby Cuban villages up to sixty miles away for signs of sickness and disease.[7]

Chaplain Anderson and the Tenth later served in the Philippines during the Philippine Insurrection as well as other duty assignments. Anderson retired from the army in 1910, and it is not entirely clear from the available evidence whether or not he was singled out specifically for early retirement by President William Howard Taft in keeping with his "new Southern policy."[8] Nevertheless, many people in the black community certainly thought so and so did Chaplain Anderson. Even though he was deeply hurt, like all the buffalo soldier chaplains, he kept his faith in the U.S. Army.

CHAPLAIN ALLEN ALLENSWORTH (1842–1914)

of the Twenty-fourth Infantry rose higher in rank than any other buffalo soldier chaplain of his day by his promotion to lieutenant colonel. He made remarkable achievements in the field of education, which were recognized by the civilian community and adopted by the army. After the end of a long and successful military career he went on to establish Allensworth, California, the first all-black community in that state which was created to be a safe place for blacks to grow and develop without confronting racism.

Allensworth was born into slavery in Kentucky. When the Civil War broke out, he ran away and joined the Forty-fourth Illinois Volunteer Infantry as a civilian nursing aide. Later, he joined the U.S. Navy, saw combat service aboard several vessels, and rose to the rank of petty officer first class. After the war, he worked his way through college and became a Baptist minister, serving several churches in Kentucky. Allensworth held firm to the black folk tradition that had made African American Christianity unique, but he was also a progressive who knew that the black church needed to evolve in this new age of freedom. The "Invisible Institution" had worked well on the old plantations of the antebellum South when blacks had no churches of their own, but now they had to deal with church budgets, property taxes, missionary work, and the establishment of colleges. The new age of freedom required new talents and abilities, especially discipline. These same qualities Allensworth had seen employed successfully while in the Union navy during the Civil War, and he now applied them to church management.

In the early 1880s, Allensworth began an active campaign to become an army chaplain by writing several congressmen. He wrote a letter to the adjutant general of the army, which contains the following fascinating statement:

> I know where the official life ends and where the Social life begins and have therefore gaurded [*sic*] against Social intrusion. As I served as a petty officer in the Navy during the Civil War, I know, to some extent, what the feelings of the officers in the Army and Navy are on this subject, and am prepared to guard [*sic*] against allowing myself in any position to give offense.[9]

To the Honorable J. P. Brown, a U.S. senator, Allensworth wrote:

> I am and have been on pleasant terms with the whites of my state . . . Allow me to further say that my Southern training has taught me enough to know how to appreciate the position of those who are my superiors: intellectually, Socially and financially, and to act according to my relation to them, without undue assumptions.[10]

These statements show that Allensworth subscribed to Booker T. Washington's accommodationist school. He knew all too well the racist views of the dominant white culture, but chose not to confront them directly. Instead, he sought to find a place for himself and for his people within that culture. Despite the later controversies over the philosophy of accommodationism, Allensworth's approach was successful. On April 1, 1886 his application was accepted, and he was commissioned as the second black chaplain since the Civil War.

Allensworth proved to be a very effective chaplain and was well received by the regiment's commander and most of the other officers of the

Twenty-fourth. However, the white troops of the Fifth Cavalry, which was colocated with the Twenty-fourth at Fort Supply, Oklahoma, were not overly enthused about his arrival, with some declaring that they would never salute a black officer. Allensworth could have brought the men up on charges, but instead he chose to preach a humorous sermon to make his point. His approach worked, and the men of the Fifth never failed to salute him again. Later when some junior white officers refused to salute him, he chose to ignore it. In time, many of these same officers were won over by the kindly chaplain and approached him in an apologetic manner after witnessing his sincerity, honesty, and earnestness in the performing of his duty.

By now, the men of the Twenty-fourth Infantry were not the only ones impressed with this black officer's hard work. After an eight-day inspection tour, an officer from the Inspector General's Office noted in his report that Chaplain Allensworth "is credited with being very energetic and greatly interested in his duties."[11] His alma mater, Roger Williams University, was delighted as well and in 1887 conferred upon him an honorary master of arts degree for being a "Christian gentleman and a man of scholastic habits."[12]

But what impressed people the most were Allensworth's efforts in education. Allensworth established a well-organized school that used the brightest soldiers as teachers. He also used creative teaching methods, such as visual aids, and developed a graded course of study for both soldiers and their children entitled, Outline of Course of Study, and the Rules Governing Post Schools of Fort Bayard, N.M. When the army could not provide him the textbooks, slates, pencils, and other supplies he needed for his students, he obtained donations from civilians or procured them from his own money. He also went beyond the basic reading, writing, and arithmetic courses required by the army and promoted the teaching of vocational skills, such as telegraphy, printing, baking, clerkship, and cooking. Allensworth's goal was to make the army into a training school for young black men, teaching them the skills needed to succeed as soldiers and as civilians after their discharge from service.

Word of his efforts soon spread and were met with enthusiasm from commanders throughout the army, and in 1889, the army passed new educational requirements for its soldiers, thanks in large part to Allensworth's efforts. In 1891, the National Education Association invited him to speak at its convention in Toronto, Canada. Allensworth's talk was a success with the members and the press, and because of this triumph, he was invited to the 1893 World Columbian Exposition in Chicago to oversee an exhibit on religious organizations.

When the Spanish-American War broke out, Allensworth remained stateside on recruiting duty. He was later deployed to the Philippines, though, along with his unit. Racism in the U.S. Army was rampant in the Philippines and was directed against both blacks and Filipinos, but Chaplain Allensworth did not "consider himself charged with the settlement of political or social questions" and instead concentrated on, in his words, "well, smaller things."[13] He quickly went to work conducting worship services, delivering mail to hospital patients, encouraging churches to write soldiers with no families, and establishing another school for the men. He also helped to create the first Christian Endeavor Society in the Philippines.

While in the Philippines, Allensworth injured his knee twice and suffered from other health problems requiring his return to the United States. In 1904, Congress passed an act that permitted chaplains to be promoted to the rank of major for the first time. Fifty-seven clergymen were on duty that year, but only four were deemed "exceptionally efficient" and advanced to that rank; Allensworth was one of the four promoted. In 1905, Congress passed another act that allowed chaplains to advance to lieutenant colonel. On April 7, 1906 Allensworth was one of only two chaplains selected for promotion. As a lieutenant colonel, he was the highest ranking black officer in the history of the United States Army. A black newspaper, the *Cleveland Gazette,* stated that his final promotion was the highest honor ever given to an Afro-American.[14]

Allensworth retired from the army in 1907 but instead of sitting back in ease, he embarked on a quest to create an all-black community in the San Joaquin Valley, thirty miles north of Bakersfield, California. The town, soon named Allensworth, started out with a purchase of twenty acres and grew to eighty acres in a few short years complete with a school, post office, library, and train station. Allensworth's dream was that this community would be a refuge where African Americans could improve themselves and develop skills free from white prejudice. The town prospered until tragedy struck in 1914. That year Allensworth was killed by a motorcycle in Los Angeles. That unfortunate event, coupled with a chronic lack of water, eventually spelled doom for the town. Today, it is a state park.

Allensworth believed that a gradual, accommodationist approach offered the best opportunity of success for African Americans much like Booker T. Washington. Allensworth's goal was reconciliation, not conquest.

CHAPLAIN THEOPHILUS G. STEWARD (1843–1924)

of the Twenty-fifth Infantry was different from the other buffalo soldier chaplains in many ways. He was the only one who was freeborn, from the North, and the product of a racially mixed family. During the Civil War he was ordained as an AME minister in his native state of New Jersey. After the war, he worked to help the freedmen in the South, rose high in the AME denomination, and, became a prolific and scholarly author.

In 1891, he obtained his commission as an army chaplain and joined the Twenty-fifth Infantry, which was then stationed at Fort Missoula, Montana. He, too, felt that the Army provided young black males with the best opportunity available for success in his day. Steward wrote that if fifty thousand more blacks would join the army for twenty-five years, the "race would be carried forward many centuries," because the military taught poor blacks "respect for law, order, and authority," something that the "church cannot teach; . . . the press can only point to; . . . the school but fairly inculcates; [but] the army teaches and enforces."[15]

Steward continued to publish even after he joined the army. Examples of his work include *The Colored Regulars in the United States Army,* a book that documented the efforts of blacks in the military from colonial times through the Spanish-American War. Another book he published was *Active Service; or Gospel Work among U.S. Chaplains.* That work contained contributions by several Regular Army chaplains who discussed topics ranging from the purpose of the army chaplaincy to practical ways in which to minister to troops. The book is important because it was one of the first of its kind and provides scholars with great insights into army life and the army chaplaincy of the era.

Steward did not accompany the Twenty-fifth Infantry to Cuba during the Spanish-American War, but he did go with the unit to the Philippines later. As noted, once in the Philippines, white soldiers wasted little time in imposing Jim Crow practices from home on both Filipinos and African Americans. Unlike Chaplain Allensworth, Steward, the northern radical, refused to "turn the other cheek" when faced with racism. When a white enlisted medic refused to salute him, Steward reported the incident to the hospital's commander. When three white enlisted soldiers insulted him along a busy street, he lectured the troops and then reported them to their commander. While en route back to the United States after the end of the fighting in the Philippines, both Steward and his son, also an officer, were told by the dining room steward that they would have to sit at a side table. Steward complained to the regimental commander who promptly invited him to sit at his table, and told his son to sit with the other junior officers.

The American strategy for winning the Philippine Insurrection included defeating the rebels in the field and winning the hearts and minds of the people through a program of nation-building, including constructing roads, hospitals, and schools for the Filipino children. The army recognized from the start that the schools were key to their pacification program and Chaplain Steward played a major role in setting up forty-three of them. That work brought him in close daily contact with the Filipino people, a task made easier by his fluency in Spanish. Soon, many young Filipino couples flocked to the Spanish-speaking chaplain seeking to get married, for under Spanish and Roman Catholic rule, marriages were expensive and difficult to obtain.

Sometimes cultural misunderstandings arose that were quite humorous. At one point a group of Filipino children insisted on singing an "American song" for the chaplain. Steward expected to hear "God Bless America" or some other edifying piece, but instead the children broke out into "Hello My Honey, Hello My Baby, Hello My Ragtime Girl" followed by "the most lively minstrel dance."[16]

By 1907, Steward was in failing health, and so he requested a medical retirement which was granted. He spent his remaining years, until he died in 1925, as professor at Wilberforce University, but still considered himself part of the U.S. Army chaplaincy and even sent a yearly report to the adjutant general.

Conclusion

Between 1884 and 1901, five black men answered the call to serve as buffalo soldier chaplains. They were each unique individuals who worked diligently to perform their chaplain duties, educate their troops, and combat racism in their own way. Though each recognized that racism existed in the army, all five believed that the military was the best opportunity for young black males of the day. They set an example of pride and dignity for the U.S. Army, the African American community, and all of America.

Notes

1. For more information on the buffalo soldiers consult the following works: William Leckie's *The Buffalo Soldiers: A Narrative of the Negro Cavalry in the West* was written in 1967 (Norman: University of Oklahoma Press) and is a standard classic. More recently, Frank N. "Mickey" Schubert has become the best and most prolific scholar authoring such works as *Buffalo Soldiers, Braves, and the Brass: The Story of Fort Robinson, Nebraska* (Shippensburg: White Mane Publishing, 1993); *On the Trail of the Buffalo Soldiers: Biographies of African Americans in the U.S. Army, 1866–1917* (Wilmington, Del.: Scholarly Resources, 1994); and *Black Valor: Buffalo Soldiers and the Medal of Honor, 1870–1898* (Wilmington, Del.: Scholarly Resources, 1997).

2. Approximately 180,000 blacks served as Union soldiers in 166 regiments. Over 2,300 Union army chaplains served in the Civil War.

3. *Cleveland Gazette,* May 13, 1898.

4. *Cleveland Gazette,* October 1, 1898.

5. Willard B. Gatewood Jr., *"Smoked Yankees" and the Struggle for Empire: Letters from Negro Soldiers, 1898–1902* (Urbana: University of Illinois Press, 1971), 83.

6. Herschel V. Cashin, *Under Fire with the Tenth U.S. Cavalry* (1899; repr., New York: F. Tennyson Neely, 1969), 291–92.

7. Chaplain William T. Anderson File, Record Group 94, National Archives, Washington, D.C.

8. The "Southern policy" was a new Republican political strategy designed to reach out and win over the Southern vote during Taft's tenure in office (1908–12). It included a more hostile attitude toward African Americans.

9. Letter from Allensworth to the Adjutant General of the Army, dated March 3, 1886, Allen Allensworth File, Record Group 94, National Archives, Washington, D.C.

10. Allensworth File, Record Group 94, National Archives, Washington, D.C.

11. Letter from Allensworth to U.S. Senator J. E. Brown, dated March 22, 1886, Allen Allensworth File, Record Group 94, National Archives, Washington, D.C.

12. Allensworth File, Record Group 94, National Archives, Washington, D.C.

13. Quoted in Earl Stover, *Up from Handyman: The United States Army Chaplaincy, 1865–1920* (Washington, D.C.: Office of the Chief of Chaplains, Department of the Army, 1977), 55.

14. Allensworth File, Record Group 94, National Archives, Washington, D.C. William J. Hourihan, "An Officer and a Gentleman: Chaplain Allen Allensworth of the Twenty-fourth Infantry," *U.S. Army Chaplain Museum Association Newsletter* (July 1989). Allensworth held the distinction of obtaining the highest rank for an African American until Charles Young was promoted to full colonel in World War I. Louis Carter became the first black chaplain promoted

to full colonel in 1936. Benjamin O. Davis Sr. became the first black promoted to general in the Regular Army in World War II, and Matthew Zimmerman became the first black chaplain promoted to general and the first black Army Chief of Chaplains in 1989.

15. Theophilus G. Steward, "Washington and Crummell," *The Colored American* (October 29, 1898). See also Steward's article entitled, "The Army as a Trained Force and the Birth of the Republic Addresses" (Cincinnati: By the Author, 1904).

16. Theophilus G. Steward, *Fifty Years in the Gospel Ministry* (Philadelphia: AME Book Concern, n.d.), 324.

DOUGLAS C. MCCHRISTIAN

"Dress on the Colors, Boys!"

BLACK NONCOMMISSIONED OFFICERS IN THE REGULAR ARMY, 1866–98

As the troops of the Tenth U.S. Cavalry charged the crest of San Juan Hill on July 1, 1898, one man sprinted ahead in the face of enemy fire, mounted the Spanish entrenchments, and planted the regimental colors. Turning to encourage his comrades, Color Sgt. George Berry shouted, "Dress on the colors, boys. Dress on the colors!" The regiment did just that, taking the Spanish positions within minutes afterward.

Berry, an old soldier with thirty years of service to his credit, typified many of the regular army noncommissioned officers of that era, particularly those in the all-black units. He enlisted in the Ninth Cavalry in 1867 and with the exception of one short break in service had been with the Ninth and Tenth cavalry regiments—the famed buffalo soldiers—ever since.

But the road to glory at San Juan Hill had not been an easy one for Berry and his comrades. In 1866, Congress proposed legislation to authorize six segregated regiments, commanded by white officers. Historian Arlen Fowler has written that many people inside and outside army circles expressed opposition, however, to the idea of recruiting blacks into the regular army because, they believed, "ex-slaves were too ignorant and cowardly to make good soldiers." While some 186,000 black men answered the call to serve the nation in so-called "Colored Volunteer" regiments during the Civil War, there were serious reservations about establishing such units in the regular army. The opponents of this measure ignored the reality that black soldiers had proven their worth in blood at such places as Fort Wagner, Cold Harbor, and Petersburg. In all, more than 38,000 blacks had died in the service of a nation that now questioned their ability, if not their loyalty.

With the passage of the act to authorize the black regiments, the army undertook the task of organizing them. The new units were designated as the Ninth and Tenth cavalry regiments and the Thirty-eighth, Thirty-ninth, Fortieth, and Forty-first infantries. The latter would be consolidated into two regiments, the Twenty-fourth Infantry and Twenty-fifth Infantry, during the general army reorganization in 1869.

Officers who applied for the vacancies in the black regiments were subjected to the scrutiny of a special examining board composed of experienced officers. Basic qualifications included at least two years of active field service during the Civil War. One-third were drawn from the regular army; the remainder from the volunteer forces. Company commanders and field-grade officers of cavalry were further required to have prior service in that branch.

Finding good men for the rank and file proved more difficult. Preference was given to veterans on active duty in the Colored Volunteers. These men could apply for an immediate discharge to re-enlist in the regulars, and some did. Raw recruits, many of them ex-slaves, flocked to the recruiting offices in hopes of gaining a better quality of life. Army pay may have been meager, but it was a great inducement to men who had previously labored for nothing. Soldiering also offered food, clothing, and shelter. Like many of their white counterparts, some blacks enlisted for the chance to go west and experience the adventure of the frontier. More importantly, the army afforded these disadvantaged black men the opportunity to gain self-respect through acceptance and responsibility, and, ostensibly, equal treatment.

However, recruiting efforts revealed that few blacks, particularly in the South, possessed initiative and a sense of self-reliance, much less any formal education. Slavery had denied them access to education. Moreover, it had engrained in them a servile attitude largely devoid of self-esteem, a critical element in developing the esprit de corps so essential to these new regiments.

Col. Benjamin H. Grierson established higher standards for his Tenth Cavalry. He ordered his officers to go to northern cities to

> recruit men sufficiently educated to fill the positions of Non-Commissioned Officers, Clerks, and Mechanics in the regiment . . . enlist all the superior men you can who will be a credit to the regiment.

Grierson's idea was that urban-bred blacks might possess a higher degree of native intelligence and sharpened wits derived from living in a city environment. Likewise, some northern blacks had opportunities to acquire formal education. Grierson also increased recruiting efforts in the former border states of Virginia, Kentucky, and Tennessee, where slavery had not been as prevalent as in the Deep South.

The importance of efficient noncommissioned officers was well-recognized throughout the army. Testifying before a special committee of the House of Representatives in 1878, 1st Lt. Edmund V. Rice stated: "Non-commissioned officers are the bone and sinew of a regiment and are of so much importance to an army that the greatest care should he taken in their selection." Rice spoke from experience beyond his rank, having had sixteen years of service, both in the volunteer forces during the Civil War and in the regular army afterward.

Among the volunteer regiments, which made up the bulk of the Union Army during the Civil War, noncoms often were men well-known to the rank and file. Recruited within the respective states, the members of these units usually hailed from the same region or county, and frequently from the same town. These men shared much in common with each other and some were close friends. While the corporals and sergeants enjoyed a degree of authority commensurate with their respective ranks, they sometimes supervised the men more as peers than as superiors.

This was not the case, however, in the regular army. Here was a no-nonsense organization whose hallmarks were duty and discipline. These were professional soldiers who were cut from different cloth than the wartime volunteers. For instance, of the six sergeants in Troop H, Tenth Cavalry in 1884, the first sergeant and all five duty sergeants were veterans having from one to three prior enlistments.

In this environment, the noncommissioned officers assumed a degree of importance beyond that seen among the volunteer units. One historian has noted: "If a single word were chosen to describe the non-commissioned officers of the Indian Wars army, that word would have to be tough." An illustration of this is found in the statement of a Twenty-fifth Infantry sergeant, Grandison Mayo, who remembered that a soldier in his company was given fifteen minutes of double-timing around the parade ground at port arms simply for having laughed in ranks.

Some soldiers were bona fide hard cases who had experienced trouble with the law and resented authority of any kind. Such men were difficult to handle under any circumstances, and even more so when serving in isolated stations on the western frontier. Not only did the army expect

the men to toe the mark, but the character of many of the individuals demanded firmness and strict adherence to the rules. For the most part,
these men were not impressionable youngsters. The average age of first
enlistment recruits in the regulars was twenty-three, and for subsequent
enlistments, thirty-two. Thus, any noncom worth his stripes had to be
able to enforce discipline, even if it meant doing so with his fists. In some
units, this was more useful than having a formal education.

Former occupations among black recruits were not so diverse as
among white soldiers. Whereas the ranks of white regiments usually
included comparatively high ratios of tradesmen, clerks, and even professional men, the majority of black recruits had been day laborers and
share-crop farmers. This factor proved to be among the detriments to
finding capable men to serve as noncommissioned officers.

The development of good noncoms in black regiments came neither
easily or quickly. One Ninth Cavalry officer wrote:

> The men knew nothing and the noncommissioned officers but little
> more. From the very circumstances of their preceding life, it could
> not be otherwise. They had no independence, no self-reliance, not a
> thought except for the present, and were filled with superstition.

The severe shortage of literate men plagued the black units for many
years. In the immediate postwar years, most companies were fortunate
to have even one man who could read and write. Invariably, this man was
appointed to be quartermaster sergeant and was given responsibility for
maintaining accountability over the company property. Historian William H. Leckie observes that most of the first sergeants were illiterate in
those early years, but the ability to manage the men was deemed more
important than administrative skills.

Not only were the NCOs relied upon to manage the men, they were
also expected to be skillful drillmasters, be able to execute minor tactics,
and to be familiar with army regulations and procedures. At target practice, they kept score and validated the men's records. In field situations,
sergeants had to be able to conduct patrol in remote regions, render reconnaissance reports, and prepare sketch maps of the country. The
added responsibility for training the noncoms in these basics, as well as
doing most of the routine paperwork, fell to the company officers in the
early years after the regiments were organized. Consequently, Leckie
suggests that the circumstances peculiar to the black regiments forced
the officers and noncoms into closer association with each other, which

could contribute to a somewhat more intimate bond than was generally experienced in white units.

The matter of education, then, became a priority in the black regiments. Recognizing this need at the outset, Congress authorized each of the black regiments to have its own chaplain. By regulation, a white regiment was authorized a chaplain only if the unit were serving "together as a whole," a condition that seldom occurred on the western frontier. Invariably, the companies of any regiment were distributed among several posts within a geographical region.

One of the chaplain's principal responsibilities was to serve as schoolmaster. The education programs in black regiments profited by attracting several well-qualified men, who took this duty seriously. When the Twenty-fifth Infantry was formed in 1869 at Jackson Barracks, Louisiana, the regiment's first chaplain, the Reverend D. Elington Barr, immediately established a school for the men. Attendance, however, was not compulsory, according to army regulations. Barr attempted to avoid conflicts with duty schedules by holding additional evening classes for the men at his own quarters. When the regiment reached the West Texas frontier, Col. George L. Andrews expressed his belief that all noncoms should know how to read and write. He reinforced Barr's efforts by ordering that all noncommissioned officers were to attend the post schools at the various stations occupied by the Twenty-fifth.

Education in the Twenty-fifth suffered a severe setback in 1872, when Barr resigned. The position lay vacant for three years before a replacement was found in Chaplain George C. Mullins. Mullins, an ordained minister with a degree from the University of Kentucky, dedicated himself to providing educational opportunities for the rank and file. He believed strongly that education was a key ingredient in helping black enlisted men to gain self-respect and dignity, and develop into good, well-disciplined soldiers. Mullins' achievements were recognized officially in 1881 when he became chief of education for the U.S. Army.

Among the black chaplains particularly devoted to soldier education was Allen Allensworth, who held a degree from Roger Williams University and had several years of experience as a teacher for the Freedmen's Bureau. Allensworth was appointed to the Twenty-fourth Infantry in 1886. Significant among his accomplishments was the development of graded curriculum, segregated into separate programs for children and for soldiers. The program for soldiers included special instructions on writing reports and preparing various company records, in addition to arithmetic, writing, and reading. This was a decided advantage for any man who aspired to become a noncommissioned officer.

A few officers in black regiments also took particular interest in improving the training of their sergeants and corporals. At Fort Davis, Texas, Lt. John Bigelow Jr., Tenth Cavalry, honed his noncoms by scheduling classes twice weekly, in addition to extra drills. These exercises provided Bigelow and his NCOs the opportunity to address specific topics relating to tactics and field service.

In perspective, the acute need for education in the black regiments contributed greatly to the development of education in the army as a whole. By 1882, the adjutant general reported, "The importance of the question of education in the army cannot be overestimated, whether we consider its immediate benefits in raising the standard of intelligence in the ranks, or its ulterior advantages to the country at large whenever the soldier reenters civil life."

The success of the army's educational programs is reflected in the case of Sgt. Emanuel Stance, Ninth Cavalry. When Stance, a former slave, enlisted in October 1866, he was barely literate. Nevertheless, he was made a sergeant almost immediately, probably for his leadership ability. At Kickapoo Springs, Texas, three and a half years later, Stance commanded a ten-man detachment in a hot fight with Comanches. Upon completion of his mission, Stance was able to render a clear, detailed written report to his superiors.

Appointment of noncommissioned officers at the company level was the province of the company commander, subject to the approval of the colonel. Each company had a complement of one first sergeant, four or five sergeants, depending upon whether infantry or cavalry, and four corporals. Companies were subdivided into four squads; each placed under the command of a noncommissioned officer, usually a sergeant.

Corporals, the lowest of the company grades, usually supervised small fatigue and police details around the post and were assigned to drill the recruits of their companies in the manual of arms and the school of the soldier. Private William Earl Smith, serving in the Fourth Cavalry in the mid-1870s, observed that a corporal's "money was well-earned by drilling recruits . . . the most disagreeable duty was surely to have a dozen green shavetails . . . No one can imagine that there is such ignorant class of men alive on this earth until he puts a dozen or so through the maneuvers and manual of arms." Certainly, the conditions were no different in the black regiments.

For those men who were willing to accept the responsibility, even a promotion to corporal carried with it considerable authority, in addition to extra pay. While a corporal's former chums might refer to him behind his back as the "knight of the double chevron," they dared not be disrespectful to his face. During a troop movement from Sheldon, Arizona, to Fort Grant, a Tenth Cavalry officer told one of his men to dismount and walk, punishment for talking back to a noncom. Such actions served to underscore the regular army's intolerance of insubordination at any level.

A duty sergeant was given assignments demanding greater responsibility and exercise of good judgment. As a chief of squad, or squad leader in modern parlance, he was directly responsible for the discipline and cleanliness of his men, and he made sure that their arms, clothing, and equipment were maintained in good order. In garrison, sergeants served as drillmasters and each took his turn serving as sergeant-of-the-guard. They also rotated within the company, usually for week-long periods, as barrack room orderlies and as supervisors over the kitchen and mess hall. Other times, sergeants were given charge of paymaster escorts, extended patrols with a dozen or so men, and guard detachments at stage stations.

The new recruit learned quickly that the first sergeant occupied the most important position in the company. The company commander, particularly in garrison, usually relied upon the first sergeant to run the company on a daily basis. The first sergeant supervised the other noncoms in the company and was expected to be familiar with all aspects of that unit's operations and logistical support. Sometimes, however, this practice was carried too far. In 1884, officer absenteeism became so acute among the Tenth Cavalry buffalo soldiers that Col. B. H. Grierson was compelled to issue an order requiring company officers to attend drills.

The first sergeant's word was law, and woe be to any soldier who dared challenge it. The rigid caste system of the Indian Wars army dictated that anyone in the company wishing to speak to the company commander was first obligated to obtain the permission of the first sergeant. The latter also had the prerogative to impose company punishments for minor infractions and to confine soldiers in the guardhouse when circumstances warranted. According to historian Don Rickey, the first sergeant occupied a position "only a little lower than that of the Almighty." To the privates in the company, especially the recruits, this was hardly an exaggeration.

A generalization can be made that most of the noncommissioned officers were, by virtue of their promotions to their respective grades, a cut above the average enlisted man. However, soldiering in the regular army did not make saints of men and the noncoms certainly were no exception. Tenth Cavalry Sgt. Thomas White, for instance, was granted a pass to go hunting in the vicinity of Fort Davis, Texas. Instead of carrying out his assignment, White spent his time with "disreputable" women at one of the neighboring dives. As a result, the sergeant was court-martialed and stripped of his rank.

In a more serious case, buffalo soldier Richard Robinson, a Twenty-fifth Infantry corporal, made insulting remarks about the wife of Sgt. Moses Marshall. A few hours later, and perhaps several drinks later, Marshall stormed back into the barracks squad room, removed his rifle from the rack, and forthwith shot Robinson through the head.

Sgt. Emanuel Stance, a buffalo soldier, referred to earlier, was awarded the Medal of Honor for his actions at Kickapoo Springs in 1870. A year later, in dark contrast to his record up to that point, Stance was reduced to the rank of private for insubordination. Throughout the remainder of his army career, Stance may just as well have had his chevrons pinned, rather than sewn, to his uniform. In what must qualify as a record, he was re-promoted to corporal and to sergeant no less than five times each. And he was reduced to the ranks an equal number of times. He made first sergeant twice, having been reduced from that grade only once. Stance's superiors obviously recognized his natural combat leadership qualities, but he was characterized by one private in the company as being "dirty mean" to his men. The historical record suggests that Stance and his subordinate sergeants may have conspired to tyrannize the men in the troop. The company commander was either unaware of the conditions, or chose to ignore them, until the situation finally exploded at Fort Robinson, Nebraska on Christmas Day, 1887. Stance's body, bearing four gunshot wounds, was found along the road leading to nearby Crawford. Although no one was ever tried for the crime, it was generally acknowledged that members of Stance's troop had murdered him in reprisal for his malicious treatment of them.

Discrimination plagued the black regiments and noncoms. One white medical officer wrote: "The impracticability of making intelligent soldiers out of the mass of negroes is growing more evident to the post surgeon every day, and his opinion is concurred . . . by their own officers when speaking with confidence. . . ." Another officer serving with black troops echoed this when he observed that, "I find, as a general thing, not more than two or three efficient [noncommissioned officers] in a troop." Integrated garrisons sometimes presented special problems when white and black troops, of necessity, shared the same duties. "It was outrageous," one officer's wife recorded, "to put white and black troops in the same little guard room, and colored sergeants over white corporals and privates."

Although the men were quartered separately, racial tensions sometimes erupted between factions serving in close contact at frontier posts. An off-duty incident between blacks and whites at Fort Larned, Kansas, nearly touched off a riot. When a stable housing Tenth Cavalry horses and equipment was put to the torch by an arsonist, the post commander arranged to transfer the black unit to another post in order to avoid further problems. Army regulations and the strict discipline enforced in the regulars, fortunately, made such confrontations relatively rare.

The distance across the parade ground separating the officers' quarters from the enlisted barracks was symbolic of the social gulf between officers and enlisted personnel, regardless of race. Consequently, personal relationships between NCOs and commissioned officers were rare. When bonds of mutual admiration and respect occurred, they were strictly formal in nature.

One Tenth Cavalry officer recognized the beneficial effect of granting special privileges to his men by providing his noncommissioned officers with a separate room in the barracks. Here, he said, during off-duty time "they could enjoy each others' society apart from the men." This officer recognized that esprit de corps among his noncoms would contribute to a sense of team spirit and company efficiency.

The shared experience of combat sometimes broke down the barriers of class and race between officers and noncoms, even if only temporarily. One such incident occurred during the Geronimo Campaign in 1886 when a troop of Tenth Cavalry buffalo soldiers was spiritedly engaged with Apaches in Sonora, Mexico. As the troopers charged dismounted up the hill defended by Geronimo's warriors, a Corporal Scott was severely wounded. The Apaches' heavy fire quickly drove the remainder of the troops to take cover. When Lt. Powhatan H. Clarke observed Scott lying in an exposed position, unable to move, he dashed out and rescued the stricken corporal. Clarke received the Medal of Honor for his action.

Another example of an officer-soldier relationship involved Tenth Cavalryman Caleb Benson, a faithful buffalo soldier private of thirty years service. Just before Benson's retirement in 1908, his officers arranged to have him promoted to first sergeant, both as an honor and to enable the old soldier to depart with a higher pension.

In combat situations, noncommissioned officers were expected to serve as examples for the more inexperienced men. Coolness under fire was especially important in the small-unit actions that typified the Indian campaigns. The conduct of the corporals and sergeants sometimes made the difference between success and failure in action.

Early in the history of the Tenth Cavalry, overworked Sgt. Charles H. Davis established a standard for the conduct of noncoms. On September 19, 1867, Davis was commanding a detachment of only nine men at a construction camp along the Kansas Pacific Railroad, west of Fort Hays, Kansas. Some seventy Cheyennes attacked the camp, killing two civilians who were some distance out on the prairie. The plucky sergeant immediately led a counterattack on foot. The audacity and accurate shooting of Davis's detachment broke up the Cheyennes and compelled them to retreat.

Another instance occurred in New Mexico during the Victorio campaign when Lt. George W. Smith led a twenty-man detachment of the Ninth Cavalry buffalo soldiers plus a party of civilians in pursuit of the elusive warriors. The Apaches ambushed the patrol, killing Smith in the first volley. Sgt. Brent Woods immediately assumed command and organized a counterattack that drove off the Apaches. He also prevented the lieutenant's body from falling into the hands of the Indians. Had Sergeant Woods failed to demonstrate responsible leadership, the situation might well have resulted in a disaster.

In January 1880, Sgt. George Jordon, Troop K, Ninth Cavalry, was ordered to lead a detachment of twenty-five men to defend the citizens of Tularosa, New Mexico Territory. Arriving at the town, Jordon put his men to work fortifying an old adobe corral. That evening, a hundred Apaches attacked and the black troopers repulsed several assaults, until the Indians finally decided they could not capture the position. For his heroism and leadership, Jordon was awarded the Medal of Honor.

The Medal of Honor was instituted in 1862 as recognition for military people who distinguished themselves by their gallantry in action. It remained the only U.S. award for heroism until after the turn of the century. During the Indian campaigns, eighteen Medals of Honor were bestowed upon enlisted men in the black regiments. It seems more than coincidental that fourteen of those were awarded to noncommissioned officers. Such a disproportionate percentage suggests that the black non-coms took their duties seriously.

The noncommissioned officers, truly the backbone of the army, had to be trained and educated to fulfill their responsibilities. In black regiments, the lack of formal education and experience that might have served as a foundation of leadership qualities made this a particularly challenging task. Nevertheless, many blacks succeeded through pride, determination, and dedication to duty. That military service presented black men with a rare opportunity for an honorable profession is reflected in the service records of Indian Wars veterans. Of the ten first sergeants in the Tenth Cavalry on the eve of the Spanish-American War, none had fewer than fourteen years of service. The majority had served from sixteen to thirty-four years each. By the 1890s, a few blacks had been promoted to coveted positions as members of the noncommissioned staff of the army.

The structured, regulated environment of the army created opportunities for self development and professional stature denied to most blacks in civilian life. Black men who made the army their profession recognized that their achievements stood for more than just individual accomplishment. They represented hope for an entire race. Symbolized by Sgt. George Berry at San Juan Hill, the black noncoms led the way. Through courage and initiative, they overcame the odds to establish a new level to which others of their race might aspire. In encouraging his comrades to press forward in the face of the enemy, Sergeant Berry's cry might well have served as a call to all black men. "Dress on the colors, boys! Dress on the colors."

Notes

William H. Leckie presents a rich operational history of the Ninth and Tenth cavalry regiments in *The Buffalo Soldiers: A Narrative of the Negro Cavalry in the West* (Norman: University of Oklahoma Press, 1967). An infantry counterpart is found in Arlen Fowler, *The Black Infantry in the West, 1869–1891* (Westport, Conn.: Greenwood Press, 1971). Fowler's work is enhanced by his treatment of some of the social aspects of black soldiers on the frontier, including a chapter devoted to education and the role of regimental chaplains. John M. Carroll, ed., *The Black Military Experience in the American West* (New York: Liveright Publishing, 1971), contains a collection of useful essays concerning the buffalo soldiers during the Indian campaigns, as well as the Spanish-American War and the Pancho Villa era. More than two decades ago the scarce official histories of the four black regiments, originally prepared in the early 1920s, were reprinted individually by the Old Army Press (Fort Collins, Colorado, 1972). These volumes, rare today in their own right, provide a wealth of basic information about the Ninth and Tenth cavalries and the Twenty-fourth and Twenty-fifth regiments. For authoritative discussions of frontier army life in general, see Don Rickey Jr., *Forty Miles a Day on Beans and Hay: The Enlisted Soldier Fighting the Indian Wars* (Norman: University of Oklahoma Press, 1963); and Edward Coffman, *The Old Army: A Portrait of the American Army in Peacetime, 1784–1898* (New York: Oxford University Press, 1986). The classic narrative work on the recipients of the Medal of Honor is *Deeds of Valor* (Detroit: Perrien-Keydel, 1905).

PART II

The Black Soldier

The selection by the editors of "Cathay Williams: Black Woman Soldier, 1866–68" by DeAnn Blanton as the first article in this section represents a contradiction, paradox, and an anomaly since all nineteenth-century blacks who served as soldiers except one was a man, legally only men could be soldiers, and even an ingenious act of deception normally should warrant little attention. However, Cathay, Cathey, or Cathy Williams who on November 15, 1866, presented herself to the St. Louis, Missouri, military recruiter as William Cathay represents the complexity and contradiction of African American life and serves as a metaphor of the black soldiering experience.

Cathay Williams had no right to join the military since her gender eliminated such service. The various spellings of her name are indicative of the inattention given to many ex-slaves by a society that had little value for them, and her cursory physical examination reflects the urgency of the nation to fill its ranks with all available manpower. The two years of service without apparent detection also suggests that artificial restrictions of race, class, and gender were false indicators of competency.

The black soldier historically has been called to duty for every major conflict on American soil, but it has been a muted call: serve with little recognition, serve for less pay, serve under white leadership, and serve only under dire circumstances. It was not until 1866 that the nation allowed black men to become a part of the standing army, and it was the buffalo soldier who would be the first to gain that distinction. These black soldiers were assigned duties in the western part of the nation for over four decades with little rotation from the region. They were called upon to fight and protect Indians; patrol stage and wagon routes; escort paymasters; build and maintain forts, roads, and telegraph lines; chase and arrest outlaws, renegades, whiskey peddlers, horse and cattle thieves; perform standard garrison duties; and maintain conformable relations with the town folk who often despised them.

Since reestablishing order on the plains following the Civil War was a central motivation for dispatching the buffalo soldier to western outposts, relations with the Indians by necessity occupied a portion of the army's attention. Many students of western history have signaled the irony of one oppressed group fighting another at the behest of their mutual oppressor. This question has generated an interesting and sometimes vitriolic debate: Did the buffalo soldiers and the Indians give each other quarter whenever possible? Many scholars have labeled the notion that either group related in any way other than combatants as romantic nonsense while some detractors have argued that very point. Some scholars have pointed to the television film, *Buffalo Soldiers,* where buffalo soldiers capture an Apache leader and his band but after a brother-to-brother powwow allow them to go free, as both sentimental and ahistorical.

The above tête-à-tête never happened, and scholars were correct to view this Hollywood version of political correctness with chagrin since in military campaigns and contests, adversaries essentially are concerned with winning and ultimate victory. Any nonmilitary consideration on its face would seem unusual and exceptional, yet the question of racial motivation sometimes was raised by the buffalo soldiers themselves. In "One Soldier's Service: Caleb Benson in the Ninth and Tenth Cavalry, 1875–1908" by Thomas R. Buecker, Caleb Benson makes what Buecker calls "a somewhat bizarre (possibly apocryphal) observation on the relationship between the black cavalrymen and the Plains Indians." (56) Private Caleb Benson as a member of the Ninth Cavalry, Company D in late 1879 was dispatched to Milk Creek, Colorado, where he was engaged in one of the major battles of the West.

The White River Utes, upset with the treatment they had received from Indian agent N. C. Meeker, attacked and killed Maj. T. T. Thornburgh and ten of his men while wounding twenty-three others. Several hundred well-positioned Ute sharpshooters kept the remaining members of the three cavalry companies and one of infantry dug in under heavy fire. The novelty of the black-faced buffalo soldiers who came to the aid of their distressed comrades may have played a decisive role in the Utes' unusual response to their arrival. According to official military reports, not a buffalo soldier (including Private Benson) was harmed as they rode down a valley fully exposed to the same Ute sharpshooters who had killed and wounded Thornburgh's troopers. It was Private Benson's contention that the Indians never shot a "colored" man unless it was necessary. He further speculated that the Indians wanted to win the friendship of the African American race and obtain their aid in campaigns against the white man.

Black soldiers did face real dangers from Indians, and many were killed by them; however, Indians were only one of the dangers they faced. A trip off post or performing garrison duties was equally dangerous. Black soldiers suffered injury and death from town folk, ranchers, former Confederates, white officers and enlisted men, and sometimes from other blacks; however, these hazards did not dissuade them from military service. While the motivation for black men joining and re-enlisting in the military differed, each soldier was mindful of the anomaly of being rejected by the very people he was there to protect.

This was true for enlisted men as it was the first black commissioned officer, Lt. Henry O. Flipper. "The Court-Martial of Lieutenant Henry O. Flipper," by Bruce J. Dinges clearly indicates a dual standard of discipline. An offense that usually generated a light reprimand for a white officer was the basis for Lieutenant Flipper's dishonorable discharge from the Army. Lieutenant Flipper mistakenly assumed that good conduct and favorable military reviews were sufficient to protect him from the shadow of servitude and racism.

The exploits that won Sgt. John Ward and Private Pompey Factor Medals of Honor are highlighted in the final article in this section entitled, "The Black Seminole Indian Scouts in the Big Bend," by Thomas A. Britten. In April 1875, Lt. John L. Bullis, with a small detachment of Black Seminole scouts, pursued a band of Comanche who had stolen about seventy-five horses. It was the heroic actions of Ward, Factor, and Trumpeter Isaac Payne, firing upon the advancing Indians, that rescued Bullis from certain death. All three men received the Medal of Honor upon Lieutenant Bullis's recommendation.

The Black Seminole scouts continued to pursue marauding Indians, Mexican bandits, horse thieves, whiskey peddlers, and smugglers until their service was no longer needed on the border in the 1890s. A few scouts, however, continued to serve until their unit was officially abolished in 1914. The Black Seminole scouts performed all the duties assigned to them with great fidelity for more than four decades of service and played an essential role in making the border safe, yet they were unable to win the respect and acceptance of their white neighbors in Texas or the American government. The promise of land that prompted the original eleven Black Seminole scouts to cross the Mexican border and join the army was never fulfilled.

The determination and sense of duty that motivated many of the buffalo soldiers did pay dividends for those who followed if not for the original men themselves. The buffalo soldiers became the pride of the black community when there were few other role models. They were a part of a military tradition embraced by African Americans in difficult circumstances and unpredictable times. However, the hope and expectations were always present that sacrifice, duty, and heroism eventually would be honored by a grateful nation and that they would someday receive the full rights of citizenship unstintingly extended to all Americans.

DEANNE BLANTON

Cathay Williams

BLACK WOMAN SOLDIER, 1866–68

On November 15, 1866 Cathay Williams became a soldier. She enlisted with the U.S. regular army in St. Louis, Missouri, intending on a three-year tour of duty. She had never been in the army before. She informed the recruiting officer that she was twenty-two years old and by occupation a cook. She named Independence, Missouri the place of her birth. When asked her name, she must have replied William Cathay. As she was illiterate, her papers read William Cathey, and by that name and spelling she would be known the rest of her army career. The recruiting officer described William Cathey that day as five feet nine inches, with black eyes, black hair, and black complexion.

An army surgeon examined William Cathey upon enlistment, and determined that the recruit was fit for duty. We can assume the exam was cursory, only checking for obvious and superficial impairments or abnormalities. If either the surgeon or the recruiting officer realized that William Cathey was female they kept the fact to themselves. It seems highly unlikely they knew the truth, because nineteenth century U.S. Army regulations forbade the regular enlistment or commissioning of women.

Other than the place of her birth, nothing is known of this woman prior to her enlistment in the U.S. Army. Information about her family life and circumstances prior to enlistment, including whether she was born slave or free, has not been found.[1] Even her age at the time of enlistment is uncertain. She might have been only sixteen years old and lied about her age, a not uncommon ploy among her male counterparts. The army in the nineteenth century hardly ever checked the veracity of age claims, or asked for proof of identity.

Her reasons for becoming a soldier are a matter of conjecture, as she never stated them. Was she fleeing an unhappy life with family or other relations? Was she an orphan? She might have had compelling reasons to change her identity, such as running from something or someone. Perhaps she viewed the army as a way to get out of Missouri, or get away from home. Maybe she found cooking for a living unsatisfactory. Or did she simply want the adventure of being a soldier?

It seems reasonable that she viewed the army as a job open to African Americans, with prospects for a decent livelihood and a semblance of respect. We can presume Cathay Williams had no substantial means of support other than herself. (There is no evidence she ever married.) She was uneducated, and therefore consigned to laboring for her wages. As a black woman in 1866, her prospects were dim and low-paying. As a black man in the army she would earn more money than a black female cook.

Whatever her motivations in joining the army, she may not have realized she was setting a precedent. While she was not the first woman to enlist in the army—women disguised as men fought in the volunteer armies of the Revolution and the Civil War—Cathay Williams may be the first to have served in the U.S. regular army in the nineteenth century. To date, she is the only *documented* African American woman who served in the U.S. Army prior to the official introduction of women.

Very little is known about the details of William Cathey's service because personnel records were not kept for regular army enlisted soldiers during the nineteenth century. The unit muster rolls, compiled every two months, rated the company as a whole, listed its members, and occasionally included comments regarding the individual soldier. The muster rolls reveal that William Cathey did not have an illustrious, or even an exciting army career. She was an average soldier. She neither distinguished herself nor disgraced her uniform while in the service. She was never singled out for praise or punishment. The opinions held of William Cathey by peers and officers is unknown. Whether she was congenial or aloof, outspoken or retiring is a mystery.

Furthermore, the records can not tell us if she faced difficulties concealing the fact she was female. It may have been easy for her. She was one of the tallest privates in her company, and she probably never experienced close physical scrutiny during her service, despite hospital visits.

The mechanics of how she successfully concealed her femininity are left to speculation. We do not know whether or not she found the necessary deception stressful.

Upon enlistment, William Cathey was assigned to the Thirty-eighth U.S. Infantry. The Thirty-eighth Infantry was officially established in August 1866 as a designated, segregated African American unit. (The Thirty-ninth, Fortieth, and Forty-first infantries were also designated black units that year.) The officers of the segregated African American regiments were white, and the regimental headquarters of the Thirty-eighth was located at Jefferson Barracks, Missouri. The Thirty-eighth through Forty-first infantries were short-lived, however. In March 1869, after William Cathey's discharge, they were consolidated into the historically familiar African American Twenty-fourth and Twenty-fifth infantries.[2]

From her enlistment date until February 1867, William Cathey was stationed at Jefferson Barracks. Her time there would have been spent in training and the daily routine of army camp life. It is uncertain, though, just how long she actually was present at the installation. On February 13, Company A of the Thirty-eighth Infantry was officially organized, and William Cathey, along with seventy-five other black privates, was mustered into that company. At the time of this organization, however, she was in an unnamed St. Louis hospital, suffering an undocumented illness. How long she was hospitalized also is not recorded.

By April 1867 William Cathey and Company A had marched to Fort Riley, Kansas. On the tenth of that month, William Cathey went to the post hospital complaining of "itch." (Army itch was usually scabies, eczema, lice, or a combination thereof, the perceived result of the filth of camp life.)[3] On April 30, she was described as ill in quarters, along with fifteen other privates. Because they were sick, their pay was docked ten dollars per month for three months, so we can presume William Cathey was not malingering. She did not return to duty until May 14, which indicates that something other than itch bothered her.

In June 1867 the company was at Fort Harker, Kansas. Indeed, the company was destined to travel. On July 20, 1867, it arrived at Fort Union, New Mexico, after a march of 536 miles. On September 7, Company A began the march to Fort Cummings, New Mexico, arriving October 1. The unit was stationed there for eight months.

It appears that William Cathey withstood the marches as well as any man in her unit. When the company was not on the march, the privates

did garrison duty, drilled and trained, and went scouting for signs of hostile Native Americans. William Cathey participated in her share of the
obligations facing Company A. There is no record that the company ever
engaged the enemy or saw any form of direct combat while William
Cathey was a member.

In January 1868 her health began deteriorating, after about eight
months off the sick list. On the twenty-seventh of that month, she was
admitted to the post hospital at Fort Cummings, citing rheumatism. She
returned to duty three days later. On March 20, she went back to that
hospital with the same complaint. Again, she returned to duty within
three days.

On June 6, the company marched for Fort Bayard, New Mexico,
completing the forty-seven mile trek the next day. This was the last fort
at which William Cathey lived during her army stint. On July 13, she was
admitted into the hospital at Fort Bayard, and diagnosed with neuralgia.
(Neuralgia was a catch-all term for any acute pain caused by a nerve, or
parts of the nervous system. It could be a symptom of a wide range of
diseases).[4] She did not report back to duty for a month. This was the last
recorded medical treatment of William Cathey while in the military.

During her military career, she was in four hospitals, on five separate
occasions, for varying amounts of time, and apparently, no one discovered that William Cathey was a woman living as a man. It seems fairly
certain in the Victorian age, in an army hospital, even out West, that the
masquerade would have been noted had it been uncovered. It is a fore-
gone conclusion that she would have been discharged from the army immediately had that discovery been made.

The fact that five hospital visits failed to reveal that William Cathey
was a woman raises questions about the quality of medical care, even by
mid-nineteenth century standards, available to the soldiers of the U.S.
Army, or at least to the African American soldiers. Clearly, she never
fully undressed during her hospital stays. Perhaps she objected to any potentially intrusive procedures out of fear of discovery. There is no record
of the treatment given her at the hospitals. There is every indication that
whatever treatments she received, they did not work.

On October 14, 1868 William Cathey and two other privates in
Company A, Thirty-eighth Infantry were discharged at Fort Bayard on
a surgeon's certificate of disability. William Cathey's certificate included
statements from both the captain of her company and the post's assistant
surgeon. The captain's statement read that Cathey had been under his

command since May 20, 1867 "and has been since feeble both physically and mentally, and much of the time quite unfit for duty. The origin of his infirmities is unknown to me." The surgeon's statement claimed Cathey was of "a feeble habit. He is continually on sick report without benefit. He is unable to do military duty. . . . This condition dates prior to enlistment." Thus, with such wording on the certificate of disability for discharge, ended the brief army career of Cathay Williams, alias William Cathey. She served her country for just under two years.

Was William Cathey as infirm as the certificate states? Those statements by the captain and the surgeon lend the impression she was perennially ill. Yet the available records, admittedly scant in detail, indicate she went for months without seeking medical treatment. Perhaps she was sick in quarters more often than recorded on the company rolls, or maybe she was ill more often than just when she went to the hospital. But if her infirmities predated enlistment, why did the recruiting officer and the surgeon in St. Louis make her a soldier?

Was she mentally feeble, as her captain claimed? That is open to debate. Her illiteracy points to a dearth of education, which is far different from stupidity or mental incapacity. One fact is certain. She was bright enough, or wily enough, to conceal the fact she was female for nearly two years. Her successful imposture argues for either some mental ability on her part, or a lack of scrutiny and observation on the army's part.

In any event, in October 1868 Cathay Williams was on her own in New Mexico, far away from any relations she may have had in Missouri, and she was sick. Some regrettably sparse information is known about her life after the army. She resumed the garb and identity of a woman, in fact of herself, Cathay Williams. She traveled to Fort Union and worked as a cook for the family of a colonel in 1869 and 1870. She then traveled to Pueblo, Colorado and worked as a laundress for a Mr. Dunbar for two years. She moved on and lived in Las Animas County, Colorado for a year, again working as a laundress. She finally settled permanently in Trinidad, Colorado, making her living as a laundress. There is some evidence she may also have found work as a nurse.

Why did Cathay Williams return to the identity of a woman working in low-paying servitude? We can only guess at her reasons. She may have been tired of living as a man. Maybe concealing the fact she was a woman became too much of a burden. Perhaps she had no choice. Her bad health likely made her incapable of the generally physically demanding manual labor available to uneducated black men working for wages. She may have viewed the somewhat less physically demanding "woman's work" her only alternative in making a living.

At some point in late 1889 or early 1890, Cathay Williams was hospitalized in Trinidad for nearly a year and a half. Again, no record has surfaced detailing the nature of this illness. She was probably indigent when she left the hospital, so she filed in June 1891 for an invalid pension based upon her military service. Her application brought to light the fact that an African American woman served in the regular army.

Her original application for the pension, sworn before the local county clerk (as was the procedure for all pension applications), gave her age as forty-one. She stated that she was one and the same with the William Cathey who served as a private in Company A, Thirty-eighth U.S. Infantry for just under two full years. She claimed in her application that she was suffering deafness, contracted in the army. She also referred to her rheumatism and neuralgia. She declared eligibility for an invalid pension because she could no longer sustain herself by manual labor. We can infer she was unemployed at the time of the application.

The clerk recorded her attorneys as Charles and William King of Washington, D.C. These two men most likely were professional pension claim handlers. There is no evidence that they over-exerted themselves on behalf of their client in Colorado.

A supplemental declaration, filed the following month in Trinidad by Cathay Williams before the county clerk, contended that she contracted smallpox at St. Louis in October 1868, and that she was still recovering from the disease when she swam the Rio Grande River on the way to New Mexico. She stated that the combined effects of smallpox and exposure led to her deafness.

There are obvious problems with the two declarations. Nowhere do the available records extant today indicate that she ever complained of, or exhibited signs of, deafness while in the army. The Pension Bureau, a forerunner of today's Department of Veterans Affairs, claimed such documentation could not be found in 1891. If Cathay Williams suffered hearing impairment during her tour of duty, no one bothered to record the fact. Given the minimal information written down about regular army privates during the nineteenth century by their commanding officers and their doctors, this is a possibility. Since Williams was illiterate, she would not have known what they wrote about her anyway.

Her claim of suffering small pox in October 1868 is even more puzzling. She was in New Mexico that month, and discharged on the fourteenth. She could not have been in St. Louis. Did the county clerk record the wrong month and year? Was Cathay Williams suffering memory lapse twenty-three years after she left the army? Did she invent this illness? The attorneys for Cathay Williams apparently never noticed the discrepancies of dates in the July 1891 declaration.

Assuming an error in recording the year of her bout with small pox does not help Williams' case. If she claimed hospitalization in October 1866, then she did not have a case for a disability pension based on that disease, as it happened before her enlistment. She could not have been hospitalized in St. Louis in October 1867, because she was in New Mexico.

William Cathey was in a St. Louis hospital in February 1867 but the reason she was there was not recorded. Her illness could have been smallpox. If Cathay Williams was mentally feeble, as her captain charged, then she easily could have been confused about the month when she gave her supplemental affidavit. Swimming the Rio Grande could have occurred only during the march from Fort Harker to Fort Union, which took place in the summer of 1867. If she had smallpox earlier that year, she conceivably still could have been feeling its effects.

The military medical records document that William Cathey suffered rheumatism and neuralgia while in the service. The pension case of Cathay Williams would have been stronger if she had claimed disability based on those two problems. Why didn't she? One wonders if her lawyers gave her any advice at all.

On September 9, 1891 a medical doctor in Trinidad, employed by the Pension Bureau, examined Cathay Williams. (His name is lost to posterity because his signature on all the paperwork is illegible.) He was charged with providing both a thorough examination of the patient, and a complete description to the Pension Bureau of her physical condition at the time of the exam. The doctor described Cathay Williams that day as five feet seven inches, 160 pounds, large, stout, and forty-nine years of age. He reported that she could hear a conversation, and therefore was not deaf. He also reported no physical changes in her joints, muscles, or tendons indicating rheumatism or neuralgia. This doctor obviously did not know that neuralgia was a problem of the nerves, not the muscles, thus raising questions of his competency.

Most horrifying, the doctor reported that all her toes on both feet had been amputated, and she could only walk with the aid of a crutch. He provided no explanation of, or ruminations concerning the cause of amputation. He may not have even asked her how, why, or when it happened. Other than her loss of toes, the doctor stated she was in good general health. While he declared the impairment caused by the amputations permanent, he gave his opinion as "nil" on a disability rating.

In addition to ordering the physical examination of Cathay Williams, the clerks at the Pension Bureau in charge of her case solicited information from her private doctors in Trinidad. Those men could not, or did not, provide the bureau with any information. So it is not known if she lost her toes during the Trinidad hospitalization, or why the procedure was necessary. While it is apparent the amputations happened after her military service, those severed toes are still another unexplained incident in the life of Cathay Williams.

In February 1892, the Pension Bureau rejected her claim for an invalid pension. Her lawyers were notified in April. In September, they rallied to their client's defense. While they conceded there was no proof she acquired deafness in the line of duty, they tried to follow up on the disability of the feet, and claimed she lost her toes due to "frosted feet." Frostbite would have qualified her for an invalid pension, if she was afflicted during her service. Her medical records do not document any such complaint. While it does get cold in Kansas and New Mexico, where she served, it also gets very cold in Colorado, where she later lived.

There is no indication of whether the case went any further, or if Williams' attorneys received any response from the Pension Bureau regarding their new claim. In any event, Cathay Williams did not receive a government disability pension based upon her military service.

The Pension Bureau rejected her claim on medical grounds, that no disability existed. Under the existing regulations, there were five lawful grounds for denial of an invalid pension. The first reason, desertion, is not valid. The second—that disability existed prior to enlistment—could have been cited by the bureau, based on the surgeon's statement on her discharge certificate that the feeble condition predated enlistment. The third reason—that disability was not due to service—also could have been cited by the bureau, as they could find no documentation of deafness, smallpox, and presumably, frostbite during her tenure in the army. Remember, she did not claim disability due to neuralgia or rheumatism. A fourth cause of denying a pension was that the service was not legal. The Pension Bureau could have attempted that excuse immediately, because the former soldier in question was a woman who had passed herself for a man in order to join the army. Enlistment of women in the military was illegal.

Instead, the Pension Bureau used the fifth reason—that no disability existed. This is questionable. Perhaps the Trinidad doctor's report, which basically stated she was fine, held the most weight in the case. But Cathay Williams *was* disabled. She could only walk with the permanent aid of a crutch. And, for different reasons, the army itself had deemed her disabled for service in 1868. The pension clerks offered no explanation for picking the "no disability" grounds for denial of the pension. The review personnel of the Pension Bureau rubber-stamped the decision, and did not raise any questions about the case. There was wide room for Cathay Williams' pension case to be disputed as the initial lack of effort and the delayed activism on the part of her lawyers certainly would be grounds for legal malpractice. The pension clerks had some other compelling reasons to doubt the circumstances of the case. The inadequate documentation of William Cathey's illnesses while in the army raised the question of the government's culpability. The conflicting statements of the application and supplemental affidavit for the pension raised the issue of Cathay Williams's credibility. The September 1891 medical report by the doctor in Trinidad denied any disability. The damning sentences on her discharge papers stated that the feeble condition predated enlistment.

The fact that the Pension Bureau chose the least defensible reason for denial, that Cathay Williams was not disabled, raises the question of how fairly and how thoroughly her case was treated. She was disabled. True, she was not an invalid in the strictest sense of the word, but as a laundress by occupation, she was severely impaired by not being able to walk and stand without aid.

Was racism or sexism at work during the pension application and review process? Did those elements play a crucial role in the denial of a pension for Cathay Williams? One can argue that racism and sexism were pervasive social attitudes in the 1890s, and the Pension Bureau did not operate in a social vacuum. It should be noted, however, that nowhere in her pension application file are any written statements that can be perceived, even marginally, as racist or sexist, and there are no derogatory remarks written about the applicant herself.

Surprisingly, the Pension Bureau never questioned identity, and never appeared to doubt that William Cathey of the Thirty-eighth Infantry and Cathay Williams of Trinidad, Colorado were one in the same. This is rather incredible. Granted, Cathay Williams was not the first woman to apply for a pension based upon military service. By 1891, the

Pension Bureau had dealt with more than one woman who disguised herself as a man and served her country during the Civil War. Women who applied for pensions based upon army service usually met with resistance, not just from the pension clerks, but from the army itself.

Why was Cathay Williams' service not questioned by the pension investigators? Was it because she produced the original discharge papers of William Cathey on demand? Was it because the alias was disingenuous, a simple switch of her first and last names, and therefore credible? Was it because her skill as a soldier was never tested on the battlefield? Or was it because she was black? The pension clerks might have found it less troubling to believe a black woman could pass as a man and do soldier duty, and more difficult to accept that white women did the same during the Civil War.

Maybe a small and brief notation in Cathay Williams's pension file fully sums it up. A clerk wrote in the margins that the question of identity was never raised, as the claim was rejected for medical reasons. This one sentence leaves open the probability that her service may have been questioned had there been no recourse to deny her claim on strictly medical grounds.[5]

It is unfortunate that so little is known of Cathay Williams. The information in her pension file together with the scattered references to her in military records is all that exists. The fragmentary references to her physical condition, however, provide some clues as to what may have caused her various ailments during the course of her adult life. It is entirely possible that Cathay Williams suffered from mild diabetes, the form that is non-insulin-dependent and not immediately life-threatening.

Untreated, mild diabetes increases the individual's susceptibility to viruses. Cathay Williams may have contracted smallpox. And another virus later in life may have caused her to be hard of hearing. If she easily caught whatever "bugs" were going around the camp or the fort, this would explain why the Fort Bayard surgeon labelled her of feeble habit. Untreated non-insulin-dependent diabetes can also affect the peripheral nerves, causing pain. We know that Cathay Williams suffered unexplained pain in the nerves, or neuralgia. Another symptom is loss of deep tendon reflexes and general muscle weakness and soreness. This could be what she and the Fort Cummings doctors diagnosed as rheumatism. The doctor in Trinidad would not have noticed any physical changes in her muscles or tendons if her pain was caused by diabetes. If Cathay

Williams was a diabetic, then the Fort Bayard surgeon was right—her illness did predate enlistment.

Mild diabetes, especially in younger patients, can be controlled with diet and exercise. We can assume that Cathay Williams did not know the cause of her medical problems any more than the variety of doctors who treated her. We can also assume that she did not have the proper diet for a diabetic. But it is interesting to note that she was healthiest when Company A was on the move, marching frequently to different posts between June 1867 and January 1868. She was getting daily exercise, which was good for a diabetic condition.

A major, and one of the final, complications of untreated diabetes is gangrene. Gangrene of the toes would explain the amputations. If the theory that Williams was diabetic is correct, then she did not have long to live after her toes were amputated.[6]

Nothing definite is known of Cathay Williams after the Pension Bureau rejected her claim. Where she lived, how she survived, her quality of life, and the date and place of her death are undetermined. She was born in anonymity, and so she died.

The 1900 federal census schedule for Trinidad, Colorado does not list Cathay Williams, nor cite any black woman with a similar name. From this we can deduce that she either left Trinidad sometime after 1892, or she died prior to the arrival of the census-takers. (Unfortunately, the statewide census for Colorado is not indexed.) Given her handicap, and the assumption she was in financial straits when she applied for the pension, it seems unlikely she relocated. It is more probable that she died sometime between late 1892 and 1900. This is especially likely if the diabetes theory is correct, as the amputations illustrate she was in the final stages of the disease.

All theorizing aside, the central and most significant fact of the life of Cathay Williams is that this African American woman set a precedent. She did it without fanfare, and in all probability, without intention. After all, she did not enter the army to prove a point, nor did she reveal the fact she was a woman from any social or political motivations. She probably entered the army to make a living, and when she filed for a pension she very likely was destitute.

Cathay Williams is an improbable pioneer, which makes her life even more significant. Her army service was not brilliant. It was short-lived, but then, she was mustered out of the army essentially through no fault of her own—she was unhealthy. Further, she was uneducated, possibly suffering a long-term debilitating disease, in lowly circumstance, and perhaps unintelligent. What little is known about her life suggests it was difficult. The importance of Cathay Williams does not lie just in the recognition that she is the only documented black woman who served in the Regular Army infantry during the nineteenth century. She set a precedent against the odds.

Historically, she prevailed, despite whatever illness, hardship, discrimination, and anonymity she faced during the course of her life. She carved a small, but symbolically important place in the history of American women, in the history of African Americans, and in the history of the U.S. Army.[7]

Notes

1. A search of the 1860 federal census schedule for the state of Missouri for information about Cathay Williams' origins was unsuccessful. Recently more information about Cathay Williams has been discovered; see "Cathy Williams' Story," *St. Louis Daily Times* (January 2, 1876); Frank N. Schubert, "William Cathay/Cathay Williams," *Voices of the Buffalo Soldier* (Albuquerque: University of New Mexico Press, 2003), 33–35; and Philip Thomas Tucker, *Cathy Williams: From Slave to Female Buffalo Soldier* (Mechanicsburg, Penn.: Stackpole Books, 2002).

2. John K. Mahon and Romana Danysh, *Infantry, Part I: Regular Army*, Army Lineage Series (Washington, D.C.: U.S. Army, 1972), 31; and Record Group (RG) 94, Records of the Adjutant General's Office (AGO), returns from regular army units, Thirty-eighth Infantry, 1866–69, National Archives and Records Administration (NARA).

3. Richard J. Dunglison, *A Dictionary of Medical Science* (Philadelphia: Henry C. Lea, 1874), 559.

4. Dunglison, *Dictionary of Medical Science*, 698.

5. The following sources were consulted in piecing together the life and military service of Cathay Williams: RG 15, Records of the Veterans Administration, pension application file SO 1032593, Cathay Williams, NARA; RG 94, AGO, carded medical records, Regular Army, 1821–84, six cards relating to William Cathey, NARA; RG 94, AGO, enlistment papers, U.S. Army, 1798–July 1894, papers for William Cathey, NARA; and RG 94, AGO, regular army muster rolls, Company A, Thirty-eighth Infantry, December 1866–October 1868, NARA. When no evidence existed in the records relating to a particular aspect of Cathay Williams' life, the questions put forth and possibilities offered are strictly the speculations of the author.

6. Sylvia A. Price and Lorraine M. Wilson, *Pathophysiology: Clinical Con-*

cepts of Disease Processes (New York: McGraw-Hill, 1986), 887–93. This textbook provided the clinical information about diabetes, and formed the basis of the author's theory that Cathay Williams was a non-insulin-dependent diabetic.

7. Special thanks to my former and present colleagues, Michael Knapp and Michael Musick, of the National Archives, Military Reference Branch, for their initial investigations into the existence of a black woman soldier. Special thanks also to Rebecca C. Young, B.S.N., who provided research assistance into the subject of diabetes, and to Marc Wolfe, friend and colleague, who proved a thoughtful sounding board and editor.

THOMAS R. BUECKER

One Soldier's Service

CALEB BENSON IN THE NINTH
AND TENTH CAVALRY, 1875–1908

In 1866 African Americans were allowed for the first time to serve in the regular U.S. military establishment. Six new regiments, including the Ninth and Tenth U.S. Cavalry, were organized. The new units were to be composed solely of black enlisted men, and so, in the post–Civil War years, recently freed slaves and other young blacks enlisted in the two cavalry regiments soon took on their famous nickname, the "buffalo soldiers."[1]

After being organized, both cavalry regiments were sent to western duty, as the Plains Indian wars riveted the nation's attention for the next quarter century. Although the duty was hard, many soldiers chose to make a permanent career in the army. Many began their service in southwestern deserts, and then later saw duty on the northern plains. The close of the century saw the western frontier army transformed to one of empire, with overseas duties in the Caribbean and the Philippines. In later years some soldiers returned to the plains states to homestead or to retire. One such professional soldier was Caleb Benson, who followed this full route between the Civil War and World War I.

Information on Caleb Benson's early life is sketchy. According to his obituary, he was born on June 25, 1861, but other dates in June 1860 or 1861 appear in his record.[2] His birthplace is listed as Aiken, South Carolina, on his first army enlistment application, but he recorded Jacksonville, Florida, on subsequent forms. His father's name was Jacob; his mother's name is unknown. There were also several sisters in the family.

When Benson was six years old, the family moved to Charleston, South Carolina. After both parents died, the teenaged Benson followed the example of many young men at the time and decided to enlist in the

U.S. Army. On February 2, 1875, at Columbia, South Carolina, he filled out enlistment papers before 1st Lt. William H. Beck, Tenth Cavalry.[3]

At this time twenty-one was the legal age for enlistment. In the case of minors, a parent or someone responsible filled out the "consent in case of minor" portion of the application. With both parents deceased, this part of Benson's paper was not used. When he signed up, declaring that "I am 21 years and 7 months of age, and know of no impediment to my serving honestly and faithfully as a soldier," he was actually only fourteen or fifteen years old. At the time recruit quotas had to be filled and re-cruiting officers were not overly inquisitive. Caleb signed the papers be-fore a witness with an "X," unable to write his name until years later. He enlisted for five years, the standard cavalry term throughout most of the post–Civil War years.

Enlistment records provide a description of the new recruit. He was five feet, four inches tall, of slight build, weighing about 135 pounds. He listed his previous occupation as a waiter. Caleb Benson's long career in the military had begun.[4]

Benson was assigned to the Ninth Cavalry, which was then stationed at posts in Texas. On May 6 he joined Company D, commanded by Francis S. Dodge, at Fort Clark as part of a draft of nineteen recruits.[5] The regiment received eighty-six new recruits that month. In Texas the Ninth Cavalry protected stage and mail lines from marauding Indians and helped establish law and order. Shortly after his arrival Benson got a taste of army life on the frontier. On June 8 his company went into the field on a scouting patrol, which lasted until June 26. While on scout the company covered 357 miles.[6]

During the winter of 1875–76 the Ninth Cavalry was ordered to the District of New Mexico. On February 26, 1876, the men of Company D left Fort Clark en route to Santa Fe. They arrived on April 30 and were immediately assigned to Fort Union, arriving at that post May 5.[7] In July Benson's company was sent north into Colorado; however, Caleb was at that time held in confinement and remained behind. He remained at Fort Union on detached duty for a year while Company D was in Col-orado and later at Fort Wallace, Kansas. In July he rejoined his company, which was detached to Ojo Caliente, scouting and guarding the Apache reservation there.[8]

In March 1878 Benson's company was ordered back to Colorado, scouting through the Rio La Plata region. In September they escorted the boundary survey between Colorado and Utah. Company D then spent the winter of 1878–79 building quarters at the new post of Fort Lewis at Pagosa Springs.[9]

Restlessness among western Utes caused Company D to be sent into the Middle Park area of Colorado to prevent "any possible collision between the Indians and settlers in that region."[10] Company D spent the summer and late fall of 1879 on field service there. In early October Private Benson was involved in one of the major battles of the West.

During the preceding months the Utes had grown increasingly angry over agent Nathan C. Meeker's attempts to force their instant acculturation. Soon it was reported that the Utes were unsettled and were starting forest fires in central Colorado. In September Meeker, fearing for the lives of agency employees, called for military protection. Troops under Maj. Thomas Thornburgh were dispatched from Fort Fred Steele, Wyoming Territory, and headed south to the White River Agency. The call for soldiers infuriated the Utes, and on September 29 Thornburgh's column of 175 soldiers was attacked at Milk Creek, fifteen miles north of the agency. Major Thornburgh was shot and instantly killed, and the supply wagons were quickly corralled. The command was surrounded and suffered heavy casualties. However, during the night couriers slipped away for help.[11]

On October 1 the couriers reached Captain Dodge's company. Dodge issued 250 rounds of ammunition and three days rations to his thirty-five men and made a forced march on Milk Creek. About 4:30 A.M. on October 2, Company D reached the besieged command, where their "arrival caused great rejoicing by the entrenched men and the newcomers were greeted with glad hand."[12] Almost immediately all of Company D's horses were shot by the Utes. Most of Thornburgh's animals met the same fate.

The combined force then settled in to defend itself. Finally, on October 5, a larger relief force under the command of Col. Wesley Merritt arrived, drove off the Utes, and ended the Milk Creek siege. Recalling the fight years later, Benson related a somewhat bizarre (possibly apocryphal) observation on the relationship between the black cavalrymen and the Plains Indians:

> While we were engaged during August and September of 1879 in the White River campaign (*sic*), two white men lost their lives in going down to the river for water to make coffee, something that the colored cooks had done without loss of life.

When the first white man left with his kettle, a soldier in our colored regiment said to him, "Before you go down there, you'd better black your hands and face,"

Scoffing at the idea, the white man left. But he did not return. Another white cook also went down to the river, and he didn't come back either.

People may think it isn't true, but the Indians never shot a colored man unless it was necessary. They always wanted to win the friendship of the Negro race, and obtain their aid in campaigns against the white man.[13]

The Milk Creek fight was costly. Major Thornburgh, nine enlisted men, and three civilian employees died, and three officers, forty enlisted men, and two teamsters were wounded. However, after Milk Creek the problems with the Utes were eventually solved through negotiations, although for several years a large number of troops were massed near the reservation.[14]

With the loss of its horses, Company D left for Rawlins, Wyoming Territory. There it boarded a train and returned to Fort Union by rail on October 23. Remounted, Benson's company spent the rest of the year scouting in the vicinity of Fort Bayard. On January 11, 1880, Benson was sent with his company on a scout. In February his five-year enlistment ended, but he was held in service, being away from any post. On March 23 he was discharged at Fort Stanton for "expiration of enlistment," seven weeks after the actual date for his discharge.[15]

After five years as a civilian during which he may have worked as a cook or baker, Benson rejoined the army. In the spring of 1885 the Tenth Cavalry was transferred to Arizona to prepare for campaigns against Geronimo and other Chiricahuas. Black troops guarded reservations and strategic points along the Mexican border, in what the soldiers called the "water hole campaign."[16] Regimental headquarters for the Tenth Cavalry was at Whipple Barracks, near Prescott, Arizona Territory, where Benson reenlisted. On June 9, 1885, he was enlisted in the Tenth Cavalry by 1st Lt. S. L. Woodward.[17] He also received an examination by an army surgeon (not the case during his 1875 enlistment), who found him "free from all bodily defects and mental infirmities."[18] On this enlistment record he stated he was twenty-four years old, far beyond the legal minimum and closer to the truth.

Benson was assigned to Troop B as a company baker.[19] His troop, under command of Capt. Robert Smither, was also stationed at Whipple Barracks.[20] On October 20 Benson received a marksman's certificate; although his scores were low, they allowed qualification. His skills with the carbine led him to be described as a "very poor shot" in a period of growing interest in marksmanship in the army.[21]

While at Whipple Barracks, his troop performed the usual garrison duties and also went out to repair government telegraph lines. In May Troop B transferred to The Post of San Carlos[22] where the men performed field and escort duty. In June details from Troop B rode 1,290 miles in pursuit of raiding Apaches. The black troops spent long weeks in the field. In November 1886 regimental returns reported, "The troops of different detachments [Troop B] marched during the month 2,490 miles." The regimental history later noted, "For most of the troops there was little glory in this campaign. Theirs was the harder duty, to prevent outbreak, rather than chase the renegades back onto their reservations. Theirs was the dismal duty to guard mountain passes, water holes and trails that did not lead to glorious fighting."[23] In December Troop B, with two other Tenth Cavalry troops, was assigned to Fort Thomas, Arizona Territory.[24]

At Fort Thomas, just before Christmas 1886, Caleb had an unfortunate accident. He was assigned to help dig a well as part of a guard fatigue duty. While he was digging, the walls caved in on him. His fellow workers quickly pulled him out of the hole and took him to the post hospital, where it was found he had a double hernia. Shortly afterward he was ordered with his troop for a long pursuit of Apache raiders. Four months later the troop camped at Fort Apache[25] where Benson checked into the post hospital. Because of his injury and the long period on horseback, he was compelled to wear a truss for the rest of his military career.[26]

From 1887 to 1890 Benson's troop shuttled between San Carlos, Fort Thomas, and Fort Apache. While at Fort Apache, he reenlisted in the Tenth Cavalry in June 1890. On this and later enlistments, his physical disability (hernia) was waived by inspecting surgeons and his troop commander. One troop commander later stated "not-withstanding this disability he continued to perform the duties of an able bodied soldier."[27] On this, his third army enlistment, he was transferred to Troop K, where he remained for the remainder of his time in the service.

In 1891 Col. J. K. Mizner requested that his Tenth Cavalry regiment be transferred out of the Southwest to new stations. He preferred to go north, as far as Kansas.[28] The War Department sent the Tenth north, but much further than Kansas, to the Department of Dakota. The Tenth found itself garrisoning frigid Forts Custer and Assinniboine in Montana, and Fort Buford[29] in western North Dakota.

Troop K arrived in Montana by rail in early May and marched thirty miles through a late spring blizzard to its new station at Fort Custer.[30] Along with regimental headquarters and Troops A, B, E, F, and G, Troop K helped form Custer's regular garrison. Life in Montana was a great relaxation for the Tenth Cavalry after hard and hot duty in the Southwest. Private Benson spent most of the summer of 1892 on detached service as a cook at the post's sawmill camp. While at Fort Custer the soldiers trained, made practice marches, and performed regular garrison duties, punctuated by several civil disorders.

On April 25, 1894, Troops B, E, G, and K hurriedly left Fort Custer on a thirty-five-mile march to Custer Station on the Northern Pacific Railroad. Arriving at 2:00 A.M. the next morning, the squadron captured a contingent of Coxey's Army, a haphazard organization of labor protesters. A number of Montana Coxeyites had commandeered a Northern Pacific train at Butte City to take them to join other protesters at Washington, D.C. After the train was captured, the highjackers were jailed, and the troops returned to post.[31]

On July 7 Troop K left its post to guard railroad property from Pullman strikers at Billings, arriving the next day. Other troops of the regiment were assigned to critical railroad points in Montana. By the end of August the strike had cooled, and Troop K returned to Fort Custer on July 29.[32]

In June 1895 Benson took a brief furlough, evidently making a trip to Fort Buford. At Buford he signed up for his fourth army enlistment, his third in the Tenth Cavalry. The 1880s were marked by the removal of hundreds of roaming Cree Indians, who had come into Montana from Canada. Their presence generated fears among the Montanans, who called on the military to remove them. In 1896 a detachment from Troop K escorted a number of Crees from Billings to the Canadian border. For several years periodic "roundups" of Crees were part of the service of the army in Montana.[33]

In April 1897 the last major Cheyenne-white confrontation occurred when a Northern Cheyenne named Whirlwind killed a sheepherder near the Tongue River Reservation. Three troops, including K, were sent to the reservation to arrest Whirlwind. Through the diplomacy of Agent George Stouch, the arrest was made and the troops returned to their stations.[34]

Fort Custer was abandoned as a military post in November of 1897. Troop K moved overland to Billings and then northwest to Fort Assinniboine, near Havre.[35] By January 1898 the regiment was united there.

In 1898 war with Spain changed things for the frontier army. The increasing threat of hostilities led the secretary of war to order the concentration of troops for an invasion of Cuba. On April 15 six cavalry regiments, including the Tenth, and most of the army's field artillery were massed at Chickamauga Park in northern Georgia. This site, established during the Cleveland administration as a maneuvering ground for regular army and National Guard units, became the preferred location for the concentration of regular army forces. Coinciding with the arrival of the regulars, volunteer regiments also gathered there.[36]

On April 29 Brig. Gen. William Shafter was ordered to move the force to Tampa, Florida, in preparation for the invasion of Cuba. Between May 9 and 14, all regular army units at Chickamauga Park left for Tampa. Because of severe overcrowding there, several regiments, including the Tenth Cavalry, were sent to Lakeland to the east, where the regiment readied for combat, drilling in the early morning or after sunset because of the intense heat. Two squadrons of the Tenth Cavalry became part of the Fifth Corps for the first invasion wave. Benson's squadron was attached to the Fourth Corps and was to remain in Lakeland, part of the second wave, which was never needed. While at Lakeland, Benson enlisted for the fifth time (on June 23). By this time army enlistments had been shortened from five years to three.

By late summer the short-lived war with Spain was over. Because the invasion was unwisely made in the summer, most of the troops sent to Cuba fell dangerously ill with fever and malaria. The army decided to move the stricken soldiers back to the United States and quickly built a convalescent camp at Montauk Point on the western tip of Long Island. In August the squadron at Lakeland brought the horses and baggage of the regiment to rejoin their returning comrades. With thousands of men being shipped to Montauk, reunited units were sent as rapidly as possible to other stations. In the fall of 1898 the Tenth Cavalry went to Huntsville, Alabama, to a large camp established for Spanish War mobilization.

During this service in the south, the Tenth Cavalry witnessed a change of white racial attitudes. As the regiment headed south before the war, one veteran recalled, "We received great ovations all along the line. Thousands of people were thronged at the places we would stop and we were treated royally."[37] While traveling from Montauk to Huntsville, the regiment even paraded in Washington before President McKinley. While in Huntsville two cavalrymen were killed by a black civilian, motivated by the rumor of a reward for every dead black soldier.[38] In January 1899 the regiment was moved to posts in Texas, with Troop K assigned to Fort Brown.[39] On the way to Texas the troop train was fired on while it passed through Mississippi.[40]

The stay of Troop K at Fort Brown was relatively short, as American forces were ordered back to Cuba to help keep order. In May the regiment sailed for Cuba to replace a volunteer regiment. The troopers considered occupation duty as the best service they had ever experienced. Troops were stationed throughout the interior of Cuba, where the soldiers occasionally pursued guerrillas and bandits. Under the governorship of Gen. Leonard Wood authority was established and eventually the regiment was consolidated at two points, Manzanillo and Holguin.[41] While Troop K was stationed at the latter place, Private Benson reenlisted for his sixth term on June 23, 1901.

In May 1902 the American forces withdrew, leaving the new Cuban government in control. The Tenth Cavalry was assigned to posts in Wyoming and Nebraska. The troops at Holguin left on May 4. Benson's troop was sent to Fort Robinson in the northwestern corner of Nebraska. On May 16, 1902, the regimental headquarters, band, and the First and Third Squadrons arrived at Robinson, much to the joy of the merchants of nearby Crawford, who always appreciated large garrisons at the post. Originally established in 1874, Fort Robinson was already one of the older western posts still utilized as troop stations.

At Fort Robinson the officers and enlisted men were housed in adobe quarters, much the same as those in the Southwest. Garrison duties, training, and practice marches occupied most of the soldiers' time. Early in the twentieth century the army made several major changes in the soldiers' uniforms and equipment. They traded their old blue uniforms for more functional khaki, and got new and more stylish dress uniforms as well. Other changes came in armament with the adoption of the 1903 Springfield rifle and the organization of machine gun platoons with every cavalry regiment.[42]

During this period there was little field service except in 1906, when part of the regiment was sent after some Utes, who had left their reservation in Utah and were heading toward South Dakota.[43] With little field duty, the black cavalrymen were able to take up athletics for the first time. Troop K won regimental championships in football and baseball. In target practice Troop K stood third for all company organizations and first in the cavalry branch.[44] Benson's aim evidently improved as he qualified for the sharp shooter's badge about this time.

By 1903 Caleb Benson had over twenty years of service in the U.S. Army. He could qualify for a pension with one more regular enlistment, because his time overseas in Cuba counted double toward retirement. However, his military career was nearly cut short while he was at Fort Robinson.

In August 1903 a detachment went to the wood reserve five miles west of the post to cut lumber. Benson was sent along as cook. While he bent over his field stove, the wind suddenly came up, causing the fire to flare, blowing ashes and flames into his face. Benson was rushed to the post hospital for treatment and it was discovered that he lost most of his eyesight. He also suffered a head injury from a fall at the time of the accident, which later caused memory loss. Although hampered by injuries, Caleb continued his service.[45]

In June 1904 he had reached another discharge date. Not ready to leave the army, he applied for reenlistment, but his application was refused by the post surgeon on account of disabilities received in the line of duty. The surgeon reasoned that besides suffering from the hernia, Benson had been thoroughly disabled by the recent stove injuries. Reenlistment was denied and Private Benson was out of the army.

Benson remained around Fort Robinson, a common practice whereby older, discharged soldiers were often supported by comrades. He also worked for an officer, assisting in the kitchen to earn his board. In 1904 he applied for a government pension since he was "unable to earn a living and depend largely on the good will of my former troop for support."[46] In order to receive the pension, Benson completed affidavits about his recent injuries and those incurred at Fort Thomas in 1886. Fellow soldiers and officers who knew that the accidents were caused in the line of duty sent similar statements. In a letter to the commissioner of pensions, Benson wrote, "After having put in the best years of my life (27) . . . I therefore beg of you to hasten assistance which of right I should have from my government."[47]

As an alternative to receiving a disability pension, Benson wanted to be allowed to reenlist in order to finish thirty years of service. Several officers of the Tenth Cavalry, besides the captain of his former troop, expressed their consent to having him enlist in their units. If not allowed to reenlist, he well deserved a pension they felt, "on account of his long, faithful and valuable service as a soldier."[48] Maj. Robert D. Read,[49] who had been Benson's captain when he was in Troop B, urged that he be permitted to reenlist to complete his thirty years and receive full retirement pay. Evidently the arguments of Benson and his former officers paid off—and it is possible his damaged eyesight improved because on January 29, 1907, he reenlisted in his old troop.

Back in the army Private Benson prepared again for overseas service. On March 1, 1907, headquarters, band, and troops A, C, D, K, and L boarded twelve passenger coaches and left Fort Robinson for San Francisco. There they boarded the transport *Thomas,* bound for the Philippine Islands. Although the war in the Philippines officially ended in 1902, the American military presence continued for many years, as army units rotated between the Philippines and the United States. The Tenth reached Manila on April 2, and Benson's Troop K with the Second Squadron took up station at Fort McKinley.

By the summer of 1908 Benson had served six regular enlistments totaling twenty-four years. With overseas duty figuring double for retirement,[50] Benson neared the thirty-year mark. At summer's end, Benson was ordered to The Presidio of San Francisco.[51] Just before his retirement, Benson was promoted to first sergeant, though all through his military career his rank had been private. (On one occasion he was rated as a trumpeter.) The higher rank gave him more retirement pay and honored his long service in the army. While he was at The Presidio, the War Department issued Special Order Number 215 on September 15, 1908, placing 1st Sgt. Caleb Benson on the retired list created by act of Congress on March 2, 1907. After thirty years of service in the Southwest, northern plains, and overseas duty in Cuba and the Philippines, Caleb Benson returned to civilian life.[52]

According to his retirement orders, "He will repair to his home." Benson decided to return to Crawford. The Quartermaster Department furnished him first class limited rail transportation to Crawford, and $4.50 for subsistence for three days of travel. On September 30 he left San Francisco for Nebraska.[53]

On March 26, 1909, Benson married Miss Percilla Smith of Crawford. Percilla was a native of Virginia and a graduate of the Hampton Institute, who had moved to Crawford from Philadelphia. At the time of the marriage she was thirty-four years old and he was forty-eight.[54] Shortly after their marriage, the Bensons filed a homestead claim about one and one-half miles northwest of Glen, just up the White River from Fort Robinson.

After living on the homestead for four years Caleb and Percilla moved to Fort Robinson. There they were both employed in the household of Capt. Henry Whitehead, Twelfth Cavalry, for several years. Whitehead had been a young lieutenant in the Tenth Cavalry in the old Montana days. Just after World War I the Bensons again worked on the post, this time for Lt. Col. Edward Calvert. In 1923 they accompanied the Calverts to Wisconsin, working for them there for a short period. About 1925 the Bensons moved to New York City, where they resided in Harlem on West 137th Street. The reason for the move is unknown. While in New York the Bensons accepted custody of a young boy, Jimmie Amos, as a foster son. Although they had no children, Caleb and Percilla gave him permission to assume their last name, and he became "Jimmie Benson."[55] During his years in New York, Caleb joined several veterans' groups, including the United Indian War Veterans, United Spanish War Veterans, and Veterans of Two or More Wars.

The Bensons moved back to Crawford in July 1934. They still owned the property near Glen. Jimmie Benson followed them to Crawford during World War II.[56]

In the summer of 1934 two stone pyramids were erected at Fort Robinson. One was in honor of the post's namesake, Lt. Levi Robinson, and its twin honored Crazy Horse, who was killed there in September 1877. Maj. Edwin N. Hardy, the post commander, planned an elaborate ceremony on September 5. A number of special guests were invited to sit on the speaker's stand, which was the back porch of the headquarters building. Several retired soldiers in the Crawford community, including Sergeant Benson, were invited to participate. Along with Sgt. W. C. Beckett, Tenth Cavalry, Benson sat beside descendants of Sioux leaders, Maj. Gen. C. H. Bash, the quartermaster general, and other luminaries such as Capt. James A. Cook and the Reverend George A. Beecher.[57] The ceremony was a poignant moment, as Fort Robinson's past and present were briefly drawn together.

On November 19, 1937, after a brief illness, Caleb Benson died of coronary thrombosis. He was seventy-six years old. His funeral was held the following Monday in the old African Methodist-Episcopal Church of Crawford with the Reverend Myers of the Nazarene Church conducting the service. He was survived by his wife, one sister, "and a host of friends." He was given a military burial at the Fort Robinson Cemetery. A squad from the American Legion post of Crawford fired the salute.[58]

In January 1938 Percilla applied for a widow's pension. At the time Caleb died, his government pension was $94.50 per month. Mrs. Benson moved to Virginia to be near her sister, and later both returned to Crawford, where they lived for many years. She died at the Grand Island veterans' hospital on August 25, 1966, and was buried with Caleb in Fort McPherson National Cemetery.[59]

Notes

1. The best single source on the organization and early history of the Ninth and Tenth Regiments remains William H. Leckie, *The Buffalo Soldiers: A Narrative of the Negro Cavalry in the West* (Norman: University of Oklahoma Press, 1967).

2. For example, the date June 24, 1860, appears on Benson's headstone at Fort McPherson National Cemetery.

3. William H. Beck served during the Civil War and was appointed second lieutenant, Tenth Cavalry, in 1867. He remained with the regiment until 1899 when he became the colonel of the Forty-ninth U.S. Volunteer Infantry. Francis B. Heitman, *Historical Register and Dictionary of the United States Army* (Washington, D.C.: Government Printing Office, 1903), 204.

4. Information on Benson's enlistment is from his enlistment records, National Archives & Records Administration (hereafter NARA). Copies on file at the Fort Robinson Museum (hereafter FRM).

5. Francis S. Dodge served as an officer with a black volunteer cavalry regiment in the Civil War. He was appointed first lieutenant, Ninth Cavalry, in 1866. He was appointed paymaster in January 1880. Heitman, *Historical Register*, 376. Fort Clark, in south central Texas, was an important link in the border defenses against hostile bands crossing from Mexico. It was not abandoned until 1946. Robert W. Frazer, *Forts of the West* (Norman: University of Oklahoma Press, 1980), 146.

6. Unless otherwise noted, all information on Ninth and Tenth Cavalry troop movements is from "Returns from Regular Army Cavalry Regiments, 1833–1916," Microfilm Publications No. 744, NARA.

7. Fort Union was established in 1857 for the protection of the Santa Fe Trail. It also served as an important supply center for posts in the region. Abandoned in 1891, it is now a national monument. Frazer, *Forts of the West*, 105–6.

8. The Post at Ojo Caliente was established near the agency for the Warm Springs Apaches in 1874. Troops were stationed there from the late 1870s to 1882. Ibid., 101.

126   THOMAS R. BUECKER

9. Fort Lewis was established to guard the Ute Reservation. In 1880 it was moved to a new site twelve miles west of Durango, Colorado. Ibid., 38.

10. John M. Carroll, ed., *The Black Military Experience in the American West* (New York: Liveright Publishing, 1971), 240.

11. Philip Sheridan, *Records of Engagements with Hostile Indians in the Military Division of the Missouri* (Washington, D.C.: Government Printing Office, 1882; Old Army Press Facsimile Edition, 1969), 88–91.

12. Carroll, *Black Military Experience*, 241.

13. *Northwest Nebraska News* (Crawford), August 9, 1934.

14. Robert M. Utley, *Frontier Regulars: The United States Army and the Indians, 1866–1890* (New York: Macmillan Publishing, 1973), 338–40.

15. Fort Stanton was established to control the Mescalero Apaches and served as an important base of operations in southwestern New Mexico. Frazer, *Forts of the West*, 103.

16. Carroll, *Black Military Experience*, 179.

17. Samuel L. Woodward served as an officer in the Civil War. He was appointed second lieutenant in the Tenth Cavalry in 1867 and served as regimental adjutant from 1867 to 1876 and 1883 to 1887. He was promoted to major, First Cavalry, in 1900. Heitman, *Historical Register*, 1059.

18. Benson enlistment papers, on file at FRM.

19. In 1883 the designation "Company" was officially changed to "Troop." In 1889 "Battalion" was changed to "Squadron."

20. Robert G. Smither served as an officer in the Civil War and was appointed first lieutenant in the Tenth Cavalry in 1867. He was promoted to captain in 1881 and retired in 1888. Heitman, *Historical Register*, 905. Whipple Barracks was located immediately north of Prescott to protect miners in the region in 1863. It was garrisoned until 1922 when it became a veterans' hospital. Frazer, *Forts of the West*, 14–15.

21. Comment written on Benson's 1890 discharge certificate, Caleb Benson Collection, Nebraska State Historical Society (hereafter NSHS). For more on army marksmanship, see Douglas C. McChristian, *An Army of Marksmen* (Fort Collins: Old Army Press, 1981).

22. The Post of San Carlos was established in 1882 for control of the Indians at the San Carlos Reservation. It was abandoned in 1894. Francis Prucha, *Guide to the Military Posts of the United States* (Madison: State Historical Society of Wisconsin, 1964), 105.

23. Edward L. N. Glass, *The History of the Tenth Cavalry, 1866–1921* (Fort Collins: Old Army Press, 1972), 26.

24. Fort Thomas was established in 1876 in connection with the removal of the Chiricahua Apaches to the San Carlos Reservation. Frazer, *Forts of the West*, 12.

25. Fort Apache was established as Camp Apache to control the Coyotero Apaches. It was designated as a fort in 1879 and abandoned as a military post in 1924. Frazer, *Forts of the West*, 3.

26. Details of the accident are from an affidavit filed by Benson on January

14, 1905, found in his pension file. Copies of this file were provided by the Department of Veterans Affairs and are on file at FRM.

27. Endorsement of Major Read on letter of February 18, 1905, from the Bureau of Pensions. Benson pension file, FRM.

28. Glass, *History of the Tenth Cavalry*, 28. John K. Mizner commanded the Tenth Cavalry from 1890 to 1897. Heitman, *Historical Register*, 718.

29. Fort Buford was established in 1866 just below the confluence of the Yellowstone and Missouri rivers for protection along the river. It was abandoned in 1895. Frazer, *Forts of the West*, 110–11.

30. Fort Custer was established in 1877 at the confluence of the Big Horn and the Little Big Horn rivers to control the Sioux and other Indians in the area. Frazer, *Forts of the West*, 79.

31. For more on Coxeyite activities, see Thomas A. Clinch, "Coxey's Army in Montana," *Montana* 15 (Autumn 1965): 2–11.

32. For more on the Pullman Strike, see W. Thomas White, "Boycott: The Pullman Strike in Montana," *Montana* 29 (October 1979): 2–13.

33. For more on the Cree removals, see Nicholas P. Hardeman, "Brick Stronghold of the Border: Fort Assinniboine 1879–1911," *Montana* 29 (April 1979): 54–67.

34. Lonnie E. Underhill and Daniel F. Littlefield, "Cheyenne 'Outbreak' of 1897," *Montana* 24 (Autumn 1974): 3041.

35. Fort Assinniboine was established in 1879 to prevent the return of Sitting Bull and his warriors from Canada and to control the Blackfeet in the region. It was abandoned in 1911. Frazer, *Forts of the West*, 79.

36. All information contained herein on the mobilization for the Spanish-American War is from Graham A. Cosmas, *An Army for Empire* (Columbia: University of Missouri Press, 1971).

37. Carroll, *Black Military Experience*, 344.

38. Marvin E. Fletcher, *The Black Soldier and Officer in the United States Army, 1891–1917* (Columbia: University of Missouri Press, 1974), 11.

39. Fort Brown was originally established in 1846, just prior to the Mexican War. Occupied by the Confederates in the Civil War, it was finally abandoned as a military post in 1944. Frazer, *Forts of the West*, 144–45.

40. Fletcher, *The Black Soldier*, 113.

41. Glass, *History of the Tenth Cavalry*, 39.

42. For more on the service of the Tenth Cavalry at Fort Robinson, see Thomas R. Buecker, "The Tenth Cavalry at Fort Robinson," *Military Images* 7 (May–June 1991): 6–10. A more detailed discussion is in Frank N. Schubert, *Buffalo Soldiers, Braves, and the Brass: The Story of Fort Robinson* (Columbia, Md.: White Mane Publishing, 1993).

43. For more on the "Ute Uprising," see David Laudenschlager, "The Utes in South Dakota, 1906–1908," *South Dakota History* 9 (Summer 1979): 233–47.

44. Glass, *History of the Tenth Cavalry*, 43–45.

45. Affidavits of Caleb Benson dated January 14, 1905, and George W. Gaines dated August 25, 1905. Benson pension file, FRM.

46. Letter, Caleb Benson to commissioner of pensions dated August 22, 1905, Benson pension file, FRM.

47. Ibid.

48. Read endorsement on letter from Bureau of Pensions dated February 18, 1905. Benson pension file, FRM.

49. Robert D. Read graduated from West Point in 1877 and was assigned to the Tenth Cavalry. He became captain in 1893 and major in the Tenth in 1903. Heitman, *Historical Register*, 819.

50. Read endorsement, February 18, 1905. Benson pension file, FRM.

51. The Presidio of San Francisco was originally established by the Spanish in 1776. It was occupied by the Americans in 1847. An important West Coast installation, it is presently slated for abandonment. Frazer, *Forts of the West*, 30–31.

52. An original copy of Special Order 215 is found with the Caleb Benson Collection, NSHS.

53. Copy of transportation order, Caleb Benson Collection, NSHS.

54. Information from copy of marriage certificate in Benson pension file, FRM; *Northwest Nebraska News* (Crawford), August 9, 1934.

55. Personal interview with Rebecca Benson, Crawford, July 28, 1992.

56. Jimmie Benson worked as a plumber at Fort Robinson during the war, after which he operated a plumbing business in Crawford until he retired. In June 1945 he married Rebecca Pierce of Tampa, Florida. In 1988 Jimmie Benson died and in the fall of 1992 Rebecca moved back to Florida.

57. "Souvenir Program–Dedication of Twin Monuments in Honor of Lt. Levi H. Robinson and Crazy Horse," copy on file at FRM.

58. *Crawford Tribune*, November 26, 1937.

59. In the summer of 1947 the Fort Robinson cemetery was moved to Fort McPherson National Cemetery. The Bensons are interred in grave F253. Caleb's headstone is a Spanish American War veteran's marker. Percilla's name and dates of birth and death are carved on the back.

BRUCE J. DINGES

The Court-Martial of
Lt. Henry O. Flipper

AN EXAMPLE OF BLACK-WHITE
RELATIONSHIPS IN THE ARMY, 1881

An aura of anxiety tinged with curiosity and prejudice gripped the tiny West Texas courtroom as a decision neared in one of the strangest trials in American military history. Throughout four exhausting weeks of examination and cross-examination, the accused officer maintained a remarkably "independent and indifferent air" betraying neither anger, fear, nor uncertainty. Now, at the conclusion of the twenty-ninth day of testimony, the young lieutenant rose slowly from his seat and walked with calm deliberation from the room. He awaited a verdict that might signal the end of a once promising military career.

Anyone who witnessed the scene must have been impressed by the blue-clad figure that emerged from the makeshift courtroom at Fort Davis, Texas, that seventh day of December 1881. At a height of nearly six feet two inches and weighing over 190 pounds, the twenty-five-year-old cavalry officer appeared, with but a single all-important exception, the epitome of the *beau sabreur* (handsome swordsman). And that solitary deviation from the romantic ideal of the gallant warrior transformed an almost unnoticed incident in the tedious annals of military justice into a momentary cause celebre and an event of enduring social and historical significance.

As the first black graduate of the U.S. Military Academy and the only officer of his race in the U.S. Army, Henry Ossian Flipper fully realized that his entire career had been a curious form of trial. From the moment in May of 1873 when he stepped from the cabin of his ex-slave parents in Thomasville, Georgia, his life embodied a bitter anomaly. As an object of curiosity, young Flipper found himself suddenly poised uncomfortably in the penetrating spotlight of national attention. The northern press delighted in lauding him as an example to be emulated by others of his race, while racist editors of his native South adopted him as a convenient butt for scorn and ridicule. But despite the often hostile interest focused upon his every action and complete social ostracism meted out by his caste-conscious class mates, Henry O. Flipper surmounted the barriers of prejudice and loneliness to graduate, fiftieth in a class of seventy-six, on June 15, 1877. A month later he accepted a commission as a second lieutenant assigned to Company A of the U.S. Tenth Cavalry.

Arriving in Houston, Texas, to join his regiment en route to Fort Sill, Oklahoma, Lieutenant Flipper discovered that the success of his struggle at West Point carried no assurance of acceptance in a white man's world. While curious Texans generally displayed proper and formal courtesy, the inexperienced lieutenant found the doors of white homes rigidly barred, presumably ensuring the sanctity of southern womanhood. Armed, however, with a firm conviction that "uprightness and intelligence" must eventually expose the absurdity of racial prejudice, Flipper departed for the Indian Territory determined to win the confidence of the officers and men of his regiment.

Such a task proved exceedingly difficult; but by the spring of 1880, when Company A entered Fort Davis, Texas, Lieutenant Flipper had demonstrated an unusual degree of military ability and earned the respect of both his superiors and the enlisted men of his troop. His performance in the Victorio War drew the praise of Col. Benjamin H. Grierson, Tenth Cavalry, and of his company commander, Capt. Nicholas Nolan. For services in the field, the black lieutenant assumed the duties of acting assistant quartermaster, post quartermaster, and acting commissary of subsistence. A bright and fruitful military career seemed assured.

Any illusions that Flipper entertained of an idyllic future in the army rapidly vanished. Clouds appeared on the horizon almost immediately upon his return from the field. (Trouble arose from his close friendship with Miss Mollie Dwyer, the young sister of Captain Nolan's bride, whom he first knew at Fort Sill and continued to ride with at Fort Davis.) Bitter resentment first emanated from Lt. Charles Nordstrom, whom Flipper described as an uneducated brute. Soon the black officer noted a marked coolness among others at the post and began to regard his fellow officers, with few exceptions, as little more than "hyenas." This unenviable situation further deteriorated in March 1881 when Col. William R.

Shafter relieved Maj. N. B. McLaughlin as post commander. Accompanying him as adjutant was 1st Lt. Louis Wilhelmi.

A distinguished veteran of the Civil War, "Pecos Bill" Shafter readily accepted postwar command of black troops on the remote and barren Texas frontier. Despite a character described as "coarse, profane [and] afflicted with a barely concealed racism," Shafter proved himself an effective leader of black soldiers, while also gaining a reputation for impulsiveness and harassment of any subordinate unfortunate enough to fall into disfavor. The colonel's controversial behavior and unorthodox disciplinary procedures ultimately tarnished his military reputation among his peers during the Spanish-American War.

Lieutenant Wilhelmi, a Prussian appointed to West Point in 1872, first met Henry Flipper at the academy. His scholastic career proved a failure, and ill health forced his resignation in December 1873. After a brief career as an insurance adjuster in Philadelphia, he secured a commission in the regular army in October 1875.

With the arrival of Shafter and Wilhelmi, the stage was set for what was to become the final act in the military career of Henry O. Flipper. Colonel Shafter immediately removed his black subordinate from duty as acting assistant quartermaster and ordered the transfer of commissary funds from the quartermaster's safe to Flipper's quarters. He also informed the young officer that he would be relieved as acting commissary of subsistence as soon as a replacement could be found. This action, Flipper later maintained signaled the beginning of a systematic campaign of persecution.

Unfortunately, no concrete evidence exists substantiating or disproving the black officer's conviction that Shafter, Wilhelmi, and Nordstrom conspired to destroy his military career. But as events during the summer of 1881 unfolded disconcerting questions arose concerning Shafter's concept of command responsibility and the motives underlying the actions of Lieutenant Wilhelmi—a man apparently adept at exploiting his colonel's weaknesses.

Despite Shafter's intention to relieve Lieutenant Flipper of his duties as acting commissary, five months passed until circumstances compelled the colonel to act. During this period, the lieutenant continued to perform the duties of his post. In response to Shafter's orders, he removed the commissary funds from the quartermaster's safe and placed them in his private quarters. The post commander also suggested, Flipper later maintained, that funds be deposited in the San Antonio National Bank, where the commissary officer could draw against them when necessary. Since the lieutenant anticipated relinquishing his post at any moment, he ignored Shafter's advice. But it was not forgotten.

Financial complexities increased on May 2, when Maj. M. P. Small, chief commissary of subsistence for the Department of Texas, notified all acting commissaries of his absence from headquarters for the remainder of the month and ordered the cessation of cash transmittals until June. Apparently interpreting this directive as applying to everything pertaining to commissary funds, Lieutenant Flipper also stopped forwarding weekly statements, pending further orders from the chief commissary. But, since Major Small remained absent from the early part of May to the last of June and again from July 4 to July 24, Lieutenant Flipper received no further communication from department headquarters until the arrival of a telegram in August requesting the transfer of all funds for the past fiscal year. Small, also noting that no weekly statements for the present fiscal year had as yet been received from Fort Davis, ordered the prompt transmission of receipts in the future.

By this time Flipper realized that something was strangely amiss, for on July 8, Colonel Shafter had ordered him to transfer all commissary funds in his possession to Major Small as soon as possible. In preparing for an inspection of his returns, Flipper apparently discovered a deficiency of $1,440.43. Although puzzled, he experienced no undue alarm as he expected he could easily submit a check for the amount of the deficit and then deposit personal funds in the San Antonio bank to cover it.

Unexpected complications soon developed. Unable to raise the required cash in the time allotted, the black officer procrastinated, hoping Homer Lee & Co., publishers of an autobiography he had written while stationed at Fort Sill, would forward royalties due him. Thus, aware that Major Small would not reach San Antonio until the end of July, Lieutenant Flipper relied upon Colonel Shafter to cast no more than a cursory glance at the invoices submitted for his signature and made entries in the weekly accounts reporting the funds "in transit." He was confident that the deficit could be covered within a matter of days.

Apparently this stratagem succeeded, and Shafter remained ignorant of his subordinate's difficulty until August 10, when Major Small informed him that no funds had arrived in San Antonio. Although the thought of deliberate misappropriation allegedly never occurred to him, the colonel reacted immediately. Recalling a glimpse of saddlebags attached to the lieutenant's horse and fearing his escape to Mexico, Shafter dispatched Lieutenant Wilhelmi with orders to return Flipper to the post.

When the young black officer reached Shafter's office, he maintained that the commissary funds were mailed on July 9. If they had not been received he could offer no explanation other than that they must have been lost in transit. Unsatisfied, the colonel ordered the lieutenant to turn over the funds in his possession to Lt. F. H. Edmunds, who was to assume the duties of acting commissary of subsistence.

An investigation followed. On the morning of August 13 Colonel Shafter notified Lieutenant Flipper that his quarters would be searched; he would, in effect, be assumed guilty of misappropriation and treated "just as though I knew you had stolen those checks." The lieutenant, presumably confident that all the money entrusted to him, with the exception of the amount covered by the $1,440.43 check, rested securely in his trunk, acquiesced to the search and even assisted lieutenants Wilhelmi and Edmunds in their efforts so as to make it as thorough as possible.

Upon entering Flipper's rooms, the officers discovered commissary checks in excess of $2,000 thrown haphazardly on a desk. In addition, weekly statements of funds for May, June, and July 1881 were uncovered in a trunk containing the lieutenant's clothing as well as articles belonging to his servant, Lucy Smith. Since the adjutant neglected to make an accurate inventory of the items removed at the time of the search, the exact amount of the funds impounded on August 13 was never verified, although Wilhelmi maintained that a discrepancy of approximately $2,070 existed between the amount listed in the weekly statements for the fiscal year 1880–81 and checks found in Flipper's possession. Armed with the evidence, the adjutant immediately detailed an armed guard to place the black officer under close arrest and confiscated all valuables, including his West Point class ring.

Informed of the results of the search, Colonel Shafter summoned Lucy Smith and ordered her stripped. He removed $2,800 in checks from her person, among which was the non-negotiable check drawn on the San Antonio National Bank. The frightened servant resolutely maintained that her employer had repeatedly cautioned her to take care that none of the papers in his quarters be disturbed, as he would hold her responsible. Lucy explained that when another woman was assigned to clean the lieutenant's rooms, she had placed the checks in her bosom and in her haste had neglected to remove them.

Doubting the veracity of the statements of both Flipper and his ser-

vant, and determined that the missing funds be repaid as soon as possible, Shafter reacted with characteristic impulsiveness and severity. On
August 15 he obtained an order from the U.S. district commissioner for
the arrest of Lucy Smith, charging her with the theft of $1,300. Author-
ities confined her in the Presidio County Jail. As for Lieutenant Flipper,
by the evening of August 13 he was lodged in a windowless 6½ × 4½-foot
cell in the post guardhouse. No visitors were allowed without the consent of the commanding officer. Such harsh treatment, unprecedented in
view of the alleged offense, evoked a sharp response from department
headquarters. Shafter was directed to confine the lieutenant "some-
where other than the guardhouse." Nor did the colonel's peremptory order
escape the attention of the commanding general of the army. When informed of Flipper's plight, Gen. William T. Sherman noted that "his
confinement to the Guard House though within the province of the post
commander is not usual unless there be reasons to apprehend an escape."
Consequently, on the evening of August 17 Shafter ordered Lieutenant
Flipper released and "placed in arrest in quarters and a sentinel over him."

However, during Flipper's confinement, Colonel Shafter did not
relent in his efforts to fathom the mystery surrounding the disappearance of the commissary funds and to make good the shortage. A telegram from the cashier of the San Antonio National Bank showed no
cash in Flipper's name. The lieutenant admitted the worthlessness of the
$1,440.43 check but explained: "I had to deceive in some way, and I took
that way to do it." Shafter cautioned him not to incriminate himself but
added that he would like to know the whereabouts of the missing money.
Flipper replied that he could not explain the loss unless the commissary
funds had been stolen from him. If such were the case, he refused to ac-
cuse any particular person. The young officer remained confident, however, that he could readily cover the deficit if allowed to speak to friends.

Shafter acceded to the request and allowed Flipper several visitors.
W. S. Chamberlain, a watchmaker at the post, asked Shafter "if it would
do Lieutenant Flipper any good to raise this money." The colonel replied, "Yes, it will save him from the penitentiary," and offered a personal
contribution of one hundred dollars. Shafter also informed the watchmaker that "he always thought Lieutenant Flipper to be an honest man,
and did not believe that he was guilty." In his opinion, there was "someone else . . . some damned nigger at the bottom of it."

Apparently convinced of the young officer's innocence, the populace
in the vicinity of Fort Davis promptly came to his assistance. A general

collection yielded $1,700 in a single day, and by August 17, the day of Flipper's release from the post guardhouse, the entire deficit of $3,797.77 had been covered. The post adjutant, however, retained possession of the lieutenant's personal effects, and Colonel Shafter insisted upon holding Flipper's watch as collateral for his one hundred dollar "loan."

In spite of full restitution of the missing funds, November 4, 1881, saw 2nd Lt. Henry O. Flipper arraigned on charges of embezzling $3,797.77 between July 8 and August 13 of that year and of "conduct unbecoming an officer and gentleman." In the list of specifications attached to the second charge, the prosecution alleged that the lieutenant lied to the post commander on July 9, 16, and 23 in falsely reporting the transmittal of the funds in question to the chief commissary of the Department of Texas. Furthermore, he had presented a fraudulent check for $1,440.43 on July 2, 1881, and made additional false statements on August 10, 1881, concerning the transmission of funds to the chief commissary. To all charges and specifications, Lieutenant Flipper entered pleas of "not guilty."

The court-martial of Henry Ossian Flipper convened inauspiciously on September 17 with the lieutenant's acceptance of a board composed of ten members. Three of these officers were currently serving with the First Infantry of which Shafter was colonel. Galusha Pennypacker, the thirty-eight-year-old colonel of the Sixteenth Infantry, presided over the court. Commissioned a captain at the age of seventeen, Pennypacker eventually earned a congressional Medal of Honor for gallantry in the Civil War and was the only general officer in the Union Army too young to vote in the election of 1864.

Brig. Gen. Christopher C. Augur, commander of the Department of Texas, detailed Capt. John W. Clous as judge advocate even though the captain was also at the time serving as acting judge advocate of the department. Clous's duties, therefore, included not only prosecution but selection of the officers serving on the court-martial board, review of the proceedings at the conclusion of the trial, and recommendation of the verdict and sentence.

On September 19, Lieutenant Flipper requested, and was granted, a delay until November 1 to provide necessary time to contact friends in the East in an attempt to raise funds to defray the expense of an adequate defense, obtain counsel, and summon and interview witnesses. These privileges had in effect been denied the accused as notification of the trial date failed to reach him until five days before the convening of the court.

Even with the temporary respite, the lieutenant's prospects remained bleak. Letters to leading African Americans in New York, Boston, Philadelphia, and Washington, D.C., failed to produce the desperately needed cash; and no civilian lawyer appeared anxious to accept the case for less than one thousand dollars. "Chagrined . . . depressed [and] helpless," Flipper resigned himself to fight yet another battle in his life alone. To his utter amazement, however, an offer of legal assistance arrived bearing the signature of Capt. Merritt Barber of the Sixteenth Infantry. Since army regulations specified that no officer could receive payment for defending another officer the impoverished and virtually friendless lieutenant gratefully accepted the captain's aid. Throughout the course of the trial, the black officer and his white defender shared quarters, forming a friendship cemented in deep mutual respect and confidence that transcended the barrier of color.

The case for the prosecution appears to have been severely handicapped from the outset by the judge advocate's inability to prove that Flipper had at any time secreted or disposed the missing commissary funds. Only Lieutenant Wilhelmi seemed confident that the black officer had consciously defrauded the government. Captain Clous did present incontrovertible evidence that the young lieutenant's carelessness and inexperience in handling his personal financial affairs left him chronically in debt. But the defense effectively responded with a stream of witnesses, ranging from colonels Shafter and Grierson, to the leading civilians in and around Fort Davis, praising Flipper's exemplary character.

Moreover, the testimony of the principal prosecution witnesses, Colonel Shafter and Lieutenant Wilhelmi, did little to facilitate the judge advocate's task. Although preferring the charges leading to the court-martial proceedings, Shafter was forced to admit, as late as November 8 that he did "not yet know where that money went to." The colonel also offered abundant evidence of a faulty memory and of extreme laxity in the supervision of post affairs. He reported that he had personally counted the commissary funds and that his signature appeared on every weekly report. Yet the statements for June 1881 bore no evidence of the commanding officer's verification.

Furthermore, Shafter could not recall whether he examined the papers removed from Flipper's quarters. When asked to identify them, he refused, stating: "I have only the word of the officer who took them that they are the articles that came from Flipper's quarters." Nor did he remember his order that Lucy Smith be stripped, the contents of his affi-

davit before the U.S. commissioner, or indeed, whether he had testified
at all. Finally, recognizing the inadequacy of the prepared memorandum
from which he was testifying, the colonel concluded with a statement
that, while he might not remember trifling events, he was certain of the
important items pertaining to the command of the post.

Lieutenant Wilhelmi's recollections proved almost as worthless to
the prosecution. Early in the trial, the adjutant set the tone of his testimony when he averred that his relations with the black officer were "of a
friendly character." Although his contact with Flipper did not extend beyond the realm of official duty, he felt that he had never exhibited the
prejudice that might be expected of persons "when they were brought
together with *them* [author's emphasis] officially." Thereafter a thinly
concealed thread of bias pervaded Wilhelmi's testimony. Eventually his
gratuitous interjections of suspicion became so manifest that Captain
Barber felt entirely justified in accusing him of harboring a grievance
"toward the accused that he had succeeded perhaps in winning laurels at
West Point which *his* sickness prevented him from obtaining, although
he had the unusual opportunity of having been turned back a year into
Mr. Flipper's class."

In his own defense, both before the court-martial board and later
before the House Committee on Military Affairs, Lieutenant Flipper
maintained that never prior to August 10, 1881, did he suspect any deficiency greater than several hundred dollars. While preparing the
funds for transmittal, however, he discovered an unexplained deficit of
$2,074.26. Because of his "peculiar situation" and knowing Colonel
Shafter "by reputation and observation to be a severe, stern man," he decided to conceal his embarrassment and "endeavor to work out the problem alone."

Although unwilling, or unable, to place responsibility for the disappearance of the funds on any specific officers, he suddenly recalled men-
acing omens previously ignored. Flipper testified that he been warned
that Shafter would grasp at the first opportunity to place him in an embarrassing position. On numerous occasions civilians at the post cautioned him that certain officers there were plotting to force him out of the
army. The state hide inspector, warning him of impending danger early
in July 1881, revealed that Lieutenant Wilhelmi, then in command of a
scouting party, boasted that he had "found a way to get rid of the nigger."

Later, as reported in the *Missouri Republican* (St. Louis) of November 3, 1883, the correspondent conducting this interview had found the

ex-lieutenant working in a steam laundry in El Paso while awaiting consideration of his case in Congress. Flipper had maintained that he knew who had stolen the commissary funds but could offer no concrete proof. Interviews with several of his fellow officers indicated the difficulties that faced the black man in his continuing struggle to obtain justice. Maj. Anson Mills of the Tenth Cavalry, whom Flipper considered a friend, stated that "Flipper was a rather popular man, kept his place and did not obtrude. I do not think he was treated exactly right, but I would not for a moment advocate his reinstatement. . . . His commission made him an officer and a gentleman, but then, you know, one couldn't meet a colored man on social equality." An unidentified officer added that "Col. Shafter was as much to blame as Flipper, for it is the duty of the commanding officer to go over the accounts and cash of his commissary before they are sent. . . . Shafter did not do this, but let Flipper run and then jumped him. . . . Flipper's points are well taken and if he were a white man he would upset the verdict and sentence; but he is a colored man, and I for one would not vote for any colored man being an officer. . . . Our wives and daughters must be considered." The article apparently created a considerable amount of controversy in El Paso and prompted a reply from Flipper addressed to "Mr. F. W. May, Newspaper Correspondent, El Paso, Texas," November 15, 1883. In this letter Flipper repeated his conviction that the money had been stolen from him by a commissioned officer and attempted to correct what he felt were misconceptions created by Mr. May's interviews.

However, Flipper contended that he failed to exercise caution even after observing Wilhelmi and others suspiciously prowling about in the vicinity of his quarters late at night. As a result, once he discovered the deficiency, Flipper determined to keep his own counsel while attempting to recoup the loss.

Concluding the argument of the defense, Captain Barber concentrated upon the motives compelling Lieutenant Flipper to mislead his commanding officer. The prosecution not only had failed to prove that his client had "intentionally, willfully [sic] and wrongfully converted the public money with which he was trusted to his own personal use and benefit," but could offer no evidence that either the government or any individual lost "a picayune" in the affair.

Moreover, the defense counsel noted that no difficulty occurred so long as the lieutenant's financial transactions remained under the close supervision of an officer experienced in business matters and cognizant of the proper administrative duties of a post commander.

Under Shafter's lax command, however, Flipper, "unexperienced in business methods . . . and careless to a fault in the management of his financial transactions, . . . believing implicitly in the honesty of everybody around him and trusting with a blind confidence that everything would come out all right, . . . was not calculated to carry on the transactions of a financial responsibility with safety to himself, except for short periods and under the supervision of those more experienced than himself." The young lieutenant thus found himself suddenly burdened with a responsibility beyond his comprehension, "which through inexperience and carelessness led to accidents which he did not foresee."

Nor did Captain Barber, in light of the black lieutenant's solitary struggle for acceptance in a white man's army, deem it peculiar that Flipper should seek to conceal his embarrassment from his mercurial colonel while attempting to rectify the situation. Pleading for understanding, the captain reminded the board of white officers: "From the time when a mere boy he stepped upon our platform and asked the privilege of competing with us for the prizes of success he had to fight the battle of life . . . alone. He has had no one to turn to for counsel or sympathy. Is it strange then that when he found himself confronted with a mystery he could not solve, he should hide it in his own breast and endeavor to work out the problem alone as he had been compelled to do all the other problems of his life?"

The defense counsel sought to bolster his plea for leniency by directing the attention of the court to the unusual degree of punishment already inflicted upon the accused. By virtue of the peculiar nature of Lieutenant Flipper's position as the only black officer in the U.S. Army, his entire career served as a focus for both benevolent and malicious public interest. Hence, forced to serve as a symbol of his race, "the very publicity of his career led him into those concealments and evasions which his embarrassments rendered necessary."

Now, once again, Flipper found himself a convenient target for the slander and castigation of the racist press of the nation. Therefore, Captain Barber concluded, "Tried and punished by the commanding officer of this post with a severity which is unexampled in the history of the service, tried and punished by the trumpet voice of the press which has heralded every idle dream of suspicion as the burden of my client's sin, he now comes before *you* to be tried again and he asks you . . . if he has not been punished enough for the errors into which he was led by circumstances."

The court apparently recognized the absence of evidence of actual theft on the part of the accused officer and yet seemed unimpressed by the defense counsel's arguments for leniency. On December 8, 1881, Henry O. Flipper was found not guilty of embezzlement but guilty of the charge of "conduct unbecoming an officer and gentleman" and was sentenced "to be dismissed from the service of the United States."

On January 2, 1882, Gen. C. C. Augur approved the proceedings of the court and its finding of guilty on the second charge. He disapproved, however, the ruling of not guilty to the charge of embezzlement, "the evidence seeming, in the opinion of the reviewing authority [Capt. John W. Clous] to fully establish the allegations in the specifications. . . ." D. G. Swaim, judge advocate general of the army, also reviewed the transcript of the court-martial and addressed a letter to Robert Todd Lincoln, secretary of war, recommending that the sentence "be confirmed but mitigated to a less degree of punishment," adding that Lieutenant Flipper evidently did not intend to defraud the government as his conduct appeared "attributable to carelessness and ignorance of correct business methods."

Furthermore, Swaim noted "that there is no case on record in which an officer was treated with such personal harshness and indignity upon the cause and grounds set forth as was Lieutenant Flipper by Colonel Shafter and the officers who searched his person and quarters taking his watch and ornaments from him, especially as they must have known . . . that there were no real grounds for such action." No evidence exists, however, indicating that the judge advocate general's recommendation of leniency reached the secretary of war. If considered, Swaim's opinion was clearly ignored. For on June 24, 1882, President Chester A. Arthur rendered final confirmation of the verdict and sentence of the court-martial board, and on June 30, 1882 the officer corps of the U.S. Army regained its "racial purity."

Thus, Henry Ossian Flipper received a painful reminder that justice for the black man was a patronizing boon granted at the whim of a white society. As Captain Barber admonished the court, "The question is before you whether it is possible for a colored man to secure and hold a position as an officer of the army. . . ." The department commander, the secretary of war, and the president of the United States, in dismissing the army's only black officer, tacitly voiced their opinion that no African American was fit to bear the responsibility and prestige attached to the uniform of an officer of the U.S. Army.

Flipper engaged in a lengthy process of attempting to be reinstated to his commission but, due to his political naiveté, was taken advantage of by several different lawyers and never accomplished his goal. At one time, he was promised an audience with President McKinley, by his current lawyer, and went to Washington, D.C. He found himself at the end of a reception line, however, and only got to shake the president's hand.

Flipper became a successful mining engineer in the Southwest, and spent quite a bit of time in Mexico and South America. Eventually, he was appointed a special assistant to the U.S. Secretary of the Interior. When Flipper died in 1940, his brother completed the death certificate. Next to the word occupation he wrote "Retired Army Officer."

Notes

This study is based primarily upon material in "Records Relating to the Army career of Henry Ossian Flipper, 1873–1882 (RRACHF), microcopy no. T 1027, roll no. 1, National Archives. In addition to numerous pieces of official correspondence, this collection includes the complete "Record of the Court-Martial of Second Lieutenant Henry O. Flipper" (RCM) and "Petition for Restoral to the Service: Statement and Brief Petitioner in the Matter of the Court-Martial of Henry Ossian Flipper, Second Lieutenant, Tenth Cavalry, U.S. Army," U.S. Congress, House Committee on Military Affairs, 55th Cong., 2nd sess., 1899.

The autobiography of Henry O. Flipper, *The Colored Cadet at West Point* (1878; repr., New York: Arno Press, 1968) remains an essential source material on his early life and cadet days. Henry O. Flipper, *Negro Frontiersman: The Western Memoirs of Henry O. Flipper, First Negro Graduate of West Point*, ed. Theodore D. Harris (El Paso: Texas Western College Press, 1963), traces the author's career from his arrival in Texas in 1877 to 1916.

Contemporary periodicals and newspapers exhibited an unusual degree of interest in the army's only black officer. Brief articles describing Flipper's progress at West Point appeared in *Harper's Weekly*, 17, no. 856 (May 24, 1873): 453, and again in 21, no. 1071 (July 7, 1877): 519. The *San Antonio Daily Express*, November 2–December 14, 1881, contains almost daily summaries of the court-martial proceedings.

Secondary sources concerned with the career of Henry O. Flipper include William H. Leckie, *The Buffalo Soldiers: A Narrative of the Negro Cavalry in the West* (Norman, Okla.: University of Oklahoma Press, 1967); and Ezra J. Warner, "A Black Man in the Long Gray Line," *American History Illustrated*, 4, no. 9 (January 1970): 30–38, both of which include brief accounts of the events leading to the black lieutenant's dismissal from the army.

Background material on the officers involved in the court-martial may be found in Francis B. Heitman, *Historical Register and Dictionary of the United States Army, from Its Organization September 29, 1789, to March 2, 1903*, 2 vols.

(Washington, D.C., 1903); Robert M. Utley, "'Pecos Bill' on the Texas Frontier," *American West,* 6, no. 1 (January 1969): 4–14, offers valuable information on the character and post–Civil War career of Col. William R. Shafter. Ezra Warner, *Generals in Blue: Lives of the Union Commanders* (Baton Rouge: Louisiana State University, 1964) contains brief biographical sketches of General Augur and Colonel Pennypacker.

Of additional assistance was correspondence with Nicholas J. Blesser, historian, Fort Davis National Historical Site, Fort Davis, Texas; Arthur Cromwell Jr., associate producer, KUON-TV, Lincoln, Nebraska; and Stanley P. Tozeski, chief, USMA Archives, West Point, New York.

THOMAS A. BRITTEN

The Black Seminole Indian Scouts in the Big Bend

The Big Bend region of Texas was the site of some of the last Indian hostilities in the American Southwest. Its rugged, mountainous geography provided excellent refuge for numerous bands of Apaches, Comanches, Kickapoos, and Kiowas: peoples who saw the Big Bend as their last refuge against the onslaught of white settlement and, consequently, were determined to make their last stand. In addition, bandits, murderers, and horse thieves established hideaways in the Big Bend, crossing and recrossing the Rio Grande to elude the authorities. American frontier troops, like their Spanish and Mexican predecessors, experienced tremendous difficulties trying to pacify the region's inhabitants and bring Anglo civilization to this last bastion of the Texas frontier.

In order to accomplish this task, the U.S. Army utilized a number of "special forces" (or nontraditional forces) in the Big Bend region of Texas. Probably the most famous of these were the buffalo soldiers of the Ninth and Tenth Cavalry Regiments. Organized after the Civil War ended, units of the Ninth and Tenth Cavalry under the command of colonels Edward Hatch and Benjamin H. Grierson periodically served in the Big Bend region in the 1870s and early 1880s.[1] In addition to the buffalo soldiers, the U.S. Army employed a number of Apache, Tonkawa, Navajo, and Pueblo scouts to aid federal troops in their campaigns against hostile Indians. These scouts proved to be indispensable assets to frontier commanders due to their familiarity with the terrain, excellent tracking ability, and intimate knowledge of Indian culture and warfare.[2] A final special force that saw action in the Big Bend were the Black Seminole Indian scouts. Their service to the army in the Big Bend has

gone relatively unnoticed, yet they played an integral part in the pacification of the region. Therefore, a review of the activities of the Black
Seminole Indian scouts in the Big Bend is needed in order to fully appreciate their contribution to the settlement of the Texas frontier.

As the name implies, the Black Seminoles were of mixed Seminole
and African American lineage. During the late seventeenth and eighteenth centuries, black slaves escaped the plantations of the Carolinas,
Georgia, and Alabama to freedom in Spanish Florida. Once there, the
Seminole Indians welcomed them as allies in the struggle against Anglo
expansion into northern Florida. When the Seminoles were relocated
to the Indian Territory in the 1830s–50s, the Black Seminoles went with
them, where their unique relationship with the Seminole Indians continued.[3]

In the latter part of 1849, the Seminole warrior Wildcat led an exodus
of discontented Seminoles, Creeks, Kickapoos, and Black Seminoles
south to Mexico where they hoped to establish a new home. The Mexican authorities welcomed these newcomers and granted them land in
northern Coahuila. In return for the land grants, the Seminoles and
Black Seminoles were enlisted for service in the Mexican Army to serve
as a buffer against bandits and hostile Comanche and Apache warriors
who frequently raided into Mexico. For the next decade, the Seminoles
and their black allies performed this duty very effectively. According to
Mexican Gen. Alberto Guajardo, the Seminoles and Black Seminoles
were "always triumphant on their expeditions" against hostile Indians.
However, by 1860 many Seminoles desired to rejoin their brethren in the
Indian Territory, and by the middle of 1861, only the Black Seminoles remained in Mexico.[4]

In June 1870, the Black Seminoles accepted an invitation from military authorities at Fort Duncan, Texas, to move back to the United States.
The U.S. Army was eager to have these capable scouts working north of
the Rio Grande, and readily employed several as scouts. For the next two
decades, the Black Seminole Indian scouts participated in dozens of engagements with hostile Indians, winning praise and commendations
from their commanders.[5]

Although the Black Seminoles were not deployed extensively in the
Big Bend until the 1880s, it was not uncommon for them to conduct
scouts west of the Pecos while they resided at Fort Clark in the 1870s. In
April 1875, for example, Lt. John L. Bullis and a small detachment of
Seminole scouts pursued a band of hostile Indians who had stolen some

horses and overtook them as they were crossing the Pecos River. Despite being well outnumbered, Bullis and the scouts attacked the Indians, killing three and wounding another. Events took a turn for the worse, however, when Bullis was thrown from his horse and lay on the ground vulnerable to the fast approaching Indians. Fortunately, he "just saved (his) hair by jumping on (his) sergeant's horse" while the scouts held off the Indians. Subsequently, Sergeant John Ward and Privates Pompey Factor and Isaac Payne received the Congressional Medal of Honor for their outstanding and heroic service during this engagement.[6]

In December 1879, Bullis and the scouts received orders to accompany a party of miners, explorers, and prospectors, outfitted by the Galveston, Harrisburg and San Antonio, International and Greater Northern, and Texas Pacific Railroad companies for an expedition to the Chinati Mountains in Presidio County. Two months prior to this, Victorio and his band of Warm Springs Apaches had slipped away from their reservation at Fort Stanton, New Mexico. For the next year, Victorio's gang left a trail of horse theft and murder stretching from southern New Mexico through northern Chihuahua and into the Big Bend. Thus, it was not surprising that the U.S. Army deemed it prudent to provide protection for railroad surveyors and miners in Southwest Texas.

On January 29, 1880, Bullis and his men reached the Chinati Mountains and set up permanent camp on Cibolo Creek. For the next three months, the Black Seminole scouts escorted and protected parties of prospectors in search of precious metals, covering over two thousand miles in the process. In addition to these duties, Bullis scouted the region around the Chinati Mountains to determine the feasibility of establishing a permanent post for the protection of miners. Bullis reported that:

> the southwest side of the Chinati Mountains has several fine springs, excellent gama grass and plenty of good wood within a short distance. A camp at one of these springs would afford the greatest protection to miners, from the fact that most of the silver leads thus found are on the southwest side.[7]

Bullis and his men frequently came across Indian trails during their tenure in the Big Bend. On March 13, a small band of Indians attacked the Gregurio Seguro family, killing nineteen-year-old José Miguel and kidnapping ten-year-old Kisetane. Bullis and his men immediately took the trail, following the Indians through the Chinati and Coyote Mountains, but lost them when the Indians killed their horses and proceeded north on foot toward the Guadalupe or Sacramento Mountains in New Mexico.

On the first of April, Bullis and the scouts broke camp and started back for home, marching along the Rio Grande with a party of prospectors, while the wagons were sent via the new road that had been built to connect Fort Clark and Fort Davis. Two weeks later, Bullis and his scouts found several Indian trails going northwest toward the Sacramento Mountains. Bullis believed the tracks were made by about two hundred horses and were about fourteen days old. The trail crossed the Rio Grande about fifty miles below San Carlos, which raised the prospect of Victorio's gang being the likely culprits. Being on escort duty at the time, and having insufficient rations, Bullis and the scouts dismissed the possibility of pursuit and proceeded on to Fort Clark. They arrived at the post on April 27 after covering an estimated 2,500 miles.[8]

The Black Seminole scouts had little opportunity, however, to enjoy visiting their families and relaxing at their homes on Las Moras Creek outside Fort Clark. In July the scouts received orders to proceed to Peña Colorado, a remote subpost established the previous year to protect the construction of a road being built between Fort Clark and El Paso, Texas. A secondary road ran northwest from Peña Colorado to Fort Davis, which provided a more practicable route to Fort Clark and the east. Peña Colorado also happened to be located on the Old Comanche Trail and was a favorite resting spot for Indians due to the availability of water and grass. The camp itself was rough and uninviting. It was composed primarily of mud and stone huts roofed with grass and adobe.

The task of repairing the facilities fell to the Black Seminole scouts and other troops unfortunate enough to be stationed there. "Isolation, boredom, and monotony characterized the enlisted man's life at Camp Peña Colorado." Due to its isolation, all available manpower was utilized to the fullest. In addition to attending drills, pulling kitchen duty, cleaning the barracks, and attending rifle practice, troops were expected to haul water, construct roads, and erect buildings. It was no surprise, therefore, that a scouting assignment was a welcome relief to camp life.[9]

In the fall of 1880 the Black Seminole scouts, together with Company K, Eighth Cavalry, commanded by Lt. William Shunk, guided and protected a group of army engineers led by Capt. W. R. Livernore. Livernore's assignment was to survey the route for the proposed Southern Pacific Railroad, which was to pass through the Big Bend on route to California.[10] For the next five years, the Black Seminoles served at Camp

Peña Colorado, conducting scouts, protecting prospectors, surveyors, and road builders, and completing the construction of post facilities. With the death of Victorio at Tres Castillos in October 1880, the threat of Apache depredations diminished but did not disappear entirely.

Throughout the summer and fall of 1881, Nana, one of Victorio's lieutenants, continued his leader's legacy of theft and destruction. This kept soldiers stationed in the Big Bend almost continuously in the saddle. During the month of August 1882 Indian depredations continued. On the night of August 15, a band of brazen Indians made off with a number of horses from Camp Peña Colorado. Although the Black Seminole scouts discovered moccasin tracks in the area, their attempt to track the Indians and recover the horses came to naught. Two weeks later, a few remnants of Victorio's band killed several cattle near Peña Colorado by shooting them with arrows. The following day they murdered a herder and some sheep ten miles east of Fort Davis.[11]

Despite the continuation of Indian depredations in the Big Bend in the early 1880s, prospectors, ranchers, and settlers continued their advance into the West Texas frontier region. With the establishment of the new road to El Paso and the construction of the Southern Pacific Railroad, continued settlement seemed inevitable. The increase of settlement in the Big Bend, however, served to exacerbate the already difficult task facing frontier troops at Camp Peña Colorado. More settlers meant more people to protect, and the number of soldiers policing the area was already paper thin.

The vulnerability of frontier settlements in the Big Bend manifested itself in November 1884, when a party of Mexican bandits attacked Brough's mining camp located five miles south of Nevill's Springs and thirty miles south of the Rosillos Mountains. Not content with simply stealing the miners' horses and cattle, the bandits ransacked the house of the Petty family and bludgeoned Mrs. Petty and her children to death with an axe. The bandits then carried off Mr. Petty's boots, rifle, pistol, and cash, although the family's cooking utensils and food were not touched. When news of the atrocity reached Camp Peña Colorado on the night of November 15, Lt. M. F. Eggleston, along with Troop M, Tenth Cavalry, and a detachment of Black Seminole scouts set out after the killers. In addition, Capt. Robert G. Smither with Troops A and B of the Tenth Cavalry were dispatched from Fort Davis. Upon arriving at Brough's mining camp on November 19, Eggleston inspected the camp and was relieved to find that some nearby cowboys had the decency to bury the bodies of the Petty family. With this unpleasant chore completed, Eggleston's force marched southeast to the San Vicente Crossing, where they awaited orders to cross into Mexico.

Meanwhile, Captain Smither and his troops were a few days behind. On November 22, Smither conducted his own inspection of Brough's mining camp while the rest of his troop continued east through Willow Canyon to Tornillo Creek. On November 24, Smither met with Lieutenant Eggleston at the San Vicente Crossing. Because the "doctrine of hot pursuit," which allowed U.S. forces to cross the Rio Grande into Mexico if in "hot pursuit" of hostile Indians, had expired and technically did not apply to Mexican bandits, Eggleston was awaiting permission from departmental headquarters at Fort Davis to cross into Mexico. On December 2, Eggleston and Smither received permission, and they proceeded south of the Rio Grande in pursuit of the bandits. Three six-mule teams and three pack mules carried a twenty-day supply of food and rations for the troops, as well as forage for the horses.

For the next several days, the Black Seminole scouts followed the trail into Mexico, encountering treacherous ravines, gravelly hills, dense fog and rain, as well as bitter cold temperatures. Many of the soldiers suffered frostbite due to the lack of proper clothing, and some were even barefooted! Nevertheless, the troops pressed the bandits so closely that they were able to recover eight head of stolen stock which they returned to Brough's mining camp. The bandits eluded capture, however, by hiding in the surrounding mountains.[12]

In hopes of curbing the rise of depredations along the Rio Grande frontier, army officials decided to establish posts closer to the border. In March 1885, Lt. Charles H. Grierson (the regimental commander's son) along with Company A, Tenth Calvary, and a detachment of Black Seminole scouts set up a base camp at Willow Springs, but soon abandoned the site due to its inaccessibility to wood and water. Later that month, a permanent camp was established at Nevill's Springs, located near the modern day Big Bend National Park headquarters at Panther Junction. For the next six years, the Black Seminole scouts constituted the primary force at this remote outpost. Nevill's Springs was connected administratively to Fort Clark, but was under the functional direction of the commanding officer at Fort Davis. Thus, when the scouts returned to Fort Clark every couple of months to draw pay and receive rations detachments from Fort Davis occupied Nevill's Springs until the scouts returned.[13]

While the Black Seminoles conducted scouts and worked on the construction of their barracks and other post facilities at Nevill's Springs, a crisis emanating from the San Carlos Reservation in southern Arizona soon embroiled them in yet another major Indian uprising. In May 1885, Geronimo, Nachez, Nana, and other recalcitrant Apaches fled the San Carlos Reservation and began attacking and raiding small settlements and ranches throughout southern New Mexico, northern Chihuahua and Coahuila, and the Big Bend of Texas. In an effort to prevent Apaches from entering into Texas from northern Mexico, Gen. George Cook ordered that troops be stationed at every major crossing point and watering hole along the Rio Grande border. Consequently, in June, Lt. George K. Hunter, commanding troops at Camp Peña Colorado and Lt. H. F. Kendall, commanding the Black Seminole scouts at Nevill's Springs, received orders to guard the region between Presidio del Norte and Presidio de San Vicente. After establishing a camp at Polvo, Texas (modern day Redford, Texas, in southern Presidio County), the Black Seminole scouts searched the region surrounding the Bofecillos Mountains for signs of hostile Apaches. In September, twenty Chiricahuas were reported moving north from Mexico, but the scouts were unable to locate them.[14]

Geronimo's surrender to Gen. Nelson A. Miles at Skelton Canyon in Sonora, Mexico in September 1886 finally ended the major Indian hostilities in the Southwest. The need for experienced and skilled scouts in the Big Bend, however, did not diminish. Bandits, horse thieves, bootleggers, and other fugitives from justice continued to roam the rugged mountains of Southwest Texas. Throughout the latter half of the 1880s, the Black Seminole scouts served as a quasi-frontier police force and patrolled the Rio Grande border region to maintain the peace.

In the autumn of 1891, the government's lease on Nevill's Springs expired. The scouts established a new base camp at Polvo where, along with a detachment of troops from Camp Peña Colorado, they kept a constant vigil for smugglers and bandits along the Rio Grande. A year or so later Camp Peña Colorado was also abandoned when law and order were established in the Big Bend.[15]

The Black Seminole Indian scouts were a vital link in the U.S. Army's efforts to pacify hostile Indians in the Southwest. From 1850–70 they served the Mexican government as a buffer against hostile Apaches and Comanches and aided the advance of civilization in northern Coahuila and Chihuahua. From 1870 to 1885 these experienced and skilled scouts were employed by the U.S. Army for duty against a host of hostile Indians. In 1874, the Black Seminoles played an integral part in the stunning defeat of the Comanches, Cheyennes, Kiowas, and Arapahoes at Palo Duro Canyon. In addition, the scouts traversed the Upper Rio Grande frontier in search of hostile Apache, Comanche, and Kickapoo Indians. By the close of the 1870s, the threat of Victorio's and Geronimo's bands of Apaches in the Big Bend region of Texas resulted in the transfer of the Black Seminoles to that troubled area. Finally, their continuing service as a quasi-border patrol from 1885 through the early 1890s enabled settlers to move into the Big Bend without fear of being attacked by outlaws.

This pattern clearly indicates the reliance of the U.S. Army on the skills of the Black Seminole Indian scouts. Although their exploits in the Big Bend region are not as well known as their daring raids into Mexico, or as their assistance during the Red River War, they were, nevertheless, important. Their service as guides for prospecting parties, guards for construction workers, and scouts of the Army laid the groundwork for the inevitable pacification of the Apaches and the spread of Anglo civilization to the Big Bend.

Notes

1. William Leckie, *The Buffalo Soldiers: A Narrative of the Negro Cavalry in the West* (Norman: University of Oklahoma Press, 1967).

2. Douglas C. McChristian, "Pueblo Scouts in the Victorio Campaign," paper presented at a symposium to honor Don Russell at the Buffalo Bill Historical Center, Cody, Wyoming, May 2–4, 1986, copy in Document File on Victorio's Campaigns, Fort Davis National Historical Site Archives, Fort Davis, Texas.

3. For a detailed history of the origins of the Black Seminoles, see Edwin McReynolds, *The Seminoles* (Norman: University of Oklahoma Press, 1957). Also see Wilton Krogman, "The Racial Composition of the Seminole Indians of Florida and Oklahoma," *Journal of Negro History* 19, no. 4 (October 1934); Kenneth Wiggins Porter, "Negroes on the Southern Frontier, 1670–1763," *Journal of Negro History* 3, no. 1 (January 1948); and Kenneth Wiggins Porter, *The Negro on the American Frontier* (New York: Arno Press, 1971). Virginia Peters, *The Florida Wars* (Ann Arbor: Archon Books, 1979), 34–36, gives an interesting analysis of the cultural similarities between the Seminole Indians and African slaves as well as a detailed account of the Seminole Wars. A history of the removal of the Seminoles and the Black Seminoles is given in Daniel F. Little-

field, *African and Seminole: From Removal to Emancipation* (London: Greenwood Press, 1977).

4. The migration and exploits of the Seminoles and Black Seminoles in Mexico are explained in Kenneth Wiggins Porter, "The Seminole [and Seminole-Negroes] in Mexico, 1850–1861," *Hispanic American Historical Review* 31 (February 1951); and in Felipe A. and Delores L. LaTorre, *The Mexican Kickapoo Indians,* Publications in Anthropology, no. 2 (Milwaukee: Milwaukee Public Museum, 1956).

5. "Major Zenus R. Bliss, C.O. Fort Duncan, to Colonel H. Clay Wood (AAG) 5th Military District," July 14, 1870, in *Report of the Commissioner of Indian Affairs 1879,* 792–93; "Copy of the Record from Letters Received Book, Dept. of Texas, 1870," File 264, Department of Texas, Seminole Negro, National Archives, RG 393 Part 1, E-4882 (hereafter cited as Group B); "Colonel Joseph Dorst, C.O., Fort Clark to (AG), Dept. of Texas," February 11, 1909, in Group B; "2nd Lieutenant Patrick Kellihan, 25th Inf., Ft. Clark," October 6, 1871, in "Letters Received Relating to Indians, 1871," National Archives, RG 393, Part 1, E-4815 (hereafter cited as Group A); "Major Zenus R. Bliss, C.O. Ft. Duncan, to (AG) Dept: of Texas," October 30, 1871, and November 10, 1871, in Group A; John M. Carroll, ed., *The Black Military Experience in the American West* (New York: Liveright Publishing, 1973); Ernest Wallace, "Ranald S. Mackenzie on the Texas Frontier," in *The Museum Journal,* ed. F. E. Green (Lubbock, Tex.: Texas Technological College, 1966), 113; Mildred Mayhall, *Indian Wars of Texas* (Waco: Texian Press, 1965), 172–74; Ernest Wallace, *Ranald S. Mackenzie's Official Correspondence,* in *The Museum Journal,* ed. F. E. Green (Lubbock, Tex.: Texas Technological College, 1963–64), 193.

6. John M. Carroll, ed., *The Black Military Experience in the American West* (New York: Liveright, 1973); *Army and Navy Courier* 2 (October–November 1926): 18–20, copy in the Clifford B. Casey Collection, Box 10, Folder 900, Archives of the Big Bend, Sul Ross State University, Alpine, Texas.

7. "1st Lieutenant John L. Bullis, 24th Infantry Commanding Seminole-Negro Scouts to AAG, District of the Nueces, Fort Clark, May 25, 1880," in "B.H. Grierson, HQ District of the Pecos to AAG, Department of Texas, September 20, 1880"; *U.S. War Department: AG Letters Received 1871–1880,* National Archives, N.A.M.P. Reel 45, Roll 568, copy in Southwest Collection, Texas Tech University. Letters Received by AGO, 1880 Annual Reports, N.A.M.P. RG 393, Roll no. 589, Microcopy no. 666, copy in Fort Davis National Historic Site Archives, Fort Davis, Texas; Bruce J. Dinges, "Colonel Benjamin H. Grierson on the West Texas Frontier," paper presented at meeting of the Texas State Historical Association and the Historical Society of New Mexico, El Paso, Texas, March 6, 1981, copy in Fort Davis National Historic Site Archives, Fort Davis, Texas.

8. "Bullis to AAG, Dept. of the Nueces, May 25, 1880."

9. Charles Judson Crane, *The Experience of a Colonel of Infantry* (New York: Knickerbocker Press, 1923), 106–107; Col. M. L. Crimmins, "Camp Peña Colo-

rado, Texas," *West Texas Historical and Scientific Society Publication* 6 (Alpine, Tex.: 1935): 8–11; AnneJo Wedin, *The Magnificent Marathon Basin* (Austin: Nortex Press, 1989), 17; Eddie Guffee, "Camp Peña Colorado, Texas 1879–1893," (Master's thesis, West Texas State University, 1976), 32–62; Richard A. Thompson, "Rainbow Cliffs: Camp Peña Colorado," paper presented, April 14–15, 1989, copy in Wedin File, Archives of the Big Bend.

10. Thompson, "Rainbow Cliffs," 15–20; Crimmins, "Camp Peña Colorado."

11. Guffee, "Camp Peña Colorado," 70–73; Arthur Gomez, *A Most Singular Country: A History of the Occupation of the Big Bend* (Salt Lake City: Brigham Young University Press, 1990), 78–79.

12. "Joint Expedition into Mexico in Pursuit of Murderers and Cattle Thieves," in *Letters Received by AGO, 1881–1889,* National Archives, N.A.M.P., Roll 317, Microcopy 689; "Captain Robert M. Smither, Troop B, Fort Davis to (AG) Department of Texas, December 16, 1884," and "2nd Lieutenant M. F. Eggleston, Troop M, Camp Peña Colorado to (AG) Department of Texas. January 9, 1885," in Fort Davis National Historic Site Archives; Gomez, *Most Singular Country,* 87–89; Guffee, "Camp Peña Colorado," 73–74.

13. Crimmins, "Camp Peña Colorado"; Guffee, "Camp Peña Colorado," 32–40; Gomez, *Most Singular Country,* 87–90; "Inventory Nomination Form for Nevill's' Springs," National Register of Historic Places, National Park Service, copy in Fort Davis National Historic Site Archives.

14. Gomez, *Most Singular Country,* 88–90; Thompson, "Rainbow Cliffs," 21–25; Guffee, "Camp Peña Colorado," 74–79.

15. Guffee, "Camp Peña Colorado," 74–79, 33–40; "Inventory Nomination National Register of Historic Places; Gomez, *Most Singular Country,* 90.

PART III

Discrimination and Violence

Discrimination and violence are no strangers to the nation nor to the American West. Individual citizens and groups in frontier communities without a constituted legal authority often took the law into their own hands. Discrimination and violence were endemic to these settlements and did not require a specific racial, ethnic, or cultural admixture to manifest itself. Human desires and selfish interests were ever present as groups and individuals vied for power, wealth, and control.

Into this unsettled and unsettling environment rode the buffalo soldiers, with orders to maintain a peace that never existed and a peace fiercely resisted by nearly every sector of society. In James N. Leiker's "Black Soldiers at Fort Hays, Kansas, 1867–1869: A Study in Civilian and Military Violence," (*Great Plains Quarterly* 17, no. 1 [Winter 1997]: 3–17) the writer states that the dangers buffalo soldiers faced in town and at the fort exceeded the dangers faced on the battlefield. The town of Hays City, an offspring of Fort Hays, attracted a rough crowd that provided the illicit entertainment and much of the mayhem that the Thirty-eighth Infantry and Tenth cavalry was to experience in western Kansas.

Hays City, a paradox for the buffalo soldiers, obligated them to provide police protection for the town and recreate with the same locals in a manner that often disturbed the peace. The isolated location, the small population, and a low level of civil authority combined with a racial mixture that tested the notion of a "liberal" Kansas. According to Leiker, an assorted amalgam of black soldiers, former Confederates, saloon keepers, gamblers, prostitutes, and a variety of deadbeats produced an explosive en-

vironment. Between 1867 and 1874, Hays City recorded over thirty homicides with nearly half involving conflicts between soldiers and civilians.

Black-white violence and the lynching of three buffalo soldiers
helped contribute to Hays City's reputation as especially dangerous for
blacks; however, the violence did not decrease when white soldiers replaced them. Violence in frontier towns was more than the sum of its
parts and defied simple racial explanations. Black soldiers at frontier
settlements heard epithets and ugly expressions on a regular basis. While
discrimination and violence were not limited to these distant outposts,
Frank N. Schubert in "Black Soldiers on the White Frontier: Some Factors Influencing Race Relations" (*Phylon* 32, no. 4 [Winter 1971]: 410–17)
adds another dimension to the issue.

While Schubert acknowledges discrimination, bigotry, and violence
as common experiences for buffalo soldiers, he suggests that mitigating
circumstances critically affected the intensity and virulence of those conflicts. The difference between hostile, benign, or even friendly relations
in frontier communities was related to the size of the town, the presence
of a local black population, and the town's relative proximity to an Indian reservation. The presence of an Indian reservation seemed not to
relate to fears of Indians hostilities, but the social position of the Indians
as the town's "niggers." The buffalo soldiers gained a higher-ranked status
since the Indians made up the bottom rung of the social-racial order.

Garna L. Christian in "Rio Grande City: Prelude to the Brownsville
Raid" (*West Texas Historical Association Yearbook* 57 [1981]: 118–32) cites
turn-of-the-century black self-confidence's collision with waxing white
supremacy. Christian further adds another factor to relations in the Rio
Grande valley: the presence of a three-tiered social order. Some Mexican Americans reasoned that to achieve a measure more social status
and mobility than newly arriving African Americans required the assumption of an orthodox racist position consistent with white Anglo leadership.
The efforts of Mexicans to avoid the lowest social position exacerbated
tensions between themselves and the buffalo soldiers.

Tensions between black soldiers and Mexicans were coupled with
hostilities of Texans who hated the federal government in general and
black military representatives of that government in particular. A linger-
ing fear of black retaliation among Texans also may have been ignited by
the sight of black men with guns. A third factor was tied to the fact that
the Rio Grande was a border region, a historic place of violence and disorder. Lax law enforcement made the Rio Grande area attractive to a va-

riety of renegade Indians, bandits, and outlaw gangs. It was in this environment where any and every buffalo soldier action was suspect.

The problematic Texas experience of black soldiers could hardly escape the scrutiny of anyone with knowledge of the past. When the Twenty-fifth Infantry was sent to Texas in 1917, battalion commander Col. William Newman tried to get the assignment changed. All the old memories lingered in the minds of many of the men, and as reported in C. Calvin Smith's "The Houston Riot of 1917, Revisited" (*Houston Review of History and Culture* 13, no.2 [1991]: 84–102), in Texas, of all the places where black soldiers served, "the documented record of 'ill treatment' and the lack of respect was greatest" (86).

It took less than a month for the worst fears and admonitions to be realized. On the evening of August 23, 1917, the Twenty-fourth Infantry confronted the police and citizens of Houston, resulting in the deaths of two black soldiers, five white policemen, and thirteen white civilians. Unlike the Brownsville Raid of 1906, there was no doubt that armed members of the Twenty-fourth left camp and engaged the Houston police and citizens, but what could not have been predicted was the government response. C. Calvin Smith painstakingly analyzes the testimony, official military records, and historical accounts of the embattled buffalo soldiers and draws a conclusion at odds with some other accounts.

The black soldiers who served in western posts throughout the nineteenth century represented a federal presence that was required but often not desired. They faced enemies from both sides of the Mexican border and found themselves often embroiled in local politics and grievances. The violence and discrimination they experienced was waiting for them as they arrived. The borderland region of Texas represented a commingling of people and cultures with predictably combustible results. It is difficult to say just how much of the disorder the buffalo soldiers experienced was directly related to their race, but it served as a lightning rod for the deep-seated political, social, and cultural resentment that infested the region.

JAMES N. LEIKER

Black Soldiers at
Fort Hayes, Kansas 1867–69

A STUDY IN CIVILIAN AND MILITARY VIOLENCE

Historians of the western army contend with many romanticized myths. Few of those myths, in recent years, have held the popular consciousness as has that of the army's first black regulars, known as buffalo soldiers. By now, the origins of the segregated regiments are quite familiar. In 1866, with the nation's acting military force having dwindled to a fraction of its Civil War size, the Republican Congress encouraged the enlistment of newly freed slaves and Northern free blacks. Assigned to remote western areas, black units played an instrumental role over the next few decades in opening the West for white settlement. Despite their important functions, uniformed African Americans continually suffered racism and discrimination from frontier civilians and even from some of their own white officers.[1]

For much of the past century, both popular culture and professional historians overlooked the buffalo soldiers. The gallant stereotype of patriotic, blue-jacketed warriors bringing civilization to the plains failed to accommodate the presence of armed blacks. Although scholars began to draw public attention toward black soldiers as early as the 1960s, the dedication of a buffalo soldier's monument at Fort Leavenworth, Kansas in 1992 fully captured the popular imagination, partly because of Colin Powell's visible involvement. The Leavenworth project was accompanied by a veritable explosion of buffalo soldier commemorations including museum displays, documentaries, newspaper and journal articles, and reenactment societies. Where once the public imagined the West only in terms of white soldiers and red Indians, the present fascination represents a positive step in defining the region as a meeting ground for numerous races and cultures, a step that scholars should applaud.

Yet not all have been enthusiastic about proclaiming buffalo soldiers' contributions to western conquest. From a Native American standpoint, lionizing the black regiments to redress historical neglect appears no more just nor progressive than the Anglo myths that excluded them. When the U.S. Postmaster General announced a commemorative buffalo soldiers stamp in 1994, representatives of the American Indian movement demanded both the stamp's withdrawal and a public apology.[2] For all the topic's recent attention, few grasp its frustrating irony: that black males, themselves victims of white prejudice, voluntarily aided the subjugation of Native peoples for the benefit of Anglo expansion. This scenario illustrates the complicated, even paradoxical, nature of American race relations. Unfortunately, significant questions are overshadowed by the topic's "contribution" aspects, helping to provide a focus for national and racial pride, a cry of "we were there too." Nor have academic historians pursued the more difficult questions as aggressively as they should. New western history, which has debunked many myths surrounding white occupation and shown its catastrophic consequences for minorities, generally ignores the army's role in western conquest. Military histories have added tremendously to knowledge about the subject but most employ traditional approaches that are more event-centered and descriptive than analytical and interpretive.

The time appears right for a serious reappraisal of the army's first black regulars, one that resists the temptation to cast them either as villainous enforcers of white oppression or heroic subjects of injustice. The former depiction rests on the questionable assumption that blacks shared whites' racist attitudes toward Indians; the latter, more common view treats them as passive victims, stoically enduring discrimination. Both rob the buffalo soldiers of conscious agency, seeing them not as historical actors but merely as "acted upon." In fact, when uniformed blacks entered the hostile racial climate of western towns, some acquiesced to white racism but others violently resisted. Although holding limited options, buffalo soldiers' individual reactions to civilian antagonism played a vital role in local race relations.

Setting the Scene

Fort Hays, located in northwest Kansas, serves as an example of black agency. Active from 1865 to 1889, its garrison protected stagecoach and railway traffic along the Smoky Hill River to Denver.[3] Stationed there in the late 1860s, troops from the Thirty-eighth Infantry and Tenth Cavalry (both consisting entirely of black soldiers) comprised the majority of the post's enlisted men up to 1869. Though engaged in several Indian battles, the average black soldier had more reason to fear civilians or even comrades than Indians; more injuries and killings resulted from altercations in camp or nearby Hays City than from combat. While Fort Hays's troubles were not unique, the unusual mingling of a predominantly black military with growing numbers of white civilians led to racial violence that mirrored and even surpassed that in other western communities.[4]

Given Kansas's early reputation among African Americans as a safe haven for freedmen, such an assertion might seem surprising. After all, Kansas had been among the first states to muster black volunteers into Union service.[5] Even after the Civil War, images of "Bleeding Kansas" and John Brown enhanced the state's prestige among Southern blacks as a place of opportunity and freedom. In the late 1870s thousands of "exodusters"—emigrants fleeing the South after Reconstruction—chose Kansas as their destination. While most exodusters found only disillusionment in the so-called "Canaan of the Prairies," active state charity organizations worked diligently to ease the refugees' plight.[6] In addition, Kansas claimed several black communities, among them Nicodemus, established in 1877 only fifty miles northwest of Hays City. If any state could have been expected to tolerate a high population of black soldiers, it should have been Kansas.

While the legacies of abolition and the Civil War may have encouraged relative openness in the state's eastern communities, however, isolated locales like Fort Hays initially shared little with Lawrence and Leavenworth. During the black units' peak enlistment in the late 1860s, the new forts and towns truly epitomized the "frontier," the peripheral edge of white settlement socially and geographically. While "frontier" as an analytical concept has been criticized for its ethnocentric connotations, the term retains usefulness for discovering how racial hatreds were transferred to the developing region.[7] By examining how the civilian community perceived and interacted with black soldiers, we can draw a clearer picture of how the black military experience helped to shape western race relations.

Understanding the reception of black soldiers in Hays City first necessitates an examination of the military and social atmosphere at Fort Hays. As Indian raids diminished by late 1867, three Tenth Cavalry companies were recalled for winter rest at Fort Riley, leaving Fort Hays largely under the protection of black infantry.[8] Because of its central location and proximity to the railroad, Fort Hays served as Gen. Philip Sheridan's administrative headquarters and a depot for goods arriving by rail during the 1868–69 campaign. Although small cavalry detachments remained until 1871, infantry comprised the garrison's majority. Thus, if Fort Hays could claim a "semi-permanent" black population up to 1869, the Thirty-eighth Infantry fit that role better than the more transient Tenth Cavalry.

Narratives often focus on the cavalry's dramatic offensive campaigns and overlook infantrymen, who performed the more routine tasks of escorting surveying parties, military prisoners, and payroll and supply shipments. Infantry also received a disproportionate share of kitchen and hospital duties and sanitation detail. Although their activities attracted less attention, they nonetheless performed hazardous tasks in isolated groups of four or five that were vulnerable to surprise attacks. Troopers knew full well the perils of their work. Complaints reached the fort commander in July 1868 about five soldiers from the Thirty-eighth assigned to protect railroad water tanks. Housed in small shelters with ten-day rations, the troops fired indiscriminately at anyone—white, black, or Indian—who ventured too close. Lest the frightened infantrymen fire on peaceful Native people and provoke conflict, officers ordered them to deal cautiously with anyone who approached rather than resorting to gunfire.[9]

Black soldiers often are depicted as victims, thereby emphasizing the army's racial prejudice. Indeed, discrimination did occur; troops frequently suffered abuse by bigoted officers and received harsher punishments than white soldiers for disciplinary offenses. The prohibition against blacks serving as officers even in their own regiments indicates the army's low initial regard for their abilities.[10] Yet deplorable conditions awaited all of the western army's enlisted men, no matter their color. None would have asserted "equality" as a goal; the military, after all, constituted a system of institutionalized inequality. But that did not negate the possibility of fair treatment from officers who interacted with the men on a daily basis. In fact, at Fort Hays, white commanders often became their troops' greatest partisans, even protecting them from hostile civilians. In a macabre way, blacks and whites stationed there achieved a certain degree of equality: both lived abominably.

Fort Hays differed little from most outposts during its first few months, consisting merely of several tents and crude huts. Its isolated location limited the range of leisure activities—not that much leisure time was available. Poor hygiene and sanitation rendered soldiers vulnerable to disease. Beginning in July 1867, a devastating cholera epidemic swept the western forts, striking the black units especially hard. Cholera killed seven men of the Thirty-eighth Infantry that summer but the Tenth Cavalry lost more than twenty men, more than half the regiment's total number of combat deaths up to 1918.[11] Conditions gradually improved after the Union Pacific Railroad reached Hays in October 1867, particularly because it brought fresh supplies and materials for building permanent structures. Yet poor health continued to sap the garrison's strength. Despite their dangerous duties, soldiers obtained medical treatment more frequently for pneumonia and other ailments than for combat injuries. Gastrointestinal illnesses were especially common; nearly a third of the post's black soldiers received treatment for diarrhea.[12]

Health officials knew that improved hygiene and fresh food would decrease these problems yet found implementing such simple improvements difficult. Quartermasters unsuccessfully tried to provide unspoiled meat, while either insects or neglect doomed the post's paltry attempt at growing its own vegetables.[13] Most enlisted men, regardless of color, cared little for personal cleanliness. Assistant surgeon William Buchannon complained that Tenth cavalrymen stacked all their dirty clothes and muddy stable equipment under the bunks, attracting flies to an already crowded and improperly ventilated barracks.[14]

Constant guard and escort duty, as well as the transient nature of army life makes such apathy seem understandable. Similarly, Fort Hays's hectic work load left enlisted men little time or inclination to attend the post school that taught reading, writing, addition, and subtraction. What leisure time existed was spent enjoying the benefits of steady pay. Earnings ranged from thirteen dollars a month for new privates to thirty dollars for noncommissioned officers. Although some men sent money to families back East, most wages purchased necessities from the post sutler's store or from local civilian merchants. A considerable amount ended up in the town's many taverns and brothels.

Drunkenness affected all troops at Fort Hays, including buffalo soldiers. Post records include many accounts of privates charged with neglecting duty or engaging in disorderly conduct while under the influence of alcohol. Perhaps because their isolated work made it easier and more tempting to sneak a drink, the Thirty-eighth Infantry seemed particularly prone to such problems. In February 1868 the commander placed

pickets to arrest all personnel who were intoxicated, created a disturbance or lacked passes signed by a superior officer. Typical punishment
for drink-related offenses involved a fine, brief incarceration, or a reduction in rank.[15]

Why the high frequency of alcohol use? The combination of disease,
separation from family, fear of Indian attack, and general loneliness
likely inspired many to seek solace from a bottle. Frontier racism made
intoxication particularly dangerous for black soldiers. Since the white
public perceived the black units as experimental at best, charges of drunkenness and immorality could easily taint black regiments' reputations.
At Fort Hays, the picket guard decreased alcohol-related offenses but
did not necessarily increase sobriety. When getting drunk on the fort became too risky, soldiers waited until payday and visited taverns in Hays
City. This proved dangerous for the black soldier since he was subject to
civilian law, not military, and white locals had extremely little patience
with unruly armed blacks.

The violent atmosphere and miserable, disease-ridden conditions encouraged many desertions from the frontier military. In 1867 more than
fourteen thousand men deserted the U.S. Army, nearly a quarter of its
total strength.[16] Most deserters disappeared successfully into civilian populations; the military simply lacked the time and manpower to pursue
runaways. Cavalrymen especially were likely to make clean breaks since
they took their horses and all the army property they could carry, including food, mules, wagons, and firearms. Elizabeth Custer described
how forty men deserted Fort Hays in one night, leaving officers fearful
that the garrison would soon lack sufficient protection.[17]

Romanticized works on buffalo soldiers point proudly to their low
desertion rates, a claim partly supported by statistics from Fort Hays.
While more than half of the Seventh Cavalry deserted in only one year,
a mere fourteen deserters were reported from Fort Hays's black regiments during its first five years.[18] Although drunkenness and insubordination were common among all enlisted men, desertion appeared primarily to be a white phenomenon. The dearth of black western settlers,
and black soldiers' distinctive appearance, made it difficult for potential
deserters to blend into nearby communities. One should not, however,
discount the more idealistic explanation that blacks' group identity and
pride discouraged desertion. Despite its pitfalls, military service offered
African American males opportunities for self-respect seldom matched
in Reconstruction America.

Desertion rates remained high throughout the post—Civil War period but peaked in 1871.[19] By then Indian resistance in the Hays vicinity had nearly disappeared, even though the fort remained a valuable transportation depot and winter quarters. As white settlement increased, a reciprocal relationship developed between the post and nearby Hays City. Town merchants provided needed goods and services while the army employed civilian laborers on construction projects. Likewise, the thousands of dollars of army pay spent in Hays City fertilized a prosperous local economy.

Beneath this symbiosis lay major currents of hostility. Hays City resembled other western communities where violence between soldiers and civilians contributed to the region's reputation for bloodshed. If Civil War veterans were praised as heroes, federal regulars, often immigrants and displaced industrial workers, were often seen as rabble.[20] The proliferation of saloons and brothels that sprang up around every military post offended new settlers' puritanical values.[21] In addition, many westerners dismissed the federal regulars as ineffective Indian fighters, even resenting their presence. One Kansan, explaining why the state militia could deal with local hostilities more effectively, ridiculed the army's ceaseless bugling, alerting enemies as soldiers prepared to attack, retreat, awake, or go to bed.[22] Uniformed soldiers frequently elicited jokes or insults from civilians, not respect. In the case of a uniformed freedman, reactions could be openly hostile, especially among former Confederates for whom buffalo soldiers provided a visible reminder of Southern defeat.

These charged emotions played out in the chaos of western communities during early years of development. Although scholarship on Kansas cattle towns emphasizes the exaggeration of violence in popular myth, Hays City, established in October 1867 as a Union Pacific terminus, lay beyond most major cattle trails, and its violence came not from rowdy Texas cattle drovers but from transients looking for profits from the railroad.[23] An eastern Kansas newspaper described Hays's citizenry in unflattering terms:

> Gamblers, pimps, prostitutes, and dead beats, run the town, and the most unblushing defiance of everything that is decent is the prevailing sentiment. One year ago, for the joke of the thing, they elected a prostitute as one of the School Board, and another Street Commissioner. How it is to be expected black or white soldiers will act

any other way when they get a taste of the lightning poison vended there is a mystery to us. We hope the authorities of the State will incur no expense in protecting any such a class as runs Hays City.[24]

Observers did not exaggerate the town's horrific level of violence; from 1867 to 1874, Hays City saw more than thirty recorded homicides.[25] During periods of ineffective civilian law enforcement, black troops served as the town guard. In late 1867, a visitor recorded that:

> Hays City is really under martial law, the town being policed by soldiers from the fort; and, what makes it trebly obnoxious to some, the soldiers are colored. They certainly have the credit, however, of maintaining quiet and general good order throughout the day and night: that is, quiet for a frontier town.[26]

Actually, the presence of federal regulars exacerbated more violence than it prevented. Nearly half of all homicides up to 1874, thirteen, resulted from altercations between soldiers and civilians.[27]

Considering the color of the troops involved, a problem arises in trying to separate "racial" violence from the larger pattern of civilian-military violence everywhere, regardless of race. Simply because an episode involved a black participant did not mean it had racial causes. The key distinction rests on whether an incident originated from some discriminatory behavior based on skin color. By that criteria, not all violence involving blacks during Hays City's first three years can be classified as racial. But the Fort Hays experience certainly shows a hardening of white opinions toward armed African Americans, reflected not only in the callous actions of local toughs but in how state newspapers reported such activity.

Black soldiers did not behave like passive victims of prejudice. The same group cohesion that discouraged black desertions encouraged a search for vengeance when a soldier was wronged or insulted. White troops shared the feud mentality that characterized fort-town relations; if an individual returned to the post bruised or bloodied, comrades shielded him from discovery until they could get revenge on his assailants.[28] For buffalo soldiers, however, the drive to retaliate appeared especially strong. During a national age of violent racism, the army's black frontiersmen upheld the doctrine of "eye for an eye." Their refusal to tolerate abuse certainly deserves a measure of admiration, but their actions ultimately intensified white prejudice, creating a cycle of hatred that resembled an ongoing blood feud.

The First Violent Encounter

The first violent encounter, initiated by townspeople, illustrates how officers generally sided with their men. Prior to the picket guard's establishment in February 1868, post commanders had to deal with the habitual problem of troops leaving the fort without permission. On December 21, 1867, a small detail was sent to retrieve all those absent without leave, most of whom were imbibing in civilian saloons. Privates Charles Allen, Thirty-eighth Company E, and John Washington, Tenth Cavalry Company I, demanded admittance to an establishment where AWOL soldiers reportedly languished. When they were refused, Allen began beating the door with his weapon. The saloonkeeper, Matthew "Red" Flinn, fired several shots, killing Allen and severely wounding Washington. The town guard, Allen's fellow infantrymen, immediately began searching for Flinn. Later the same evening a local named Cornelius Doyle accosted Corp. Albert E. Cropper, Thirty-eighth Company G, cursing him and shouting that "any damned nigger soldiers hunting Red" would be killed. The argument ended when Doyle apparently attempted to draw his pistol and Cropper fatally shot him with his rifle.[29]

While Allen's death produced no great uproar, talk immediately filled the streets about lynching Cropper. Civilian newspapers described Doyle's shooting far differently than the official military report. The *Hays City Railway Advance* claimed Doyle gave Cropper no "provocation whatever," a charge repeated by a Hays resident in a hearsay letter to the *Lawrence Tribune*.[30] Following his arrest and preliminary hearing, Cropper was transferred to the post guardhouse for his own protection. Meanwhile, fort commander Capt. Samuel Ovenshine had arranged with county authorities to offer a reward for Red Flinn, who had left the county and later was located near Leavenworth.[31]

Whether Cropper really acted in self-defense cannot decisively be determined from the disparate accounts, even though his record shows no history of similar trouble.[32] Yet the fact that disparate accounts exist at all reveals how differently the civilian and military communities perceived the incident. Already suspicious of the patrol guard, residents now thought the army had protected a murderer. To prevent further hos-

tility, Ovenshine withdrew the patrol and returned Hays City to the jurisdiction of civil law, the inefficiency of which only contributed to Cropper's eventual acquittal. By the time the district court reconvened after a
six-month hiatus, only one witness to Doyle's shooting remained in the
county, and Cropper's case was dismissed for lack of suitable jurors.[33]

The killings of Allen and Doyle commenced years of hostility between the fort and town. While Cropper awaited trial, minor conflicts
between black soldiers and white townsfolk continued through 1868, the
same year Hays City came under control of an organized vigilante group.
The vigilance committee visited perceived troublemakers and ordered
them to leave town. Despite their stated purpose of establishing peace,
vigilantes only increased local violence; thirteen documented murders
occurred in 1869, the town's peak year for homicides.[34] While most eastern Kansas newspapers denounced the situation, at least one, the *Lawrence Tribune*, partly defended vigilante activity by declaring that lax
law enforcement required citizens to protect themselves. In recalling the
army's protection of the "murderer" Cropper, the writer implied the
committee's real purpose was to defend the community from black soldiers.[35] In a state known for its supposed racial liberality, press coverage
of events in Hays City paralleled what Democratic newspapers said
about Southern race relations: armed, aggressive blacks, protected by a
disliked federal military, posed threats to public safety. The *Leavenworth
Daily Commercial* even likened the violence to southern "black outrages"
provoked by radical Republicans.[36] Attitudes became even more "Confederate sounding" after a murder by black soldiers in early 1869 led to
one of Kansas's few known racial lynchings.

Leading to a Lynching

Civilian and military accounts concur that the events of January 5–7 began when privates Luke Barnes, Lee Watkins, and James Ponder were refused admission into a local brothel. Prostitutes, in Hays at least, rarely
discriminated on skin color, so more than likely the men's disruptive behavior prompted the refusal. All three belonged to the Thirty-eighth Infantry, Company E, and at least two, Watkins and Ponder, had enlisted
together in Nashville and spent detached service away from the post, protecting railroad camps.[37] Later that evening, the trio invaded the shop of
a black civilian barber named John White. Hiding from the men's rage
while they drunkenly smashed his shop, White heard the troops boast

that they planned to get revenge for the deaths of their comrades by killing the next white man they saw. Wandering into the street, the trio opened fire on a Union Pacific watchman named James Hayes, a citizen of Leavenworth. Shot in the stomach, his spine severed, Hayes lived until the following morning, describing his assailants only as "two niggers."[38]

Evidence against Barnes, Watkins, and Ponder would have been extremely meager without John White's testimony. Accompanied by the county sheriff and a federal marshal on January 6, White identified the three out of a lineup of the entire garrison, explaining the vandalism to his shop and their stated intent to kill a white person. The barber's testimony placed the post commander, Lt. Col. Anderson Nelson, in a precarious position. Authorities insisted Nelson release the three to civilian custody rather than placing them under military protection like Cropper. Besides the resentment such an action would generate among his troops, Nelson must have known about the defendants' tenuous safety in a Hays jail cell, especially with the vigilance committee in operation. With tensions between soldiers and civilians running high, Nelson decided on a conciliatory gesture and permitted county police to assume custody of the privates, who were arraigned later that day before a justice of the peace and placed under overnight guard.

Luke Barnes, Lee Watkins, and James Ponder never saw their case brought to trial. During the evening of January 6–7, a mob stormed the jail, overpowered the guards, and seized the prisoners from their cells. One account reported the mob's size as between seventy-five and one hundred, all with masks or darkened faces. The vigilantes hanged the men from the ties of a railroad bridge half a mile west of town. Union Pacific employees discovered their bodies the next morning.

Eastern Kansas newspapers, long contemptuous of Hays City's vigilante tradition, suddenly applauded the lynching. In James Hayes's hometown of Leavenworth, the *Daily Commercial* delighted in providing a detailed and hearsay version of the hanging:

> Sometime during the night the vigilantes released the mokes from prison and indulged them in a dance in mid-air in which they executed a treble shuffle, something of a novelty in negro breakdowns which are chiefly remarkable for merely a double shuffle. No doubt existed of the guilt of the parties, as they sloshed around extensively brandishing their Springfield rifles, and threatening vengeance on the whites.

The men and brethren appear to be rather airy out on the
plains, . . . Let us have peace![39]

The likelihood that Barnes, Watkins, and Ponder would have been convicted and executed anyway illustrates this incident's strong racist motives. Hays City's high number of homicides shows remarkable tolerance
for violence—except when perpetrated by blacks. Rather than simply
hanging three killers, the lynching issued a statement that racial norms
concerning troublesome blacks would be enforced illegally if necessary.

Retaliation for Lynching

Unlike other racial lynchings, however, the January 1869 episode involved U.S. soldiers, not usually known for meekness in the face of violence. Troops of the Thirty-eighth Infantry performed the unpleasant
task of retrieving their comrades' bodies and preparing them for burial.[40]
Rather than intimidating soldiers, the lynching only enraged both the
officers and enlisted men. Lieutenant Colonel Nelson, whose disastrous
decision had placed the three within vigilante reach, responded with his
own retaliatory measures. On January 14 Nelson sent a Thirty-eighth
detachment into Hays City to arrest all persons out after curfew. Black
soldiers raided a ballroom and arrested fifty-one people, jailing them
overnight at the fort guardhouse. Nelson later wrote Governor James
Harvey that because of the rumored plots against his men, he intended
to close the saloons and livery stables and even declare martial law if necessary.[41]

Such drastic steps became unnecessary as a short-lived calm ensued
following the lynching. In late January, rustlers stole several head of livestock from the post herd. The troops—their tempers running high—
blamed locals for the theft. On February 6 Tom Butler, a white ex-
quartermaster's employee who had been fired on suspicion of stealing,
left town following the Union Pacific tracks East. When a mule was reported missing the next day, officials dispatched a search party that consisted of the quartermaster and post surgeon, a civilian detective and
numerous employees, and ten soldiers from the Thirty-eighth Infantry.
Tracking and cornering Butler at a water tank, the group choked him
with a rope until he confessed to participation in a rustling gang. The
party then divided, with fort officials and employees in one group and the
black troops escorting Butler in another. Likely recalling their friends'

treatment a month earlier, the soldiers shot Butler and left his corpse in an abandoned house. The mule he supposedly had stolen turned up wandering a few miles from the fort.[42]

Clearly an act of revenge, Butler's murder illustrates the complicity of white military authorities. Tired of incessant attacks on the army's men and property, white officers willingly sided with black troops in using Butler as an example, frustrating any designation of the violence as purely racial. A Hays citizen summarized the situation: "There has been for some time much unpleasant feeling existing between the authorities of Hays City and Ft. Hays, commenced by the hanging of the three negro soldiers by the Vig's. . . ."[43] Indeed, the bad blood between fort and town transcended race, reflecting a larger pattern of antipathy characterizing civilian-military relations. In April, during the Nineteenth Kansas Cavalry's station at Fort Hays, white troops congregated nightly in Hays City, engaging in brawls and shootings with locals. As both the size and number of violent episodes increased, large gangs of black and white soldiers marched the streets armed en masse. Meanwhile, fort officials exercised little control over the troops' nightly sojourns.[44]

Shootout and Rampage

In May 1869 two years of animosity climaxed in an armed confrontation that shared many features with modern race riots. Newspapers claimed that black soldiers planned to burn Hays City to the ground, a possibility in the wake of the lynching. Yet because the troops had just been paid and drunkenness and fighting often accompanied receipt of wages, it appears the violence began with the alcohol. According to admittedly biased civilian sources, several black infantrymen tried to break into a brothel from which they earlier had been refused admission. A scuffle began, with troops lining up in battle formation and opening fire into nearby homes and businesses. Townspeople returned the fire, shooting from doors and windows and exchanging more than four hundred shots in about half an hour.[45]

At this point, fort officials finally took decisive action, dispatching soldiers from the Fifth Cavalry to quell the disturbance and ordering all infantrymen hack to the post.[46] As white cavalrymen attempted to break up the melee, several residents embarked on a rampage against Hays City's few black civilians. Vigilante ruffians ordered all black families out of town and murdered two African American barbers. Of the newspapers that reported the atrocities, only the *Kansas Daily Commonwealth* voiced contempt for the deed:

> Hays City has added another laurel to its garland of infamy. The other night—after the affray—a full account of which appeared in our special dispatches—was ended and the soldiers had been withdrawn. a party of roughs deliberately hunted down and murdered two peaceful and unoffending barbers. who were citizens of the town, and as quiet and harmless men as it afforded. Honest and decent men will want for language to express their indignation at this brutal and cowardly outrage.[47]

Apparently, the two barbers became the only fatalities during the evening's chaos. The post surgeon recorded no gunfire injuries but newspapers reported six wounded civilians, including a U.S. deputy marshal, and a white trooper from the Seventh Cavalry.[48]

While the events of May 1 definitely had racial motivations, classifying them as a "race riot" is not quite accurate, occurring as they did during a period of vigilante activity. In its coverage of the incident, the *Commonwealth* even pointed out that not all the discord derived from blacks' or even the military's proximity:

> it is certain that human life and limbs are altogether too unsafe in that locality. Every trifling dispute is settled by an instantaneous appeal to the pistol or the knife. All things considered. Hays City is one of the best places to move away from that can be found upon the globe.[49]

Buffalo soldiers proved a contributing but not determinative factor in the town's history of conflict. In late April and early May, the Thirty-eighth companies relocated to new assignments on the Mexican border, leaving Fort Hays with fewer than a hundred troops by summer of 1869.[50] Even so, the community's reputation for bloodshed continued, with friction between soldiers and civilians remaining a constant. In 1871, a saloon brawl involving white troops escalated into gunfire, resulting in the death of the county sheriff.[51]

One should not isolate racial tensions from their larger social context and exaggerate their importance over other causes of violence. Yet the buffalo soldiers' presence did produce long-lasting hostility toward the black population. As the *Daily Tribune* stated, "Hays City seems to have many of the same ideas that unreconstructed rebels have, to wit:

that negroes have no rights which a white man is bound to respect."[52] Following their eviction in May 1869, some black families were permitted to return, a decision most later regretted. In March 1871, four residents were arraigned for invading the home of an elderly black woman and raping her. Whites expressed disgust that the men were arrested on the word of "colored people." Fearing for their safety, the fort commander permitted all black families to relocate into dugouts on the post for protection, with troops once again sent into town to restore order.[53] The 1869 lynching and other such episodes firmly established the area's reputation as an unsafe place for African Americans. An observer in 1909 commented on the community's white homogeneity:

> no negro has ever ventured to make Hays a place of residence. An occasional straggler has worked a few days in town, but the history of the place has appealed too strongly to his imagination for him to remain.[54]

Conclusion

Fort Hays's predominantly black garrison and its hostile relationship with citizens in Hays City provide an example of how civilian-military social interaction helped to transfer racial hatreds to the newly conquered region. The years from 1867 to 1869 saw African Americans' introduction to regular army life, the beginning of a twenty-year process in which they would forcibly help to seize western lands from American Indians. Prejudice always remained a factor in their lives but as the Hays City experience indicates, their active involvement in a local cycle of hatred obscured whatever achievements whites might have recognized and intensified racist paranoia.

Whether black soldiers' participation in an occupying army deserves praise or criticism, of course, remains a matter of individual perspective and moral judgment, an arena in which the historian can claim no particular authority. Yet if history teaches any lesson, it is that one group's pride may be another's tragedy. As Vernon Bellecourt has asked, "Which do we value more, a wildly bastardized fable of progress and equality, or truth? Justice is the act of conscious, informed human beings."[55] In the recent rush to reveal the buffalo soldiers' past, historians should not forget the dual importance of understanding their legacy, lest new myths be created similar to those that once depicted white soldiers like Custer as heroes. Furthermore, the buffalo soldiers existed not only as enlistees in the fight against Indians but as actors in a complex theatre of negotiations framed by civilian whites' racism and the usual conflicts between army and civilians in a garrison town. Just as ethnocentric interpretations once regarded black history as insignificant, romanticizing the buffalo soldiers' experience not only perpetuates distortion, but it also robs them of the right to be judged not as representatives of an entire race but as human beings capable of human error.

Notes

1. For an overview of the black cavalry's official duties, William H. Leckie's *The Buffalo Soldiers: A Narrative of the Negro Cavalry in the West* (Norman: University of Oklahoma Press, 1967) has become a classic. Arlen L. Fowler's *The Black Infantry in the West, 1869–1891* (Westport, Conn.: Greenwood Press, 1971); and John M. Carroll's edited collection, *The Black Military Experience in the American West* (New York: Liveright Publishing, 1971) also provide valuable descriptive information. For more recent works that deal with black soldiers' reception in civilian communities and their relationships with white officers, see Monroe Lee Billington, *New Mexico's Buffalo Soldiers, 1866–1900* (Niwot, Colo.: University Press of Colorado, 1991); and Frank N. Schubert's *Buffalo Soldiers, Braves, and the Brass* (Shippensburg, Penn.: White Mane Publishing, 1993).

2. Vernon Bellecourt, "The Glorification of Buffalo Soldiers Raises Racial Divisions between Blacks, Indians," *Indian Country Today* (May 4, 1994): 5(A).

3. For general information on Fort Hays, see Leo Oliva, *Fort Hays, Frontier Army Post, 1865–1889* (Topeka: Kansas State Historical Society, 1980). Robert M. Utley's *Frontier Regulars: The United States Army and the Indian, 1866–1891* (Lincoln: University of Nebraska Press, 1984) provides a thorough discussion of the late 1860s campaigns.

4. Studies of the buffalo soldiers' impact on local race relations commonly focus on specific forts and communities. For useful examples, see Monroe Lee Billington, "Black Soldiers at Fort Selden, New Mexico, 1866–1891," *New Mexico Historical Review* 62 (1987): 65–80; Thomas R. Buecker, "Confrontation at Sturgis: An Episode in Civil-Military Race Relations, 1885," *South Dakota History* 14 (Fall 1984): 238–61; Michael J. Clark, "Improbable Ambassadors: Black Soldiers at Fort Douglas, 1896–1899," *Utah Historical Quarterly* 46 (1978): 282–301; and Ronald G. Coleman, "The Buffalo Soldiers: Guardians of the Utah Frontier, 1886–1901," *Utah Historical Quarterly* 47 (1979): 421–39.

5. Dudley Taylor Cornish, "Kansas Negro Regiments in the Civil War," *Kansas Historical Quarterly* 20 (May 1953): 417–29. For a more detailed discussion of the black volunteers, see Cornish, *The Sable Arm: Black Troops in the Union Army, 1861–1865* (Lawrence: University of Kansas Press, 1956); and Joseph

T. Glatthaar, *Forged in Battle: The Civil War Alliance of Black Soldiers and White Officers* (New York: Free Press, 1990).

6. Robert Ahearn, *In Search of Canaan: Black Migration to Kansas, 1879–80* (Lawrence: University Press of Kansas, 1978); and Nell Irvin Painter, *Exodusters: Black Migration to Kansas after Reconstruction* (New York: Alfred A. Knopf, 1971).

7. For discussion of the frontier concept, see Patricia Nelson Limerick, Clyde A. Milner II, and Charles E. Rankin, eds., *Trails: Toward a New Western History* (Lawrence: University Press of Kansas, 1991).

8. December 1867 monthly returns show Companies E and G, Thirty-eighth Infantry, and Companies F and I, Tenth Cavalry, to be present. Of the 435 enlisted men, 285 belonged to black regiments. Headquarters, Tenth Cavalry, Special Order No. 139, Fort Riley, Kansas, 26 November 1867, Letters Received (LR), Fort Hays (FH), National Archives Microfilm Publication (NAMP), T-837, roll 5; and Post Returns, Fort Hays, December 1867, Adjutant General's Office (AGO), Record Group (RG) 94, NAMP, 113.

9. Brevet Major E. A. Belger to Major John Yard, Tenth Cavalry, Post Commander of Fort Hays, 16 July 1868, LR, FH, NAMP, T-713, roll 5.

10. Descriptions of prejudice are available in Billington, *New Mexico's Buffalo Soldiers* (n. 1 above), 181–201; and Arlen L. Fowler, *Black Infantry in the West* (n. 1 above), 114–39. Jack D. Foner's "The Negro in the Post–Civil War Army," in *The United States Soldier between Two Wars: Army Life and Reforms,1865–1898* (New York: Humanities Press, 1970), 127–47, describes army and civilian attitudes toward the black units in attempts to replace them with integrated regiments.

11. James N. Leiker, "Voices from a Disease Frontier: Kansans and Cholera, 1867," *Kansas History* 17 (Winter 1995): 236–53; and Roman Powers and Gene Younger, "Cholera on the Plains: The Epidemic of 1867 in Kansas," *Kansas Historical Quarterly* 37 (1971): 351–93; Post Returns, FH, July and August 1867, AGO, RG 94, NAMP, roll 3; Edward L. N. Glass, *The History of the Tenth Cavalry, 1866–1921* (Fort Collins: Old Army Press, 1972), 95.

12. Monthly Registers of the Sick and Wounded, FH, NAMP, and T-713. Dysentery, rheumatism, bronchitis, syphilis, and gonorrhea were also prevalent.

13. Oliva, *Fort Hays* (n. 3 above), 57.

14. Report of William Buchannon, Assistant Surgeon, July 14, 1868, Monthly Surgeon's Reports, FH, NAMP, T-837, roll 3.

15. General Order no. 8, February 21, 1868, General Orders, FH, NAMP, T-713, roll 20.

16. For discussion of army desertion rates in the post–Civil War period and their causes, see Foner, *United States Soldier* (n. 10 above), 6–10, 222–24.

17. Elizabeth Bacon Custer, *Tenting on the Plains* (New York: Charles L. Webster, 1887), 695. This edition should not to be confused with the 1895 abridged version, which contains no reference to the forty deserters.

18. Monthly Post Returns, FH, 1866–71, AGO, RG 94, NAMP.

19. Foner, *United States Soldier* (n. 10 above), 222–23.

20. For public perceptions of federal regulars, see ibid., 59–75.

21. Billington, *New Mexico's Buffalo Soldiers* (n. 1 above), 181–82.

22. *Leavenworth Daily Conservative,* July 10, 1867.

23. For the myth of violence, see Robert R. Dykstra, *The Cattle Towns* (Lincoln: University of Nebraska Press, 1966). For a more recent revisionist example, see Ty Cashion's "(Gun)Smoke Gets in Your Eyes: A Revisionist Look at Violent Fort Griffin," *Southwestern Historical Quarterly* 99 (July 1995): 81–94.

24. *Junction City Weekly Union,* May 8, 1869.

25. James D. Drees, "The Hays City Vigilante Period, 1868–1869" (Master's thesis, Fort Hays State University, 1983), 105–7.

26. *Kansas Daily Tribune,* November 26, 1867.

27. Drees, "Hays City Vigilante Period" (n. 25 above), 8.

28. Elizabeth Custer, *Following the Guidon* (New York: Harper and Brothers, 1890), 155.

29. Capt. Samuel Ovenshine, Fifth Infantry, Post Commander, FH, to Brevet Capt. M. Howard, Fort Harker, February 2, 1868, Letters Sent (LS), FH, NA, RG 393 (Continental Commands), Part 5; *Atchison Daily Free Press,* January 4, 1868 (quoted).

30. *Kansas Daily Tribune,* December 25, 1867; *Railway Alliance,* December 24, 1867.

31. Ovenshine to J. M. Soule, Esq., Justice of the Peace, and J. E. Walker, Pres. of Ellis Co. Board of Commissioners, January 30, 1868, LS, FH, NA, RG 393, Continental Commands, Part 5; Ovenshine to Howard (n. 29 above).

32. Muster rolls show Cropper as born in Baltimore, aged twenty-one at time of enlistment in May 1867, and having been promoted to corporal within six months. He was discharged in 1870 at expiration of service and reenlisted twice, joining the Ninth Cavalry in 1875. Enlistment records describe his character as "excellent." Unit Muster Rolls, Thirty-eighth Infantry, Company G, 1868, RG 94, NA; and Enlistment Papers, RG 94, NA.

33. *Railway Alliance,* December 24, 1867; *Kansas Daily Tribune,* January 10, 1869.

34. Drees, "Hays City Vigilante Period" (n. 25 above), 8. Of many local histories of Hays City's "gunfighter period," this provides the most thorough discussion of vigilante violence and its causes.

35. *Kansas Daily Tribune,* January 10, 1869.

36. *Leavenworth Daily Commercial,* January 9, 1869.

37. Information on Barnes, Watkins, and Ponder was obtained from Unit Muster Rolls, Thirty-eighth Infantry, Company E, 1868–69, NA, RG 94.

38. Lt. Col. Anderson Nelson, Fifth Infantry, Post Commander, FH, to Governor James Harvey, January 18, 1869, LS, FH, NA, RG 393, Part 5. This contains the first official mention of the lynching by military personnel but since Nelson did not elaborate, detailed information in this and the following paragraphs derives from civilian newspapers. *Leavenworth Times and Conservative,* January 9, 1869, provided a very brusque summation. *Leavenworth Daily Commercial,* January 9 and 12, 1869, delivered the most factual details but also the

most editorial comment, praising civilian law officers' handling of the matter. Though the papers vary in their reporting, all agree, including *The Kansas Daily Tribune,* January 10, 1869, on the points presented here.

39. *Leavenworth Daily Commercial,* January 9, 1869.

40. *Kansas Daily Tribune,* January 10, 1869.

41. *Leavenworth Times and Conservative,* January 16, 1869; Nelson to Harvey, (n. 38 above).

42. *Kansas Daily Tribune,* February 19, 1869.

43. Ibid.

44. Drees, "Hays City Vigilante Period" (n. 25 above), 42.

45. Both the *Leavenworth Times and Conservative,* May 4, 1869, and *Kansas Daily Tribune,* May 8, 1869, claimed the blacks had a predetermined plan to burn the town.

46. 1st Lt. Mason Carter to Capt. J. W. Clous, Thirty-Eighth Infantry, May 3, 1869; and Carter to Capt. Sam Ovenshine, May 3, 1869, LS, FH, NA, RG 393, Part 5.

47. *Kansas Daily Commonwealth,* May 6, 1869, reprinted in *Junction City Weekly Union,* May 8, 1869.

48. *Kansas Daily Commonwealth,* May 4, 1869; *Leavenworth Daily Times and Conservative,* May 4, 1869; *Kansas Daily Tribune,* May 8, 1869; and Monthly Register of the Sick and Wounded, May 1869, FH, NAMP, T-837, roll 3A.

49. *Kansas Daily Commonwealth,* May 4, 1869.

50. Post Returns, April 1869, FH, NAMP, T- 713, roll 20.

51. *White Cloud Chief,* July 27, 1871.

52. *Kansas Daily Tribune,* May 8, 1869.

53. Maj. Gen. Gibson to Acting Assistant Adj. Gen., Headquarters, Department of the Missouri, Fort Leavenworth, March 4 and 5, 1871, LS, FH, NA, RG 393, Part 5.

54. James Beach, "Old Fort Hays," *Kansas Historical Collections* 11 (1909–10): 580.

55. Bellecourt, "Glorification of Buffalo Soldiers" (n. 2 above), 5(A).

FRANK N. SCHUBERT

Black Soldiers on the White Frontier

SOME FACTORS INFLUENCING RACE RELATIONS

A body of literature concerning the use of black soldiers on the post–Civil War frontier has emerged in recent years. Some of these new studies have focused on the black soldiers themselves and others have dealt with them tangentially to other central topics.[1] However, all of the works share one common characteristic. They have left largely untouched the question of what formed the attitudes of white frontier communities toward black soldiers.

All the factors that shaped the responses of frontier communities to black military garrisons may never be fully discerned. However, a study of the role of black soldiers in Wyoming, one of the frontier states in which they served, indicates that the varying conditions of frontier life played an important part in the development of white attitudes. The suggestions are tentative but may prove useful in evaluating relations between black troops and white civilians elsewhere in the frontier West.

To state that the white response was racist involves no unnecessary risks. Whites who migrated westward certainly carried their bigotry with them.[2] After black regiments were added to the regular army in 1866, distaste for black troops was therefore practically inevitable. As one professional soldier observed, "The national prejudice has followed the flag across [to] the Pacific Ocean."[3]

The Ninth Cavalry first arrived in Wyoming in 1885, a year in which seventy-four black Americans were lynched in the United States.[4] Between 1885 and 1912, the last year for black troops in Wyoming until World War II, Southern states codified their racism while the rest of the nation watched.[5] Two months after the last black troops left Wyoming,

Woodrow Wilson, who later permitted the segregation of most black employees of the federal government, was elected president.[6]

The spread of blatant racism in this period did not bypass Wyoming. The 1887 territorial code authorized optional segregation in school districts which had fifteen or more "colored children." Article VII of the state's 1890 constitution provided assurance to the contrary: "In none of the public schools. . . . shall distinction or discrimination be made on account of sex, race or color."[7] However, the choice was still available in 1940.[8]

Not all of Wyoming's racist actions provided options. Citizens of the state lynched five black Americans, and, in 1913, prohibited racial intermarriage for the second time.[9] Indeed, it seems that the "Equality State's" participation in the mainstream of American racism was restricted more by the small number of black residents than by its own inclinations.[10] Given this context, a generally racist response to the black regulars is neither surprising nor unusual. More interesting and more important for assessments of frontier race relations are the variations in the reaction to the troops and the different conditions of frontier life that they reflect.[11]

Johnson County in the rural northern part of Wyoming had demonstrated its contempt for blacks with "coon dances," before the Ninth Cavalry's 1885 arrival. The local newspaper, the *Big Horn Sentinel*,[12] recorded two such affairs in the year prior to the arrival of the black cavalrymen. Reporting of the first gala was especially detailed:

> A "coon dance" was given at the Oriental by the ladies of the House this week and was a successful as well as a novel amusement. There being no real "coons" in Big Horn, the ladies and gents blacked their faces with burnt cork and had a regular plantation breakdown. Lots of fun was had by all in attendance. "Laugh and grow fat" is the maxim of the Big Horn people.[13]

The Big Horn people were not laughing when the men of the Ninth arrived. Their hostility was clear: "The colored regiment has arrived at Fort McKinney. Wonder if it has darkened Buffalo."[14] The arrival of the Ninth converted bemused contempt into open hostility. The coming of black prostitutes in the following year converted hostility into frank advocacy of segregation. Editor E. H. Becker of the *Sentinel* began his attack by railing against "the nigger houses of prostitution, conducted openly on Main Street," in one issue and concluded in the next that, "the better class of citizens are determined to see that the color line is drawn at least in regard to who shall occupy buildings in the principal business part of town."[15]

The newspaper did not indicate adoption of Becker's solution of relocating the houses of prostitution, known as "hog ranches" among the troops, or of any other solution. What is significant is that the presence of the black cavalrymen and the black prostitutes, who were sure to follow, acted as a catalyst on Editor Becker and probably many other citizens of Buffalo. Becker's newspaper moved from tongue-in-cheek comments on "coon dances" in 1884 and 1885 to a serious and open racism in the advocacy of segregation in the Buffalo business district in 1886.

This blatantly hostile response to the black soldiers and camp followers was probably made inevitable by the composition of the population of the cattle-ranching county. Only 12 of the 637 residents recorded in 1880 were black. Virtually all of the remainder were native-born whites with a sprinkling of foreign-born but no other nonwhites.[16] The blacks were clearly regarded and treated as unwelcome intruders.

The Ninth Cavalry returned to northern Wyoming in the late spring of 1892. Their mission was to restore calm in the wake of the Johnson County cattle war.[17] They established Camp Bettens in Sheridan County, just forty miles northeast of their previous station at Fort McKinney and five miles from Suggs, a small town in which they confronted an even more intense hatred than in Buffalo. They were verbally harassed and two soldiers were denied accommodations in the local hotel while one was refused a shave by a town barber. The insults reached a climax when a local white, with drawn gun, asked a soldier, "Ain't your mother a black bitch?"[18] The troopers responded to the provocations by shooting up the town, killing two horses in the process and suffering one fatality themselves.[19] Once again the black cavalrymen had served in practically all-white rural Wyoming; once again the response was a deep and unrelenting hatred, this time leading to violence and death.[20]

The response of Cheyenne, the Wyoming town with the largest population and the greatest number of black residents, was more subtle and varied. Cheyenne had been exposed to black Americans in its earliest days. Three hundred blacks worked with the Union Pacific construction gangs, which laid track into Wyoming in 1867 and began the development of the territory.[21] A black entrepreneur, Barney L. Ford, had played a significant part in the town's early development; and a black barber, William Jefferson Hardin, had represented the city in the territorial legislature.[22] From its rude beginnings, Cheyenne had a substantial black population with its own social institutions, including two churches.[23]

When the first black troops, four companies of the Twenty-fourth Infantry, arrived in 1898, both of the city's newspapers simply ignored them until they went away. The next black contingent in the city, men of the Tenth Cavalry, were ignored by one paper, the *Wyoming Tribune*, and tentatively approved and put on probation by the other. The *Cheyenne Daily Leader* observed that, "The men seemed to be an intelligent class of Negroes, and will probably make a good record while at Fort [D. A.] Russell."[24] That paper withdrew its provisional approval five years later, after an alleged rape and a few fights, with the terse comment: "the good record is ruined."[25] The cavalrymen had flunked their test. No white unit, regardless of its record or activities in Cheyenne, ever had to undergo such an examination or live up to expectations of five continuous years of good behavior.

When the entire Ninth Cavalry arrived in Cheyenne in 1909, the same paper, perhaps overawed by the presence of nine hundred armed black men, decided that the troops had a respectable tradition and did not pose a threat to the peace of Cheyenne, as many citizens feared.[26] Even the *Tribune* broke its silence to note that, "the impression the Ninth Cavalry, the crack colored regiment now stationed at Fort Russell, is making on Cheyenne people is excellent."[27]

Cheyenne was still more interested in crimes committed by black soldiers than by whites. In December, 1911, the *Tribune* gave obviously disproportionate emphasis to black deserters. A black escapee from the Ninth, apprehended in Chicago, received front-page billing and a headline, "Negro Deserter Is Caught in Chicago"; news of the capture of two white soldiers in Pine Bluffs, Wyoming, was buried in an inside-page column, "News in Brief," along with twenty other small items.[28] The town's relatively large population, continued exposure to black Americans, and the availability of a black social structure with which the troopers could intermingle cushioned the impact of the arrival of black troops at Fort Russell. Thus Cheyenne did not regard the men as manifest intruders and local editors could respond with other than blatant hostility. They could and did ignore the troops, establish a facade of rationality and test their behavior, or offer an empty acceptance. The nature and size of Cheyenne's population permitted the expression of racism in more diverse and more genteel ways than in rural, northern Wyoming.

The reaction of the Lander community in west-central Wyoming to the black troopers more closely resembled decency than the response of any other Wyoming town.[29] Lander was a small, virtually all-white settlement with one significant feature differentiating the town from similar communities in the state. It was located adjacent to an Indian reservation, the Shoshoni and Arapahoe reserve on the Wind River.[30] This single difference—the reservation Indians displayed no tendency toward insurrection—appears to have been fundamental in shaping the attitudes of the local whites. They had probably developed, prior to the arrival of the black soldiers, what Professors Daniels and Kitano call a two-category racial system, in which the reservation Indians were, of course, the lower of the two categories. The townspeople accepted the blacks to maintain that dichotomy: "One of the gravest dangers in a three-or-more category system, where one group remains superior, is the realistic fear within that group of a coalition among the disadvantaged."[31] In effect, Lander already had its "niggers," and to further enhance the position of the blacks in the community their mission was to garrison the Wind River Reservation, or to keep down the "niggers."

Lander's commemoration of the departure of the Ninth Cavalry for Chickamauga and preparation for duty in Cuba, on April 20, 1898, clearly demonstrated the town's appreciation for the soldiers as well as its patriotism. The entire town was decorated with flags and bunting and a large delegation, led by the mayor and the town's cornet band, met the troopers on the outskirts of town. The men paraded down Main Street, accompanied by the firing of weapons and the blaring of trumpets, as they made their way through Lander. The local newspaper recorded the sentiments of the town: "We are sorry to see the soldier boys leave the post and hope that the war to which they marched will in some manner be averted and that there will be no need of them encountering any of the dangers of war."[32]

Units of the Tenth Cavalry arrived for service at Fort Washakie four years later. The newspaper took special notice of 2nd Lt. Benjamin O. Davis, who led the advance party: "A colored lieutenant, belonging to the troop of colored soldiers now on their way up from Rawlins, passed through the city on the way to the post."[33] During Lieutenant Davis's tour of duty at Lander, which lasted until his 1905 promotion to first lieutenant and reassignment to Fort Robinson, Nebraska, he was treated exactly as the white officers of his unit by the local paper. The *Clipper* noted his shopping tours in the city, just as it did the excursions of other officers, and did not again mention that he was black.[34]

When the Tenth departed in 1907, Lander and the black troopers were still on excellent terms. The *Clipper* never reported any violence and unit records do not indicate that any of the troops spent time in the local jail: "No complaints of any kind were made against them . . . at any time while they were stationed at the Post."[35] In no other Wyoming town did the black troops meet such a favorable community response. However, even Lander could not avoid racial stereotypes and degrading slang names in discussing the troops, whose minstrel performance was billed as "original Darky Melodies by original darkies," and who were "always a happy-go-lucky sort," perhaps slightly better than the local conception of the cheerful, carefree, and irresponsible black civilian.[36]

The experience of the black regiments in Wyoming may be typical of their experience throughout most of the western frontier. Manifestations of racism in the Southwest were apt to be more brutal than on the Northern frontier; the Cheyenne, Wyoming, experience certainly offers no explanation for the Houston, Texas, riot of 1917.[37] With this obvious exception, racism in western cities, which were conditioned to the presence of some blacks, probably manifested itself in more subtle and varied ways than it did in isolated agricultural regions, like those in northern Wyoming. Racism may have been mildest and whites most tolerant of black soldiers in communities near Indian reservations.[38] In fact, the Indian reservation may well have exerted a greater positive influence on black and white relations than American egalitarian rhetoric or the frontier itself.

Notes

1. Most notable is William H. Leckie's *The Buffalo Soldiers: A Narrative of the Negro Cavalry in the West* (Norman, Oklahoma, 1967). Other studies of varying quality and significance include Jean I. Castles, "The West: Crucible of the Negro," *Montana, the Magazine of Western History,* 19 (November 1969): 83–85; Jack D. Forbes, *Afro-Americans in the Far West: A Handbook for Educators* (Washington, D.C.: Government Printing Office, 1970); Donnie D. Good, "The Buffalo Soldiers," *American Scene* 10 (April 1970); Thomas D. Phillips, "The Black Regulars," in *The West of the American People,* ed. Allan G. Bogue, Thomas D. Phillips, and James E. Wright, 138–43 (Itasca, Ill.: Peacock Publishers, 1970), 138–43; Dale T. Schoenberger, "The Black Man in the American West," *Negro History Bulletin,* 32 (March 1969): 7–11; Donald Smyth, "John J. Pershing at Fort Assiniboine," *Montana* 18 (Winter 1968): 19–23; Robert M. Utley, "'Pecos Bill' on the Texas Frontier," *American West* 6 (January 1969): 4–13, 61–62.

2. Eugene H. Berwanger has shown that racism did not decline with West-

ward movement. *The Frontier against Slavery: Western Anti-Negro Prejudice and the Slavery Extension Controversy* (Urbana: University of Illinois Press, 1967).

3. Capt. Matthew F. Steele, "The 'Color Line' in the Army," *North American Review* 183 (December 21, 1906): 1288. Captain Steele, an 1883 graduate of the U.S. Military Academy, served with white units throughout his career.

4. Peter M. Bergman, *The Chronological History of the Negro in America* (New York: HarperCollins, 1969), 296. The Ninth was one of four black regiments in the regular army. The others were the Tenth Cavalry and the Twenty-fourth and Twenty-fifth infantry regiments.

5. August Meier and Elliott Rudwick, *From Plantation to Ghetto* (New York: Farrar Straus Giroux, 1968), 157, 164.

6. John Hope Franklin, *From Slavery to Freedom* (New York: Alfred A. Knopf, 1964), 446.

7. John W. Blake, Willis Van Devanter, and Isaac P. Caldwell, eds., *Revised Statutes of Wyoming* (Cheyenne: Daily Sun Steam Printing House, 1887), 836. There are no indications that a school district ever exercised the option.

8. Charles S. Mangum Jr., *The Legal Status of the Negro* (Chapel Hill: University of North Carolina Press, 1940), 81.

9. Jessie P. Guzman, ed., *Negro Yearbook* (New York, 1952), 227. The first territorial legislature had outlawed intermarriage in 1869. That statute was repealed in 1882. Lewis L. Gould, *Wyoming: A Political History, 1868–1896*, Yale Western Americana Series (New Haven: Yale University Press, 1968), 26.

10. Wyoming's black population from 1880 to 1910 ranged from 1.0 percent to 1.5 percent of the general population. U.S. Department of Commerce, Bureau of the Census, *Negro Population, 1790–1915* (Washington, D.C.: Government Printing Office, 1918), 105.

11. Troopers of the Ninth garrisoned Fort McKinney near the county seat of Buffalo from 1885 to 1890. Professor Leckie considers the assignments to have been a "long promised rest . . . after eighteen years of distinguished service in the Southwest." *The Buffalo Soldiers,* 251.

12. *Big Horn Sentinel,* December 20, 1884, 3; July 25, 1885, 3. The weekly moved from Big Horn to Buffalo in November, 1885.

13. Ibid, December 20, 1884, 3.

14. Ibid, August 22, 1885, 3.

15. Ibid., July 31, 1886, 3; August 7, 1886, 3.

16. U.S. Department of the Interior, Census Office, *Compendium of the Eleventh Census: 1890,* 1.413, 515.

17. See T. A. Larson, *History of Wyoming* (Lincoln, Neb.: University of Nebraska Press, 1965), 269–78, for a brief, judicious account of the Johnson County War.

18. Official Report of Suggs Disturbance, June 18, 1892 (National Archives, Record Group 94); *Buffalo Bulletin* June 23, 1892, 3; Testimony of Private Abraham Champ, Report on Suggs Disturbance of Acting Inspector General, to the Assistant Adjutant General, Department of the Platte, June 28, 1892 (National Archives, Record Group 94).

19. Robert A. Murray, "The United States Army in the Aftermath of the Johnson County Invasion: April through November 1892," *Annals of Wyoming* 38 (April 1966): 59–75, is the best published account of the Suggs incident; but see Frank N. Schubert, "Racial Violence on the Western Frontier: Black Cavalry in the Johnson County War," soon to appear in the *Western Historical Quarterly.*

20. Only three of Sheridan County's 1,972 residents in 1890 were nonwhite. No population data for Suggs, which lasted only from 1891 to 1893, is available, Census Office, *Compendium of the Eleventh Census: 1890,* 1.523,

21. Charles H. Wesley, *Negro Labor in the United States 1850–1925* (New York: Vanguard Press, 1927), 102.

22. Forbes Parkhill, *Mister Barney Ford: A Portrait in Bistre* (Denver: Sage Books, 1963), 145–49, 172–74; *Cheyenne Daily Sun,* November 9, 1879, 2.

23. In 1900, 2.1 percent of Cheyenne's 14,000 residents were black; in 1910, 5.8 percent of the town's 11,300 people were black. Census Office, *Twelfth Census of the United States, 1900, Population,* 1.608; Bureau of the Census, *Negro Population, 1790–1915,* 105. The churches were Allen Chapel, African Methodist Episcopal Church (1875), and the Second Baptist Church (1882).

24. *Cheyenne Daily Leader,* August 18, 1902, 3.

25. Ibid., February 22, 1907, 7.

26. Ibid., May 18, 1909, 4.

27. *Wyoming Tribune,* July 1, 1909, 4. Thomas Phillips has suggested that much of the apprehension over the arrival of black soldiers in western towns was caused by the fear that the troops would turn their weapons on the residents. Perhaps Phillips could have suggested further that this apprehension was based on feelings of guilt for the treatment of blacks, "The Black Regulars," 139.

28. *Wyoming Tribune,* December 2, 1911, 1, 3.

29. Troopers of the Ninth garrisoned nearby Fort Washakie in 1885–91 and 1895–98.

30. Fremont County, of which Lander was the seat, had three blacks in its 1900 population of 5,347. The 1910 population of 11,822 included thirty-two blacks. Census Office, *Twelfth Census of the United States, 1900, Population,* 1.608; Bureau of the Census, *Thirteenth Census of the United States 1910,* 1.246.

31. Roger Daniels and Harry H. L. Kitano, *American Racism: Exploration of the Nature of Prejudice* (Englewood Cliffs: Prentice-Hall, 1970), 98–99. Other methods of preventing a coalition of the disadvantaged have been used. See William S. Willis, "Divide and Rule: Red, White and Black in the Southeast," *Journal of Negro History* 48 (July 1963): 157–76.

32. *Fremont* (Lander*) Clipper,* April 22, 1898, 4.

33. Ibid., August 22, 1902, 1; Organizational Returns, Tenth Cavalry, August, 1902 (National Archives, Record Group 94). Davis, who later became the first black general in the U.S. armed forces, died on November 25, 1970.

34. *Fremont Clipper,* December 19, 1902, 1; April 10, 1903, 1.

35. Ibid., February 22, 1907, 1.

36. Ibid., April 19, 1897, 4; August 29, 1902, 4.

37. Phillips, "The Black Regulars," 139. Phillips's argument that the civilian

reaction to black garrisons depended largely on the geographic origins of the local residents appears simplistic. He offers no documentation for this contention, either in the article cited or in his "The Black Regulars: Negro Soldiers in the United States Army, 1866–1891" (Ph.D. diss., University of Wisconsin, 1970).

38. Professor Leckie has verified the author's hypothesis concerning white communities near Oklahoma reservations. Letter from William H. Leckie to the author, March 9, 1970.

GARNA L. CHRISTIAN

Rio Grande City

PRELUDE TO THE BROWNSVILLE RAID

While historians continue to debate culpability in the notorious Brownsville Raid of August 1906, a strikingly similar incident that occurred seven years earlier at neighboring Rio Grande City goes virtually unnoticed.

In the early 1970s John D. Weaver and Ann J. Lane retrieved the Brownsville affray from historical oblivion with separate investigations of the clash that resulted in the death of a civilian and the expulsion from military service of 167 members of the black Twenty-fifth Infantry. While Lane raised doubt concerning the official verdict which sentenced the soldiers, Weaver challenged it so effectively that the government reversed its former position under aroused public pressure and granted honorable discharges and monetary compensation to the several survivors in 1973.[1]

While responsibility for the Brownsville tragedy cannot be established on the basis of other events, an appropriate frame of reference may be drawn from the milieu that surrounds actions of a related time and origin. Several conflicts between civilians and black soldiers along the Mexican border preceded that at Brownsville, two of which involved other units of the Twenty-fifth Infantry. Members of Company D assaulted a peace officer at Laredo in October, 1899; enlisted men from Company A killed a lawman at El Paso in February, 1900. Sandwiched between was the clash at Rio Grande City, where Troop D of the Ninth Cavalry fired on the town in November, 1899. Each encounter followed allegations from soldiers of racial discrimination and police harassment, countered by citizens' complaints of obnoxious military conduct.[2]

While in each case the black soldiers constituted recent arrivals to the Texas border posts, they were no strangers to frontier Texas of the post–Civil War era. The state marked one of the first destinations of the Ninth and Tenth Cavalry and the Twenty-fourth and Twenty-fifth Infantry after their creation in 1866 when eastern locales pointedly refused to receive them. The remote Indian and bandit-ridden stretches of the Rio Grande and West Texas grudgingly acknowledged their worth in guarding railroads, stringing telegraph lines, and pursuing marauding Apaches and outlaws. Where the dangers lessened, such as at Fort Concho in 1881, white supremacy spurred racial attacks reminiscent of the Southeastern United States. The era ended by the early 1880s with the completion of the western railroads and the pacification of the Indians. Accordingly, the war department pressed the troops beyond the Texas border into the lesser settled western territories."[3]

The black units that returned to Texas following the Spanish-American War only outwardly resembled the soldiers who had tracked the red man into Arizona more than a decade earlier. Battlefield conditions in Cuba had hardened their resolve and congressional awards demonstrated their valor. In tune with the new Negro of the twentieth century who would leave his docility in European trenches, the veterans of San Juan Hill and El Caney stood poised to assume their dormant constitutional prerogatives.[4]

Ironically, the blacks' mood of exhilaration and expectation coincided directly with the surge of white supremacy, which reached epic proportions at the turn of the century. A complex maze of events, buttressed by pseudoscientific racial theories and political opportunism, was at that moment pushing the African American ever lower on the socioeconomic scale, North and South. Far from comforting the racists, the blacks' heroics in the Caribbean unsettled their smug superiority, provoking them to challenge the African American's newly won self-confidence.[5]

Texas counted its share of such persons in 1899. Confederate veterans had elected a string of officials who largely held the antebellum view of appropriate race relations. Nor was the bias restricted to white Anglo-Saxons. Along the Mexican border many Hispanics had adopted the predominant position on race, some to a more striking degree than their mentors. The Mexicans, believed a military inspector, accepted as inevitable an inferior relationship with the white establishment but rallied against adding the newly arrived blacks to their list of betters. Thus a symbiotic relationship of racial prejudice developed between whites and Hispanics toward the blacks. The Mexicans sought acceptance from the leadership by assuming the orthodox racial view while also enhancing their limited social mobility at the expense of the few black residents. Anglo public officials in turn, often courted the favor of the Latinos by openly siding with them against the soldiers.[6]

Other factors rankled some Hispanics. Mexican women, particularly those of easy virtue, often befriended the black soldiers, sending Latin tempers soaring. The towns of South Texas at century's end drew like a magnet societal dregs from both sides of the border who engaged in an assortment of nefarious activities. To them the military presented an obstacle to their profitable pursuits. For this reason white community leaders sometimes demonstrated less disdain for black soldiers than otherwise would be the case, trading one set of racial concerns for another. Nowhere was it truer than on the South Texas border that underdogs are not always natural allies.[7] Law officers at Rio Grande City stoutly denied allegations of brutality, brandishing records of the justice of the peace court, which they claimed repudiated such charges.[8] Prior to the initial clash of October 17 involving soldiers and townsmen in a gambling hall, lawmen, consisting of an Anglo sheriff, a deputy sheriff of mixed ancestry, and several deputies of Mexican descent, made nine arrests in a five-month period.[9] The peace officers considered neither the number of arrests, the nature of the charges, largely disturbances of the peace, nor the extent of punishment, often the minimum fine, to be excessive. The court cleared two soldiers of charges in that period and received fines as low as one dollar from others.[10]

The army, however, viewed the matter differently. The post commander, Lt. E. H. Rubottom, placed so little confidence in the peace officers that he refused to treat with any except Sheriff W. W. Shely. An investigating military officer noted that the soldiers paid court costs in every instance in addition to the fines and believed that the lawmen tolerated and protected the societal parasites who constantly exploited the soldiers. The servicemen repeatedly complained of disparaging racial remarks uttered by lawmen and even federal officials while in their presence. Without question they considered most of the community leadership as well as the citizenry to be aligned against them.[11]

If a showdown between town and fort proved unavoidable, the garrison on the very outskirts of the population had little to support itself except guns. Though Rio Grande City, a backwater seventy-five miles from the nearest railroad, counted barely twelve hundred and fifty inhabitants, Troop D of the Ninth Cavalry comprised less than a tenth of that number. The post commander, the sole officer aside from the medical examiner, was a youthful second lieutenant who had not been commissioned into service until June of 1899. His age, inexperience, and association with black troops earned him little respect in town, where some unjustly accused him of excessive drinking.[12]

Not surprisingly, the first serious confrontation between soldiers and townspeople, on October 17, prompted widely-differing interpretations in the two sectors. Civilians accused enlisted men of rushing the gaming tables with their guns, the account accepted by local authorities and carried by the press. The two arrested soldiers told of being attacked by Mexican gamblers while standing innocently on the street. The court imposed a formidable fine of fifty dollars each on the two African Americans and then jailed them for inability to pay. Whatever the cause of the melee, four soldiers sustained wounds, two by gunshot and two by knives.[13]

The gambling hall debacle threw up a watershed in community-military relations at Rio Grande City, deeply embittering both sides. The press reports, circulated statewide by the *Galveston News,* hardly pacified matters, depicting the soldiers as clearly the instigators and somewhat inflating the number of casualties. Several soldiers reported to Lieutenant Rubottom threats by lawmen to shoot "every nigger" seen in town on the following payday.[14]

Rumors of impending violence rebounded between town and fort over the next month following the clash. Reports circulated mainly by town women that residents were hoarding ammunition in preparation for an attack on Ringgold unnerved the soldiers. Citizens, in turn, repeated among themselves stories pointing to a military raid on Rio Grande City. Payday, November 20, enjoyed the distinction of the most commonly assumed target date by both sides. News from Laredo of a contingent of black soldiers from Fort McIntosh assaulting a peace officer, in that nearby city, further heightened tensions.[15]

Lieutenant Rubottom, lending credence to the rumors of a civilian attack, acted to ward off trouble. On November 17, he ordered the entire troop to remain within the garrison and closed the post to all visitors save those on regular business. Three days later, Rubottom increased the guard. Then began the baffling chain of events that climaxed in violence and a series of investigations by the army, the state of Texas, and a grand jury, finally culminating in frustrating inconclusion.[16]

Though warped by inexperience and over reliance on the assurances of enlisted men, partly due to an injury that hindered his mobility, Rubottom's perceptions corroborated the statements of the enlisted men. During the day several guards reported to him sightings of Mexicans lurking in the chaparral in the vicinity of the post. In the afternoon the mail carrier told Rubottom of being fired upon as he carried the mail from the fort to town. Several black women, claiming they had been driven by hostile residents from the town, took refuge on the reservation.[17]

Evening wrought a deterioration of the already troubled situation. The post commander cautioned the men to remain "quiet and sober" and not fire a shot except in defense of the garrison. About seven o'clock, immediately past sunset, Rubottom heard several shots near the post from the direction of town, barely six hundred yards away. He identified the sounds as reports from forty-fives, rather than emissions from Krag-Jorgensen rifles as used by the army. The officer hastily placed the entire troop on guard, along with a sergeant in charge of each. He instructed them to remain inside the reservation and "not to fire unless fired upon."[18]

The lieutenant followed those unconventional orders with even more remarkable ones a half hour later when he witnessed a recurrence of gunfire from the town. After ordering more volleys in the direction of the firing, Rubottom as a last resort had the Gatling gun placed at the gate, angled somewhat to the left of the town, and directed its fire upon that site for several minutes. "This was sufficient to stop their firing entirely," stated the officer matter-of-factly, "and no more shots were fired by either side."[19]

The remainder of the evening proved anticlimactic. Rubottom left the troops on guard all night and attempted to wire department headquarters, only to find the lines down at Laredo. The next morning he telegraphed the commanding officer at Fort Brown and eventually contacted San Antonio, thereafter filing hourly reports. Rubottom, with the consent of the department commander, assumed control of the local telegraph, preventing "several false communications from certain citizens." He notified the county judge that a second attack from townsmen "would meet with extreme measures" and conferred with local officials, who pledged cooperation.[20]

If, however, the post commander thought the issue settled, he soon realized his folly. Newspapers around the state headlined the story, the prestigious *Galveston News* under the banner, "War on Negro Troops" and "The Negroes Terrorized the Place." Subsequent news coverage turned on the indignant reaction of the town as well as communities around the state. Governor Joseph Sayers, a Confederate veteran, demanded the transfer of the black troops from Texas and in the same breath called for both military and state investigations. Lieutenant Rubottom's questionable decision to employ the Gatling gun sparked considerable excitement, as local officials and residents clamored that the soldiers had faked an attack on the post in order to exact vengeance on a peaceful citizenry.[21]

Two investigators, Cyrus Roberts, colonel of the U.S. Army, and Thomas Scurry, adjutant general of Texas, converged on the site. The men represented constituencies with quite different viewpoints. From the outset the military played down the clash as, in the words of an army official at Washington, of "no occasion for any uneasiness on the part of the state or local authorities." The soothing words fell on deaf ears of state and local authorities, however, as a crescendo arose from the populace for removal of the troops. The press speculated that Roberts and Scurry likely would arrive at contrasting conclusions on culpability in the matter.[22]

Despite their divergent backgrounds, the two inspectors amicably cooperated, exchanging notes and testimony and coordinating their investigations. Roberts and Scurry encountered little hesitation on the part of either civilians or soldiers to testify. On the morning of November 25, they met with the county judge in the latter's office to obtain statements from the townspeople and local officials. Present also were two army officers from forts Brown and McIntosh, recently dispatched to Ringgold. The sheriff examined eight witnesses, including two Hispanic teenagers and a woman, a baker, the deputy sheriff, a deputy U.S. marshal, and a physician.[23]

Sheriff Shely, who had been out of town on the day of the shooting, elicited virtually identical testimony from the witnesses. All claimed that the soldiers had fired without provocation with the intention of harming the residents because of imaginary grievances against some of the citizenry. The boys claimed to have gathered two-and-a-half pounds of empty shells and a few Krag cartridges in the bushes outside the fort the day following the shooting. Their statement implied that the soldiers had fired at the citizenry at close range off the military reservation.[24]

The testimony directly conflicted with the accounts told by the troops and cast some doubt in Colonel Robert's mind. He noted that the deputy marshal and deputy sheriff had alienated the soldiers while making allegedly unnecessary and brutal arrests. Reliable evidence showed the baker had lied when he claimed having been present at the fort during the firing. The colonel also discovered that another youngster had collected shells near the gate and inside the post fence, raising the question of whether all in fact were found in that area.[25]

The military personnel matched the citizenry in its zeal to testify, Roberts and Scurry, singly or in combination, questioned fifteen members of Company D, the post commander, an Indian scout, and townswomen who verified their version of the facts. Each man insisted that the post received a burst of gunfire from the direction of Rio Grande City shortly after sundown, while several swore having seen Mexicans skulking near the post that afternoon. Mary McPherson, a white woman, stated that she and her nine-year-old daughter sought refuge at the fort on the day of the shooting after sighting armed men in town.[26]

Nor did the soldiers' testimony escape criticism from the investigator essentially representing the other faction. The state adjutant general noted one instance of bullet damage within the reservation, which apparently resulted from firing inside the post, rather than from without as claimed by the troops. Scurry also doubted the ability of the quartermaster sergeant to identify figures, as he claimed, two hundred yards away on a dark night.[27]

Despite speculation to the contrary in the press, the two investigators reached surprisingly similar conclusions. They filed reports expeditiously and within days of each other, Scurry on November 30 and Roberts on December 3. Predictably, the tones varied, with the military report somewhat more understated than that of the state. Each was a bit more skeptical of the credibility of the witnesses of the other constituency than of its own. On the crucial issue of culpability, however, Scurry and Roberts frankly admitted lack of knowledge.[28]

The army and the state both discounted the twin rumors of conspiracy to assault the other. Neither placed much emphasis on the importance of the first shot, Scurry admitted, "The evidence is too conflicting for me to undertake to say by whom the shots from the outside were fired or from what particular locality; nor . . . at what time the shooting in the direction of the Post began . . . [or] whether before or after the firing from the Post began." Roberts assumed that the soldiers had fired in retaliation but placed greater weight on the tensions that existed between the garrison and the town prior to the firing.[29]

The investigators concurred that Lieutenant Rubottom, removed from duty in the aftermath of the incident, acted with impropriety in his unusual defense of the fort. They agreed that a proper course of action would have compelled him to summon local officials at the first sign of danger and to contemplate force only if the peace officers refused aid. In their judgment Rubottom's permission to distraught soldiers to fire if fired upon constituted a grievous error.[30]

Neither inspector, however, recommended stern measures against the young post commander. Rather than proposing disciplinary action against the officer, Roberts advised attaching him to the command of a seasoned officer. Prophetically, the colonel predicted that local officials might seek indictments against the garrison.[31]

Colonel Roberts forcefully recommended the abandonment of Fort Ringgold, citing lack of military necessity, the formidable cost of operation, and the exploitation of the soldiers by undesirable civilians and biased peace officers. He stated, "there can be no question of the bitter antagonism existing towards colored soldiers on the part of the Mexican population. . . . I have little doubt the feeling against any colored troops would be the same." He believed that many of the local officials shared such prejudice, while others such as Sheriff Shely publicly sided with those of that sentiment in order to maintain support from the populace. Of the troops, Roberts said, "They are without exception proud of their position as United States soldiers and inclined to assert their privileges to the fullest and especially in a community like the one in which they are located at Fort Ringgold."[32]

Public outcry against the soldiers over the next several months contrasted sharply with the dignified and restrained tone of the reports. While the investigators had judiciously prepared their statements, newspapers engaged in speculation and freely quoted irate residents.[33]

The prospect of abandoning Fort Ringgold, rather than withdrawing black troops for white, by no means pleased all locals. This was to be expected in a town economy heavily dependent on government purchases of hay, wood, and other military supplies. Indeed, rumor had the army abandoning all the remaining posts along the lower Rio Grande. Laredoans particularly took umbrage, viewing the assertion as a move by the army to spite South Texans. Col. Chambers McKibbin, commanding the Department of Texas, approved Robert's recommendations for Ringgold specifically. At Galveston he candidly stated to the press, "The class of people that infest Ringgold come across the Rio Grande from Mexico and simply live off the soldiers. They bleed every cent of the soldiers' pay and are a constant source of trouble and annoyance."[34]

As Colonel Roberts had feared, the Starr County grand jury sched-

uled a review of the assault, creating a new dimension of wholesale indictments. Colonel McKibbin wired Governor Sayers: "This the military authorities cannot permit as it would destroy all control over troops
at post." The state executive warmly responded, "If the troops at Fort
Ringgold cannot be controlled should a judicial investigation be had . . .
the sooner these troops be discharged the better it will be for the service."
Sayers laid the blame for "the late troubles at that Post" largely on "the in-
competency of the officer in command." The Texan launched into a bit-
ing defense of states' rights, pledging "to do everything within my power
to secure the arrest and trial of all persons" indicted by a state court. He
denied the existence of a single federal or state statute that granted military personnel immunity from duly charged civil tribunals.[35]

The intensity of the state's argument stemmed in part from a series
of events of the past several months, which had heightened the friction
between the army and Texas citizenry. The beating of a Laredo peace
officer by soldiers from Fort McIntosh in mid-October had sparked civic
reaction in that locale equal to sentiment at Rio Grande City and aggra-
vated racial anguish statewide. When the mayor of Laredo demanded the
removal of the black troops, Senator Charles Culberson stopped short of
endorsing that position. Culberson represented the view of much of the
populace, desiring a replacement of the troops by whites in place of outright abandonment of the fort. When a Laredo grand jury returned indictments against two soldiers hostility toward the men prompted the
court to remove the trial to San Diego and the army to transfer the garrison to San Antonio. South Texans who erroneously believed the latter
action constituted a permanent abandonment of Fort McIntosh grew
more indignant toward the military. Accordingly, the press seized every
word of the exchange between the governor and the commander.[36]

The vehemence with which the state defended its position gave
pause to Colonel McKibbin, who sought to limit the areas of disagree-
ment in a disclosure to the adjutant general at Washington; He clarified
his original intention "to notify him [Sayers] of another phase of the
troubles . . . with the sole object of preventing disorders." The governor's
injection of state sovereignty McKibbin judged "a forced consideration."
He emphasized to his superior the fact that no civil authority had attempted to serve any process on anyone at the garrison and concluded
wryly, "Governor Sayers' letter was read by me in the public press before
the original was received."[37]

McKibbin indeed was correct regarding the absence of judicial proceedings against Ringgold, as the Star County grand jury failed to issue indictments after a heated review of the incident. Nevertheless, it lashed at the actions of Lieutenant Rubottom and his command as "without the slightest provocation and reason." The grand jury asserted that only "the reticence of witnesses and the suppression of material facts" prevented the return of wholesale indictments against the military. "If this is the discipline and control of the United States army," lamented the report, "God help us and all others thus at the mercy of such responsibility." [38]

Despite the forebodings, the Rio Grande City controversy peaked short of the public outcry and drastic governmental action that followed the Brownsville affair. Rather than abandoning Fort Ringgold, as suggested by colonels Roberts and McKibbin, the army continued its operation intermittently until 1944. Without further incident one set of black troops replaced another before the post temporarily closed in 1906. Lieutenant Rubottom survived the threat to his career, finally retiring as a lieutenant colonel in 1920, following service in the Philippines and in wartime France. [39]

Nevertheless, the bitter remnants of Rio Grande City could not have escaped the collective memories of South Texas garrisons and towns in the mere seven years that preceded the Brownsville crisis. The jolting similarities in the mutual suspicions that anticipated the clashes, the contradictory assertions of guilt and innocence, the stark nature of the confrontations, and the immediate public rejection of the black troops formed a grim pattern of events present in both instances. Indeed, the actual motivation for the Brownsville Raid may well have rested on some instigator's perception of the former conflict. Coinciding with an acceleration of racial tension nationally, the latter so deeply penetrated the social fabric as to obscure the significant antecedent. Retrieval of the Rio Grande City episode from the historical dustbin permits greater illumination of the darker corners of racial relations at the turn of the century, which spawned such tragedies as that at Brownsville, Texas.

Notes

1. John D. Weaver, *The Brownsville Raid* (New York: W. W. Norton, 1970); Ann J. Lane, *The Brownsville Affair: National Crisis and Black Reaction* (Port Washington, N.Y.: Kennikat Press, 1971); *New York Times*, September 29, 1972; November 18, 1973.

2. *Galveston Daily News*, October 20, 1899; November 22, 1899; *El Paso Herald*, February 17, 1900.

3. Jack D. Foner, "Black in the Post-Civil War Army," in *Blacks and the Military in American History: A New Perspective* (New York: Praeger Publishers, 1974), 54, 73; William H. Leckie, *The Buffalo Soldiers: A Narrative of the Negro Cavalry in the West* (Norman, Okla.: University of Oklahoma Press, 1967), 11, 72, 81, 82, 259; John M. Carroll, ed., *The Black Infantry in the American West* (New York: Liveright Publishing, 1971), 67–71, 84–87, 92–93, 96–97, 277–78; Arlen L. Fowler, *The Black Infantry in the West: 1869–1891* (Westport, Conn.: Greenwood Publishing, 1971), 18, 24, 32–36; Marvin E. Fletcher, *The Black Soldier and Officer in the United States Army: 1891–1917* (Columbia: University of Missouri Press, 1974), 26, 38, 45; John H. Nankivell, *History of the Twenty-fifth Regiment, United States Infantry, 1869–1926* (New York: Negro Universities Press, 1969), 35; J. Evetts Haley, *Fort Concho and the Texas Frontier* (San Angelo, Tex.: San Angelo Standard Times, 1952), 235–37.

4. Foner, *Blacks and the Military*, 74.

5. C. Vann Woodward, *The Strange Career of Jim Crow* (New York: Oxford University Press, 1966), 67–109; Foner, *Blacks and the Military*, 76–82; Willard B. Gatewood Jr, "Negro Troops in Florida, 1898," *Florida Historical Quarterly*, 49 (July, 1970): 8.

6. Lt. Col. Cyrus Roberts to the adjutant general, San Antonio, Texas, December 4, 1899, RG 393, National Archives.

7. Ibid.; *Galveston Daily News*, November 22, 1899; George B Hufford to Gen. Nelson A. Miles, Laredo, Texas, November 22, 1899, AGO file 298752, RG 94, National Archives.

8. *Galveston Daily News*, October 20, 1899, November 22, 1899; *El Paso Herald*, February 17, 1900; Weaver, *Brownsville Raid*, 18.

9. Frank N. Schubert, "Black Soldiers on the White Frontier: Some Factors Influencing Race Relations," *Phylon* 32, no. 4 (Winter 1971): 415; Fletcher, *Black Soldier*, 25; Weaver, *Brownsville Affair*, 9; Roberts to adjutant general, December 4, 1899, NA; *Galveston Daily News*, November 20, 1899.

10. Statement from Docket Justice Court Showing All Cases of Troopers Tried Before Justice Since Arrival of Present Troop, Starr County, Texas, 1899, Texas State Archives; Adjutant Gen. Thomas Scurry to Joseph D. Sayers, Governor of Texas, Austin, Texas, November 30, 1899, Texas State Archives.

11. Scurry to Sayers, November 30, 1899, T.S.A.; Lt. Col. C. S. Roberts to the Commanding Officer, Department of Texas, San Antonio, Texas, December 3, 1899, National Archives.

12. Roberts to Commanding Officer, December 3, 1899, N.A.

13. Ibid.; Statement from Docket, *Galveston Daily News*, October 23, 1899.

14. *Galveston Daily News*, October 23, 1899.

15. 2nd Lt. E. H. Rubottom to Adjutant General Department of Texas, Fort Ringgold, Texas, November 23, 1899, AGO files 296983, RG 94, National Archives; Scurry to Sayers, November 30, 1899; *Galveston Daily News*, October 20, 1899.

16. Rubottom to Adjutant General, November 23, 1899, NA.

17. Ibid.

18. Ibid.

19. Ibid.

20. Ibid.

21. *Galveston Daily News,* November 22, 1899; November 23, 1899; November 24, 1899; November 26, 1899.

22. *Galveston Daily News,* November 23, 1899 "quotation," November 26, 1899.

23. Scurry to Sayers, November 30, 1899, T.S.A.; Roberts to Commanding Officer, December 3, 1899.

24. Ibid.

25. Roberts to Commanding Officer, December 3, 1899, N.A.

26. Scurry to Sayers, November 30, 1899, T.S.A.

27. Ibid.

28. Roberts to Commanding Officer, December 5, 1899, N.A.; Scurry to Sayers, November 30, 1899, T.S.A.

29. Ibid.

30. Ibid.

31. Ibid.

32. Roberts to Commanding Officer, December 3, 1899, N.A.

33. *Galveston Daily News,* November 23, 1899 (first quotation); November 24, 1899 (second quotation); November 30, 1899 (third quotation).

34. Ibid., November 23, 1899; December 7, 1899; Col. Chambers McKibbin to the Adjutant General, San Antonio, Texas, December 4, 1899, AGO file 296983, RG 94, National Archive.

35. Joseph D. Sayers to Gen. Chambers McKibbin, Austin, Texas, December 18, 1899, AGO file 296983, RG 94, National Archives.

36. C. A. Culberson to Secretary of War, Washington, D.C., November 16, 1899, AGO file 296983, RG 94, National Archives; Pritchard to Adjutant General, Fort McIntosh, Texas, November 10, 1899, ibid; McKibbin to Adjutant General, San Antonio, Texas, November 20, 1899, ibid.

37. Col. McKibbin to the Adjutant General, San Antonio, Texas, December 19, 1899, AGO file 296983, RG 94, National Archives; *Galveston Daily News,* December 19, 1899.

38. *Galveston Daily News,* December 19, 1899.

39. Fort Ringgold Texas (1848–61, 1865–1906, 1917–44), RG 393, Records of the U.S. Army Commands (Army Posts), National Archives; Garry D. Ryan to author, Washington, D.C., June 15, 1978. The order to close Fort Ringgold in 1906 preceded the Brownsville Raid.

"Behold a stranger at the door,
He gently knocks, has knocked before,
has waited long, is waiting still,
You treat no other friend so ill."
    —from a hymn by Joseph Grigg

C. CALVIN SMITH

The Houston Riot of 1917, Revisited

Black Americans, and especially black soldiers, have always been committed to the American creed of freedom and democracy for all. Anytime the nation has found itself threatened by a foreign enemy, black men have been among the first to volunteer their services in its defense. Black soldiers took pride in their military record and the black community accorded them a place in the highest level of social respectability. However, many whites, especially in the South, believed blacks were inferior and should not be allowed to wear the uniform of the armed forces, which they held so dear. Whites were also disturbed by the attitude of pride and self-worth exhibited by black soldiers, which they interpreted as arrogance and a threat to Jim Crowism. Black soldiers were not wanted in the South because, as Senator James K. Vardaman of Mississippi put it, "whites are opposed to putting arrogant, strutting representatives of the black soldiery in every community."[1]

In 1916, with the United States entry into World War I almost a certainty and the induction of large numbers of blacks into the military likely to follow, Vardaman and a group of Southern congressmen sponsored a bill to prevent the enlistment of blacks in the armed forces or the reenlistment of those already in uniform. The measure, however, was defeated because of the strong opposition of the Secretary of War, Newton D. Baker, who argued that passage of the statute would be unwise since "black soldiers have performed brave and often conspicuously gallant service for the nation since the American Revolution."[2] Baker, more informed than the congressmen, knew the United States was destined to enter the European war and that all available manpower would be needed. Veteran black soldiers serving in the armed forces in 1916 were not unaware of the efforts of white Southerners to oust them, but they were men who were proud of their record in the armed forces and were determined to live up to the standards established by their predecessors. They were also aware that the nation, especially white southerners, had little respect for their service and treated "no other friend so ill."

Of all the places where black soldiers served, the documented record of "ill treatment" and lack of respect was greatest in Texas. Perhaps that was because Texas served as one of the border states between the United States, unstable Mexico, and the revolution-racked republics of Central America. In the 1890s and early 1900s, U.S. troops were sometimes dispatched from Texas to wars and hot spots in those countries and a significant number of those soldiers were black. Following the Spanish-American War of 1898, the all-black Tenth Cavalry, which had served with distinction during the war, was transferred to Texas for duty. While traveling by train between Huntsville and San Antonio, the soldiers suffered unprovoked sniper fire from resentful white civilians. The frequency and intensity of the attacks were so great that their white commanding officer was forced to request the War Department to provide a military escort for his troops so they could "pass through an area which they were supposed to protect without danger from hidden assassins."[3]

The unwarranted attack upon black soldiers in 1898 was not an isolated incident; in fact, it was part of a recurring pattern of hostility toward black troops in Texas. In 1906, 167 members of the all-black Twenty-fifth Infantry, stationed at Brownsville, Texas, were dishonorably discharged and imprisoned after being accused of conducting a random and unprovoked raid upon the city. The fact that the raiders were never identified by any investigative body, civilian or military, and that the white commanding officers of the accused testified that a roll call during the incident revealed that all their men were in camp with clean, unfired weapons made little difference in their fate.[4] To the local community, justice had been done. Their views were succinctly expressed by a local newspaper editor when he wrote: "Whatever may be the value of black troops in wartime, in peacetime they are a curse to the country."[5]

The attitude of Texans toward black soldiers had changed little when the United States entered World War I in April 1917. Following passage of the Selective Service Act in May of that year, which removed the army's quota system that limited black enlistments to their percentage of the total population and opened the service to the mass enlistment of blacks, military officials recognized the potential for conflict if black recruits were sent into Jim Crow Southern communities for training. Initially, army officials decided against sending black recruits into the South for training and tours of duty, especially those from the North, because they feared "embarrassing difficulties will arise in places of public entertainment from the demands of these troops who are associated with white contingents in Northern states, and are accustomed to a situation which they are sure not to find in the neighborhood of Southern camps."[6] This decision was revoked in early August by Newton D. Baker, who believed it conflicted with established military tradition. However, Baker was cognizant of the potential racial problems that could arise from his decision and ordered commanders of Southern camps to "exercise discretion and judgement to prevent any difficulty from arising from this cause."[7]

Hoping to minimize the potential for racial conflict between black troops and local white communities in the South, the War Department ordered the all-black Third Battalion, Twenty-fourth Infantry, U.S. Army to Houston, Texas, for a tour of guard duty during the construction of nearby Camp Logan. They arrived July 28, 1917. It was an assignment that neither the black troops nor their white officers wanted, because of the reputation Texans had in regard to their treatment of black soldiers. Col. William Newman, battalion commander, tried to get the order revoked because:

> I had already had an unfortunate experience when I was in command of two companies of the 24th Infantry at Del Rio, Texas, in April 1916, when a colored soldier was killed by a [Texas] ranger for no other reason than that he was a colored man; that it angered Texans to see colored men in the uniform of a soldier.[8]

Newman's view was shared by many of his officers. "Every time we have been in Texas we have had trouble," commented Capt. Lindsey Silvester, commanding officer of Company K of the Twenty-fourth.[9] And Cecil Green, a black sergeant with the battalion, said the troops "expected trouble in Houston from [white] mobs" from the very beginning.[10] Newman's superiors attempted to allay his fears and those of his men by informing them that the Houston Chamber of Commerce had assured the War Department that black troops would be received by the citizens of Houston "in a spirit of patriotism."[11]

When the Third Battalion, Twenty-fourth Infantry, arrived in Houston it entered a community that was already rife with racial tension caused by the strict enforcement of Jim Crow laws, police brutality, and white civilian resentment of the troops because they were replacing a detachment of the all-white Texas National Guard. Black citizens in Houston, in all walks of life, had little to say that was positive about race relations in the city. "Having a home [in Houston] is all right," a black Houston physician told a National Association for the Advancement of Colored People (NAACP) reporter, "but not when you never know when you leave it in the morning if you will really be able to get back to it at night." Similar sentiments were expressed by Elijah C. Branch, a black Houston minister, who said, "law abiding citizens feared the police in getting over the city at night more than they feared the highwayman."[12] The soldiers of the Twenty-fourth were not welcomed and were expected, by local authorities and civilians, to behave in the same fashion as local blacks, accepting brutality, harassment, and insulting racial epithets without retaliation or comment. According to the battalion's commander, the general attitude among local police and white civilians was that the men's status as soldiers was negated by their race. He reported that white construction workers at Camp Logan "lost no opportunity to refer to the 24th Infantry as 'niggers;' the city police and people generally did the same . . . and no efforts were made in any respect to discourage the use of this appellation."[13]

The common use of the word "nigger" by local civilians and police was particularly offensive to the men of the Twenty-fourth, the majority of whom had spent the previous two years in the Philippine Islands (Manila) and in Cheyenne and Columbus, New Mexico, areas where they faced little or no racial discrimination. Colonel Newman knew his men would have a difficult time in Houston since "the Texan's idea of how a colored man should be treated was just the opposite of what these Twenty-fourth Infantrymen had been used to."[14] News from Waco, Texas, of an almost violent confrontation between black soldiers and white civilians in that city on July 29, the day after the Twenty-fourth arrived in Houston, did little to reduce growing racial tension. In an effort to reduce white hostility toward his troop, Newman ordered all of his men disarmed, including the battalion's military police, and stored the arms under lock and key. He believed the unarmed troops would be viewed as less of a threat to local whites and reduce the possibility of retaliation on the part of the soldiers for acts of injustice and humiliation. The only members of the Twenty-fourth allowed to carry weapons were the guards on duty around the outskirts of Camp Logan, and they were allowed only their rifles and five rounds of ammunition.[15] Newman's early efforts to reduce white hostility toward his troops did little good. Capt. David E. Van Natta, one of the troops' white officers, wrote: "At different times since August 17, the date of my arrival at Camp Logan [the troops had arrived on July 28], I have heard various people talking about the colored troops being here. The sentiment was very strongly against them or any more colored troops being sent here for any purpose."[16] Less than a month after their arrival in Houston, the incident most feared by the War Department and the officers and men of the Twenty-fourth Infantry occurred. On the night of August 23, 1917, soldiers from the Twenty-fourth clashed with white police and civilians in Houston, a confrontation that resulted in the death of twenty people: two black soldiers, five white police officers, and thirteen white civilians.

Professional historians have devoted little time to analyzing the causes and consequences of the Houston incident. The first published accounts were written by biased and emotionally charged journalists and other individuals who were more interested in presenting their interpretation of the incident rather than a balanced account.[17] In recent years more balanced accounts have been written. Arthur E. Barbeau and Florette Henri's *The Unknown Soldiers: Black American Troops in World War I* (Philadelphia: Temple University Press, 1974) is one of the more interesting historical treatments of the incident. However, the most definitive studies published to date are "The Houston Mutiny and Riot of 1917" (*Southwestern Historical Quarterly* 76 [1973]: 418–39) and *A Night of Violence: The Houston Riot of 1917* (Baton Rouge: Louisiana State University Press, 1976), both by Robert V. Haynes.[18]

All studies of the Houston incident agree on most of the basic facts: a small group of soldiers from the Twenty-fourth were involved in a violent confrontation with white police and civilians of Houston, sparked by police brutality and the use of the term "niggers." However, Haynes accepts the military authorities' conclusion that the violence grew out of a planned conspiracy, carefully concealed by a manufactured fear of a white mob attack, of revenge against the police on the part of experienced soldiers.[19] Haynes argues that the cry heard in the soldiers' compound, "They are coming! The mob is coming," moments before the outburst of gunfire from the camp was a signal for the attack upon Houston to begin. He also argues that Sgt. Vida Henry, who apparently committed suicide after the attack on Houston, was the plotter and leader of the conspiracy. His arguments depend on his acceptance as fact the testimony given during the trials: testimony from white civilians, police, white officers of the battalion, and from black soldiers who were alleged participants in the affair and served as witnesses for the prosecution in return for immunity. A careful reading and analysis of the official documents relative to the Houston incident clearly shows both bias on the part of many of the witnesses and distortion of the testimony on the part of the military. Reexamination of the circumstances and the conflicting stories of those involved suggests instead that the conspiracy theory was a convenient measure to place exclusive blame on the soldiers and not actual fact.

The night of August 23, 1917, was indeed one of violence but it did not grow out of a planned attack on the white police of Houston by angry, revenge-seeking black soldiers; rather, it was a spontaneous outburst triggered by weeks of having to endure insulting racial epithets, by police brutality, and by the fear in the camp of an imminent mass mob attack by angry white Houstonians and the belief that such an attack had been launched. The fuse that ignited the explosion of that tragic night was lit at approximately 2:35 P.M. when Corp. Charles W. Baltimore, a black military policeman, approached two city policemen, Lee Sparks and Rufus Daniels, and inquired about the brutal arrest of a black soldier earlier that day. According to Baltimore, he asked, "in what I thought to be a respectful tone of voice what had been the trouble with the [black] soldier they had just arrested."[20] Patrolman Sparks, who had a reputation as a bully and "Negro Baiter," answered Baltimore's inquiry by shouting, "Don't you like it?" Before the startled soldier could explain, Sparks attacked him with his service revolver. In an attempt to escape the rain of blows, Baltimore ran, was fired at, pursued, caught, and severely pistol-whipped. Sparks later justified his actions on the grounds that the victimized soldier had approached him roughly and was using profanity. However, Rufus Daniels, Sparks's partner, refused, in sworn testimony, to confirm Sparks's story. He said that he had not heard any profanity while Baltimore was talking to his partner.[21]

Following the Baltimore incident, rumors quickly spread that the soldier had been killed and that a white mob was planning an attack upon Camp Logan. The rumors of Baltimore's death and the resulting tension in Camp Logan attracted the attention of Maj. Kneeland S. Snow who had assumed command of the Twenty-fourth Battalion on August 20. According to Snow, he and his white officers immediately "realized we were sitting on a powder-keg" and began "doing everything in our power to keep it from being touched off." Snow, accompanied by Capt. Haig Shekerjian, who was in charge of military police, proceeded to police headquarters to investigate the Baltimore affair. There they found Baltimore severely beaten, but alive. Subsequently, they were able to secure his release by convincing Chief of Police Clarence Brock that the injured soldier had been carrying out his duties as a military policeman when he questioned the arrest of another soldier. Brock also promised the officers that Patrolman Sparks would be suspended for his unwarranted attack upon Baltimore, and that he would order his men to refrain from referring to the soldiers as "niggers" since that appeared to be the source of most of the friction.[22]

During their return to Camp Logan, Snow informed Baltimore of Brock's promise and requested that he relay the information to the men. Snow also informed his white officers of Brock's promise. To prevent an accidental clash between his men and white Houstonians, Snow canceled all passes for the evening and posted extra guards to make sure that no one left camp without authorization. After taking these precautions, Snow and his officers believed they had defused the explosive situation and that the camp would be back to normal the next day.[23] Tension, however, remained high in the camp since many of the inexperienced soldiers and their black officers feared that they had been disarmed so that they could not defend themselves from the white mob attack they believed would occur at any moment.

The cause of widespread fear in Camp Logan of a white mob attack has never been fully explained. Haynes has argued that this fear was part of a planned conspiracy and was manufactured by those involved in planning the attack upon Houston, in order to create panic and give their plans a reasonable chance for success. He draws this conclusion from conflicting testimony given to the Houston Civilian Board of Inquiry, which was organized after the incident to investigate its causes, and to military courts by frightened black youths, revenge-seeking white police and civilians, and military officials who were trying to clear themselves of any and all responsibility for the incident.[24] It was upon these highly questionable sources that Haynes constructed his conspiracy theory. These people, by Haynes's own admission, and according to the report of one of the army's chief investigators of the incident, Col. G. O. Cress, were asked leading questions with suggested answers by prosecutors who wanted to prove the incident was premeditated and not a spontaneous reaction to weeks of humiliation and an imminent fear of physical violence.[25]

A careful analysis of the official report by military investigators reveals that the soldiers' fear of a white mob attack was genuine and that there was no conclusive proof the fear was deliberately created by alleged conspirators against the city of Houston to mask their plans. From the moment the Twenty-fourth arrived in Houston, the soldiers were under immense pressure because, according to Colonel Newman, "there was a disposition on the part of the citizens not to respect a uniform [when worn by a black soldier] and that the situation was much more trying than they had ever been made to face."[26] Newman's views were shared by Colonel Cress who reported that "the attitude among . . . the white citizens generally is, in substance, that a nigger is a nigger, and that his status is not effected by the uniform he wears."[27] These attitudes often resulted in acts of brutality against the defenseless soldiers by police and civilians when, according to Col. Newman, "it was clearly not the soldier's fault."[28]

To understand the fear of attack felt by the men of the Twenty-fourth on the night of August 23, an examination of the events surrounding the suspension of Patrolman Sparks and his reaction is necessary. Long before the arrival of the Twenty-fourth in Houston, Sparks had developed a reputation as a "brutal bully" and a "Negro Baiter" who was not satisfied with the socioeconomic advantages whites enjoyed over blacks. He was a man who missed no opportunity to use brutality to put those he viewed as "uppity" blacks in their proper place. This sadistic conduct was apparently endorsed by Sparks's superiors since there is no evidence to indicate any effort was made to alter his behavior.[29] Since Sparks had never been disciplined for his treatment of blacks, he was shocked when informed by Chief Brock that he was being suspended due to the Baltimore incident and he angrily accused Brock of being a Negrophile. "Any man that sticks up for a nigger," Sparks yelled at his supervisor, "is no better than a nigger."[30]

Sparks's suspension was not only a blow to his ego, it also threatened him economically. He had only recently returned to duty after a ten-day suspension, without pay, for "improper remarks made to a white woman," and could not afford another one.[31] Sparks was clearly not a man who hid his feelings and he faulted the black soldiers for his fate, publicly berated his chief, and talked of getting even. In a city where public hostility toward black troops was at an all-time high, the angry explanations of his position, which Sparks undoubtedly would have made to white civilian associates to garner their support, could easily have led to rumors of retaliation among them. Since whites often disregarded the presence of black onlookers, such as servants, when discussing racial issues or airing hostility toward other blacks, it is quite possible that black civilians informed the men of the Twenty-fourth about the threats of revenge against them: thus accounting, in part, for the soldiers' heightened fear of attack.

The intense fear of an attack by a mob of white Houstonians engulfing Camp Logan on the night of August 23 cannot be dismissed, as it is by Haynes and some military investigators, as something generated by a small group of revenge-seeking black soldiers to conceal their plans for an attack upon the city. Nor can the charge that the cry, "They are coming! The mob is coming," be interpreted as a covert, coded signal to the men to begin such an attack. "That those who went out of camp employed this alarm, 'the mob is coming,' as a means of starting the riot," reported Col. G. O. Cress, "could not be ascertained, but all circumstances point to the fact that the men left back in camp . . . were obsessed with the idea that a mob of citizens from Houston would attack them."[32] The cry was followed by gunfire and by a mad scramble for weapons and a mass exodus from camp by approximately 150 frightened and inexperienced soldiers, but the evidence indicates that the camp was indeed fired upon by outside forces.

The men left in camp, after the first shots were fired, clearly believed they were under attack and seized their weapons and began to return fire indiscriminately. According to one of their white officers, "the only way to get the men to stop shooting was to shake them and make them realize that they were actually shooting at each other and not some mythical mob of white citizens."[33] The soldiers had only army rifles at their disposal but the initial shots fired near Camp Logan, testified L. E. Gentry, a local white policeman, "didn't sound like rifles to me." An examination of those wounded in and near Camp Logan also revealed that "these wounds resulted from gun shot [weapons of nonmilitary issue] and not rifle fire."[34] An examination of bullets fired into homes near Camp Logan on the night of the "alleged riot" also revealed that they had been fired from nonmilitary weapons.[35] This, combined with the examination of bullets in the camp and Gentry's testimony, substantiates the statement by soldiers left in the camp that those who disobeyed orders and left the camp did so in order to form a skirmish line around the camp to meet their attackers.

The conspiracy theory is further weakened by the testimony of R. E.

Lewis before the Houston Civilian Board of Inquiry. According to Lewis, a local attorney who lived near Camp Logan, a small group of men passed his home after the initial shooting and he inquired of them "What was going on?" One of them replied, "Oh we are shooting up the whites; we haven't but a little time to stay here; (but) we are no negroes." Lewis then testified that "one of the men raised his rifle and said, 'You know how far and how fast one of these magazine rifles can shoot?'"[36] Lewis did not identify the men he talked to on that dark and rainy night as black or white. However, the fact that they left Lewis unharmed clearly indicates that they were not an angry group of black soldiers on a mission of revenge against whites. Were these men, armed with rifles, members of the Texas National Guard, which the Twenty-fourth replaced, along with other whites (Haynes's "mythical" white mob)? Was the attack upon Camp Logan an attempt to duplicate the Brownsville incident of 1906? The evidence is clear that Camp Logan had been fired into by outside forces and that the frightened soldiers panicked, seized their weapons, and left camp to meet their assailants. It was not an organized or planned exit since the soldiers left camp "hollering and yelling like a mob."[37] Such an exit does not indicate that it was one planned by experienced or veteran black soldiers.

Haynes has argued that Sgt. Vida Henry and a small group of supporters planned and organized the attack upon Houston. This view was first advanced by military authorities who, Haynes admits, deliberately distorted the sworn testimony of the two chief officers of the Twenty-fourth Battalion, Commander Snow and Chief of Military Police Captain Shekerjian, in order to produce a conspiracy theory. Both men testified that Sergeant Henry was the one who warned them of possible trouble on the night of August 23, but in order to identify Henry as the organizer of the incident and leader of the rebellious men, top army officials concluded that the officers had made a mistake and that someone else had given the warning. Accepting the distorted military view, Haynes goes on to argue that Henry was indeed the principal conspirator, that he deliberately deceived his superiors, tricking them into seizing all weapons in camp in order to create fear among the men, arranged for the cry "the mob is coming" to be shouted in camp as a signal for action on the part of his followers, and planned to use his position as a first sergeant to lead more men from the camp into Houston on a mission of revenge.[38]

The argument that Sergeant Henry led the men in such a conspiracy is unsupported either by reliable, documented evidence or by Henry's character and attitudes. Based upon his military record prior to the incident, Henry was one of the few members of the Twenty-fourth who was enjoying his stay in Houston. According to Col. William Newman, who was in command of the Twenty-fourth until August 20, Henry told him that he was fond of the city because "he had met more high-class colored people in Houston than he had ever seen before."[39] Newman described Henry as a man of unquestioned loyalty who had been given responsibilities that were beyond his capabilities. "I thought he was unoffensive and not forceful enough to be a First Sergeant of a company," said Newman. Major Snow, Newman's successor, held similar views of Henry, whom he described as illiterate but courteous. Snow also testified that it was Henry who first warned him of trouble.[40] In light of the sworn opinions of Colonel Newman and Major Snow, it is inconceivable that Sergeant Henry had the desire, courage, or ability to organize a full-fledged rebellion against military authority and the city of Houston.

All who identified Sergeant Henry as the leader of the soldiers' attack upon Houston were frightened men who testified under grants of immunity from prosecution or promises of leniency from military prosecutors. The witnesses responded to questions that were worded to elicit a preconceived response.[41] It is beyond question that Henry participated in the incident. However, his decision to do so was made after failing to prevent the troops from seizing weapons and from disobeying orders to remain in camp. According to Colonel Cress's investigation and report on the incident, the soldiers who bolted the camp after the initial shooting "were not in any formation when they left but appear to have halted and, at least partially, organized on the street just east of camp."[42]

In all probability Henry was among the men who panicked and, once outside the camp, realized that a serious military offense had taken place that would bring the severest of punishments. He, therefore, decided to make the crime fit the harsh punishment that surely awaited the men when the camp returned to normal and made the decision to direct their actions. This was a spur-of-the-moment decision rather than a coldly premeditated plot. Once the decision had been made Henry realized its gravity, which explains why he took his own life on the streets of Houston rather than give the army the pleasure of dictating his execution.

The other soldiers who participated in the Houston confrontation were not as fortunate as Henry. In the aftermath of the disturbance the entire Third Battalion, Twenty-fourth Infantry, was immediately transferred to Camp Furlong in Columbus, New Mexico, where 118 men were arrested, charged with murder and mutiny, and held for trial by General Court-Martial. The purpose of a military court-martial, as the history of such events has shown, is to convict—and 110 of the accused were ultimately convicted. The men were tried in three groups: 63 on November 1, 1917; 15 on December 17, 1917; and the last 40 on February 18, 1918. The trials resulted in twenty-eight death sentences, thirteen of which were secretly carried out on December 11, 1917, before the cases could be reviewed and without notification to the respective families. President Woodrow Wilson reluctantly commuted ten of the remaining death sentences to life imprisonment after his office was flooded with letters protesting the earlier executions and requesting leniency for those who remained on death row. Those not given the death penalty were sentenced to the federal prison in Leavenworth, Kansas, to serve terms that ranged from two years to life.

When the fate of those soldiers sentenced to death because of their alleged involvement in the Houston affair became public knowledge, the black community reacted with fury. Blacks on the street openly talked of revenge and the nation's black press refused to condemn what the white press described as "one of the most disgraceful mutinies of American troops in our history."[43] Instead, black newspapers angrily attacked what they believed to be military injustice. *The Crisis,* the journal of the National Association for the Advancement of Colored People, which served as the organization's national voice, described the executed soldiers as "martyrs for the cause of democracy."[44] Similar views were expressed by the *Baltimore Crusader;* the *Messenger,* a socialist publication in New York City edited by Asa P. Randolph and Chandler Owen; and the *New York Age,* a publication founded by the well-respected T. Thomas Fortune. Fortune was a strong supporter of the philosophy of Booker T. Washington and counted among his supporters prominent politicians such as Senator Thomas C. Platt of New York and former President Theodore Roosevelt. An editorial in the *Age* angrily declared that "strict justice has been done, but full justice has not been done. And so sure as there is a God in heaven, at some time and some way full justice will be done."[45]

All of the 110 men sentenced to death or imprisonment by the military courts-martial proclaimed their innocence. The night of the incident was dark and rainy, making it impossible for the white officers of the Twenty-fourth to identify individual participants.[46] Neither did the courts-martial produce any evidence to identify individuals. Subsequently, the accused were convicted upon military speculation and the conflicting testimony of seven frightened black soldiers, one of whom was so scared that he "defecated in his breeches" on the night of the incident.[47] These men were pressured to admit that they were participants in the affair and were promised leniency in return for their testimony against other suspected participants. The goal of army prosecutors was to prove that the Houston incident was unprovoked, premeditated, and that the white officers of the Twenty-fourth bore no blame. With the aid of the seven black soldiers, the prosecution was able to ensure that all the white officers of the battalion were officially relieved of any responsibility for the incident.

If the white officers bore no responsibility, who was responsible for the Houston incident? The easy answer is that the soldiers were responsible since they disobeyed orders and took up arms against civilians. This was the official position taken by the War Department. In his studies of the incident, Haynes accepts the War Department's position but also broadens the responsibility. He argues that local business leaders and public officials shared some of the responsibility due to economic greed (the profits to be made from the construction of Camp Logan) and an unwillingness to sacrifice political popularity to guarantee fair treatment to soldiers. Haynes also criticizes Chief of Police Brock for his inability to control his men and eliminate police brutality. But Haynes's hardest indictment is reserved for the soldiers, whom he denounces for their decision to fight violence with violence. The urge to defend oneself when under attack, a natural urge propelled by intense fear, is not a factor in Haynes's analysis, since he dismisses their reactions to the attack of their encampment by an irate mob in favor of a conspiracy theory. There is no question that some of the inexperienced soldiers from the Twenty-fourth, reacting to what the evidence indicates was a mob attack, panicked and reacted with violence toward their attackers. That, however, was a reaction to violence and not its cause. The ultimate responsibility, therefore, rests with those who deliberately set in motion the forces that ended in violent confrontation.

The War Department and the white officers of the Twenty-fourth bear much of the responsibility for the bloodshed in Houston. The Secretary of War, Newton D. Baker, reversed a decision made by army officials not to send black troops into the South for military training and tours of duty, in full recognition of the potential problems. Top army officials and lesser officers then failed to carry out his directive that they "exercise judgement and discretion" to prevent clashes between their men and the local white population. Conflict between black soldiers and whites in Houston was assured when the War Department decided to send sixty-five experienced, noncommissioned officers from the Twenty-fourth to commission officer training school at Fort Des Moines, Iowa. According to Brig. Gen. J. L. Chamberlain, these men were "the very best material among the noncommissioned officers of the regiment and included the Regimental Sergeant Major, the Battalion Sergeant Major, the First Sergeant, and three other Sergeants from Company I, the company in which the mutiny started." Subsequently, "many of the non-commissioned officers and many of the men left with the regiment were new men," not experienced soldiers as Haynes and others have charged.[48] Those elite noncommissioned officers from the Twenty-fourth who were attending officer training school believed that if they had been with their men, the Houston incident would never have occurred. They even volunteered to "give up their prospects for commissions so as to return to the regiment and redeem its reputation."[49]

The War Department was also responsible for transferring command of the Twenty-fourth from Col. William Newman, an officer with experience in commanding black troops, to Maj. Kneeland S. Snow, an inexperienced officer, who, according to Haynes, was more concerned about his golf game and Houston's nightlife than he was with the welfare of his men.[50] Snow took command of the Twenty-fourth two days before the tragedy of August 23 and miserably failed to execute Baker's directive to use "judgement and discretion" to prevent trouble between black troops and the local white population. Due to these actions, significant responsibility for the Houston tragedy must fall on the shoulders of the War Department, which blinded by military tradition and racism, ignored an excellent opportunity to play a major role as an agency of model race relations and progressive social change.

In view of the economic importance of Camp Logan to the Houston economy, Baker and army officials could have forced local officials to treat the men of the Twenty-fourth with dignity and respect, even within the confines of a Jim Crow community. However, the War Department did not believe that its duty was to work for improved race relations in the civilian community or the army. This was clearly communicated to Emmett J. Scott, Baker's black assistant for minority affairs, in the aftermath of the Houston incident when he asked Baker to implement more humane racial policies in the army. "There is no intention on the part of the War Department," Baker replied, "to undertake at this time a settlement of the so-called race question."[51] Despite the War Department's lack of concern and poor decision-making, however, the ultimate responsibility for the Houston incident rests on the shoulders of local police, the business community, and political leaders.

It was the Houston business community that successfully lobbied the War Department for Camp Logan and it was the construction of the camp that ultimately brought the all-black Twenty-fourth Infantry to the city. Camp Logan was an economic boon for Houston, contributing approximately sixty thousand dollars weekly to the local economy.[52] Local leaders wanted more and were negotiating with the War Department for an aviation school. In fact, the announcement that the city had been awarded the school was made on August 21, 1917, one day before the incident. During the negotiations business leaders were aware of growing problems between white civilians, police, and the black troops at Camp Logan but refused to report them to the War Department for fear of losing the aviation school and having the operations of the camp severely restricted.[53] This was clearly revealed in an unsigned editorial in the *Houston Post* following the explosion at Camp Logan. According to the editorial: "The only explanation of toleration of this insolent and disorderly conduct [any display of pride and independence by blacks was viewed as insolent and disorderly conduct by many local whites] is that those who knew of it thought it best to endure patiently rather than run the risk of losing the camp by flooding the War Department with complaints."[54]

The Houston business community, represented by the local Chamber of Commerce (which had assured the War Department that the black soldiers would be treated with respect by local whites), allowed the pursuit of profits from government wartime expenditures to override its civic responsibility. Treating black soldiers with respect would not have seriously challenged the local Jim Crow laws, which the white community cherished. Had business and political leaders pressured local police authorities into reining in a brutal, out of control police force, clashes might have been minimized and violence averted. Instead, business leaders not only failed to intervene but refused to report problems with the Twenty-fourth to the War Department in order to protect their profits. It was this failure of courage and political leadership, fueled by greed that paved the way for what is commonly known as the Houston Riot of 1917.

In 1921, Congressman D. R. Anthony of Leavenworth, Kansas, introduced a resolution into the U.S. House of Representatives requesting Secretary of War John W. Weeks to review the cases of the sixty-three soldiers still imprisoned as a result of the Houston tragedy to determine if they were eligible for pardons or clemency. Weeks reported that the cases of the imprisoned soldiers had been reviewed in the spring of 1920 by the Department of Psychiatry and Sociology at the U.S. Disciplinary Barracks, Fort Leavenworth, Kansas, and that the prison psychiatrists had issued a negative report. According to the report:

> Practically all of these prisoners deny participation in the mutiny or events occurring in the city of Houston on August 23, 1917. It seems to us that the conspiracy continues among these men. In view of the serious nature of the offenses of which these men were convicted, it is believed that it would be distinctly prejudicial to discipline and the interest of the services to grant any clemency at this time.[55]

In denying clemency, the army refused to consider the fact that the accused had not been positively identified by anyone as actual participants in the Houston affair. The protests of innocence might have been truth, rather than an obstinate conspiracy. Nor did the army consider the mitigating circumstances that led to the incident.

In the aftermath of World War I, the war fought to "make the world safe for democracy," the vast majority of black Americans readily agreed with Emmett Scott, Baker's Assistant Secretary of War for Black Affairs, when he commented in 1933: "as one who recalls the assurances of 1917 and 1918 . . . I confess personally a deep sense of disappointment, of poignant pain that a great country in time of need should promise so much and afterward perform so little."[56] And the remnants of the Twenty-fourth who bravely fought and died in the war while their brothers languished in prison could say to America with conviction that "you treat no other friend so ill."

Notes

The hymn text appearing at the beginning of this chapter was quoted in Kelley Miller, *The Disgrace, of Democracy: An Open Letter to President Woodrow Wilson* (Washington, D.C.: Howard University Press, 1917), 14. Copies of this publication are located in Record Group 165, War Department General Staff,

Military Intelligence Division, 1917–41, Box 69, Negro File, National Archives, Washington, D.C.

1. Quoted in David M. Kennedy, *Over Here: The First World War and American Society* (New York: Oxford University Press, 1980), 159.

2. Mary F. Berry and John W. Blassingame, *Long Memory: The Black Experience in America* (New York: Oxford University Press, 1982), 308.

3. Ibid.

4. For detailed accounts of the Brownsville incident see John D. Weaver, *The Brownsville Raid* (New York: W. W. Norton, 1970); Ann J. Lane, *The Brownsville Affair: National Crisis and Black Reaction* (Port Washington, N.Y.: Kennikat Press, 1971); and Lewis N. Wynne, "Brownsville: The Reaction of the Negro Press," *Phylon* 33 (Summer 1972): 153–60.

5. Quoted in Berry and Blassingame, 311. In 1972, more than sixty years after the incident, the army cleared the records of those accused of raiding Brownsville and declared their original conviction a gross injustice.

6. Newton D. Baker, Secretary of War, to President Woodrow Wilson, August 17, 1917, *The Papers of Woodrow Wilson*, vol. 43 (Washington, D.C.: Library of Congress, 1955), 506.

7. Ibid.

8. The comments of Col. William Newman are included in an investigative report on the Houston incident of 1917 by Col. G. O. Cress entitled "Investigation into the disciplinary conditions in 3rd Battalion, 24th Infantry, while on duty in Houston, Texas, July 26 to August 25, 1917." The report is dated October 5, 1917, see Record Group 407, Records of the Adjutant General's Office, 1917–25, Box 1277, Folder 4, National Archives. Cress and a number of other military officials filed multiple reports on the Houston incident, hereafter cited by name of correspondent, date, and record group number.

9. Quoted in Robert V. Haynes, *A Night of Violence: The Houston Riot of 1917* (Baton Rouge: Louisiana State University Press, 1976), 53.

10. "Statement of Sergeant Cecil Green to Colonel G. O. Cress, August 30, 1917, in an investigative report by Colonel Cress entitled "Investigation of the Trouble at Houston, Texas, Between the Third Battalion, 24th Infantry, and the Citizens of Houston, August 23, 1917," Record Group 393, U.S. Army, Southern Department, Box 364, File 370.61, National Archives.

11. See Newman's statement in Cress Report, October 5, 1917, RG 407.

12. Martha Gruening, "Houston: An N.A.A.C.P. Investigation," *Crisis* 15 (November 1917): 19; Haynes, *A Night of Violence*, 85.

13. Cress Report, October 5, 1917, RC 407.

14. Report of Col. William Newman to Inspector General of the Army, September 20, 1917, Record Group 407, Records of the Adjutant General's Office, 1917–25, Box 1277, National Archives.

15. Ibid.

16. Report of Capt. David E. Van Natta, Second Illinois Infantry, to Inspector General of the Army, September 25, 1917, Record Group 393, U.S. Army,

Southern Department, Records of the Judge Advocates General, Box 364, File 370.61, National Archives.

17. See *The Outlook*, September 5, 1917; *Literary Digest*, September 29, 1917; Gruening, 14–19.

18. Robert V. Haynes, "The Houston Mutiny and Riot of 1917," *Southwestern Historical Quarterly* 76 (1973): 418–39; Haynes, *A Night of Violence*.

19. Haynes, "The Houston Mutiny," 430 n53.

20. For the sworn statements of Lee Sparks and Charles Baltimore, see Cress Report, September 13, 1917, RG 393.

21. Ibid.

22. Cress Report, October 5, 1917, RG 407.

23. Major Snow's account of events leading up to the confrontation on the night of August 23 is located in Cress Report, September 13, 1917, RG 393.

24. See testimony of Chief of Police Clarence E. Brock in Newman Report, September 20, 1917, RG 407; and the testimony of Cleo Lockhart, age fifteen, Edna Topper, age thirteen, and Flassy and Bessie Chancey, ages fifteen and sixteen respectively, Record Group 153, Records of the Judge Advocate, NNG-73–543, General Courts-Martial, Federal Records Center (Microfilm), Suitland, Maryland.

25. Cress Report, October 5, 1917, RG 401.

26. Newman Report, September 20, 1917, RG 407.

27. Cress Report, September 13, 1917, RGS 93.

28. Colonel Newman's comments are quoted in Cress Report, October 5, 1917, RG 407.

29. Haynes, *A Night of Violence*, 93.

30. Ibid., 102.

31. Testimony of Chief Clarence C. Brock before the Houston Civilian Board of Inquiry, August 24, 1917, p. 217 of transcript, Record Croup 393, U.S. Army, Southern Department, Box 364, File 370.61, National Archives. Haynes has argued that Sparks was suspended for using abusive language in front of a black housewife while arresting her teenage son. This appears very unlikely in view of the record of unrestrained police brutality blacks endured in Houston. By Haynes's own admission, Sparks's supervisors had made no effort to control his abusive behavior prior to the Baltimore incident (*A Night of Violence*, 93.) Furthermore, Sparks apparently continued his career of brutality toward blacks. Three days after the Camp Logan tragedy, Sparks shot and killed a black Houstonian. Although indicted for murder, Sparks was quickly acquitted by the jury (Haynes, "The Houston Mutiny and Riot of 1917," 478 n76).

32. Cress Report, September 13, 1917, (5), RG 393.

33. Haynes, *A Night of Violence*, 125.

34. Testimony of Patrolman L. E. Gentry before the Houston Civilian Board of Inquiry, p. 25 of transcript; Maj. K. S. Snow to Brig. Gen. John A. Hulen, "Report on Circumstances Attending the Mutiny," August 24, 1917, Record Group 393, U.S. Army, Southern Department, Box 364, National Archives.

35. Haynes, "The Houston Mutiny," 429 n49.

36. Testimony of R. E. Lewis before the Houston Civilian Board of Inquiry, p. 97 of transcript, August 24, 1917, RG 393.

37. Haynes, *A Night of Violence,* 136–39.

38. Ibid.

39. Statement by Newman, October 1, 1917, in Cress Report, October 5, 1917, RG 407.

40. Testimony of Maj. K. S. Snow, September 27, 1917, Record Group 407, Records of the Adjutant General's Office, Box 1277, Folder 4, National Archives.

41. Haynes, *A Night of Violence,* 258.

42. Cress Report, September 13, 1917, RC 393.

43. *The Outlook* (September 5, 1917), 10; *Literary Digest* (September 29, 1917), 4–5.

44. *The Crisis* (October 17, 1917), 284–85.

45. These papers are quoted in John Hope Franklin, *From Slavery to Freedom: A History of Negro Americans* (New York: Knopf, 1980), 330.

46. Cress Report, September 13, 1917, RG 393.

47. Haynes, *A Night of Violence,* 261–62, 277, 304.

48. Brig. Gen. J. L. Chamberlain, Inspector General, U.S. Army to Adjutant General, September 26, 1917, Record Group 407, Records of the Adjutant General's Office, Box 1277, National Archives.

49. Ibid.

50. Haynes, *A Night of Violence,* 91.

51. Newton D. Baker, Secretary of War, to Emmett J. Scott, September 30, 1917, quoted in Kennedy, 159.

52. Edgar A. Schuler, "The Houston Race Riot, 1917," *Journal of Negro History* (July 1944): 304.

53. Ibid.

54. Ibid.

55. John W. Weeks, Secretary or War, to the Honorable Julius Kahn, U.S. House of Representatives, December 6, 1921, Record Group 233, House Committee on Military Affairs, 67th Congress, Houston Riot Cases, HR67A-F28.1, National Archives.

56. Quoted in, Kennedy, 284.

PART IV

Community of Soldiers

Buffalo soldiers in the American West, reared in a segregated society that offered black citizens few of the benefits available to their white counterparts, developed a community of black soldiers. Their duty hours were often tedious and boring; off-duty diversions were primarily limited to their own company. They quickly learned (if such learning were necessary) that for meaningful and enjoyable lives while on military duty they must rely on each other. White and black soldiers seldom mixed, and the segregated society placed considerable obstacles in the paths of black soldiers who joined in any type of activity with whites on or off the base. Segregation led to the adoption of black community strategies and activities that brought support for each other. While the U.S. military offered opportunities not available in Jim Crow-dominated civilian society and most recreational activities took place within the segregated unit, black soldiers did meet with both civilian and military whites for occasional duties, events, and activities.

Black soldiers received a double dose of negative responses from the citizenry, first because they were soldiers and second because they were black. Sometimes they could lose their lives. Black soldiers off base who became embroiled in a dispute at a bar or gambling house might well be killed by a white civilian. Suppliers, within and without the military, took advantage of their precarious position: Products sent to the camps for black soldiers might spoil overly soon, and inferior animals and other supplies were issued to the black troops. Yet, the use of black soldiers to prevent violence garnered compliments and favorable opinions from the citizenry who benefited. Numerous examples existed of mutual enjoyment; black musical bands impressed and performed for the local citizens, and the bands were invited by them to community gatherings. Athletic events, especially baseball competition, led to mutually agreeable relationships between black soldiers and the larger community.

An exceedingly important factor in the ability of buffalo soldiers to lead hospitable communal lives was the geographic location of their camps. The worst place to serve, as noticed by episodes in our chapter on discrimination and violence, was Texas. Texas' Southern heritage of slavery, racism, and hatred of black soldiers led to many violent confrontations. While the New Mexico frontier experience witnessed confrontations between black soldiers and citizens, there was also mutual engagement and interchange. The New Mexico black soldiers ultimately relocated to Utah, where black soldier and white community relations were quite satisfactory, as Michael J. Clark persuasively points out in "Improbable Ambassadors: Black Soldiers at Fort Douglas, 1896–99."

Fort Douglas was located in an attractive setting near Salt Lake City; the black troops for the most part were welcomed by the white community, and the site already featured a reasonably sized black community. Recreational activities included societies and clubs, athletics, bands, and virtually no black-white conflicts or struggles. At the beginning of the Spanish-American War, the black soldiers of the Twenty-fourth Infantry were among the first groups to be sent to Cuba, where they performed well and were received back with a great welcome in the United States and in Salt Lake City. The war left its imprint on the participants, and the postwar buffalo soldiers seemed more disenchanted with life; disciplinary violations increased. Shortly, the members of the Twenty-fourth (1899) were sent to fight in William McKinley's Philippine-American War. Overall, their favorable experience and behavior at Fort Douglas led them to be called "Improbable Ambassadors."

Black soldiers of the Twenty-fifth Infantry, located at Fort Missoula, Montana in the 1890s, discovered one other reason to enjoy their position as black soldiers when they participated in the great bicycle experiment. As Charles M. Dollar showed in "Putting the Army on Wheels: The Story of the Twenty-fifth Infantry Bicycle Corps," under the leadership of Lieutenant Moss, the army formed the Black Bicycle Corps, an experimental group to ascertain whether the bicycle could be used efficiently to move infantrymen and equipment. Trips generally were marked with hardships; mud, rough roads, wind, and tire blowouts especially frustrated the black bicyclists, but there were good experiences as well. Friendly people greeted them along the way, and when they entered St. Louis a big celebration resulted. The experiment was successful. The use of black soldiers in the bicycle corps illustrated that the military, as opposed to society in general, usually did not let racism determine the role and function of soldiers. While discrimination seemed to dominate civilian society, the military frequently enabled black soldiers to receive equitable treatment.

By the late nineteenth century, athletics also became an entry to community activities, allowing blacks to engage with whites in positive ways, as Marvin E. Fletcher argues in "The Black Soldier Athlete in the United States Army, 1890–1916." The most popular sport was baseball but other sports included football, basketball, boxing, and track and field. Normally, competition took place within the regiment, but games were held between black regimental teams and white civilian and military teams. To enhance a sense of community for black soldiers, leisure time activities such as billiards, bowling, and ice skating (depending on location) gave them periods of recreation. Overall, athletic events between white and black teams created a venue for interrelations between white and black, whether civilian or military, that was mostly positive. There were other results. In at least one instance, a black defeat of white teams led a white military officer to argue that blacks should not be allowed to compete (especially against whites) because it was unseemly for an inferior race to defeat a superior race. However, as Fletcher put it, "as a result of the opportunities provided by the recreation and competitive sports programs within the military, blacks had a chance to show their talents" (25), an opportunity denied them in the society at large.

Athletics were not the only way in which blacks in the military could assist improved race relations between black and white; music offered another avenue. Horace D. Nash, in "Community Building on the Border: The Role of the 24th Infantry Band at Columbus, New Mexico, 1916–1922," discusses the achievements of the military band while stationed at Columbus, New Mexico, prior to and during World War I. Despite the fact that, as in much of the nation, social activities were segregated, at Columbus a high degree of tolerance existed and black and white residents jointly attended most public affairs, largely as a result of the black soldiers' band. The Twenty-fourth Infantry band performed at integrated activities. The band also aided in the growth of a spirit of community, while at the same time providing blacks with a sense of pride. Black band members participated in wartime community efforts, fundraisers, Red Cross drives, holiday celebrations, Juneteenth, and a wide range of other community events. On the base, the band played for social groups, dances, activities organized by black women, and various gatherings designed to improve morale and a sense of community. The band became a source of pride for the entire town, and by providing entertainment for blacks at segregated events, the infantry band helped create a more active and dynamic black community.

Whether as a result of a favorable location, determined and successful military action, athletics, music, or their own internal efforts, black soldiers in the American West from the Civil War through World War I developed a pride and a spirit of community, which enabled them to better enjoy life and to survive in a military set in a segregated, and too often racist, society.

MICHAEL J. CLARK

Improbable Ambassadors

BLACK SOLDIERS AT FORT DOUGLAS, 1896-99

Although the record is clear, few people know that on the east bench, overlooking Salt Lake City and touching the boundaries of the University of Utah, more than six hundred Black people—soldiers of the U.S. Twenty-fourth Infantry, wives, children, and others—lived, worked, and attended school for almost four years in one of the most attractive locations in the western United States. Twenty-one graves in the little Fort Douglas cemetery, with weatherworn markers that become less legible each year, serve as quiet reminders that Black people exceeded the geographical boundaries historians have generally assigned them. Two additional graves mark the resting place of Black cavalrymen from the famous Ninth Cavalry stationed at Fort Duchesne, Utah, prior to the turn of the century and at Fort Douglas following the departure of the Twenty-fourth Infantry.

Although Black U.S. Army regiments were stationed throughout the West for almost a century after the Civil War, knowledge that they were a regular and integral part of the army is not widespread.[1] During the Civil War, Black units served throughout the Southwest; and after 1866, members of the Twenty-fourth Infantry, Twenty-fifth Infantry, Ninth Cavalry, and Tenth Cavalry served as far north as Vancouver, British Columbia, as far west as the Presidio in San Francisco, and as far south as Mexico. Black men in uniform, as well as their wives and children, were prominent in Fort Bayard, New Mexico; Fort Grant, Arizona; Fort Douglas, Utah; Fort Duchesne, Utah; Fort Logan, Colorado, Fort Missoula, Montana; Fort Davis, Texas; and numerous other posts throughout the West and served in some cases to augment comparatively small Black civilian populations.

The relative dearth of published material on the army's Black rank-and-file and the considerable difficulties involved in uncovering information may partially account for the limited attention given Black enlisted men. Additionally, officers and cavalry units have been considered more attractive by writers and historians. This does not mean that Black units and their men have gone entirely unobserved. Their critics appear to have been more vocal, if not more numerous, than their eulogizers. As late as 1900, Black soldiers continued to be characterized as "illiterate," "lazy," "a drinker," "a gambler," "set apart by nature," "a natural horseman," and inconsequential in the development of the West.[2] Subsequent discussions by historians have challenged these characterizations, but the definitive study is yet to be made.

In attempting to delineate in more detail the presence of the Twenty-fourth Infantry in Utah, the author's examination of local newspapers and army records for that period raised several questions that warranted further investigation: why was the Twenty-fourth stationed in Utah? what impact did the unit have upon Salt Lake City? what was it like to be a Black soldier during this period? where did the men come from? how did the presence of Black soldiers affect the development of Salt Lake City's Black community and its historical presence in Utah? were there any long-term effects of the regiment's presence in Utah?

During early September 1896 word circulated between military posts that the adjutant general was considering a plan to relocate several regiments. Although details of the proposed reassignment of troops were not fully known, there were those soldiers who wished for new duty assignments and those who were anxious to remain where they were. Some civilian populations refused to cheer the pending change. In Salt Lake City, for example, the Sixteenth Infantry, a white unit, grudgingly prepared to leave Fort Douglas for Boise Barracks and Fort Sherman in Idaho and Fort Spokane, Washington. According to a local newspaper report, the unit's football and baseball teams were greatly disappointed because they had hoped to win championships in Utah.[3] In addition, younger soldiers were probably concerned with leaving girl friends, and older soldiers faced the prospect of moving families and household effects. A group of Salt Lake City residents, after attending a dance at Fort Douglas, "went home happy and expressed sorrow at its being the last dance they would attend at the post for several years."[4]

The Fifteenth Infantry, as luck would have it, was transferred from Illinois to forts in the Southwest that had been garrisoned by the Twenty-fourth Infantry. These New Mexico and Arizona posts had reputations for being "hellholes," and members of the Fifteenth Infantry were probably convinced that they were being punished for some wrongdoing. On the other hand, it appears likely that most members of the Twenty-fourth Infantry were happy with the regiment scramble and felt that, after thirty years, the unit was finally getting in Fort Douglas the kind of duty station it deserved. At that point, all four of the army's so-called Black units—each unit had white officers—were stationed in the West.[5]

The arrival of the Twenty-fourth Infantry in Salt Lake City more than doubled Utah's Black population. The Ninth Cavalry, stationed at Fort Duchesne in Utah County, had 584 Black soldiers, and the Twenty-fourth's strength was rather constant at 512. One may speculate that Utah's total Black population, civilian and military, exceeded eighteen hundred in the fall of 1896 and reached twenty-three hundred in 1898 after the Twenty-fourth returned from the Spanish-American War.

Both rumor and fact preceded the arrival of the Twenty-fourth Infantry in Salt Lake City, and some citizens expressed concern, or at least interest, at news appearing in the *Salt Lake Tribune* and *Salt Lake Herald* reporting the War Department's decision to station the Twenty-fourth at Fort Douglas.[6] On September 20, 1896, almost one month before the advance companies of the Twenty-fourth arrived in Salt Lake City, the *Tribune,* in an editorial entitled, "An Unfortunate Change," voiced attitudes that Black soldiers would ultimately have to confront during their tour of duty in Utah. The editorial reflected upon the close ties that had existed between the city and members of the Sixteenth Infantry and implied that such relationships would not be possible with members of the Twenty-fourth. It also pointed out that the residential portion of the city lay between the central city and Fort Douglas. As a result, "colored" soldiers would have to travel on streetcars to and from the post, and this would bring them in direct contact with whites and especially with white women. The editorial argued that there were differences between Black and white soldiers when they were drunk. A Black soldier "will be sure to want to assert himself" when on a car with white ladies. It would be best, the editorial concluded, to lay the facts before the secretary of war and

> he might still be induced to make the change and send the colored men to some other station where they would be just as comfortable, where they would not be a source of apprehension and discomfort to the people of a large city like this.[7]

Following the editorial lead, Senator Frank J. Cannon met with Secretary of War Daniel S. Lamont and asked that some regiment other than the Twenty-fourth be sent to Fort Douglas. According to the *Deseret News*, at least a part of Senator Cannon's appeal to the secretary had to do with the undesirability of locating "a colored regiment" in the immediate neighborhood of the University of Utah. However, the secretary, although sympathetic to Cannon's appeal, "found it impossible to change the order."[8] The *Salt Lake Herald* must have reflected what was on the minds of a good many citizens when it reported: "Some people say that there is a good deal of politics mixed up in the move of the Twenty-fourth Infantry to Fort Douglas."[9] Julius F. Taylor, a Black and editor of the *Broad Ax*, noted that Secretary of War Lamont was a Democrat and for that reason would not withdraw the order to transfer the Twenty-fourth.[10] Taylor's speculation is not persuasive, and it appears that politics played no significant part in the secretary of war's decision.

In addition to criticizing Senator Cannon for his part in trying to prevent the Twenty-fourth from being stationed at Fort Douglas, Taylor was critical of the *Salt Lake Tribune* for being the only newspaper in Salt Lake City to raise "any sort of objection to the location of the Twenty-fourth." Taylor also charged the *Tribune* with being "the accepted organ of the Republican party."[11] By way of contrast, the *Salt Lake Herald* editorialized on October 10, 1896, "Glory and Honor to the Sixteenth Infantry! Welcome to the Twenty-fourth Infantry." The *Herald*'s welcome indicated that there was no unified view regarding the Black soldiers. Some opposed their coming, others did not. Depending on the source, the issue was considered racial, political (owing, possibly, to the recently fought battles over statehood and the practice of polygamy), or a matter of reward for meritorious service.

William G. Muller, a white officer of the Twenty-fourth, in his unpublished history of the regiment, considered the *Salt Lake Tribune*'s editorial the most prominent occurrence connected with the unit's tour of duty in Utah. Although he could not recall the dates the regiment was stationed at Fort Douglas, he did recollect that feelings against the "negro soldiers" were "bitter" and prejudiced. Later, he observed, when the regiment returned to Salt Lake City from Cuba, "it had the hearts of the people."[12] Muller also remarked that a year after the Twenty-fourth's arrival the *Tribune* printed what amounted to an apology to the unit.

Morale may have been an important factor in the relocation of the Twenty-fourth Infantry. During the thirty years the regiment was stationed in the southwestern territories, various requests had been made for transfer to more desirable duty stations. In January 1895 the requests became more specific, asking for a "station near a large city." George W. Murray, apparently a civilian supporter of the Twenty-fourth, in a memorandum to the secretary of war, offered several key points for consideration: (1) the difference in treatment between Black and white units; (2) "every unit in the infantry regiment in the Army has had or now have [*sic*], a station near a large city except the Twenty-fourth"; and (3) "depression and demoralization results [*sic*] from service too long in the wilderness."[13] Murray's memorandum was received in the adjutant general's office on February 7, 1895, and was submitted to Lt. Gen. J. M. Schofield in command of the army. He suggested that "this regiment be given a northern station if it is found practicable to do so."[14]

No immediate action followed Murray's recommendation to Secretary of War Lamont, but on January 22, 1896, Col. J. Ford Kent, commanding officer of the Twenty-fourth, added to what must have been an increasing number of requests to have the Twenty-fourth moved to a northern station. Writing from the regiment's headquarters at Fort Bayard, New Mexico, Col. Kent requested a "good station" and announced that "a natural feeling prevails that it is on account of their color that the regiment is debarred from the better locations."[15] Kent sought support for his request by noting that Gen. Schofield, by then "the late Commanding General," had supported his request. Schofield had given a favorable endorsement for relocation on February 15, 1895, and had inspected Kent's post in May. Kent in his letter to the adjutant general noted that Schofield informed him in May that "it had been decided, in the event of a possibility in changes in station, that the 24th Infantry should be sent to Fort Douglas . . ."[16] Several months passed before the final decision was made.

In September 1896 the *Salt Lake Herald* reported: "Colored Men Will Come."[17] The response was primarily one of surprise, for the change had not been expected until spring. The city was alive with discussion of the pending arrival of the "Colored Gentlemen" from forts Bayard and Huachuca.[18] The uncharitable editorial that had appeared in the *Salt Lake Tribune* on September 20 was followed on September 23, 1896, by an article entitled, "Capt. Hoffman's View," which reflected favorably upon the Twenty-fourth Infantry. Capt. William Hoffman, apparently a resident of Salt Lake City, said he was acquainted with the regiment and that its members were "well-behaved." "The men will keep to their own race," he said, and "we generally will know only the officers and their families." After his own regiment, the Eleventh, Hoffman volunteered, the "Twenty-fourth is my very first choice" Hoffman did not discuss how he became acquainted with the merits of the Twenty-fourth, but his views may have moderated the more impetuous citizen's concerns over the prospect of having uniformed Black soldiers walking the streets of Salt Lake City. Captain Hoffman concluded "that there is no chance whatever that the War Department order will be changed." If Hoffman's belief in the army's intractability and Senator Cannon's "Vain Attempt to Have Them Sent Elsewhere"[19] did not convince the people of Salt Lake City that the arrival of the Black soldiers was imminent, the debarkation at the train station "of about 100 colored women and a number of dark sports who follow the regiment from post to post" must have.[20] "Fifty enlisted men were married and brought their families with them."[21] It is difficult to estimate how many children and other civilians arrived in connection with the unit. Most families lived on or near the post.

Individuals present the story of the Twenty-fourth in a much different way. Solomon (Black Sol) Black, for example, claimed "to have been the youngest soldier in the late war [Civil War]," and said "he was still wearing knee pants when he went in as a drummer boy."[22] The son of Louis Black, he was born in Rome, Georgia, on August 10, 1854, and enlisted in the Black Forty-fourth Infantry at the age of twelve. One month later the youngster, less than five feet three inches tall, was detailed as a musician and served as a fifer and drummer boy until he was discharged on April 30, 1866. Four years later he enlisted in the Twenty-fourth Infantry and completed six enlistments before retiring on May 1, 1897. Like many of his fellow soldiers, Black served in both the infantry and the cavalry (Tenth). After leaving Salt Lake City, he returned to Texas, married Emily Drake who was twenty-five years his junior. He died on December 11, 1932, at the age of seventy-eight and was buried at the National Cemetery.[23]

A fellow soldier with a less certain past, and perhaps a good candidate for development as a folk hero, was Thomas W. Taylor who was born in Freetown, Africa (Sierra Leone), on January 17, 1870.[24] "He is only plain Tommy Taylor to the boys in blue," wrote Annabel Lee for the *San Francisco Call*, "but he is called Prince by his kith and kin, and one day he will be king. And that is why this story is told. It is a true dramatic of a royal household." Taylor claimed to be a Zulu prince whose real name was Jerger Okokudek ("Death-Leaves-One"). According to his story, he left "Kafirland," won medals from Cambridge University (which he attended with his ten sisters), married Rosella Williams, French daughter of one of the professors, came to the United States, and joined the Twenty-fourth at Fort Barrancas, Florida, to learn the arts of modern war so that he could return to his homeland and free his people.[25] Taylor's story, while intriguing, raises more questions than it answers. Freetown, for example, is located on the northwest coast of Africa, a considerable distance from the traditional homeland of the Zulus, and the name "Okokudek" tends to be more of Yoruba origin. Taylor's statement that he enlisted in 1899 does not square with military records that state he enlisted on March 12, 1896. Unfortunately, his military service records will not be available for scrutiny by historians for some time.

Another infantryman, Parker Buford, served thirty years in the Twenty-fourth. He was born in Giles County, Tennessee, January 30, 1842. Buford's son, James J. Buford, also served in the unit. In 1898 the Buford family lived on the perimeter of Fort Douglas at 333 South Thirteenth East. A number of other Black families lived in the general area.[26] Discharged from the army in 1898; the elder Buford continued to live in Salt Lake City until his death in 1911. He is buried in the Fort Douglas Cemetery. His wife, Eliza Elizabeth Buford, lived in Salt Lake City until 1920, when she moved to Pasadena, California, dying there at the age of ninety. Thornton Jackson, also a member of the Twenty-fourth and a long-time resident of Salt Lake City, witnessed Mrs. Buford's military pension application."[27]

Thornton Jackson was a good friend of Sgt. Alfred Rucker, according to Rucker's daughter Viola Rucker Dorsey who was born in the Fort Douglas hospital on January 24, 1896. The Rucker family lived on the post, and the children attended the Wasatch School on South Temple. After retirement, Rucker "drove a dobby wagon for the officers' wives." The "Lee, Irvine and Atchison families lived close by," Mrs. Dorsey recalled, and her father "liked Fort Douglas." He was a "very stern, very noisy" person. When President Warren G. Harding visited Salt Lake City, Sergeant Rucker "stepped out and saluted the president during the parade. He was wearing his blue uniform and Harding stopped the parade to meet him." Viola married George Dorsey whose father was stationed at Fort Duchesne with the Ninth Cavalry.[28]

Other individuals could be singled out, but suffice it to say that most of the Twenty-fourth Infantry lived in Utah for only a short period of time. Those who made Utah their home raised families, sent their children to school, and planted traditions.

According to newspaper reports, the new residents of Fort Douglas were pleased with their assignment and "gratified at having been transferred from Texas to the promised land."[29] Members of the unit apparently wanted the people of Salt Lake City to have a good impression of them, for as one member of the regiment stated: "I do not say this from conceit, but you will find our regiment better behaved and disciplined than most of the white soldiers. It is not an easy matter to get 600 men together without there are one or two unruly fellows among them."[30]

Some questioned whether the newly arrived Black chaplain connected with the unit, Allen Allensworth, should be considered an officer. In some accounts he was considered the exception to the all-white officer ranks. Others regarded him much like a civilian. Born a slave in Louisville, Kentucky, Allensworth was appointed to the position of army chaplain by President Grover Cleveland. The fact that Allensworth was picked by a Democratic president endeared him to Julius Taylor, editor of the *Broad Ax*, and gave Allensworth the distinction of being the only Black army chaplain at that time."[31] Allensworth was married and had two daughters, Eva and Nellia.

The arrival of the Twenty-fourth was not without its impact upon the city's Black community. When the soldiers arrived on the Union Pacific, it was reported that "almost every colored resident in the city" met them at the station."[32] There would be greater contact between the fort and the Black citizens of the city in the months to come.

The Black regiment was newsworthy. There was considerable talk about its band that over a three-year period would entertain thousands of Utah's citizens, "its crack drilling," and the ability of many of its members in athletics, both track and baseball.[33]

Julius Taylor, energetic gadfly editor, was quick to report on his meetings with members of the regiment:

> After we had mingled with a great many members of the Twenty-fourth Regiment, we came to the conclusion that they would rather crawl in bed with a thousand rattlesnakes rather than to associate with the following well-known negro haters and high priests of the g.o. Lilly white party: C. C. Goodwin, Esq. editor of that well-known negro-hating sheet, the *Salt Lake Tribune;* P. C. Lannan, ex-butcher and manager of the same; Ex-Mayor George M. Scott;

Ex-banker James H. Bacon; Hon. James Glendinning and the Hon. Frank J. Cannon.[34]

It is unlikely that "a great many" enlisted men would become so quickly attuned to the political situation in the city and the personalities involved. Taylor, however, rarely missed an opportunity to take C. C. Goodwin and Frank J. Cannon to task, whatever the issue.

Concern over how the newly arrived soldiers would make use of the diversions the city had to offer was probably great. The city boasted a number of establishments that might appear attractive to the soldier looking for some way to pass the time. One, located "on the east side of Commercial Street, near Second South," was called the "policy shop" and allegedly offered gambling, food, and liquor. There, according to a newspaper account, "Merchants, street-loungers, youth, prostitutes and even men in the employ of the city contribute their mite in the hope of fabulous winnings."[35] Yet, the strictness of military discipline and the earnestness of white officers and top sergeants in enforcing it limited the pursuit of pleasure somewhat. According to the *Broad Ax:*

> Rev. Allensworth desires to inform the good people of our beautiful city that he would be more than pleased if all the saloons, gambling houses and immoral houses should absolutely refuse to entertain the negro soldiers, for he believes that there are a thousand white men who are willing to go to hell with the black man, but there are a very few who care to go to heaven with him. He hopes that the police will arrest every brazen faced woman, be she black or white, who attempts to travel on the Street cars to and from the fort.[36]

Despite Allensworth's appeal, Black soldiers did make use of the city for saintly as well as more mundane purposes.

With the regiment well settled at Fort Douglas, "Chaplain Allensworth and a member of the *Broad Ax* staff visited with President Wilford Woodruff head of the Mormon Church," four days before Christmas in 1896. Woodruff, said "that he in common with the rest of our citizens desired to welcome all the members of the Twenty-fourth regiment to our city."[37] The church leader made it clear that he was welcoming the Black members of the regiment as well as its white officers. The Mormon position had been stated earlier in response to an article appearing in the Deming, New Mexico *Headlight* and reprinted in the *Deseret Evening News* that asserted:

Mormons never thought much of the children of Ham and it has been one of their doctrines that the soul of a negro could never reach the exaltation of future bliss. The regiment will probably be ordered away in the course of a couple of years.[38]

The *News,* which had apparently quoted the article in order to refute it, retorted:

The *Headlight* is altogether wrong in its statement of Mormon doctrine; there is nothing in the teachings of the Latter-day Saints to justify the assertion quoted. . . .[39]

Military routine at Fort Douglas offered little excitement for the enlisted members of the Twenty-fourth Infantry. While in the Southwest the regiment's duties had included "expeditions against the Indians . . . guarding strategic points, building roads, hunting horse thieves, and doing anything else which called for hard work and no fame."[40] By contrast, the Utah experience included practice marches, attendance at the post school, exercises in the gym during periods of cold weather, work at improving the post's water waste, maintenance of the post garden, janitorial work, clerk duties, work in the post exchange, drills, commissary work, maintenance of post stables, and blacksmithing. From time to time, an enlisted man might have an opportunity for detached service or recruiting and travel, for example, to Fort Logan, Colorado, or to one of the eastern cities.

For all of its regularity, however, enlisted men appeared to prefer military over civilian life and there was a high percentage of reenlistments. The average number of enlisted men in the regiment between February 1, 1897, and April 1, 1898, was 513. During that time, the average number of probable vacancies was approximately twelve per month. In many cases, however, the vacancies failed to materialize as individuals changed their plans and remained in the service or accepted discharge and reenlisted within a short period of time. The post band was apparently considered excellent duty. For the same period, the average number of probable vacancies in the band amounted to slightly more than one-half vacancy per month."[41] One controversy that may have affected vacancies during the months of November and December came in reaction to the treatment received by an enlisted man, Private Barnes, from Captain Augur. Augur had struck Barnes because he "was not doing his job." Apparently, Barnes had witnesses and was prepared to press his case against Augur. In a letter to the commanding officer of Company D, Twenty-fourth Infantry, the company adjutant declared that Colonel Kent had investigated the occurrence and observed that "Augur was sorry." The adjutant stated that "Kent seems to be supporting his officer."[42] Barnes's fellow enlisted men displayed their displeasure by indicating they would not, in some cases, reenlist.

Private Barnes's willingness to bring charges against a white officer provides a rare glimpse at the activities and encounters that produced courts-martial and other disciplinary measures. The attractiveness of disciplinary problems as news items makes it possible to get a closer look at the atmosphere that existed at the post as well as to determine, to some extent, what the soldiers did on their frequent visits to the city. However, disciplinary measures were fewer before the unit's departure for the Spanish-American War in Cuba than after the men returned.

In addition to his military routine at Fort Douglas, the Black soldier was involved in various societies and clubs, athletics, and other activities. A number of enlisted men belonged to "Noah's Ark Lodge, G.U.O. of O.F., which is the lodge of the Twenty-fourth Infantry." Lt. Peter McCann, who before January of 1899 was a first sergeant in the Tenth Cavalry, helped set up the lodge when he served with the Twenty-fourth while it was stationed in New Mexico.[43] In addition to Noah's Ark Lodge, some soldiers belonged to the Society of Prognosticators, organized while the regiment was stationed at Fort Bayard, New Mexico.[44] Like many of the soldiers' societies, the Society of Prognosticators "operated under rules known only to the organization. . . ."[45] A less secret society composed of enlisted men was the Christian Endeavor Society. This group met once a week and invited guests to speak on a variety of topics. On one occasion, Miss Nellia Allensworth, daughter of the post chaplain, spoke on "Confidence."[46] Mr. Wake of Salt Lake City, on another occasion, chose as his topic "Our Missionary Work."[47] The society regularly invited members of the Allensworth family and Sgt. James M. Dickerson to speak. The Frederick Douglass Memorial Literary Society was also active on the post. It sponsored instrumental solos, lectures, and debates on such topics as: "Resolved, that there is no future for the negro in the United States" (the debate was decided in the affirmative).[48] This society also supported an amateur dramatic club.[49] Enlisted men also joined the Love and Hope Lodge No. 3858, which had ninety-five members. Affiliated with the "Grand United Order of Odd Fellows, a Colored order," the lodge was founded at Fort Huachuca, Arizona, near the Mexican border. In Salt Lake City the soldiers founded "city lodges of the order" and on occasion participated in events with civilians. W. W. Taylor, editor of the *Plain Dealer*, and Horace Voss were members of city lodges.[50]

The Williams and Prince Minstrel Company was organized by the men at Fort Douglas and provided entertainment at the post as well as in the city.[51] Dancing was another favorite activity. Enlisted men gave "hops" and invited Black civilians; a dancing school was conducted by Corporal and Mrs. Batie;[52] and the New Year's holiday in January 1898 provided an occasion for the enlisted men to hold a masquerade ball at the post.[53] Post social life demonstrates the extent to which Black civilians and soldiers mingled and the lengths to which the Black soldier went to improve the quality of his life and that of his fellow soldiers. There was enough activity on the part of enlisted men that the *Salt Lake Herald* could report, "enlisted men want their own social hall for entertainment and dances and to hold meetings of their secret clubs."[54]

Athletics were also important to the men. Sports fans from the city followed the Fort Douglas baseball team, the Colored Monarchs, which competed against the Ninth Cavalry's team from Fort Duchesne and civilian teams from Salt Lake City. The team's popularity led the Salt Lake City Street Car Company to donate on occasion ten dollars "to the post baseball fund." Individual players had their followers in the city, but sometimes, as in the case of James Flowers, "a good athlete and baseball player lacked the necessary qualifications of a soldier." Baseball "cranks" were disappointed when Flowers was dishonorably discharged from the service.[55]

The reputation of the Twenty-fourth Infantry's band—heralded by some as the best in the army—reached Salt Lake City before the regiment. The band was as well received as the athletic teams. The *Salt Lake Herald* reported that members of the band "seem to feel they are a part of this city and it is their duty to do all they can to make matters pleasing."[56] At least one officer at the post was less pleased than were Salt Lake City citizens about the use of the band. "I am aware," one first lieutenant lamented in a letter that found its way to the adjutant general's office, "that a regimental band has other purposes for its existence than the furnishing of music for a post dance once a week." He obviously wanted the band to play exclusively at the post to prevent "unpleasant mixing of blacks and whites," apparently at establishments in the city.[57]

Senior officers at the post were decidedly interested in maintaining a good image and went to great lengths to see that requests from the city were accommodated. As a result, the band played for civic occasions when its presence was requested. In addition, individual bandsmen performed community services. Bandsman Walter F. Loving, for example, orchestrated music for a group called the High School Minstrels, and the music was played at the New Grand Theatre. Apparently a gifted musician, Loving gave free vocal lessons and directed concerts.[58]

A year after the Twenty-fourth Infantry arrived in Utah, the *Salt Lake Tribune* printed an editorial that represented a change in its view regarding the Black soldiers. When the regiment's transfer had been announced, the *Tribune* recalled, the newspaper had complained that

> Fort Douglas lies above and beyond the most pronounced residence portion of the city and that soldiers would ride on cars, drunk as well as sober, and that an intoxicated colored soldier is more offensive than an intoxicated white soldier.

Admitting that this judgment had proved false, the editorial continued that the soldiers had been well behaved, had "less rowdy characteristics" than any white regiment, and were less addicted to drinking.[59] The editorial represented an achievement for the Twenty-fourth. Relations had been good between the post and the community and, officially, at least, everyone appeared satisfied.

Almost nineteen months after the regiment's arrival in Utah the routine of post life at Fort Douglas was interrupted by speculation that should it become necessary to send troops to Cuba, the four "colored" regiments would be the first to depart for the war zone. "It is acknowledged," reported the *Denver News*, "by men of experience in southern climates that white men from the cool regions of the northern states would fare badly in the treacherous climate of Cuba." The Colorado paper's prophecy that Black units would be "given ample opportunity to win glory" was accurate.[60] One month later "both officers and men seemed to be rubbing up a trifle on Spanish for they accosted one another with 'Buenos noches, compadre' and 'adios' was the parting salutation."[61] As enlisted men and officers prepared to depart and some wives and children prepared to visit relatives in the East, events at the post were reported with regularity and fanfare.

The announcement of the Twenty-fourth's orders to prepare to depart for Cuba had its impact upon some Salt Lake City citizens:

Local dealers generally are deploring the issue which makes it necessary for the companies to leave Fort Douglas as by them is distributed each month in this city about $8000 . . . There is a class that is perfectly willing to see them go, but the merchant is not numbered among them.

On a less mercenary note, patriotic civilians wanted to know exactly when the Twenty-fourth would leave, for "Everybody wants to see Uncle Sam's men when they start to battle for the honor of their country. . . ." The description of an infantryman preparing to leave the post is classic.

One soldier had his kit spread out on the floor of the veranda in front of his barracks. It contained besides the usual camp equipment, a cracked blue mug with a gilt label, "From One Who Loves You" running diagonally across its face. An inscription on the photograph gave Mobile, Ala., as the place where it was taken, and as the soldier rolled up his belongings he softly hummed:

> "Down Mobile, down Mobile,
> How I Love 'at pretty yellow gal,
> Down Mobile."

As with so many enlisted men of the Twenty-fourth Infantry, this soldier, for the purposes of history, had no name. Like many others he was hundreds of miles from home, away from his loved ones, preparing to go to war. That same day the post band gave one of its last performances:

The sun from its lofty elevation in the western sky, shot a glint of gold through the newfledged leaves in the trees around the bandstand and touched the uniforms of the players with a stream of glory.[62]

Interest in the movement of the troops was intense throughout the city. It was reported that they would leave on April 19, at 7:30 P.M., but their departure was put off for a day. The delay disappointed thousands of citizens who had prepared to see the regiment off. The Twenty-fourth did leave on April 20, however, and the newspapers estimated that "15,000 to 20,000 people were on and about the depot grounds."[63] Included in that throng were wives, children, and girl friends who "sat for hours under the trees with their soldier lords and sires."[64]

As reported in the *Salt Lake Tribune* the following day, "The element of color seemed entirely eliminated."[65] An editorial in the *Deseret Evening News* spoke of the "mighty coincidence" of Blacks freeing Cubans through war, as Blacks were freed themselves that "will mark another epoch in the tremendous evolution of human society."[66] Ladies, reported the *Salt Lake Tribune,* who did not like to ride on streetcars with Black soldiers were, on the preceding day, shaking the hands of these same soldiers. William Gibson of Vernal who was at the depot, recalled that he had seen Patrick F. Connor march through the city in 1862. Having seen both marches, he said he was "satisfied."[67]

Members of the Twenty-fourth Infantry distinguished themselves in Cuba. That campaign does not fall within the scope of this study, but it may be important to note that the work done with yellow fever patients had lasting effects. "Out of the 456 men who marched to Siboney, only 24 escaped sickness . . . and of this number, only 198 were able to march out." As a result, within "the most famous regiment of African blood since Hannibal slaughtered 70,000 Romans," thirty-six suffered death and many more men were to carry lifelong disabilities resulting from yellow fever.[68]

On September 2, 1898, the Twenty-fourth returned to Fort Douglas amid cheers of their countrymen, and by December the war was officially over. The strength of the command was increased to 958 men, the warm welcome receded, and the routine of the post was quickly resumed. There were differences, however. Approximately half of the enlisted men at the fort were new to Salt Lake City; because of the acceleration in recruitment for the war effort, the average age for soldiers at the fort was probably lower than it had been; and reenlistments, transfers, and discharges increased. In general, the soldiers seemed to exhibit a slightly different attitude, restlessness.

When the Twenty-fourth arrived at Fort Douglas in 1896, members of the unit seemed well satisfied with the change in station. Subsequent reports indicated that a general feeling of well-being continued. However, just prior to the unit's departure for Cuba the *Broad Ax* reported:

> Within the past ten days we have conversed with a number of the Twenty-fourth regiment and they all expressed a great desire to get away from Salt Lake City and to be located at some other point where it would be more congenial for them and their families.

The report is not surprising. It was as difficult for Black people to live in Utah as it was in most other states at the turn of the century. If Taylor was accurate in reflecting the general attitude of Black soldiers toward Salt Lake City, his report offers considerable contrast between what appeared to be the feeling at the time of the regiment's departure for Cuba and the confessed feelings of "a number of the Twenty-fourth regiment."[69]

The record is not clear. As mentioned earlier, the officers of the Twenty-fourth, as well as enlisted men, were sensitive about the Utah assignment and sought to make sure that there were few negative incidents involving Black soldiers. Prior to the unit's departure from the Southwest, Colonel Kent had made it clear that measures would be taken to prevent confrontations between enlisted men and Caucasian residents of Salt Lake City. Soldiers were only to visit the city in full uniform, curfews would be enforced, soldiers would not be able to work in the city, and they were to defer to whites as a matter of policy. The regiment's record, prior to its departure for Cuba, indicates that measures devised for maximum discipline were effective when coupled with the apparent desire on the part of enlisted men to make a good showing.

Experience in a national war and volunteer work in yellow fever camps in Cuba, however, was bound to have some impact on the soldiers. They had risked their lives and some of their fellows had died. It is conjecturable that the returning soldiers felt less reticent and more like they had earned a better place in society. Two enlisted men, Beverly Perea[70] and a Sergeant Williams, had been made commissioned officers only to be reduced to ranks again. Additionally, the unit faced the prospect of being sent to the Philippines. These factors appeared to affect the enlisted men. One thing is certain: disciplinary problems increased.

Not long after the regiment's arrival in Utah, on November 17, 1896, H. B. Ballantyne and W. P. Gunn had the dubious distinction of being the first members of the Twenty-fourth to appear in the Salt Lake City police court. Both were fined for drunkenness, and Gunn received an additional fine for "packing a machete in such a manner as to lay himself liable to carrying a concealed weapon."[71]

Few soldiers followed the path of Ballantyne and Gunn until after the regiment's return from Cuba when a dozen enlisted men were cited for a variety of infractions in the first few months of 1899. These offenses and the punishments included: offensive and indecent language to a noncommissioned officer (fine and fifteen days), scandalous conduct in the presence of ladies (two months at hard labor), assault upon another soldier (fine and twenty days), fraudulent enlistment (dishonorable discharge), theft and desertion (one year at Fort Leavenworth prison). From the examples cited one can see that scandalous conduct in the presence of ladies—which probably meant the use of distasteful language on a streetcar—was a relatively serious offense, more so than assault upon another soldier. Community relations were obviously considered important, and infractions involving civilians, especially ladies, were handled firmly.[72]

That soldiers would engage in various types of misconduct does not seem unusual, but racial stereotypes tended to prevail in newspaper reports of such incidents. For example:

> George Warren, a colored soldier, and Robert Brooks, a colored porter, stole a suit of clothes from another colored man and were captured by Sergt. Burbidge. During the trial yesterday the judge was compelled to listen to a ten minutes' display of oratory on the part of Warren, whose subject was: "Craps, and how they should be played to he successful." Warren was sentenced to thirty days, while Brooks who pawned the clothes, was given fifty days. "Golly, thirty days to say nuffin 'bout what I'll get when I reaches de fote," said Warren as he ambled away.[73]

Even as military and civilian officials were dealing with the little flurry of disciplinary problems among the enlisted men in early 1899, rumors were circulating that the Twenty-fourth would be transferred soon. The rumors proved true, and the men soon took up new assignments in San Francisco, Alaska, Montana, Washington, and Vancouver, British Columbia. Two detachments of twenty-five men each were sent to Sequoia and Yosemite parks in California "for the benefit of the health of the colored men, many of whom are nearly broken down from the effects of Cuban fever."[74] And in July 1899 four companies of the Twenty-fourth arrived in the Philippines for a three-year tour of duty.

The Twenty-fourth Infantry, departing on two occasions from Utah, first for the Spanish-American War and second for the campaign in the Philippine Islands, may be the most prominent U.S. Army regiment to serve from the state. The unit has not, however, been regarded as a regiment having close ties with the state. Personal relationships that may have been established during the regiment's stay at Fort Douglas have been obscured by time, and the Twenty-fourth Infantry, the "buffalo soldiers," remain indistinct in local memory. The fanfare of the unit's arrival in Salt Lake City, its participation in jubilee celebrations and other state occasions, the baseball games, concerts, and other human dramas struggle to become part of the states history. Perhaps this is as it should be. Few of the soldiers made Utah their home, and not many of their descendants live in the Beehive State today.

Nevertheless, members of the Twenty-fourth, perhaps over fifteen hundred different individuals, were significant additions to the Salt Lake City population in both an economic and a social sense. The economic impact of the regiment upon the surrounding community was, of course, a duplication of the contact of prior and subsequent military units. Socially, however, the local community, for the first time in history, experienced the influx of a relatively large and cohesive military group that greatly augmented the already existing Black community. Although the Twenty-fourth Infantry had not been located near a large city for a thirty-year period and Salt Lake City had never had a large Black population, the two sides managed. Generally speaking, suspicion and uncertainty gave way to confidence and resolution, stereotypes to a tenuous familiarity and with the advent of war, the two worlds met in the camp of self-interest. Black soldiers, members of the Ninth Cavalry and Twenty-fourth Infantry and later, the Twenty-fifth Infantry, became improbable ambassadors. More than two thousand different soldiers carried a like number of versions about their stay in the "Great Basin Kingdom" to the far corners of the United States.

Notes

1. Oswald Garrison Villard, "The Negro in the Regular Army," *Atlantic Monthly* 91 (1903): 724. Villard observed that "It was not until the battle of Santiago . . . that the bulk of the American people realized that the standing army comprised regiments composed wholly of black men. Up to that time only one company of colored soldiers had served at a post east of the Mississippi."

2. Ibid. The notable success of Black jockeys in the Kentucky Derby between 1875 and 1902 may have contributed to one stereotype. See, for example, Middleton Harris, *The Black Book* (New York: Random House, 1974), 151. Earlier there was discussion in the U.S. Senate regarding the ability of Blacks as horsemen. During a debate Sen. Henry Wilson of Massachusetts observed that Blacks "are the best riders in America connected with our army. We have some colored regiments west of the Mississippi that were raised in Kentucky, who understand the management of horses as well as any man in this country, admirable riders." U.S. Congress. Senate. "Military Establishment." *Congressional Globe.* 39th Cong., 1st sess., March 14, 1866, 1385.

3. *Salt Lake Tribune,* September 27, 1896.

4. *Salt Lake Tribune,* October 4, 1896.

5. U.S. Congress. House. *Annual Report of the Secretary of War.* 54th Cong., 1st sess., 1895, 84. The Ninth Cavalry and Twenty-fourth Infantry were stationed in Utah, the Tenth Cavalry and Twenty-fifth Infantry in North Dakota and Montana.

6. *Salt Lake Tribune,* September 19, 1896: "The order from Washington first reached Fort Douglas in the press dispatches and caused considerable surprise, not to say consternation. There had been considerable gossip in army circles during the summer, foreshadowing a change, but it had about died down, and the close of the summer season led the people at the post to suppose that no change would be made until spring." See also *Salt Lake Herald,* September 19, 1896.

7. *Salt Lake Tribune,* September 20, 1896.

8. *Deseret Evening News,* October 8, 1896.

9. *Salt Lake Herald,* September 21, 1896.

10. *Broad Ax,* October 30, 1897. In 1896 there were two newspapers run by Blacks, the *Broad Ax* and the *Plain Dealer.* Taylor apparently backed the Democratic Party while the *Plain Dealer* backed the Republican Party. Taylor seemed to think that Lamont supported Blacks and would not change the transfer order. Taylor's position appears unusual as the Republican Party, "the party of Lincoln," was overwhelmingly supported by Black voters until the New Deal.

11. *Broad Ax,* October 31, 1896. It is difficult to ascertain whether Taylor constructed or accepted a local view regarding the Republican Party or by coincidence viewed both the *Tribune* and the Republicans critically. The issue may warrant greater investigation if Taylor's view of the Republican Party was widely shared by Blacks in the West.

12. William G. Muller, *The Twenty-fourth Infantry: Past and Present* (1923; repr., Ft. Collins, Colo.: Old Army Press, 1972), 12.

13. Murray to Daniel S. Lamont, January 31, 1895, Records of the Office of the Adjutant General, General Correspondence, 1890–1917, AGO 1500, RG 94, National Archives, Washington, D.C.

14. Schofield to Murray, February 15, 1895, ibid.

15. Kent to adjutant general, January 22, 1896, ibid.

16. Ibid.

17. *Salt Lake Herald,* September 19, 1896.

18. *Salt Lake Herald,* September 20, 1896.

19. *Deseret News,* October 8, 1896.

20. *Salt Lake Tribune,* October 11, 1896.

21. *Broad Ax,* September 24, 1896.

22. *Salt Lake Tribune,* May 9, 1897.

23. Registers of Enlistments in the U.S. Army, 1798–1914, Microcopy Nos. 108, 110, 170, RG 94. In addition to enlistment registers, this record group also includes declarations for pensions, marriage certificates, copies of death certificates, and applications for reimbursement, a great deal of information is contained on each form.

24. Ibid., Microcopy No. 216.

25. *San Francisco Call,* July 2, 1899.

26. See R. L. Polk's *Salt Lake City Directory, 1898.*

27. Pension Application Files for the U.S. Army, RG 94.

28. Interview with Mrs. Viola Dorsey, February 5, 1976.

29. *Salt Lake Herald,* October 16, 1896.

30. *Salt Lake Tribune,* October 16, 1896.

31. *Broad Ax*, October 21, 1896.

32. *Salt Lake Tribune*, October 23, 1896.

33. *Salt Lake Tribune*, October 16, 1896.

34. *Broad Ax*, October 24, 1896.

35. *Salt Lake Tribune*, March 28, 1896.

36. *Broad Ax*, October 24, 1896.

37. *Broad Ax*, December 26, 1896.

38. *Deseret Evening News*, October 22, 1896.

39. Ibid.

40. John M. Carroll, ed., *The Black Military Experience in the West* (New York: Liveright Publishing, 1971), 92.

41. Adjutant, Twenty-fourth Infantry, to commanding officer, Company D, Twenty-fourth Infantry, October 23, 1897, Letters Sent, Adjutant Generals Office, 1897–1906, RG 94.

42. Ibid.

43. *Salt Lake Tribune*, January 20, 1899.

44. *Salt Lake Tribune*, January 11, 1899.

45. Ibid.

46. *Salt Lake Tribune*, February 6, 1898.

47. *Salt Lake Tribune*, February 20, 1895.

48. *Salt Lake Tribune*, January 11, 1899.

49. *Salt Lake Tribune*, February 6, 1898.

50. *Salt Lake Tribune*, May 3, 1897.

51. *Salt Lake Tribune*, February 3, 1899.

52. *Salt Lake Tribune*, April 2, 1899.

53. *Salt Lake Herald*, January 4, 1898.

54. *Salt Lake Herald*, January 31, 1897.

55. *Salt Lake Tribune*, May 20, 1897, March 5, 1899; *Salt Lake Herald*, June 7, 1897.

56. *Salt Lake Herald*, June 1, 1897.

57. Company B, Twenty-fourth Infantry, to adjutant general, November 28, 1896, Letters Sent, Company B, Twenty-fourth Infantry, September 6, 1895 to May 19, 1899, RG 94.

58. *Salt Lake Tribune*, January 23, February 6, 1898.

59. *Salt Lake Tribune*, October 24, 1897.

60. *Denver News* as compiled in "Journal History of the Church" March 15, 1898, Archives Division, Historical Department, Church of Jesus Christ of Latter-Day Saints, Salt Lake City. A year and two months later on May 18, 1899, the *Salt Lake Tribune* reported: "The removal of the companies of the Twenty-fourth to Alaska but goes to illustrate the uncertain side of a soldiers life. Just a little more than a year ago, the government concluded to send the men to Cuba, for the reason that black men can stand the hot weather better. Now they are sent to the other extreme and the reason is given that they can withstand the cold weather with much less discomfort than the white men."

61. *Salt Lake Tribune*, April 16, 1898.

62. *Salt Lake Tribune,* April 20, 1898.

63. *Deseret Evening News,* April 20, 1898.

64. *Salt Lake Tribune,* April 20, 1898.

65. *Salt Lake Tribune,* April 21, 1898.

66. *Deseret Evening News,* April 21, 1898.

67. *Salt Lake Tribune,* April 21, 1898.

68. Theophilus G. Steward, *The Colored Regulars in the United States Army* (New York: Arno Press, 1964), 221–25, 235; A. Prentiss, ed., *The History of the Utah Volunteers in the Spanish-American War and in the Philippine Islands* (Salt Lake City: Tribune Job Printing, 1900), 125.

69. *Broad Ax,* April 23, 1898.

70. Beverly Perea to adjutant general, March 9, 1908, Records of the Office of the Adjutant General, General Correspondence, 1890–1911, AGO 127989, RG 94.

71. *Salt Lake Herald,* November 17, 1896.

72. See, for example, *Salt Lake Tribune,* January 8; February 6, 14, 28; March 14; April 9, 1899.

73. *Salt Lake Tribune,* January 24, 1899.

74. *Salt Lake Tribune,* May 1, 1899.

CHARLES M. DOLLAR

Putting the Army on Wheels

THE STORY OF THE TWENTY-FIFTH INFANTRY BICYCLE CORPS

In the late nineteenth century the widespread popularity and use of bicycles inevitably led to experiments in military use of them. The first experiment came in Europe in 1875 when the Italian Army demonstrated the value of having bicycles carry dispatches during field maneuvers. Later, the armies of Belgium, France, Austria, Germany, Switzerland, Spain, Holland, Russia, and England incorporated military cyclists into various units.[1] In addition to courier service reconnaissance operations, some units used a multicycle (double tandems of bicycles attached to a two wheel cart) to transport tools, construction materials, and guns.[2] Medical units even had bicycle ambulances, which consisted of a stretcher connected between two bicycles.

In spite of the success of military cycling in Europe, similar tests and experiments in America did not take place until the early 1890s. The major impetus for testing the military value of cycling came in 1891 from Gen. Nelson A. Miles, who at the time was commander of the Department of Missouri and stationed at Chicago, Illinois. In October 1891 Miles was in New York City and attended a six-day bicycle race at Madison Square Garden. On October 21, 1891, the *New York Times* carried a story in which Miles stated his interest in bicycle couriers for the U.S. Army. He noted that the bicycle was quiet, reliable, and unlike horses did not have to be fed and watered. The key question, he said, was whether riders should be light and slim like cavalry soldiers or large like the enlisted men in the infantry. Until the stamina of riders of bicycles in military exercises was demonstrated, the utility of bicycles in military activities remained uncertain.[3]

On November 25, 1891 General Miles instructed Col. R. E. A. Crofton, commander of the Fifteenth Infantry at Fort Sheridan, Illinois, to organize a detachment of one officer and nine noncommissioned men to conduct experiments using bicycles provided by the Pope Bicycle Company at no expense to the government. Lt. W. T. May was placed in charge of the detachment which immediately began a training program that was conducted indoors because of snow and ice on the roads. However, in early January 1892, the Adjutant General's Office of the Department of the Army directed that the experiment cease because General Miles' instructions involved testing military equipment that only the secretary of war could approve.[4]

On January 29, 1892, General Miles requested the secretary of war to permit continuation of the experiment. He noted that there were no mounted troops at Fort Sheridan if it were necessary to move a small detachment of soldiers quickly. In addition, he considered it quite important that an opportunity existed to test the use of the bicycle for military purposes without any cost to the government. "As they [bicycles] are being used for nearly all roads at favorable seasons of the year between the Atlantic and the Pacific, I consider it quite important to demonstrate their utility by practical use in the military service."[5]

Finally, almost a month later, Miles's request was approved by the acting secretary of war. In the meantime, based upon the orders Col. Crofton received from the Adjutant General's Office, Lieutenant May had discontinued the experiment. On February 4, 1892 he submitted a report in which he noted that even though the experiment had been conducted indoors because of the weather, he considered it successful. He hoped that during the spring and summer months unlimited tests would be possible.[6]

Apparently, General Miles's success in gaining approval of the acting secretary of war was short-lived since Lieutenant May did not continue the experiment.[7] Nevertheless, Miles continued to take advantage of opportunities to promote the testing of bicycles for military use. In May 1892 he sent a message from his headquarters in Chicago to New York City by relays of riders provided by the League of American Wheelmen, a private organization of bicycle sportsmen. On May 31, 1892, General Miles was the speaker at a banquet in Chicago honoring Charles L. Burdett, president of the League. The subject of his speech was military cycling and Miles noted with some satisfaction that the day before men from the Fifteenth Infantry stationed at Fort Sheridan had conducted a practice march on bicycles from Pullman to Chicago. The riders carried full military equipment and covered the fifteen miles in one hour and twenty-five minutes. Miles also noted that these bicycle experiments "demonstrated the wretched conditions of the American roads." Such efforts, he asserted, "have demonstrated to the country that we need good avenues in order that our people may move from one part of the country to the other, and that they may have means of bringing their products to the market."[8]

Despite Miles's strong advocacy of better roads throughout the country and the use of bicycles in military exercises, no full-scale experiment was conducted. However, his promotion to the position of major general commanding the army in 1895 changed this. In his first annual report to the secretary of war in 1896, Miles recommended that one full regiment be equipped with bicycles. Furthermore, he stated that it was his intention "to use to some extent troops stationed at different posts to make practice marches and reconnaissances, and thereby obtain a thorough knowledge of their own country, especially the topographical features, conditions of the roads, sources of supplies, and all information of military importance."[9]

The value of bicycles for these forced marches was obvious, and it was logical for Miles to encourage experimentation. One of the more ambitious undertakings was conducted by 2nd Lt. James A. Moss of the Twenty-fifth Infantry. After graduating from the U.S. Military Academy at the bottom of his class in June of 1894, Moss, who was a white Southerner from Lafayette, Louisiana, was assigned to the Twenty-fifth Infantry, an all-black enlisted men's unit stationed at Fort Missoula, Montana. During the summers of 1896 and 1897 twenty of these enlisted men helped prove that Moss's and Miles's ideas about the military use of bicycles had practical merit.

Although Moss's assignment was typical for someone who had graduated at the bottom of his class, his strong commitment to military cycling made it a particularly good assignment for him. Col. Andrew S. Burt, commanding officer of the Twenty-fifth Infantry, was an enthusiastic advocate of athletic sports among soldiers. Furthermore, bicycles were used widely on the fort and in Missoula. In April 1894 the *Daily Missoulian* reported that "Like in Missoula, half of the people at the fort are on bicycles and a person without a wheel is out of the times as it were."[10] Within a month of Moss's arrival informal bicycle drills were being practiced at the fort. A highlight of the Fourth of July program in

1895 was a bicycle drill by twenty soldiers of the Twenty-fifth Infantry.[11] However, it was not until General Miles formally recommended establishment of a special bicycle regiment that Moss secured official organization of the Twenty-fifth Infantry Bicycle Corps, the first of its kind in the regular army.[12] The objective of the corps was to test thoroughly the practicality of the bicycle for military purposes in a mountainous country.

The corps, consisting of eight enlisted men and Lieutenant Moss, spent July and early August of 1896 on practice rides and exercises involving getting over fences and fording streams. Climbing a nine-foot fence in twenty seconds soon became standard for the corps. At the command "Jump fence," the soldiers at the head of each file would lean their bicycles against the fence and pull themselves over. The soldiers behind would pass over both bicycles and then climb over the fence. Each soldier would then move his bicycle to his assigned location and assume the position "Stand to bicycle." Shallow streams were forded by dismounting and rolling the bicycles through the water. In deeper water two soldiers in a single file would hang a bicycle on a long pole resting on their shoulders and carry it across.

The first trip the corps made that summer was to Lake McDonald and back, a distance of 126 miles. The round trip to Lake McDonald was completed in three and a half days and proved a severe test of both the men and the bicycles. In his official report, Moss noted that the trip was completed under "the most adverse circumstances." Heavy rains, strong winds, deep mud, steep grades, and impassible roads that frequently forced the men to push their bicycles made the trip dreary and exhausting. Frequent punctures, burst tires, broken pedals, loose rims, and lost chains added to their difficulties.[13] Despite the grueling ordeal, the men learned a great deal about military cycling, which helped to prepare them for their next trip.

Immediately upon returning to Fort Missoula the corps began preparations for a trip to Yellowstone Park and return via Fort Assinniboine—a distance of some eight hundred miles.[14] Even though rations were to be picked up every 150 miles or so, it was necessary to pack enough food to last four days. This additional weight, along with the extra bicycle parts that Moss considered necessary after the Lake McDonald trip, added several pounds to the weight of each bicycle (from seventy-five to seventy-nine pounds). Moss hoped to avoid delays caused by stopping to repair punctures through use of nine puncture-proof tires supplied by the Advance Tire Company.

Early on the morning of August 15, 1896, the Twenty-fifth Infantry Bicycle Corps left Fort Missoula en route to Yellowstone Park. On the first day out the corps covered forty-two miles in almost eight hours of actual travel time despite riding into a wind most of the day and rolling their bicycles along a railroad track for several miles to avoid steep grades. As Moss made clear in his daily field reports, this was no pleasure jaunt. August 17 was a typical day:

> Left camp 6:18 A.M. Struck a mountain ¼ mi. from camp. Grade quite steep. At 7 o'clock delayed 30 mins. fixing Sgt. Green's gun and knapsack. Reached Avon 9 A.M. At 10 A.M. delayed 5 mins. fixing puncture. 10:10 Forman broke his seat spring. Delayed 10 minutes. 10:55 A.M. delayed 25 mins. fixing puncture. Reached Elliston 11:30 A.M. Stopped here until 1 o'clock, when we left for Helena. Sun very hot. Had to stop in the shade several times. Delayed about 45 mins. by these stops. Roads very stony and nearly all up grade. Reached Blossburg 3 P.M. Left for Helena 4 P.M. Reached summit of Main Divide of the Rocky Mountains at 4:20. Reached foot of summit at 4:45. Stopped here about 15 mins. The grade was so steep that we could not ride down—had to roll our wheels the whole way down—had to use brakes until we had cramps in our fingers, to prevent wheels from getting away from us—was, without doubt, hardest work so far on the trip. At 5:15 stopped 10 mins. to fix puncture. A few minutes later, delayed from 6:30 to 7 P.M. fixing three punctures. Reached Fort Harrison 7:30 P.M. Distance travelled, 44 miles.[15]

Tires continued to be a problem, especially after the non-resilient puncture-proof tires were replaced with conventional tires. Moss calculated that punctures and burst tires delayed the corps seven hours one day. Later he wrote that until a resilient puncture-proof tire was available, military cyclists during times of actual enemy attack would "dread the enemy's tacks nearly as much as his bullets."

In spite of these difficulties the corps reached Yellowstone Park on August 25, ten days after leaving Fort Missoula. They spent five days leisurely touring the park and viewing the geysers and other points of interest. In his official report of the trip Moss wrote that he took a picture of a bear on a bicycle and that "several tourists came to camp to take pictures of the bicycle corps." He summed up the reaction of the corps: "Soldiers delighted with the trip—treated royally everywhere—thought the sights grand."

The return trip to Fort Missoula (which was not all downhill) was made in eight days. At 7:45 P.M. on September 8, the corps rolled into the fort after a day of riding, which Moss called "by far the hardest on the whole trip." However, this did not end the summer activities of the corps. After resting for three days, the bicyclists joined the Twenty-fifth Infantry and the Tenth Cavalry in a joint practice march. Moss set up a system of bicycle relays between himself and Col. Andrew S. Burt, commander of the Twenty-fifth Infantry. In addition, members of the corps thoroughly reconnoitered the country along the line of march. Frederic Remington, who was accompanying the Tenth Calvary, reported that, while "It is heavy wheeling and pretty bumpy on the grass," the Bicycle Corps "manage far better than one would anticipate."[16]

At the conclusion of the practice march Lieutenant Moss prepared a report detailing the corps' experience in using bicycles under such trying circumstances as bad roads, inclement weather, and mountainous terrain. His report was sent to the adjutant general of the Department of Dakota. General Miles, who was aware of the activities of the Twenty-fifth Infantry Bicycle Corps, expressed interest in seeing Moss's report, which was forwarded in early November to the adjutant general of the army. Meanwhile, Lieutenant Moss had decided to take a leave of absence from the middle of December to late February. Sometime in early January he was in Washington, D.C., and received from General Miles the suggestion that he plan a more extensive trip for the coming summer. On January 22, 1897, he wrote to General Miles requesting permission for the following: (1) to be placed on special duty in Washington until April 15 so that he could study the literature on bicycles at the Bureau of Information and visit the leading bicycle manufacturers and tire factories in the East; (2) to organize a bicycle corps of twenty soldiers and one surgeon under his command; (3) to select the members of the corps from among soldiers stationed at Fort Missoula; (4) to make a trip from Fort Missoula to St. Louis and return carrying arms, ammunition, and rations; and (5) to secure the needed bicycles from a manufacturer at no expense to the government.[17]

On February 2 General Miles submitted the request to Secretary of War Russell Alger with the endorsement that Lieutenant Moss shows "excellent qualifications for the work" and that "this proposition was submitted at my instance. . . ." The secretary returned the request to Miles on March 12 with the notation that the matter be postponed until a puncture-proof tire had been fully tested. In the meantime, on the strength of General Miles's endorsement, Moss had gone to the Spalding Bicycle Company at Chicopee Falls, Massachusetts, to make arrangements for twenty-two Spalding military bicycles with special equipment. Given this situation and his own interest in the project, General Miles returned the request to the secretary with the comment that Lieutenant Moss had studied the matter of puncture-proof tires carefully and had brought to his office samples of tires that seemed satisfactory. Furthermore, since the government would incur no expense in the use of the bicycles, he recommended that the test not be postponed. Finally, on May 4, the secretary of war approved the project.

Moss returned to Fort Missoula to select the soldiers who would make the trip and to await shipment of the bicycles from the Spalding Company. Five of the twenty enlisted men chosen from a group of forty volunteers were veterans of the trip to Yellowstone Park the year before. For most of the remaining fifteen "general reliability and physical condition" rather than knowledge of cycling must have guided Moss in his selection since he noted that some of them were poor riders and one learned to ride only one week before the corps left for St. Louis.[18] The twenty enlisted men were divided into two squads headed by lance corporals William Haynes and Abram Martin. Sgt. Mingo Sanders was acting first sergeant of the corps.[19] Joining Moss as second in command was a fellow white officer, Dr. James M. Kennedy, assistant post surgeon at Fort Missoula, who shared Moss's interest in cycling.[20] The bicycles, which arrived on June 4, had been specially equipped according to Moss's instructions. Steel rims replaced the wood rims used the previous summer and gear cases protected the chains from dirt, mud, rocks, and accidental loss. Hard leather frame cases that fit into the diamonds of the bicycles contained rations, spare parts, tools, and other items. Three of the cases were made of metal and were so designed that, when removed from the bicycle and the rations taken out, each case formed two separate parts, providing a total of six cooking utensils. Except for one soldier with a shotgun, each enlisted member of the corps carried a rifle, a belt, a bayonet, and fifty rounds of ammunition. The rifles were worn slung across the back. Luggage carriers mounted on the fronts of all but two bicycles were used to pack a blanket, a shelter tent half and poles, and various personal effects. Two riders packed these items in tin coffee pots measuring eighteen inches by nine inches, which were attached to the handlebars of their bicycles.

Food for the trip consisted of the standard military field and travel rations, which included flour, baking powder, salt, pepper, dry beans, coffee, sugar, bacon, canned beef, and baked beans. Moss arranged with the Quartermasters Department to send rations to points along the road, which were about one hundred miles apart. This meant that the corps carried only a two-day supply of food. Although this was an incentive to travel the planned fifty miles per day, it also meant that with difficult travel conditions the men might have to travel on empty stomachs.

The travel route Moss laid out called for the corps to ride easterly along the Northern Pacific Railroad to Billings, Montana. At this point they would veer southward somewhat and follow the Burlington Railroad through Wyoming, South Dakota, and Nebraska into Missouri and along the Mississippi River to their destination of St. Louis. Moss claimed that this route would permit a thorough test of the durability and practicality of the bicycle as a means of transportation for troops. All of the arrangements were in order for what Moss and others believed would be a historic trip. With this in mind he decided to add another member to the corps, an official reporter and photographer. He chose Edward H. Boos, an experienced twenty-three-year-old cyclist from Missoula whose father was publisher of the *Daily Missoulian.* Plans called for Boos to send regular reports on the corps' progress to leading newspapers across the nation.

At 5:30 on Monday morning, June 14, 1897, the Twenty-fifth Infantry Bicycle Corps left for St. Louis. They reached their destination about 6 P.M. on Saturday, July 24, having traveled nineteen hundred miles at an average of forty-six miles per day. With the exception of actually being under fire, the corps experienced all of the hardships of a campaign. According to Moss's account they suffered from thirst, hunger, and the ill effects of alkali water, cold, heat, and loss of sleep.

On the second morning out, the corps began their ride in rain and mud, which turned into snow and sleet later in the day as they reached the Great Divide of the Rocky Mountains. Once they reached lower elevations heat became the problem. In Nebraska it was 110 degrees in the shade. In fact, it was so hot that the sand blistered the feet of two soldiers as the corps pushed their bicycles through 170 miles of sandhills.

In parts of Wyoming and South Dakota and in virtually all of Nebraska, the water was alkali. Sometimes for stretches of a hundred miles or more the only water fit to drink was in railroad water tanks. When the corps did not follow the railroad tracks they had a choice of alkali water or no water at all. Lieutenant Moss became so ill from the effects of drinking alkali water that he could not ride. Surgeon Kennedy assumed command until Moss had recovered sufficiently to catch up with the corps by train four days later.

Usually the rations lasted less than the planned two days, with the result that the men frequently did not have enough to eat. Mud and rain so delayed the corps between Billings, Montana, and Fort Custer, Montana, the next ration station, that they ran out of food. After a miserable night in a deserted Indian cabin near Pryor Creek, the men had a breakfast of weak coffee and a piece of burnt bread. That day they rode forty-two miles to Fort Custer.

Probably the three most trying hardships were the mud, the rough roads, and a wind that always seemed to blow into the faces of the riders. In his official report Moss wrote, "The wind is one of the worst and most discouraging things to contend against." Every time it rained, which was frequent in Montana and Wyoming, the dirt roads, or what there was of them, turned into gumbo mud. Since the bicycles could not be ridden through this mud, which was very heavy and sticky, they had to be rolled. Very slow progress was made, as the wheels would clog with mud after only a few turns. The men were able to move their bicycles by walking with a knife in one hand and using the other to guide the bicycles, stopping every few feet to cut the mud off. Sometimes it was easier to carry the bicycles.

Even where there was no mud the roads generally were very rough. Boos reported that in one section of Montana where the road was too rough even for walking the bicycles, the corps used a nearby railroad track bed. However, the track bed provided little relief since the railroad ties were being replaced and the space between them had not been filled in. For more than twenty miles they pushed their bicycles over railroad ties, which were between six inches and two feet apart, experiencing one severe jolt after another.[21] Moss reported that on the average, the corps had to dismount every seven miles because of road conditions. He estimated that the men walked between three and four hundred of the nineteen hundred miles to St. Louis.[22]

Frequently Moss would ask residents of a town that the corps passed through about the condition of roads only to learn that "the judgment of some people of what constitutes a good road is sadly at fault." A road, town residents considered "all right, . . . we found . . . to be anything but decent."[23] Moss also noted that the condition of roads was an index to the people of the communities through which we passed. Where the roads were properly graded and well-worked, the inhabitants were well informed, used modern farming impliments (*sic*), had fine wind-mills and other conveniences. On the other hand, where the roads were in a bad condition and evidently much neglected, the people were narrow-minded, devoid of any knowledge of the topography of the country, and behind the times in everything.[24]

Life on the road for the Twenty-fifth Infantry was not all hardship. Frequently the meager fare of military rations was supplemented by purchases of eggs and milk from farmers. Occasionally flour was traded for freshly baked bread. One night the corps enjoyed a "grand supper" of fried rabbit, shot earlier in the day, boiled eggs purchased from a farmer, and the usual rations. In Nebraska when the corps stopped at a farm house for water, the farmer and his wife were so delighted to see them that they insisted the men should stop long enough to have bread and milk. When the bread was gone all of the cakes and cookies in the house were also served.

Such farm houses and farm families were few and far between. Until the corps reached Missouri, their route took them through desolate areas where the drudgery of the trip was broken only by an occasional humorous incident or the warm welcome of townspeople. For example, outside Parkman, Montana, the corps came upon three elderly women in a wagon occupying the center of the road who kept their team going fast enough so that the men could not pass easily, but yet too slow for their normal bicycle speed. When Lieutenant Moss asked for his half of the road, the women laughed at him and continued down the middle of the road. Shortly, there was an opportunity to pass, and the corps whirled past the women. In a dispatch, reporter Boos described the scene: "The women were so surprised and astonished that they forgot about their horses, which took fright and ran off in the rough ground."[25] Actually, this was a bit of male chauvinism. Both Lieutenant Moss and reporter Boos were members of the League of American Wheelmen and should have known that their abrupt passing had frightened the horses, not the women, and that they had violated one of the "Rules of the Road" members of the league subscribed to.

When the corps was a mile or so from a town they would stop and wait for stragglers before regrouping in formation and riding into town. Thus, even with their tattered uniforms and dirty bicycles the men made an excellent impression when local wheelmen greeted them and escorted them into town. Usually they stayed long enough to inquire about local road conditions or to pick up rations and bicycle parts. Invariably the townspeople would question the men closely and inspect their bicycles with great interest. Sometimes this interest took an unexpected turn, as was the case in Big Timber, Montana, when an enthusiastic veteran greeted the corps and insisted that they have a drink with him in a local bar. Finally, after the men had enjoyed the old veteran's hospitality for an hour, Lieutenant Moss managed to get them back to their bicycles to resume the ride. On another occasion, when the corps stopped in Lincoln, Nebraska, in the middle of the day for their usual lunch and rest period, they were surrounded by so many people especially cyclists inquiring about details of the trip, that rest was out of the question.[26]

The Bicycle Corps arrived in Crawford, Nebraska, on Saturday afternoon, July 3, at the height of a Fourth of July celebration. The *Crawford Nebraska Journal* described the scene: "It was nearly 4 o'clock when the corps started down Second Street at a lively gait. Professor Gungl's Ninth cavalry band greeted them with the strains of Annie Laurie as only that band can play that piece, while thousands of spectators who lined the sidewalks on either side of the street rent the air with the wildest cheers to speed them on their journey."[27] A less congenial welcome came in part of Missouri which had been pro-Confederate during the Civil War. Late one evening reporter Boos asked an elderly farmer whether the corps could camp on his land. The farmer looked at the soldiers and then asked, "Be you fellows Union soldiers?" "I guess we are," was Boos' answer. The old farmer said, "Then you can pile right off a this land." As the troops started to mount up, someone from the house shouted, "Hey, wait a minute—you can camp there below the pig sty."[28]

Of course the warmest welcome came when the corps reached St. Louis. The *St. Louis Globe Democrat,* which had printed Boos' dispatches and kept readers informed of the corps' progress, devoted full pages to the trip on the Sunday and Monday after their arrival.[29] Hundreds of cyclists greeted them when they arrived late Saturday afternoon, and as many as ten thousand spectators visited their campground over the next several days.

For more than a week the Twenty-fifth Infantry Bicycle Corps was the center of attention, but the adulation ended quickly. Lieutenant Moss submitted a preliminary report to General Miles in which he requested permission for the corps to ride to Minneapolis and then return to Fort Missoula by train. However, General Miles was out of the country and permission was denied. Instead, they were ordered to return to

Fort Missoula by train.[30] Late in the afternoon of August 19, 1897, the men of the Bicycle Corps returned to Fort Missoula. When they had left more than two months earlier the *Daily Missoulian* had carried a lengthy article describing their departure. Now the newspaper devoted three brief lines to their return. The big news was the discovery of gold in Alaska. The men of the Twenty-fifth Infantry Bicycle Corps were no longer the heroes of the day.

But the story of the Bicycle Corps does not end here. On February 7, 1898, Lieutenant Moss requested permission from the adjutant general to organize another bicycle corps that spring for the purpose of making a trip from Fort Missoula to San Francisco.[31] Moss's commanding officer, Col. Andrew S. Burt, added an interesting endorsement to the proposal. In a personal letter to George Meiklejohn, the assistant secretary of war, he suggested that the proposed trip would call favorable attention to "colored soldiers" as they passed through the country. He added:

> It is well known there is prejudice against the colored man and when he appears in uniform it is like shaking a red flag against a bull. It is a wise policy to educate the people to become familiar with the colored man as a soldier. . . . Is it not better—is it not fairer to the colored soldier as well as to the people that the masses should be familiarized with the sight of a 'nigger' in uniform? The expedition proposed by Lieutenant Moss would be a fine educator. The one he made last year to St. Louis (think of it—a 'nigger soldier' in 'sesesh' Missouri!!) had a very happy effect. The men by their behavior won the respect of everybody.[32]

By this time, war with Spain seemed imminent and further bicycle tests were judged unnecessary. Later that year Lieutenant Moss was transferred to the Twenty-fourth Infantry and saw duty in Cuba. In October of 1898 he proposed the organization of a bicycle company of one hundred soldiers who would patrol Havana once it was occupied by American troops. After pointing out the advantages of speed and mobility in courier service, he noted that "in case of riots or other disturbances of any kind, a number of cyclists, armed with rifles and rapid fire guns (such guns have been mounted on tandems and tricycles and tested with the greatest success) could be moved to the seat of disturbance with inconceivable rapidity." He estimated that the cost of equipping a corps of one hundred men would be between four and eight thousand dollars. He concluded his proposal by noting that "After three years of practical and theoretical work, I have compiled plans for the organization of a cycling service and the specifications for a military bicycle, all of which are at the disposal of the War Department." Lieutenant Moss's proposal was rejected.[33]

As popular interest in bicycles crested in America in the late 1890s, a number of individuals in the U.S. Army and various state National Guard units proposed and conducted experiments in military cycling. However, only the trip of the Twenty-fifth Infantry Bicycle Corps can be considered a successful experiment. Several factors help to account for this success. Gen. Nelson A. Miles was a staunch advocate of such experimentation and tests, and without his support and intervention at several critical points it is unlikely that Moss and his men could have carried out such an ambitious undertaking. Another factor of some consequence was that Moss was impartial in dealing with bicycle manufacturers. Moss's commanding officer, Col. Andrew Burt, noted in his endorsement of Moss's proposed ride to San Francisco in 1898 that his "absolute honesty of purpose puts him beyond the manipulation of any one or any syndicate of manufacturers."[34] Furthermore, Moss's reports clearly demonstrate that he was a careful planner who paid attention to detail. Such attention did not preclude his promoting public interest in the 1897 trip through the arrangements he made for Edward H. Boos to accompany the corps as the official reporter. It was Boos who sent periodic dispatches to the *St. Louis Globe Democrat*. Finally, Moss's own courage and determination to complete the ride to St. Louis were crucial. As he noted in a personal letter to Gen. Samuel Breck, who Moss credited with assistance in "getting my scheme through," "if I don't ride into St. Louis on a bicycle at the head of my command, it will be because I have been taken back to Ft. Missoula on a stretcher."[35]

Of course it was the enlisted men of the Twenty-fifth Infantry Bicycle Corps and not just Moss who made the trip. Their courage and determination in following his leadership made the trip a success. Unfortunately, there is not extant contemporaneous documentation (other than biased stereotype references) that reveals how they viewed the bicycle trip. Although their names are known, they remain "unknown" to us today. This brief recounting of the experiences of this handful of black soldiers and their white commanding officer in the glorious days of cycling seems appropriate in view of the revival of interest in adult use of bicycles in the United States today.

Notes

1. Henry H. Whitney, "The Adaption of the Bicycle to Military Uses," *Journal of the Military Service Institution* 17 (1895): 543–51.

2. Charles Turner, "Military Cycling," *The Outing Magazine* 17 (1891): 194. Turner includes a picture of a twelve-person multicycle.

3. *New York Times*, October 21, 1891.

4. File No. 23672, Records of the Adjutant General's Office, Record Group 94, National Archives (hereinafter cited as RG 94, NA).

5. Ibid.

6. Ibid.

7. May was reassigned to the post of regimental adjutant on April 30, 1892. Nevertheless, he wrote a manual that applied the general principles of the Infantry Drill Regulations to bicycles. The manual includes instructions on how to mount and dismount properly, ride in a circle, ride in columns, and stack cycles. The manual also provided cycle maintenance and bugle music appropriate for a bicycle detachment. See William T. May, *Cyclist's Drill Regulations* (1892).

8. The full text of this speech is in Albert Augustus Pope, *The Bicycle in the Army* (1894).

9. "Report of the Major General Commanding the Army" in *Report of the Secretary of War, 1896*, vol. 1, 69. In October of 1895, General Miles's Aide-de-Camp, Capt. Francis Michler, conducted a survey of the number of officers and enlisted men in the various departments who could ride a bicycle. Col. A. S. Burt, commander of the Twenty-fifth Infantry, reported that at Fort Missoula three officers and seventy-eight enlisted men could ride bicycles.

10. *The Daily Missoulian*, April 16, 1894.

11. *The Daily Missoulian*, July 4, 1896. Since this article does not identify any of the twenty soldiers, it is assumed that Moss was among the group.

12. Moss submitted his request to organize and conduct military experiments with bicycles on April 13, 1896. In his endorsement, dated April 21, 1896, Col. Burt noted that "I am desirous of seeing the plan submitted by Lieutenant Moss carried out. I think it will be a valuable experiment to the service under the conditions of the surrounding company." Burt also noted that he had instructed Moss to correspond with the "large manufacturers of wheels in this country" regarding the use of bicycles for the proposed experiment. The Spalding Bicycle Company agreed to provide the bicycles at no cost to the government. On May 12, 1896, the project was approved by the Acting Engineer Office, Department of Dakota. See File No. 2635, Records of the U.S. Army Continental Commands, 1821–1920, Record Group 393, National Archives (hereinafter cited as RG 393, NA). Also see *The Daily Missoulian*, July 11, 1896.

13. This account is taken from Moss's official report, File No. 46408, RG 94, NA. Also see James A. Moss, *Military Cycling in the Rocky Mountains* (1897).

14. *The Daily Missoulian*, Aug. 15, 1896.

15. File No. 46408, RG 94, NA.

16. "Vagabonding with the Tenth Horse," *Cosmopolitan* 22 (February, 1897): 347–54.

17. File No. 50038, RG 94, NA.

18. File No. 60178, RG 94, NA.

19. The remaining enlisted men were Mus. Elias Johnson, privates John Findley, George Scott, Hiram L. B. Dingman, Travis Bridges, John Cook, Frank L. Johnson, William Proctor, Elwood Forman, Richard Rout, Eugene Jones, Sam Johnson, William Williamson, Sam Williamson, John H. Wilson, Samuel Reid, and Francis Button.

20. Kennedy was a native of Abbeville, South Carolina. He had been appointed post surgeon in 1893 and Fort Missoula was his second assignment.

21. *The Daily Missoulian*, July 10, 1897.

22. *St. Louis Globe-Democrat*, July 27, 1897.

23. "25th Infantry Bicycles Corps," *United States Army and Navy Journal* (Aug. 7, 1897): 903.

24. File No. 60178, RG 94, NA.

25. *St. Louis Globe-Democrat*, July 11, 1897.

26. *Nebraska State Journal*, July 15, 1897.

27. *Crawford Nebraska Journal*, July 9, 1897.

28. "History of Fort Missoula, Montana," (author unknown), unpublished manuscript, p. 28. Copy in possession of the writer.

29. *St. Louis Globe-Democrat*, July 25, 1897.

30. File No. 60178, RG 94, NA.

31. File No. 70545, RG 94, NA.

32. File No. 2166, RG 94, NA. Col. Burt added in a postscript: "We don't use that word 'nigger' here. Why I have used it above is to more clearly illustrate my meaning."

33. File No. 70545, RG 94, NA.

34. File No. 2166, RG 94, NA.

35. Ibid.

MARVIN E. FLETCHER

The Black Soldier-Athlete
in the U.S. Army, 1890–1916

Today white Americans find nothing unusual in reading about or seeing Blacks and whites compete against each other in athletics. The same could not be said of the years between 1890 and 1950. Segregation made interracial sports competition infrequent. Athletics in the army was a major exception to this generalization. The army, in segregating the men of its units, created the conditions that permitted Blacks and whites to compete against each other. Blacks took advantage of the opportunity and showed Americans how much segregation deprived athletics of skilled and competent people. In addition, the competition and recreation programs made army life more attractive for the Black soldier.

For many reasons the period from 1890 to 1916 has rightly been called the worst in U.S. history for Blacks. Politically, legally, and economically their status continually grew worse. Neither of the national political parties displayed much interest in their vote or their welfare. In the South, where most of them lived, restrictions such as the literacy test and the poll tax, made it very difficult for them to vote. Most Blacks were landless sharecroppers, never able to get out of debt to the white landowner. Segregation became more complete after having been given sanction by the decision of the U.S. Supreme Court in *Plessy v. Ferguson* (1896). Athletics was but one of the many areas hurt by such segregation.

Not very much is known about the Black athlete in this period. There was some interracial competition but in only a few sports. At this time baseball was the only sport with many professional players. A handful of Blacks played in the International League in the 1880s, but by the early 1890s none were allowed to compete.[1] At the same time all-Black teams competed in the white leagues, but these were soon eliminated also.[2] By the early part of this century Blacks were restricted to all-Black leagues. While on occasion they were able to compete against barn-storming white major leaguers, for the most part whites simply ignored them.[3] On the amateur level Blacks attending schools such as Rutgers, Brown, Amherst, and Harvard took part in a variety of sports includ-ing football, basketball, and track and field.[4] Some Black schools (such as Howard University) also had organized competition but here again whites avoided or ignored them. Few Blacks had the opportunity to enter ath-letic programs or compete against others. The U.S. Army provided Blacks with this chance.

Created in 1866, the Ninth and Tenth Cavalry and the Twenty-fourth and Twenty-fifth Infantry were all-Black units. Not until the end of the Indian Wars, in 1890, did the Army as a whole have much time for anything besides Indian fighting. During the following twenty-six years of peace, before World War I, there was more time for recreation, in-cluding athletic competition. In addition, the army moved out of the small, western posts it had occupied during the Indian Wars and into large camps near the urban areas of the United States, the Philippines, and Hawaii. These changes in the army's mission and location resulted in a growth of athletic activities within and between regiments.

One of the most popular sports in America at this time was baseball. Organized activity ranged from intra-regimental competition to games between Black regimental teams and white military and civilian teams. Within the Black regiments competition for a position on a company or regimental baseball team was always keen. On one occasion the chaplain of the Tenth Cavalry reported that the Black soldiers were concentrat-ing so seriously on baseball that they did not even get drunk or cause disturbances.[5] The unit officers (who were most often white men) took advantage of this attitude as a means of discipline: bad behavior meant exclusion from competition.[6] The officers also encouraged and coached the teams, but rarely played on them and then only on the company level.[7] Uniforms generally were purchased with money from the troop or regimental fund. For example, Troop D, Ninth Cavalry, chose blue uni-forms with dark blue socks.[8]

Competition between regiments was keen and took place wherever two units could get together. When the Tenth Cavalry was stationed at Fort Ethan Allan (near Burlington, Vermont) they scheduled a game with the Fifth Infantry, located then at Plattsburg Barracks, New York.

In order to reach the site of the game in New York, the regiment hired a steamer for the trip across Lake Champlain. Over two hundred men and their families made the trip and watched with pleasure as their team beat the Infantry 11 to 4.[9] When several units gathered, a tournament was often played. During breaks between the training problems of the 1903 Fort Riley, Kansas, maneuvers, a regimental baseball tournament was set up. Though many teams, Black and white, were entered, it finally narrowed down to the two Black regiments present: the Tenth Cavalry and the Twenty-fifth Infantry. In the climatic game, the Twenty-fifth won 4–3 in ten innings.[10] The Twenty-fifth and the Twelfth Infantry were involved in a series of games that spanned two continents. In 1898, during the build-up for the Spanish-American War, many regiments gathered at the training camp at Chattanooga. A game, before several thousand spectators, resulted in an easy victory for the whites. The next games in the series were played several years later in the Philippines. The Blacks promptly avenged the defeat.[11] More often than not, something in addition to pride was at stake in the games. The Twenty-fifth's team arrived in Manila in 1901 and challenged any team to a game for "Money, marbles or chalk, money preferred."[12] It was not an idle gesture. The Twenty-fourth's team, in similar circumstances, won enough money in bets during maneuvers at Pine Camp, New York, to keep them well supplied with funds for drinks.[13]

The best Black army baseball team represented the Twenty-fifth Infantry. They won many games against all types of competition. This is evident from a contemporary (1914) description of the regiment's amusement hall in Hawaii: "Every bit of wall space was covered with banners won by the companies, battalions, and the regiment in athletic contests during many years past."[14] In that year they won the army championship of Oahu, Hawaii, with a record, in league competition, of nine won and one lost.[15] In 1916 they ran up a record of forty-two wins and two losses, not only against military squads, but also civilian teams like Santa Clara University and the Olympic Club of San Francisco. Al Earle of the Spalding Company then proposed to sponsor the regiment's team in a series of games on the West Coast. The army vetoed this proposal. They said that "there is no special end of military athletic training served thereby."[16]

The Twenty-fifth's 1916 schedule points out that competition was not limited to military opponents. The Black regimental teams played both civilian amateur and professional teams, and did quite well for themselves. The Tenth Cavalry team lost a game to the University of Vermont by a score of 5–1, but then beat a team from St. Michael's College, also in Vermont, by a score of 4–2. The local paper described the soldiers' pitcher in the latter game as a man with "lots of speed and a large repertoire of plain and fancy curves. Besides striking out 11 men he had the college boys pretty well scared."[17] Games were often arranged with amateur teams from the nearby communities. The Ninth Cavalry, in typical fashion, greatly impressed a team from Park City, Montana. The civilians, "hitherto invincible," drew two thousand spectators to a game with the Browns, the Ninth's team. "Each of the Brown's wore a rabbit's foot as a mascot, with which they made some mysterious motions before playing." The Blacks won 9–8.[18] The Black regimental teams also played professionals. The Ninth's team defeated a group of white pros from Walla Walla, Washington.[19] The Cuban Stars, a Black professional team, had the elements on their side in a game with the Tenth Cavalry at Fort Ethan Allen in May, 1911. The temperature hovered near freezing and a stiff north wind carried snow flurries. The soldiers blamed the weather for the errors that caused their 3–2 defeat.[20] The closeness of the score against a good professional team as well as the general performance of the Black teams is an indicator of the quality baseball played by the Black athletes.

While baseball was the most often mentioned organized sport in the newspaper accounts of the activities of the Black soldiers, other team sports such as football and basketball were not neglected. While stationed at Fort Riley, Kansas, troops of the Ninth Cavalry each fielded a football team. In 1906 Troop K won the regimental league with a good defense; its goal line was crossed only once during the season.[21] Competition also existed on the interregimental level. A team formed by the Twenty-fifth Infantry easily beat one from the Tenth Cavalry 49–0 in a game played in 1904.[22] Basketball as a competitive activity had just begun to develop in the period under discussion. As a result few posts were properly equipped for the game. The Tenth Cavalry got their chance when they were assigned to Fort Ethan Allen and they took advantage of it. Interest was quite great "and almost every evening one or two games were played in the gymnasium."[23] As in the other sports, there were several levels of competition. In 1911 the machine gun platoon was the winner of the intraregimental competition, not losing a single game.[24] A regimental team was formed in that year and traveled to New York City to play a Black All-star team. In the pregame publicity the team from

Vermont was billed as 'The Champion Basketball Team of the U.S. Army.'[25] The *New York Age*, a Black newspaper, reported the game:

> The boys in blue proved as tricky as the horses they ride, and whenever an All-Star player attempted to tackle a cavalryman by jumping on his back he was usually given a quick excursion through the air. Medical aid and sticking plaster were called into use several times, and one soldier had a sweet short dream in the second half, but no one was seriously injured.

Though the Black soldiers were heavier, the All-Stars were faster and won 30–14.[26] Though other Black units may have played football or basketball, no accounts of such games were found.

The other major type of regimental as well as individual organized athletic activity within the Army at this time was track and field. One group of events in this category directly related to military skills (i.e., tent pitching), while others were more conventional events (i.e., the high jump).

Competitions involving military related skills took place at army maneuvers and within the army created geographic departments. The Fourth of July, 1908, was the date and Pine Camp was the scene for such a field day. The competition among the many army and national guard units was won by the Twenty-fourth Infantry, who received a cash prize of $88.00 for their efforts.[27] Cavalry related activities included bareback tug of war and mounted wrestling.[28] During the tug of war finals at Fort Riley in 1907, (this time held without horses), Troop B, Ninth Cavalry, faced a team from the Twenty-fifth Battery, Field Artillery, with a cash prize of fifty dollars at stake. The competition was indecisive until an officer, in an effort to cool down the artillery team, doused them with a bucket of water. The Blacks took advantage of the slippery floor and quickly won the contest.[29]

Regular track competition also brought out the hidden talents of the Blacks. Victories were won despite the fact that most of the soldiers had no training in the skills required. The winner of the 220 yard dash at a military track meet held in Denver, Colorado, in 1896, is a good example of this situation. An army observer thought that the Black private from Troop B, Ninth Cavalry, "with training could have equaled the world's record of amateur runners, as he had not been taught how to start."[30] Apparently some effort was made to develop such skills, for in 1916 Private Gilbert, of the Twenty-fifth Infantry, ran the 100 yard dash in 9.6 seconds, equaling the amateur mark at that distance.[31] The Black soldiers also did quite well in inter-regimental competition. In 1915 a soldier from the Twenty-fifth won the 220 and 440 yard races at the Army-Navy Championship Track and Field Meet held in conjunction with the Panama-Pacific Exposition in San Francisco.[32] In 1908 the three geographic departments in the Division of the Philippines each held a track meet to determine the regiment that would participate in the division meet. For example, the meet held in the Department of Luzon involved teams from the Third, Ninth, and Tenth Cavalry, the Fifth Field Artillery, and the Twenty-sixth, Twenty-ninth, and Thirtieth Infantry.[33] The competition in this meet, as in the other two department meets, was won by a team from a Black regiment: the Ninth Cavalry in the Department of Luzon, the Twenty-fourth Infantry in the Department of the Visayas, and the Twenty-fifth Infantry in the Department of Miridanao.[34] The 1908 divisional competition that followed was won by the Twenty-fourth Infantry with a score of 42 points.[35] All of these victories by Black athletes bothered at least one white officer. He expressed his feelings in a letter to *The Army and Navy Journal:* "Surely this is a matter for some thought on the part of those who are responsible to the nation for the maintenance of its prestige and for its defense."[36]

Several meanings can be read into this note. The one that is least probable, given the racial ideas of the time, was that the country would benefit if Blacks would be encouraged to enter more athletic meets. More likely this officer, and probably many others, was worried about the influence of Blacks in athletics. In his view whites, once displaced by Blacks, would not be able to compete against their animal-like opponents. The army paid no heed to the questions raised by this white officer. Consequently, the following year the Blacks in the Philippines added to their laurels. In the 1909 divisional meet George Washington, a soldier from the Twenty-fifth Infantry won the 100 yard dash and the 220 and 880 yard races. For his efforts he was awarded the gold medal for the best all-round athlete at the meet. Afterwards he was challenged by Corporal Andrews, a soldier from the British Legation in Hong Kong. After beating the British soldier, Washington was declared champion runner of the Far East.[37] The success of Blacks in the army track events again showed that segregation denied America great athletic talent.

One type of competition that the army handled much the same as civilian society in this period was boxing. There were bouts between Black soldiers and white soldiers and civilians. In addition, the Black soldiers showed a great deal of interest in Black professional boxers, such as Joe Gans and Jack Johnson, both champions of their weight class. In 1909 Sgt. Oscar Morgan, Twenty-fifth Infantry, beat a white soldier from the Field Artillery for the heavyweight crown of the Philippine Islands.[38] The Philippines was also the site of a real "slugging match" between Steinberg of the Thirtieth Infantry and Murray of the Ninth Cavalry. While the referee's attention was directed outside the ring, according to a report published in *The Army and Navy Journal*, Murray got in a low blow. This enraged spectators and a melee started. The fighting outside the ring became worse when Murray was given the decision on a KO in the third round.[39] However, not all Black soldier boxers were successful in the ring. In January 1912 the Seattle Athletic Club and the Twenty-fifth Infantry put on two three-round boxing matches, apparently pitting white civilians against the soldiers. The Blacks fared poorly against their skilled white opponents. They lost both bouts.[40] Black professional boxers were quite successful in this period and the soldiers evidenced great interest. Movies of the Joe Gans-Battling Nelson lightweight championship fight of 1908 attracted a big crowd to the post exchange at Fort Ethan Allen when the Tenth Cavalry sponsored a showing.[41] The soldiers, like Blacks as a whole, showed a great deal of interest in the career of Jack Johnson, the first Black heavyweight champion. Johnson won the championship in 1908 and two years later Jim Jeffries, "the great white hope," came out of retirement to challenge him. The fight was held in Reno, before a crowd of twenty thousand spectators, but many others around the nation displayed interest. The Black soldiers stationed at Fort Lawton, Washington, stayed by the telegraph to keep up with the action. When Johnson won, with a KO in the fifteenth round, the soldiers rejoiced. William P. Evans, a white officer, vividly recalled the event: "I can hear yet the cheer when Johnson scored and finally won."[42] All the way across the country at Fort Ontario, New York, the Blacks in the Twenty-fourth Infantry celebrated Johnson's victory with a party in the barracks.[43]

Other athletic activities of the Black soldiers depended upon leisure time, the climate, and proper facilities. Individual recreation activities were more common but less reported than team competition. Such activities as ice skating, bowling, gymnastics, and billiards, at one time or another, helped the soldiers pass their leisure moments during the winter months. Winter provided the climate and opportunity for ice skating. At Fort Keogh, Montana, as at other northern and western posts, two ice skating rinks, with walls of frozen snow, were created on the parade ground. One rink was reserved for officers and their families, while the other was used by enlisted men and their families.[44] The soldiers of the Tenth, while at Fort Keogh and at Fort Custer, Montana, kept the rinks in constant use.[45] Skating was not confined to the post area, however. Two sergeants of the Tenth, J. Graham and S. T. Dorsey, skated thirty miles down the Little Horn River to the Crow Agency, an Indian reservation.[46] At Fort Assinniboine, Montana, the men of the Tenth set up a bowling alley in the post amusement hall.[47] Gymnastics occupied the winter months of the Blacks at several western posts: Fort Custer, Montana, and Fort Mackenzie, Wyoming. According to local reports, Troop B, Tenth Cavalry, began the winter season at the gym in January, riding the wooden horse, climbing the greasy pole, and bursting the boxing glove.[48] During the winter of 1904 another unit of the same regiment gave an evening of "athletic entertainment" at the gym at Fort Mackenzie.

> They danced, walked, lay down, sat and kneeled on a slack wire, turned handsprings over three or four men, sometimes using only one hand; others by grasping one another by the ankles became a human wheel, and rolled around the room; others played on the horizontal and parallel bars with such rapidity that it was hard to tell when one feat was finished or another commenced.[49]

Billiards also drew the soldiers' attention. In 1897 the men of the Tenth stationed at Fort Custer held a wintertime tournament. The championship was decided between two members of Troop B—Peter Francis and Rand Harris.[50] Summer recreation centered around baseball, but much of the time was taken up by practice marches and maneuvers, especially after 1899.

For Black civilians the period between 1890 and 1916 was terrible. In athletics, as in many other aspects of life, they were generally excluded. In the army Black soldiers were also segregated, by regiments, but competition in sports occurred. This was a crucial difference. As a result of the opportunities provided by the recreation and competitive sports programs within the military, Blacks had a chance to show their talents. They responded by participating and doing well, competitively in all types of sports. This success, made known to Black civilians through the Black and white press, helped to recruit new Black soldiers. It made the army an attractive alternative to civilian life. Most importantly, the participation and competition of the Black soldier athletes demonstrated that America was losing excellence by excluding its Black population. It took a long time for civilian society to catch up with the military. Today we see the results all the time.

Notes

1. Robert Peterson, *Only the Ball Was White* (New Jersey: Englewood Cliffs, 1970), 44.

2. Ibid., 49.

3. Ibid., 66.

4. Edwin B. Henderson, *The Negro in Sports* (Washington, D.C.: Associated Publishers, 1939); for accounts of blacks in competition with whites in football, see pp. 86–113, basketball, pp. 128–33; track, pp. 45–47, 65–67.

5. Document File #53910, October 1901, Records of the Adjutant General's Office, Document File 1890–1917, National Archives, Record Group 94. Hereafter documents in this series will be cited as AGO #_____.

6. Oswald Garrison Villard, "The Negro in the Regular Army," *Atlantic Monthly,* 91 (June 1903): 727.

7. John H. Nankivell, *History of the Twenty-Fifth Regiment, United States Infantry, 1869–1926* (Denver: Smith-Brooks Printing, 1926), 164.

8. *Army and Navy Journal* (August 18, 1910): 1212. Hereafter cited as *ANJ.*

9. *ANJ* (May 17, 1913): 1151.

10. *ANJ* (November 7, 1903): 242.

11. Nankivell, 166.

12. *Manila Times* (May 1, 1901), as quoted in *ANJ* (June 22, 1901): 1049.

13. *Army and Navy Review* (June 27, 1908): 11. Hereafter cited as *ANR.*

14. *ANJ* (September 12, 1914): 57.

15. *ANJ* (August 29, 1914): 1675.

16. AGO #2494843.

17. *ANJ* (June 17, 1911): 1280; *Burlington* (Vermont) *Free Press* (May 6, 1910).

18. *ANJ* (May 29, 1897): 723.

19. *ANJ* (May 9, 1903): 904.

20. *Burlington Free Press* (May 4, 1911).

21. *ANR* (March 3, 1906): 2. See also *ANJ* (December 3, 1904): 341.

22. *ANJ* (December 10, 1904): 371.

23. *ANJ* (January 21, 1911): 611.

24. *ANJ* (February 25, 1911): 774.

25. *New York Age* (February 2, 1911).

26. *New York Age* (March 30, 1911).

27. *ANJ* (July 11, 1908): 1243.

28. *Colored American Magazine* (June 8, 1905): 25.

29. *ANJ* (February 9, 1907): 658.

30. AGO, #53445.

31. *ANJ* (March 18, 1916): 945.

32. *ANJ* (September 11, 1915): 59.

33. *ANJ* (January 18, 1908): 530.

34. *ANJ* (February 8, 1908): 595.

35. *ANJ* (March 14, 1908): 728.

36. *ANJ* (February 8, 1908): 595.

37. *The Freeman* (Indianapolis, Ind.) (May 1, 1909).

38. Ibid.

39. *ANJ* (February 6, 1909): 632.

40. AGO #1874272.

41. *Burlington Free Press* (September 16, 1909).

42. William P. Evans, questionnaire, 1966, in possession of the author.

43. *ANJ* (July 16, 1910): 1385.

44. *ANJ* (January 11, 1896): 325.

45. *The Enterprise* (Omaha, Neb.) (February 13, 1892).

46. *The Enterprise* (January 23, 1897).

47. *ANJ* (March 12, 1904): 731.

48. *The Enterprise* (January 18, 1896).

49. *ANJ* (March 12, 1904): 729.

50. *The Enterprise* (January 23, 1897).

HORACE DANIEL NASH

Community Building on the Border

THE ROLE OF THE TWENTY-FOURTH INFANTRY
BAND AT COLUMBUS, NEW MEXICO, 1916–22

The black military units created by Congress immediately after the Civil War played prominent roles in settling the West. In the last two decades a number of works have recognized the contributions of these regiments; however, most have dealt primarily with the military experience of blacks on the frontier in the post–Civil War era.[1] In the twentieth century these same black regiments continued their tradition of military service in the West when the Mexican Revolution brought black soldiers to duty along the Mexico-United States border.

On March 9, 1916, Mexican Revolutionary Pancho Villa and a band of his followers launched an attack on Columbus, New Mexico, a small, isolated community in Luna County, three miles north of the Mexican border. Subsequently, the United States organized a punitive expedition under Gen. John J. Pershing to pursue Villa into Mexico. Two black regiments, the Tenth Cavalry and the Twenty-fourth Infantry, were part of the expedition.[2] Following the withdrawal of the Punitive Expedition from Mexico on February 5, 1917, the white Twelfth Cavalry and the black Twenty-fourth Infantry were stationed at Columbus.[3]

By the end of March 1917, nearly 1,500 soldiers (1,170 black and 249 white) were stationed at Camp Furlong, just south of the railroad tracks in Columbus. Three years later in March 1920, there were 4,109 enlisted men at the base, including 3,599 black and 510 white soldiers, and seventy-five officers (one black officer) present for duty. During the military buildup the civilian population of Columbus exploded, from barely 700 in 1916 to over 2,500 by 1920.[4] At its height Columbus represented one of the single largest black military communities ever to reside in the West.

Although some social activities at Columbus were segregated, blacks and whites jointly attended most public affairs and a high degree of tolerance prevailed between the races.[5] While military bands had a tradition of community service and involvement,[6] at Columbus they took part in most local events, performing at movies and in theater productions, boxing matches and baseball games, YMCA concerts and dances, and parades and holiday celebrations.[7] Either the overwhelming numbers of the Twenty-fourth Infantry or the quality of its band resulted in it participating to a greater extent than the Twelfth Cavalry band in local activities. By performing at integrated activities, the Twenty-fourth Infantry band helped foster harmonious race relations and the spirit of community, while providing blacks with a sense of pride and vibrant social life.

A great deal of interaction between the civilian and military community centered on wartime community efforts. Two months after the Punitive Expedition left Mexico, the United States declared war on Germany. During the war the people of Columbus, like those across the state and nation, were active in raising funds for the Red Cross. Blacks played a role in many of these fundraising affairs, especially members of the Twenty-fourth Infantry band. On June 19, 1917, the band provided music for a dance given by the Finance Committee of the Red Cross. Many of the townspeople as well as a number of officers and their wives from both the Twelfth Cavalry and the Twenty-fourth Infantry attended the dance. According to the newspaper, "This was the first time this band had been heard for a local affair and the music made by our colored boys was highly enjoyed by all." The event raised about fifty dollars. The presence of the band was the only indication that blacks attended this activity.[8]

In May 1918 the Red Cross organized another drive to raise funds, and the black community of Columbus and Camp Furlong was involved in these efforts. The Red Cross regional office in Denver, Colorado, assigned Luna County a quota of $7,000, including a quota for Columbus of $1,400. The first meeting of the local fundraising committee was held at Meadow's Drug Store, where they discussed strategy and different plans for the campaign. Chaplain Alexander W. Thomas, the black chaplain of the Twenty-fourth Infantry, was selected to manage the drive among blacks.[9]

As part of the campaign, a series of fundraising activities were scheduled for the week of May 20–27, including three fundraisers featuring the Twenty-fourth Infantry band. The black musicians gave their first performance in the form of a concert at the Columbus Theater on

Wednesday night, May 22. The following evening the "colored people" gave a dance that was well-attended and financially a huge success. On Friday night the band performed for a dance at the Chamber of Commerce building. Due in part to their efforts, the fundraising campaign was a success as the people of Columbus had exceeded their quota by raising over $2,200. The local newspaper praised Chaplain Thomas and the other Red Cross committee members for their efforts.[10]

In August the Junior Red Cross held a carnival that included food and dancing. The music for the event was jointly provided by the Twelfth Cavalry and the Twenty-fourth Infantry bands. The program also included a vocal solo by the mayor's talented daughter, Treva Blair.[11]

Often musicians from the Twenty-fourth Infantry played at dances held by regimental officers. These affairs generally took place in the town of Columbus and were widely attended by civilians. One such occasion occurred on George Washington's birthday in 1918, when the officers of the Twenty-fourth held a dance at the Moline Recreation Hall. Guests from nearby Deming, New Mexico, and El Paso, Texas, attended the party. The following month another dance was held and a large number of out-of-town visitors also were present.[12]

Typically, holiday celebrations and special events included civilian and military, black and white, members of the town. These celebrations usually featured a full schedule of sporting activities, parades, and picnics. Dances, often a part of these festivities, were probably segregated. Some events, however, were particularly unique to Columbus. On March 9, 1919, a memorial service was held for the victims of Pancho Villa's raid. Among the speakers was Chaplain Thompson of the Twelfth Cavalry, and the Twenty-fourth Infantry band provided music for the service. A variety of military and civilian officials participated in the well-attended program, including Mayor John R. Blair and Col. G. Arthur Hadsell, commander of Camp Furlong.[13]

The holiday celebration for July 4, 1919, was planned by a biracial committee composed of civilians, military personnel, and representatives of several welfare groups. Since segregated YMCA and War Camp Community Service (WCCS) facilities existed at Columbus, representatives from the black and white branches of these organizations were included on the committee. Titus Alexander (black) and H. J. Packard (white) represented the WCCS; M. F. Mitchell (black) and S. E. Shull (white) represented the YMCA. Other members of the committee were Col. George W. Biegler, chairman; Mayor John Blair; J. H. Culley of the

American Red Cross; and Willard E. Holt, President of the Chamber of Commerce.[14]

An enormous crowd attended the Independence Day festivities. Lt. Col. Paul R. Manchester, grand marshal, and his mounted staff led a parade through the town, with Colonel Hadsell and the Twenty-fourth Infantry and Colonel Biegler and the Twelfth Cavalry following behind. The bands of both units also participated, and at the intersection of Main and Broadway streets the column halted and played "The Star Spangled Banner." Afterward, a large American flag was unfurled by Blanche Ritchie, whose father W. T. Ritchie was killed in Pancho Villa's raid. The citizens of Columbus "with their splendid industrial floats and decorated automobiles" followed the military procession in the parade. The day was filled with field events, baseball, cowboy sports, and boxing. Later, the Twelfth Cavalry band gave a "patriotic" concert at the corner of Main and Broadway, which was followed by speeches from Mayor Blair, who presided as master of ceremonies; Lt. James A. McCarthy for the military; Titus Alexander (the black WCCS representative) for the welfare organizations; and Willard Holt for the Chamber of Commerce. In the evening various balls and receptions were held at the army post.[15]

Later in the year a special celebration was held that indicated increasing peaceful border conditions. On September 16 Columbus citizens commemorated Mexican National Independence Day with a parade. About thirty automobiles, predominately decorated with the Mexican national colors, paraded through Columbus led by a U.S. Army band. Later a barbeque dinner was served, and then the crowd, including Colonel Biegler and Mayor Blair, crossed the international border to continue the celebration in the town of Palomas. In the evening, back in Columbus, the Twenty-fourth Infantry band provided music for a free dance at the Khaki Club, the black entertainment facility provided by the WCCS.[16]

One holiday celebration unique to the black community at Columbus was "Juneteenth," which was celebrated each June 19 to commemorate emancipation.[17] On June 19, 1919, Columbus blacks held a picnic at nearby Hermanas Grove to honor the day; however, many black soldiers were unable to attend. Earlier, a large contingent of soldiers was sent to El Paso, Texas, to prepare for a confrontation with Pancho Villa's forces at Juarez, Mexico. Still, some soldiers marked the occasion in El Paso with blacks in that city at festivities at Washington Park. The musicians of the Twenty-fourth Infantry were among those invited to participate.[18]

Military bands performed at a wide variety of community events. Minstrel shows had been a popular form of entertainment among Americans for many years, and Columbus citizens enjoyed these programs, too. On February 23, 1917, the men of the recently arrived Twenty-fourth provided a free minstrel show in the Columbus Theater. The regimental band provided the music for the show, with a quartette from Company F offering "many pleasant selections." The event was widely attended by the citizens of Columbus and military officers and their wives.[19] Although one historian has suggested that early members of the Twenty-fourth Infantry objected to minstrel shows and refused to perform, records indicate that black soldiers at Columbus participated in these shows.[20]

In August 1918 the Twenty-fourth Infantry band gave a concert at Camp Furlong's YMCA building, initiating a regular concert series that proved popular among soldiers and civilians alike. The performances featured the regimental bands from the Twelfth Cavalry and the Twenty-fourth Infantry, which rotated concerts. An estimated 1,875 soldiers and civilians attended the Twenty-fourth Infantry's performance at the end of the month.[21]

Smaller orchestras consisting of members from the Twenty-fourth Infantry band provided music for a variety of functions in the black community. On October 29, 1919, the Dunbar Literary Circle held a Halloween ball for nearly five hundred guests at the Twenty-fourth Infantry Khaki Club, purported to be "one of the largest and most elaborate affairs yet given in the city for some time." The facility was artistically decorated for the occasion, and "many of the novel and charming costumes were in evidence." The most striking feature of the evening was the search for several two and one-half dollar gold pieces hidden throughout the hall. One of the Twenty-fourth's orchestras provided the music, which was directed by "Musician of the First-Class [Robert] Thaddieous."[22]

Black women, mostly wives of black soldiers, formed a variety of social clubs at Columbus, among them the Twenty-fourth Infantry Women's Club, the Star Club, the Lilly White Club, the Silver Leaf Whist Club, and the Willing Workers. But the women's club activities sometimes included men, and on more than one occasion members of the Twenty-fourth Infantry Women's Club had refreshments and dancing with their husbands after their meeting. Members of the regimental band usually furnished music.[23]

Musicians from the Twenty-fourth also performed at private parties and affairs held by members of the black community. Whist parties and dances were the most popular as were birthdays and anniversaries of the higher-ranking enlisted men and their spouses. On June 3, 1920, Mrs. S. I. Prince, wife of Sergeant Prince of Company I, celebrated her birthday at Camp Furlong's Service Club. The party included whist and other games and dancing to melodies provided by members of the Twenty-fourth Infantry band. Among the numerous guests were several members of the local black community, including Mrs. J. Hubbard, a representative of the local Red Cross, and Ruby Craig, hostess of the Service Club.[24]

Religious activities were an important dimension of the black community at Columbus, and the Twenty-fourth Infantry band participated at many services. The local African Methodist Episcopal (AME) mission enjoyed broad support from soldiers and civilians in the town. In August 1918, the black civilian and military community sponsored a charity ball featuring the regimental band to raise funds for the mission.[25]

In April 1920 World War I personnel reductions forced the transfer of the Twelfth Cavalry, leaving only the Twenty-fourth Infantry at Camp Furlong. Gradually, the army began to reduce the number of soldiers assigned along the New Mexico section of the international border. The Twenty-fourth Infantry band retained its prominent role in providing music at a variety of functions, not only in Columbus but also at other area towns. On Memorial Day in 1921 the band played at Fort Bayard (near Silver City), and in November 1921 it played at the Armistice Day rodeo and celebration at Deming. Smaller orchestras consisting of Twenty-fourth Infantry band members continued to regularly perform at dances and social functions in the black community.[26]

In early 1920 the Columbus Theater Orchestra was formed, consisting of black members of the military and civilian community. Besides providing music for movies, the band performed at a variety of functions either separately or as a group. Soon renamed the Elite Jazzers, on July 23 they played at a dance for blacks at the Khaki Club, and two weeks later at a dance for whites. The owner of the Columbus Theater, James L. Greenwood, arranged to have the orchestra furnish jazz music at dances and rallies for the Luna County Democratic Party. The Democrats proposed activities in every "city, village, and hamlet" in Luna County, and Greenwood believed that the orchestra would draw large crowds. On September 17, 1920, the orchestra provided the music for the Democratic Party's rally and dance at nearby Hondale, and the following night it played for a huge political rally in the national guard armory at Deming. Not about to forget their organizational roots, on December 5, 1920, the orchestra performed classic and other music in a program at the Columbus Theater.[27]

In November 1920 band members formed a union and established price guidelines: "Dances—per man for the first three hours $5 and $1 for each hour over. Deming prices—$10 per man till midnight. Silver City prices—$15 per man until 1 A.M. El Paso prices—$7.50 for three hours." The new union elected William Warren as president and R. Jackson as secretary-treasurer.[28] Other black bands also existed, and in the summer of 1921 the Excelsior Orchestra, composed of members of the Twenty-fourth Infantry band, advertised "music for any occasion." The band often performed at the Khaki Club.[29]

Relations in Columbus between blacks and whites were not necessarily the ideal of racial harmony; however, a much better relationship developed and existed there than in many parts of the United States.[30] Inevitably, some residents did object to the presence of black soldiers. But business and community leaders realized the military was the economic base of the town, and if the Twenty-fourth Infantry were removed from Columbus, it was unlikely they would be replaced by white troops. This knowledge no doubt contributed a great deal to the furtherance of satisfactory relations between civilians and black soldiers.

The Twenty-fourth Infantry's presence at Columbus was the continuation of a long and proud tradition of black military service in the West. While stationed at Columbus, musicians from the Twenty-fourth Infantry band participated in concerts and provided other entertainment, performing at segregated and integrated events and functions. They consistently provided music for movies and boxing matches and at a wide variety of events, from parties and parades to fairs, rodeos, and holiday celebrations. Throughout the Twenty-fourth Infantry's stay at Columbus, its regimental band played an integral role in local activities, helping to foster community spirit and assist in maintaining harmonious race relations. Moreover, the band was a source of inspiration and pride for civilian and military blacks, and by providing entertainment for blacks at segregated events, the band helped create a more active and dynamic black community. Ultimately, reductions in the armed forces and peace along the international border led to the removal of black troops from Camp Furlong in late 1922. While the withdrawal of the Twenty-fourth Infantry signaled the end of an era for the town, the experience of its soldiers and band members illustrate some measure of racial cooperation and understanding through turbulent times.

Notes

1. Lawrence B. DeGraaf, "Recognition, Racism, and Reflections on the Writing of Western Black History," *Pacific Historical Review* 44 (February 1975): 22–51; Roger Nichols, ed., *American Frontier and Western Issues: A Historiographical Review* (Westport, Conn.: Greenwood Press, 1986), 208–209, 215, 263–64. For works dealing with black soldiers in the West, see John M. Carroll, ed., *The Black Military Experience in the American West* (New York: Liveright Publishing, 1971); Marvin E. Fletcher, *The Black Soldier and Officer in the United States Army, 1891–1917* (Columbia: University of Missouri Press, 1974); Jack D. Foner, *Blacks and the Military in American History* (New York: Praeger Publishers, 1974); Arlen L. Fowler, *The Black Infantry in the West, 1869–1891* (Westport, Conn.: Greenwood Publishing, 1971); and William H. Leckie, *The Buffalo Soldiers: A Narrative of the Negro Cavalry in the West* (Norman: University of Oklahoma Press, 1967). For accounts of blacks serving in New Mexico in the late nineteenth century, see three works by Monroe L. Billington, "Soldiers at Play: Fort Bayard, 1887–1896" (unpublished manuscript); "Black Soldiers at Fort Selden, New Mexico, 1866–1891," *New Mexico Historical Review* 62 (January 1987): 65–80; and "Civilians and Black Soldiers in New Mexico Territory, 1866–1900: A Cross-Cultural Experience," *Military History of the Southwest* 19 (Spring 1989): 71–82.

2. For a good discussion of the Punitive Expedition, see Clarence C. Clendenen, *Blood on the Border: The United States Army and the Mexican Irregulars* (New York: Macmillan, 1969); and Robert B. Johnson, "The Punitive Expedition: A Military, Diplomatic, and Political History of Pershing's Chase After Pancho Villa, 1916–1917" (Ph.D. diss., University of Southern California, 1964). See also William G. Muller, *The Twenty-fourth Infantry Past and Present: A Brief History of the Regiment Compiled from Official Records, under the Direction of the Regimental Commander* (n.p., 1923; Rep., Fort Collins, Col.: Old Army Press, 1972); L. Albert Scipio II, *Last of the Black Regulars: A History of the Twenty-fourth Infantry Regiment (1869–1951)* (Silver Springs, Md.: Roman Publications, 1983); and Edward L. N. Glass, *The History of the Tenth Cavalry, 1866–1921* (Tucson, Arizona: Acme Printing, 1921; rep., Fort Collins, Colorado: Old Army Press, 1972).

3. Black soldiers in the Ninth and Tenth cavalries performed duty on the border prior to Villa's Raid and the Punitive Expedition. The Ninth Cavalry at Douglas, Arizona, since September 1912, and the Tenth Cavalry at Fort Huachuca, Arizona, since November 1914, were stationed along the border to enforce neutrality laws and protect U.S. interests since the outbreak of the Mexican Revolution in 1910. See Ninth Cavalry Returns, September 1912–

December 1915, and Tenth Cavalry Returns, November 1914–1916, Returns from Regular Army Cavalry Regiments, 1833–1916, Microcopy Number 744, Records of the Adjutant General's Office, Record Group 94, National Archives. Also see Glass, *History of the Tenth Cavalry*, 65–66; Post Returns, Columbus, New Mexico, July 1914–February 1916, Post Returns, Hachita, New Mexico, December 1915–July 1916, Post Returns, Camp Furlong, New Mexico, March–July 1916, Returns from U.S. Military Posts, 1800–1916, Microcopy Number 617, Records of the Adjutant General's Office, Record Group 94, National Archives, and Post Returns, Camp Furlong, New Mexico, March 1916–December 1922, Records of the Adjutant General's Office, Record Group 407, National Archives. (Hereafter cited as Post Returns, Camp Furlong, RG 407.)

4. Post Returns, Camp Furlong, RG 407, March 1917, March 1920. The only black officer at Camp Furlong was the chaplain of the Twenty-fourth Infantry.

5. Horace D. Nash, "Blacks on the Border: Columbus, New Mexico, 1916–1922," (Master's thesis, New Mexico State University, 1988), 170–74.

6. For a general history of military bands, see William Carter White, *A History of Military Music in America* (New York: Exposition Express, 1944), especially 90–108. Unfortunately this work does not specifically mention the bands of the black military regiments. For a brief account of military bands in the West during the late nineteenth century, including those of the black regiments, see Thomas Railsback and John P. Langellier, *The Drums Would Roll: A Pictorial History of U.S. Army Bands on the American Frontier, 1866–1900* (London: Arms and Armour Press, 1987). For other accounts of black regimental musicians, see Billington, "Soldiers at Play," 5–7; Billington, "Black Soldiers at Fort Selden," 65–66; Billington, "Civilians and Black Soldiers," 78–81; Fletcher, *Black Soldier and Officer*, 86–88; and Fowler, *Black Infantry*, 62–64.

7. Nash, "Blacks on the Border," 170–74.

8. *Columbus Courier*, June 22, 1917. In July 1918 the army increased its authorization for regimental bands from thirty-eight to forty-eight members. In 1922 the authorization was reduced to thirty-six. White, *History of Military Music*, 100–105.

9. *Columbus Courier*, May 10 and 24, 1918. Chaplain Alexander W. Thomas, Methodist Episcopal (black), was assigned as chaplain to the Twenty-fourth Infantry in autumn 1917.

10. Ibid., May 17, 24, 31, 1918.

11. Ibid., August 16, 1918.

12. Ibid., February 22, March 29, 1918.

13. Ibid., March 7, 14, 1919.

14. Ibid., June 13, 27, July 11, 1919. The segregation of WCCS and YMCA facilities was nationwide practice. See Arthur S. Barbeau and Florette Henri, *The Unknown Soldiers: Black American Troops in World War I* (Philadelphia: Temple University Press, 1974), 41; Charles Flint Kellogg, *NAACP: A History of the National Association for the Advancement of Colored People*, vol. 1, 1909–1920 (Baltimore: The Johns Hopkins University Press, 1967), 259; and Emmett J.

Scott, *Scott's Official History of the American Negro in the World War* (n.p., 1919; repr., New York: Arno Press, 1969), 386–87, 398–407.

15. *Columbus Courier,* July 11, 1919.

16. Ibid. September 12, 19, 1919.

17. On June 16, 1865, Union Gen. Gordon Granger declared the end of slavery in Texas from Galveston. Nash, "Blacks on the Border," 126–27. Most black communities celebrate January 1 as Emancipation Day, the day the Emancipation Proclamation went into effect in 1863. Fletcher, *Black Soldier and Officer,* 87.

18. *Columbus Courier,* June 13, 20, 27, 1919; *El Paso Herald,* June 19, 1919.

19. *Columbus Courier,* February 23, 1917; Alvin F. Harlow, "Minstrel Shows," in *Dictionary of American History,* vol. 4, rev. ed. (New York: Charles Scribners Sons, 1940, 1976), 359; Billington, "Soldiers at Fort Bayard," 7; Fowler, *Black Infantry,* 84. For a detailed history of minstrels, see Edward Le Roy Rice, *Monarchs of Minstrelry, from "Daddy" Rice to Date* (New York: Kenney Publishing, 1911).

20. Fletcher, *Black Soldier and Officer,* 100; *Columbus Courier,* March 8, 1917, August 30, September 27, October 4, 1918.

21. *Columbus Courier,* July 26; August 9, 23, 1918.

22. Ibid., October 10, November 7, 1919; Safe Deposit Record Cards, Columbus State Bank Records, Luna County Courthouse, Deming, New Mexico. Thaddieous was a member of the Twenty-fourth Infantry band.

23. *Columbus Courier,* April 18, May 30, June 6, 13, July 4, 18, 25, August 1, 8, 15, 22, September 5, 1919, January 23, 30, March 12, June 3, 4, 7, 20, December 3, 1920.

24. Ibid., November 14, 19, 1919, January 23, 30, March 12, June 3, 4, 7, 20, December 3, 1920.

25. Ibid., November 24, 1916, February 16, 1917, August 16, 1918, May 30, June 6, 13, September 19, 1919; *Deming Headlight,* October 28, 1921.

26. *Columbus Courier,* July 23, September 28, October 25, 1920; *Deming Graphic,* August 9, 1921; *Deming Headlight,* June 2, 10, 1921.

27. *Columbus Courier,* July 23, 30, September 24, December 5, 1920.

28. Ibid., November 5, 1920.

29. *Columbus Mirror,* June 21, July 5, 15, 22, 1921; *Deming Headlight,* July 15, 22, 1921.

30. Gerald D. Nash, *The American West in the Twentieth Century: A History of an Urban Oasis* (Albuquerque: University of New Mexico Press, 1977), 73; John Hope Franklin, *From Slavery to Freedom: A History of the Negro Americans,* 5th ed. (New York: Alfred A. Knopf, 1947, 1980), 323–60; Chaplain's Monthly Reports, Alexander W. Thomas, January 1919, Box 7, Record Group 247, Office of the Chief of Chaplains, National Archives. For more detail on race relations in Columbus, see Nash, "Blacks on the Border," and "Investigation, Twenty-fourth Infantry, Columbus 1922," file in the Governor Merritt C. Mechem Papers, New Mexico State Records Center and Archives, Santa Fe, New Mexico.

BRUCE A. GLASRUD AND
MICHAEL N. SEARLES

Buffalo Soldiers

A BIBLIOGRAPHY

Adams, Thomas Richard. "The Houston Riot of 1917." Master's thesis, Texas A&M University, 1972.

Alexander, Charles. *Battles and Victories of Allen Allensworth*. Boston: Sherman, French, 1914.

Amos, Preston E. *Above and Beyond in the West: Black Medal of Honor Winners, 1870–1890*. Washington, D.C.: Potomac Corral, The Westerners, 1974.

———. "Military Records for Nonmilitary History." *Afro-American History: Sources for Research*. Edited by Robert L. Clarke. Washington, D.C.: Howard University Press, 1981. 65–73.

Andrews, George. "The Twenty-fifth Regiment of Infantry." In *The Army of the United States: Historical Sketches of Staff and Line with Portraits of Generals-in-Chief*, edited by Theo. F. Rodenbaugh and William L. Haskin (New York: Argonaut Press, 1966): 697–99.

Andrews, George L. "West Point and the Colored Cadets." *International Review* 9 (November 1890): 477–89.

Arnold, Paul T. "Negro Soldiers in the United States Army." *Magazine of History* 10 (August 1909): 61–70; (September 1909): 123–29; (October 1909): 185–93; 11 (January 1910): 1–12; (March 1910): 119–25.

Austerman, Wayne Randolph. "Black Regulars: The 41st Infantry in Texas, 1867–1869." Master's thesis, Louisiana State University, 1971.

Bailey, Anne J. "A Texas Cavalry Raid: Reaction to Black Soldiers and Contrabands." *Civil War History* 35 (1989): 138–52.

———. "Was There a Massacre at Poison Spring?" *Military History of the Southwest* 20 (Fall 1990): 157–68.

Bailey, Linda C. *Fort Missoula's Military Cyclists: The Story of the 25th U. S. Infantry Bicycle Corps*. Missoula: Friends of the Historical Museum at Fort Missoula, 1997.

Bailey, Sedell. "Buffalo Soldiers (Black Troops of the 9th and 10th Cavalries)." *Armor* 83 (January/February 1974): 9–12.

Ball, Larry D. *The Wham Paymaster Robbery of 1889: A Story of Politics, Religion, Race, and Banditry in Arizona Territory.* Tucson: Arizona Historical Society, 2000.

Banks, Leo W. "The Buffalo Soldiers." *Arizona Highways* 71 (January 1995): 35–37.

Barbeau, Arthur E. "The Black American Soldiers in World War I." Ph.D. diss., University of Pittsburgh, 1970.

Barbeau, Arthur E., and Florette Henri. *The Unknown Soldiers: Black American Troops in World War I.* Philadelphia: Temple University Press, 1974.

Barr, Alwyn. "The Black Militia of the New South: Texas as a Case Study." *Journal of Negro History* 63 (July 1978): 209–19.

Barrow, William. "The Buffalo Soldiers: The Negro Cavalry in the West, 1866–1891." *Negro Digest* 16 (July 1967): 34–37, 89.

Baumler, Mark F., and Richard V. N. Ahlstrom. "The Garfield Monument: An 1886 Memorial of the Buffalo Soldiers in Arizona." *Cochise County Quarterly* 18 (Spring 1988): 3–34.

Bellecourt, Vernon. "The Glorification of Buffalo Soldiers Raises Racial Divisions between Blacks, Indians." *Indian Country Today* (May 4, 1994): 5 (A).

Bennett, Charles. "The Buffalo Soldiers and the Apache War Chief." *El Palacio* 101 (Summer 1996).

Berlin, Ira, ed. "The Black Military Experience, 1861–1867." In *The Black Military Experience. Series II of Freedom: A Documentary History of Emancipation, 1861–1867*, 1–34. Cambridge: Cambridge University Press, 1982.

Berthrong, Donald J. *The Cheyenne and Arapaho Ordeal.* Norman: University of Oklahoma Press, 1976.

———. *The Southern Cheyennes.* Norman: University of Oklahoma Press, 1963.

Berwanger, Eugene H. *The Frontier against Slavery: Western Anti-Negro Prejudice and the Slavery Extension Controversy.* Urbana: University of Illinois Press, 1967.

Bigelow, John Jr. *On the Bloody Trail of Geronimo.* Los Angeles: Westernlore Press, 1968.

———. "The Tenth Regiment of Cavalry." In *The Army of the United States: Historical Sketches of Staff and Line with Portraits of Generals-in-Chief*, edited by Theo. F. Rodenbaugh and William L. Haskin, 288–97 (New York: Argonaut Press, 1966).

———. "Tenth Regiment of Cavalry." *Journal of the Military Service Institution of the United States* 13 (January 1892): 215–24.

Billington, Monroe Lee. "Black Soldiers at Fort Selden, New Mexico, 1868–1891." *New Mexico Historical Review* 62 (January 1987): 65–80.

———. "Black Cavalrymen and Apache Indians in New Mexico Territory." *Fort Concho and the South Plains Journal* 22 (Summer 1990): 55–75.

———. "Buffalo Soldiers in the American West." In *African Americans on the Western Frontier.* Edited by Monroe Lee Billington and Roger Hardaway, 54–72. Niwot, Colo.: University Press of Colorado, 1998.

———. "Civilians and Black Soldiers in New Mexico Territory, 1866–1900: A

Cross-Cultural Experience." *Military History of the Southwest* 19 (Spring 1989): 71–82.

———. *New Mexico's Buffalo Soldiers, 1866–1900*. Niwot, Colo.: University Press of Colorado, 1991.

Black, Lowell D., and Sara H. Black. *An Officer and a Gentleman: The Military Career of Lieutenant Henry O. Flipper*. Dayton: Lora, 1985.

Blanton, DeAnne. "Cathay Williams: Black Woman Soldier 1866–1868." *Minerva: Quarterly Report of Women and the Military* 10 (Fall/Winter 1992): 1–12.

Blassingame, John W. "The Organization and Use of Negro Troops in the Union Army, 1863–1865." Master's thesis, Howard University, 1961.

———. "The Recruitment of Negro Troops in Missouri During the Civil War," *Missouri Historical Review* 58 (April 1964): 326–38

Bluthardt, Robert F. "The Buffalo Soldiers at Fort Concho, 1869–1885." *Texas Heritage* (Spring 2002).

Bond, Anne Wainstein. "Buffalo Soldiers at Fort Garland." *Colorado Heritage* (Spring 1996): 28–29.

Bond, Horace Mann. "The Negro in the Armed Forces of the United States Prior to World War I." *Journal of Negro Education* 12 (Summer 1943): 268–87.

Bowmaster, Patrick A. "Buffalo Soldier Emanuel Stance Received the Medal of Honor and Became a Legend." *Real West* 9 (February 1997): 32–34, 83–84.

Boyd, Thomas J. "The Use of Negro Troops by Kansas during the Civil War." Master's thesis, Kansas State University, 1950.

Branley, Bill. "Black, White, and Red: A Story of Black Cavalrymen in the West." *Soldiers* 36 (June 1981): 44–48.

Britten, Thomas A. *A Brief History of the Seminole-Negro Indian Scouts*. Lewiston, N.Y.: Edward Mellen Press, 1999.

———. "The Dismissal of the Seminole-Negro Indian Scouts, 1880–1914." *Fort Concho and the South Plains Journal* 24 (1992): 54–77.

———. "The Seminole-Negro Indian Scouts in the Big Bend." *Journal of Big Bend Studies* 5 (1993): 67–77.

Brown, Wesley A. "Eleven Men of West Point." *Negro History Bulletin* 19 (April 1956): 147–57.

Buchanan, John Stauss. "Functions of the Fort Davis Military Bands and Musical Proclivities of the Commanding Officer, Col. B. H. Grierson, Late 19th Century." Master's thesis, Sul Ross State College, 1968.

Buecker, Thomas R. "Confrontation at Sturgis: An Episode in Civil-Military Race Relations, 1885." *South Dakota History* 14 (Fall 1984): 238–61.

———. "One Soldier's Service: Caleb Benson in the Ninth and Tenth Cavalry, 1875–1908." *Nebraska History* 74 (Summer 1993): 54–62.

———. "Prelude to Brownsville: The Twenty-fifth Infantry at Fort Niobrara, Nebraska, 1902–06." *Great Plains Quarterly* 16 (Spring 1996): 95–106.

———. "The Tenth Cavalry at Fort Robinson, 1902–1907." *Military Images* 7 (May-June 1991): 6–10.

Bullard, Robert Lee. "The Negro Volunteer: Some Characteristics." *Journal of the Military Service Institution of the United States* 29 (July 1901): 27–35.

Butler, Ron. "The Buffalo Soldier." In *The Best of the Old West: An Indispensable Guide to the Vanishing Legend of the American West*, 116–20. Austin: Texas Monthly Press, 1983.

———. "The Buffalo Soldier: A Shining Light in the Military History of the American West." *Arizona Highways* 48 (March 1972): 2–10.

Cage, James C., and James M. Day. *The Court Martial of Henry Ossian Flipper: West Point's First Black Graduate*. El Paso: El Paso Corral of the Westerners, 1981.

Carlson, Paul H. *The Buffalo Soldier Tragedy of 1877*. College Station: Texas A&M University Press, 2003.

———. *"Pecos Bill": A Military Biography of William R. Shafter*. College Station: Texas A&M University Press, 1989.

———. "William R. Shafter, Black Troops, and the Finale to the Red River War." *Red River Valley Historical Review* 3 (Spring 1978): 247–58.

———. "William R. Shafter, Black Troops, and the Opening of the Llano Estacado, 1870–1875." *Panhandle-Plains Historical Review* 47 (1974): 1–18.

———. "William R. Shafter Commanding Black Troops in West Texas." *West Texas Historical Association Year Book* 50 (1974): 104–16.

Carroll, H. Bailey. "Nolan's 'Lost Nigger' Expedition of 1877." *Southwestern Historical Quarterly* 44 (July 1940).

Carroll, John M., ed. *The Black Military Experience in the American West*. New York: Liveright Publishing, 1971.

———. *Buffalo Soldiers West*. Fort Collins: Old Army Press, 1971.

———. "Lieutenant Henry Ossian Flipper." *The Black Military Experience in the American West*. Edited by John M. Carroll, 347–52. New York: Liveright Publishing, 1971.

Cashin, Herschel V. *Under Fire with the Tenth U.S. Cavalry*. New York: F. Tennyson Neely, 1899. Reprint. 1969.

Castel, Albert. "Civil War Kansas and the Negro," *Journal of Negro History* 51 (April 1966): 125–38.

———. "The Fort Pillow Massacre: A Fresh Examination of the Evidence." *Civil War History* 4 (March 1958): 37–50.

Castles, Jean I. "The West: Crucible of the Negro." *Montana, the Magazine of Western History*, 19 (November 1969): 83–85.

"Cathy Williams Story." *St. Louis Daily Times*. January 2, 1876.

Chase, Hal J. "Struggle for Equality: Fort Des Moines Training Camp for Colored Officers, 1917." *Phylon* 39 (Winter 1978): 297–310.

Chew, Abraham. *A Biography of Colonel Charles Young*. Washington: R. L. Pendleton, 1923.

Chorlian, Meg., ed. "Buffalo Soldiers." *Cobblestone* (February 1995): 1–49.

Christian, Garna L. "Adding on Fort Bliss to Black Military Historiography." *West Texas Historical Association Year Book* 54 (1978): 41–54.

———. *Black Soldiers in Jim Crow Texas, 1899–1917*. College Station: Texas A&M University Press, 1995.

———. "The Brownsville Raid's 168th Man: The Court-Martial of Corporal Knowles." *Southwestern Historical Quarterly* 93 (1989): 45–59.

———. "The El Paso Racial Crisis of 1900." *Red River Valley Historical Review* 6 (Spring 1981): 28–41.

———. "The Ordeal and the Prize: The 24th Infantry and Camp MacArthur." *Military Affairs,* 50 (April 1986): 65–70.

———. "Rio Grande City: Prelude to the Brownsville Raid." *West Texas Historical Association Yearbook* 57 (1981): 118–32.

———. "The Twenty-fifth Regiment at Fort McIntosh: Precursor to Retaliatory Racial Violence." *West Texas Historical Association Year Book* 55 (1979): 149–61.

———. "The Violent Possibility: The Tenth Cavalry at Texarkana." *East Texas Historical Journal* 23 (Spring 1985): 3–15.

Cimprich, John, and Robert C. Mainfort Jr. "The Fort Pillow Massacre: A Statistical Note." *Journal of American History* 76 (December 1989): 830–37.

———. "Fort Pillow Revisited: New Evidence about an Old Controversy." *Civil War History* 28 (December 1982): 293–306.

Clark, Michael J. "Improbable Ambassadors: Black Soldiers at Fort Douglas, 1896–1899." *Utah Historical Quarterly* 46 (1978): 282–301.

———. "U.S. Army Pioneers: Black Soldiers in Nineteenth Century Utah." Ph.D. diss., University of Utah, 1981.

Clement, Thomas J. "Athletics in the American Army." *Colored American Magazine* 8 (January 1905).

Clendenen, Clarence C. *Blood on the Border: The United States Army and the Mexican Irregulars.* New York: Macmillan, 1969.

———. "The Punitive Expedition of 1916: A Re-Evaluation." *Arizona and the West* 3 (1961): 311–20.

Coffman, Edward M. *The Old Army: A Portrait of the American Army in Peacetime, 1784–1898.* New York: Oxford University Press, 1986.

Coleman, Ronald G. "The Buffalo Soldiers: Guardians of the Utah Frontier, 1886–1901." *Utah Historical Quarterly* 47 (1979): 421–39.

Cook, Lawrence Hugh. "The Brownsville Affray of 1906." Master's thesis, University of Colorado, 1942.

Cornish, Dudley Taylor. "Kansas Negro Regiments in the Civil War." *Kansas Historical Quarterly* 20 (1953): 417–29.

———. *The Sable Arm: Negro[Black] Troops in the Union Army, 1861–1865.* 1956. Reprint, New York: W. W. Norton, 1966.

———. "To Be Recognized as Men: The Practical Utility of Military History." *Military Review* 58 (February 1978): 40–55.

———. "The Union Army as a Training School for Negroes." *Journal of Negro History* 37 (1952): 368–82.

Cox, Clinton. *The Forgotten Heroes: The Story of the Buffalo Soldiers.* New York: Scholastic, 1993.

Crimmins, Col. Martin L. "Captain Nolan's Lost Troop on the Staked Plains." *West Texas Historical Association Year Book* 10 (October 1934): 68–73.

———. "Colonel Buell's Expedition into Mexico in 1880." *New Mexico Historical Review* 10 (April 1935): 133–42.

———, ed. "Shafter's Explorations in Western Texas, 1875." *West Texas Historical Association Year Book* 9 (October 1933): 82–96.

Daniel, Wayne. "The Many Trials of Captain Armes." *Fort Concho Report* 13 (Fall 1981): 5–16.

———. "The 10th at Fort Concho, 1875–1882." *Fort Concho Report* 14 (Spring 1982): 7–14.

Daniels, Roger, and Harry H. L. Kitano. *American Racism: Exploration of the Nature of Prejudice.* Englewood Cliffs: Prentice-Hall, 1970.

Davis, Benjamin O. Jr. *Benjamin O. Davis, Jr., American: An Autobiography.* New York: Penguin Books, 1992.

Davis, John P. "The Negro in the Armed Forces of America." In *The American Negro reference Book,* 590–661. Englewood Cliffs, N.J.: Prentice-Hall, 1966.

Davis, Lenwood G., and George Hill, comps. "Blacks in the American West." In *Blacks in the American Armed Forces, 1776–1983: A Bibliography,* 34–46. Westport, Conn.: Greenwood Press, 1985.

DeGraaf, Lawrence B. "Recognition, Racism, and Reflections on the Writing of Western Black History." *Pacific Historical Review* 44 (February 1975): 22–51.

Dietrich, Barbara, comp. "The Buffalo Soldiers on the Western frontier: Bibliography." International Museum of the Horse. http://www.horseworld.com/imh/buf/buftoc.htm.

Dinges, Bruce J. "Colonel Grierson Invests on the West Texas Frontier." *Fort Concho Report* 16 (Fall 1984): 2–14.

———. "The Court-Martial of Lieutenant Henry O. Flipper: An Example of Black-White Relationships in the Army." *American West* 9 (January 1972): 12–17, 59–61.

———. "The Irrepressible Captain Armes: Politics and Justice in the Indian-Fighting Army." *Journal of the West* 32 (April 1993): 38–52.

———. "New Directions in Frontier Military History: A Review Essay." *New Mexico Historical Review* 66 (January, 1991): 103–16.

———. "Scandal in the Tenth Cavalry: A Fort Sill Case History." *Arizona and the West* 28 (Summer 1986): 125–40.

Dixon, David. *Hero of Beecher Island: The Life and Military Career of George A. Forsyth.* Lincoln: University of Nebraska Press, 1994.

Dobak, William A. "Black Regulars Speak." *Panhandle-Plains Historical Review* 47 (1974): 19–27.

———. "Civil War on the Kansas-Nebraska Border: The Narrative of Former Slave Andrew Williams." *Kansas History* 6 (1983): 237–42.

———. "Fort Riley's Black Soldiers and the Army's Changing Role in the West, 1867–1885." *Kansas History* 22 (1999): 214–27.

Dobak, William A., and Thomas D. Phillips. *The Black Regulars, 1866–1898.* Norman: University of Oklahoma Press, 2001.

Dollar, Charles M. "Putting the Army on Wheels: The Story of the Twenty-fifth Infantry Bicycle Corps." *Prologue* 17 (Spring 1985): 7–24.

Downey, Fairfax. *The Buffalo Soldiers in the Indian Wars.* New York: McGraw Hill, 1969.

Du Bois, W. E. B. "An Essay toward a History of the Black Man in the Great War." *The Crisis* 18 (June 1919): 63–87.

Dunlay, Thomas W. *Wolves for the Blue Soldiers: Indian Scouts and Auxiliaries with the United States Army, 1860–1890.* Lincoln: University of Nebraska Press, 1982.

Early, Charity Adams. *One Woman's Army: A Black Officer Remembers the WAC.* College Station: Texas A&M University Press, 1989.

East, Brebda K. "Henry Ossian Flipper: Lieutenant of the Buffalo Soldiers," *Persimmon Hill* 23 (Summer 1995): 68–69.

Eppinga, Jane. "Henry O. Flipper in the Court of Private Land Claims: The Arizona Career of West Point's First Black Graduate." *Journal of Arizona History* 36 (Spring 1995): 33–54.

———. *Henry Ossian Flipper: West Point's First Black Graduate.* Plano, Tex.: Republic of Texas Press, 1996.

Erwin, Sarah, ed. *The Buffalo Soldier on the American Frontier.* Tulsa: Thomas Gilcrease Museum Association, 1996.

Everly, Elaine C. "Red, Black, and White: The U.S. Army at Columbus, GA." In *Soldiers and Civilians: The U.S. Army and the American People.* Edited by Garry D. Ryan and Timothy K. Nenninger, 104–13. Washington, D.C.: National Archives and Records Administration, 1987.

Finley, James P. *The Buffalo Soldiers at Fort Huachuca.* 3 issues. Fort Huachuca, Ariz.: Huachuca Museum Society, 1993–96.

———. "Buffalo Soldiers at Fort Huachuca: Military Events in the American Southwest from 1910–1916," *Huachuca Illustrated* 1 (1993).

Fisher, Mike. "The First Kansas Colored: Massacre at Poison Spring." *Kansas History* 2 (Summer 1979): 121–28.

———. "Remember Poison Spring." *Missouri Historical Review* 74 (April 1980): 323–42.

Fleming, Elvis Eugene. "Captain Nicholas Nolan: Lost on the Staked Plains." *Texana* 4 (Spring 1966): 1–13.

Fletcher, Marvin E. *America's First Black General: Benjamin O. Davis, Sr., 1880–1970.* Lawrence: University Press of Kansas, 1989.

———. *The Black Soldier and Officer in the United States Army, 1891–1917.* Columbia: University of Missouri Press, 1974.

———. "Army Fire Fighters." *Idaho Yesterdays* 16 (1972): 12–15.

———. "The Black Bicycle Corps." *Arizona and the West* 16 (1974): 219–32.

———. "The Blacks in Blue: Negro Volunteers in Reconstruction." Master's thesis, University of Wisconsin, 1964.

———. *The Black Soldier and Officer in the United States Army, 1891–1917.* Columbia: University of Missouri Press, 1974.

———. "The Black Soldier Athlete in the United States Army, 1890–1916."

Canadian Journal of History of Sport and Physical Education 3 (December 1972): 16–26.

———. "The Black Volunteers in the Spanish-American War." *Military Affairs* 38.2 (April 1974).

Flipper, Henry Ossian. *The Colored Cadet at West Point.* 1878. Reprint, edited by Sara Dunlap Jackson. New York: Arno Press, 1968.

———. *Negro Frontiersman: The Western Memoirs of Henry O. Flipper, First Negro Graduate of West Point.* Edited by Theodore D. Harris. El Paso: Texas Western College Press, 1963.

Foner, Jack D. "Blacks in the Post-Civil War Army." In *Blacks and the Military in American History: A New Perspective,* 52–71, 266–267. New York: Praeger Publishers, 1974.

———. "The Negro in the Post-Civil War Army." In *The United States Soldier between Two Wars: Army Life and Reforms, 1865–1898,* 127–47, 195–201. New York: Humanities Press, 1970.

Forbes, Jack D. *Afro-Americans in the Far West: A Handbook for Educators.* Berkeley: Far West Laboratory for Research and Development, 1967.

Fowler, Arlen L. *The Black Infantry in the West, 1869–1891.* Westport, Conn.: Greenwood Publishing, 1971.

Franklin, John Hope. *From Slavery to Freedom.* New York: Alfred A. Knopf, 1964.

———. "Soldier and Student." In *George Washington Williams: A Biography,* 1–11, 285–87. Chicago: University of Chicago Press, 1985.

Frierson, Eugene P. "An Adventure in the Big Horn Mountains; or, the Trials and Tribulations of a Recruit." *Colored American Magazine* 8 (April 1905): 196–99; (May 1905): 277–79; (June 1905): 338–40.

Fuchs, Richard L. *An Unerring Fire: The Massacre at Fort Pillow.* Rutherford, N.J.: Fairleigh Dickinson University Press, 1994.

Fuller, Charles. "The Brownsville Raid." *Literary Cavalcade* 30 (January 1978): 9–23, 28–39.

Gatewood, Willard B. Jr. "Black Americans and the Quest for Empire, 1898–1903." *Journal of Southern History* 38 (1972): 545–66.

———. *Black Americans and the White Man's Burden, 1893–1903.* Urbana: University of Illinois Press, 1971.

———. "John Hanks Alexander of Arkansas: Second Black Graduate of West Point." *Arkansas Historical Quarterly* 46 (Summer 1982): 114–32.

———. "Negro Troops in Florida, 1898." *Florida Historical Quarterly* 49 (July 1970): 1–15.

———. *"Smoked Yankees" and the Struggle for Empire: Letters from Negro Soldiers, 1898–1902.* Urbana: University of Illinois Press, 1971.

Geary, James W. "Afro-American Soldiers and American Imperialism, 1898–1902: A Select Annotated Bibliography." *Bulletin of Bibliography* 48.4 (1990): 189–93.

———. "Buffalo Soldiers and American Scouts on the Western Frontier, 1866–1900: A Select Annotated Bibliography." *Ethnic Forum* 15 (1995): 153–61.

Glasrud, Bruce A. "Buffalo Soldiers in Oklahoma." In *Encyclopedia of Oklahoma History and Culture.* Oklahoma City: Oklahoma Historical Society, 2007.

———. "Enforcing White Supremacy in Texas, 1900–1910." *Red River Valley Historical Review* 4 (Fall 1979): 65–74.

———. "Josephine Leavell Allensworth." In *African American Women: A Biographical Dictionary,* edited by Dorothy C. Salem, 9–10. New York: Garland Publishing, 1993.

———. "Soldiers." In *Exploring the Afro-Texas Experience: a Bibliography of Secondary Sources about Black Texans,* 49–58. Edited by Bruce A. Glasrud and Laurie Champion. Alpine, Tex.: SRSU Center for Big Bend Studies, 2000.

———. "Western Black Soldiers since *The Buffalo Soldiers:* A Review of the Literature." *Social Science Journal* 36 (1999): 251–70.

Glasrud, Bruce A., and William H. Leckie. "Buffalo Soldiers." In *African Americans in the West: A Bibliography of Secondary Sources.* Edited by Bruce A. Glasrud, 32–53. Alpine, Tex.: SRSU Center for Big Bend Studies, 1998.

Glass, Edward L. N. *The History of the Tenth Cavalry, 1866–1921.* Tucson: Acme Printing, 1921.

Glatthar, Joseph T. *Forged in Battle: The Civil War Alliance of Black Soldiers and White Officers.* New York: Free Press, 1990.

Good, Donnie D. "The Buffalo Soldiers." *American Scene* 10 (April 1970).

Greene, Robert Ewell. "Colonel Charles Young, Soldier and Diplomat." Master's thesis, Howard University, 1972.

———. *The Early Life of Col. Charles Young, 1864–1889.* Washington, D.C.: n.p., 1973.

———. "The Indian Campaigns, 1866–1890." In *Black Defenders of America, 1775–1973,* 109–22. Chicago: Johnson Publishing, 1974.

Grinde, Donald A. Jr., and Quintard Taylor. "Red v. Black: Conflict and Accommodation in the Post Civil War Indian Territory, 1865–1907." *American Indian Quarterly* 8 (1984): 211–29.

Gruening, Martha. "Houston: An N.A.A.C.P. Investigation." *Crisis* 15 (November 1917): 19.

Gustafson, Marsha L. "The Buffalo Soldiers: Heroes That History Forgot." *Persimmon Hill* 23 (Summer 1995): 64–67.

Gwaltney, William W. "The Making of *Buffalo Soldiers West.*" *Colorado Heritage* (Spring 1996).

———. "The Story of the Seminole-Negro Indian Scouts." *Lest We Forget* 4 (October 1996): 9, 12, 14.

Hagan, William T. *United States-Comanche Relations: The Reservation Years.* New Haven: Yale University Press, 1976.

Haley, J. Evetts. *Fort Concho and the Texas Frontier.* San Angelo, Tex.: *San Angelo Standard Times,* 1952.

Hall, Linda B., and Don M. Coerver. *Revolution on the Border: The United States and Mexico, 1910–1920.* Albuquerque: University of New Mexico Press, 1988.

Hall, Martin Hardwick. "Negroes with Confederate Troops in West Texas and New Mexico." *Password* 13 (Spring 1968): 11–12.

Hardaway, Roger D. "Buffalo Soldiers." In *A Narrative Bibliography of the African-American Frontier: Blacks in the Rocky Mountain West, 1535–1912,* 107–42. Lewiston, N.Y.: Mellen Press, 1995.

Hardeman, Nicholas P. "Brick Stronghold of the Border: Fort Assinniboine, 1879–1911." *Montana: The Magazine of Western History* 29 (Spring 1979): 54–67.

Hargrove, Hondon B. *Buffalo Soldiers in Italy: Black Americans in World War II.* Jefferson, N.C.: McFarland, 1985.

Harris, Theodore D., ed. *Black Frontiersman: The Western Memoirs of Henry O. Flipper.* Fort Worth: Texas Christian University Press, 1997.

———. "Henry Flipper and Pancho Villa." *Password* 6 (Spring 1961): 39–46.

———. "Henry Ossian Flipper: The First Negro Graduate of West Point." Ph.D. diss., University of Minnesota, 1971.

———. "Henry Flipper and Pancho Villa." *Password* 6 (Spring 1961): 39–46.

———. *Negro Frontiersman: The Western Memoirs of Henry O. Flipper, First Negro Graduate of West Point.* El Paso: Texas Western College Press, 1963.

Haynes, Robert V. "The Houston Mutiny and Riot of 1917." *Southwestern Historical Quarterly* 76 (1973): 418–39.

———. *A Night of Violence: The Houston Riot of 1917.* Baton Rouge: Louisiana State University Press, 1976.

———. "Unrest at Home: Racial Conflict between White Civilians and Black Soldiers in 1917." *Journal of the American Studies Association of Texas* 6 (1975): 43–54.

Heinl, Nancy G. "Colonel Charles Young: Pointman." *Crisis* 84 (May 1977): 173–79.

Henderson, Edwin B. *The Negro in Sports.* Washington, D.C.: Associated Publishers, 1939.

Henri, Florette, and Richard Stillman. *Bitter Victory: A History of Black Soldiers in World War I.* New York: Doubleday, 1970.

Heuman, William. *Buffalo Soldier.* New York: Dodd, Mead, 1969.

Higginson, Thomas Wentworth. *Army Life in a Black Regiment.* 1870. Reprint, New York: W. W. Norton, 1984.

Hollandsworth, James G. *The Louisiana Native Guard: The Black Military Experience during the Civil War.* Baton Rouge: Louisiana State University Press, 1995.

Hovey, H. W. "The Twenty-fourth Regiment of Infantry." In *The Army of the United States: Historical Sketches of Staff and Line with Portraits of Generals-in-Chief,* edited by Theo. F. Rodenbaugh and William L. Haskin, 695–96. New York: Argonaut Press, 1966.

Hunter, John Warren. "Mutiny of Negro Soldiers at Fort Concho, 1882." *Hunter's Magazine* (December 1911): 4–5, 13.

———. "A Trooper of the Ninth Cavalry." *Frontier Times* 4 (April 1927): 9–11.

Hurtt, C. M. "The Role of Black Infantry in the Expansion of the West." *West Virginia History* 40 (1979): 123–57.

Hutchison, Grote. "The Ninth Regiment of Cavalry." *The Army of the United*

States: Historical Sketches of Staff and Line with Portraits of Generals-in-
Chief,* edited by Theo. F. Rodenbaugh and William L. Haskin, 280–87.
New York: Argonaut Press, 1966.

International Museum of the Horse. "The Buffalo Soldiers on the Western
Frontier." http://www.horseworld.com/imh/buf/buftoc.htm.

Jackson, James W. "The Black Man and Military Mobilization in the United
States, 1916–1919." Master's thesis, California State University, Hayward,
1970.

Jackson, Sara Dunlap, ed. *Henry O. Flipper, The Colored Cadet at West Point.*
Reprint, New York: Arno Press, 1968.

Jefferson, Robert Franklin. "Making the Men of the 93rd: African-American
Servicemen in the Years of the Great Depression and the Second World
War, 1935–1947." Ph.D. diss., University of Michigan, 1995.

Johnson, Barry C. *Flipper's Dismissal: The Ruin of Lt. Henry O. Flipper, U.S.A.,
First Coloured Graduate of West Point.* London: Privately printed, 1980.

Johnson, Harry. "Buffalo Soldiers: The Formation of the Ninth Cavalry Regiment, July 1866–March 1867." Master's thesis, U.S. Army Command and
General Staff College, 1991.

Johnson, John Allen. "The Medal of Honor and Sergeant John Ward and Private
Pompey Factor." *Arkansas Historical Quarterly* 29 (Winter 1970): 361–75.

Johnson, Robert B. "The Punitive Expedition: A Military, Diplomatic, and Political History of Pershing's Chase After Pancho Villa, 1916–1917." Ph.D.
diss., University of Southern California, 1964.

Jones, H. Conger. "Old Seminole Scouts Still Thrive on Border." *Frontier Times*
11 (1934): 327–32.

Joseph, Harriett Denise. *The Brownsville Raid.* Brownsville, Tex.: Texas South-
most College, 1976.

Justice, Glenn. *Revolution on the Rio Grande: Mexican Raids and Army Pursuits,
1916–1919.* El Paso: Texas Western Press, 1992.

Kachel, Douglas. "Fort Des Moines and its African-American Troops in
1903/1904." *Palimpsest* 74 (Spring 1993): 42–48.

Katz, William Loren. "The Black Infantry and Cavalry." In *The Black West: A
Documentary and Pictorial History of the African American in the Westward Expansion of the United States,* 199–244. New York: Simon and Schuster, 1996.

———. "Six New Medal of Honor Men." *Journal of Negro History* 53 (January
1968): 77–81.

Kellogg, Charles Flint. *NAACP: A History of the National Association for the Advancement of Colored People.* Vol. 1, 1909–1920. Baltimore: Johns Hopkins
University Press, 1967.

Kelton, Elmer. *The Wolf and the Buffalo.* Fort Worth: Texas Christian University Press, 1986.

Kenner, Charles L. *Buffalo Soldiers and Officers of the Ninth Cavalry, 1867–1898:
Black and White Together* (Norman: University of Oklahoma Press, 1999

———. "Guardians in Blue: The United States Cavalry and the Growth of the
Texas Cattle Industry." *Journal of the West* 34 (January 1995): 40–54.

————. *Soldiers and Officers of the Ninth Cavalry, 1867–1898: Black and White To-gether.* Norman: University of Oklahoma Press, 1999.

Kesting, Robert W. "Conspiracy to Discredit the Buffalo Soldiers: The 92nd Infantry in World War II." *Journal of Negro History* 72 (Winter 1987).

Kinevan, Marcos E. *Frontier Cavalryman: Lieutenant John Bigelow and the Buf-falo Soldiers in Texas.* El Paso: Texas Western Press, 1997.

Knapp, George E. *Buffalo Soldiers at Fort Leavenworth in the 1930s and Early 1940s.* Fort Leavenworth: Combat Studies Institute, 1991.

————. "Buffalo Soldiers, 1866 through 1890." *Military Review* 72 (July 1992): 65–71.

Krapf, Kellie A., and Floyd B. Largent Jr. "The Black Seminole Scouts: Soldiers Who Deserve High Praise." *Persimmon Hill* 24 (Winter 1996): 73–75.

Lamkin, Patricia E. "Blacks in San Angelo: Relations between Fort Concho and the City, 1875–1889." *West Texas Historical Association Year Book* 66 (1990): 26–37.

Lamm, Alan K. "Buffalo Soldiers Chaplains: A Case Study of the Five Black United States Army Chaplains, 1884–1901." Ph.D. diss., University of South Carolina, 1995.

————. "Buffalo Soldier Chaplains of the Old West." *Journal of America's Mil-itary Past* 26 no. 1 (1999): 25–40.

————. *Five Black Preachers in Army Blue, 1884–1901.* Lewiston, N.Y.: Edwin Mellen Press, 1998.

Lane, Ann J. *The Brownsville Affair: National Crisis and Black Reaction.* Port Washington, N.Y.: Kennikat Press, 1971.

Langellier, John P. *Men A-Marching: The African American Soldier in the West, 1866–1896.* Springfield, Penn.: Steven Wright Publishing, 1995.

Langellier, John P., and Alan M. Osur. "Chaplain Allen Allensworth and the 24th Infantry, 1886–1906." *Smoke Signal* no. 40 (Fall 1980): 189–208.

Laughlin, David. *Buffalo Soldiers: An Ilustrated 30 Year History of the 10th Regi-ment of the U.S. Cavalry.* Tucson: Blue Horse Productions, 1991.

Leckie, William H. "Black Regulars on the Texas Frontier, 1866–1885." *The Texas Military Experience.* Edited by Joseph G. Dawson, 86–96, 219–21. College Station: Texas A&M University Press, 1995.

————. "Buell's Campaign." *Red River Valley Historical Review* 3 (Spring 1978): 186–93.

————. *The Buffalo Soldiers: A Narrative of the Negro Cavalry in the West.* Nor-man: University of Oklahoma Press, 1967.

————. "Forward." In *The Black Infantry in the West,* rev. ed., by Arlen L. Fowler, xvi. Norman: University of Oklahoma Press, 1996.

————., ed. *Indian Wars of the Red River Valley.* Sacramento: Sierra Oaks, 1986.

————. "Ninth United States Cavalry." *Handbook of Texas Online.* http://www.tsha.utexas.edu/handbook.

————. "Tenth United States Cavalry." *Handbook of Texas Online.* http://www.tsha.utexas.edu/handbook.

Leckie, William H., and Shirley A. Leckie. *The Buffalo Soldiers: A Narrative of the Black Cavalry in the West,* Rev. ed. Norman: University of Oklahoma Press, 2003.

————. *Unlikely Warriors: General Benjamin Grierson and His Family.* Norman: University of Oklahoma Press, 1984, 1998.

Ledbetter, Barbara A. Neal. *Fort Belknap Frontier Saga: Indians, Negroes, and Anglo-Americans on the Texas Frontier.* Burnet, Tex.: Eakin, 1982.

Lee, Irvin H. *Negro Medal of Honor Men.* New York: Dodd, Mead, 1967.

Lee, Ulysses. *The Employment of Negro Troops.* Washington, D.C.: Office of the Chief of Military History, 1966.

Leiker, James N. "Black Soldiers at Fort Hays, Kansas, 1867–1869: A Study in Civilian and Military Violence." *Great Plains Quarterly* 17 (Winter 1996): 3–17.

————. *Racial Borders: Black Soldiers along the Rio Grande.* College Station: Texas A&M University Press, 2002.

Levstick, Frank R. "William H. Holland: Black Soldier, Politician, and Educator." *Negro History Bulletin* 36 (May 1973): 110–11.

Lewis, Francis E. "Negro Army Regulars in the Spanish-American War: Smoked Yankees at Santiago de Cuba." Master's thesis, U.S. Army Command and General Staff College, 1969.

Lindenmeyer, Otto. "Black and Red: The Frontier Wars, 1870–1890." In *Black and Brave: The Black Soldier in America,* 59–65. New York: McGraw-Hill, 1970.

Logan, Rayford W. *The Betrayal of the Negro from Rutherford B. Hayes to Woodrow Wilson.* New York: Collier Books, 1965.

Longacre, E. G. "Philadelphia Aristocrat with the Buffalo Soldiers." *Journal of the West* 18 (April 1979): 79–84.

Lowe, Albert S. "Camp Life of the Tenth U.S. Cavalry." *Colored American Magazine* 7 (1904): 203–208.

Lowry, Jack. "Buffalo Soldiers." *Texas Highways* 36 (February 1989): 40–47.

Lynk, Miles. *The Black Troopers, or the Daring Heroism of the Negro Soldiers in the Spanish-American War.* New York: AMS Press, 1971.

Mangum, Charles S. Jr. *The Legal Status of the Negro.* Chapel Hill: University of North Carolina Press, 1940.

Maraniss, David. "Buffalo Soldiers: Forgotten Black Heroes of the Old West." *Washington Post Magazine* (January 20, 1991): 15–21, 30–36.

Marszalek, John F. Jr. *Assault at West Point: The Court-Martial of Johnson Whittaker.* New York: Macmillan, 1972; reprint, New York: Collier Books, 1994.

————. "A Black Cadet at West Point." *American Heritage* 12 (August 1971): 30–37, 104–6.

————. "The Black Man in Military History." *Negro History Bulletin* 36 (October 1973): 122–25.

Marszalek, John F. Jr., and Horace D. Nash. "African Americans in the Military of the United States." In *The African American Experience: An Historiographical and Bibliographical Guide,* edited by Arvarh E. Strickland and Robert E. Weems Jr., 231–54. Westport, Conn.: Greenwood Press, 2001.

Martinal, Doris. "The Negro Raid." *Texas History Teachers Bulletin* 14 (December 1927): 129–33.

Matthews, James T. "Always in the Vanguard: Patrolling the Texas Frontier with Captain Louis Carpenter and Company H of the Tenth Cavalry." *West Texas Historical Association Year Book* 75 (1999): 110–19.

———. "Traveling Over an Unknown Trail: Company H of the Tenth Cavalry at Fort Davis, 1875–1885." *Journal of Big Bend Studies* 12 (2000): 93–104.

McChristian, Douglas C. "'Dress on the Colors, Boys!': Black Noncommissioned Officers in the Regular Army, 1866–1898." *Colorado Heritage* (Spring 1996): 38–44.

———., ed. *Garrison Tangles in the Friendless Tenth: The Journal of First Lieutenant John Bigelow, Jr., Fort Davis, Texas.* Bryan, Tex.: J. M. Carroll, 1985.

———. "Grierson's Fight at Tinajade las Palmas: An Episode in the Victorio Campaign." *Red River Valley Historical Review* 71 (Winter 1982): 45–63.

———., ed. *Roster of Non-Commissioned Officers of the Tenth Cavalry.* Reprint, Bryan, Tex.: J. M. Carroll, 1983.

McClung, Donald R. "Henry O. Flipper: The First Negro Officer in the United States Army, 1878–1882." Master's thesis, East Texas State University, 1970.

———. "Second Lieutenant Henry O. Flipper: A Negro Officer on the West Texas Frontier." *West Texas History Association Year Book* 47 (1971): 20–31.

McMiller, Anita Williams. "Buffalo Soldiers: The Formation of the Tenth Cavalry Regiment from September 1866 to August 1867." Master's thesis, U.S. Army Command and General Staff College, 1990.

Meltzer, Richard. "On Villa's Trail in Mexico: The Experience of a Black Cavalryman and a White Infantry Officer, 1916–1917." *Military History of the Southwest* 20 (Spring 1990): 23–42; 21 (Fall 1991): 173–90.

Miles, Donna. "They Ranged the Old West as Buffalo Soldiers." *Soldiers* 45 (July 1990): 42–44.

Miles, Susan. "Fort Concho in 1877." *West Texas Historical Association Year Book* 35 (1959): 29–49.

———. "The Soldiers' Riot." *Fort Concho Report* 13 (Spring 1981): 1–20.

Miller, Robert H. *The Buffalo Soldiers.* Vol. 2, *Reflections of a Black Cowboy.* Englewood Cliffs: Silver Burdett, 1991.

———. *Buffalo Soldiers: The Story of Emanuel Stance.* Morristown, N.J.: Silver Burdett, 1995.

Moebs, Thomas T. *Black Soldiers—Black Sailors: Research Guide on African-Americans in U.S. Military History, 1526–1900.* 4 vols. Chesapeake Bay: Moebs, 1994.

Monnett, John H. *The Battle of Beecher Island and the Indian War of 1867–1869.* Niwot: University Press of Colorado, 1992.

Moore, John H. *The Cheyenne Nation: A Social and Demographic History.* Lincoln: University of Nebraska II: Press, 1987.

Moore, Kenneth Bancroft. "Fort Pillow, Forrest, and the United States Colored Troops in 1864." *Tennessee Historical Quarterly* 54 (Summer 1995): 112–23.

Moskos, Charles C. "Success Story: Blacks in the Military." *Atlantic Monthly* 257 (May 1986): 64–72.

Muller, William G. *The Twenty-fourth Infantry: Past and Present.* Ft. Collins, Colo.: Old Army Press, 1972.

Mulroy, Kevin. "The Seminole Negro Indian Scouts." In *Freedom on the Border: The Seminole Maroons in Florida, the Indian Territory, Coahuila, and Texas,* 107–32. Lubbock: Texas Tech University Press, 1993.

Murray, Robert A. "The United States Army in the Aftermath of the Johnson County Invasion: April through November 1892." *Annals of Wyoming* 38 (April 1966): 59–75.

Myers, Lee. "Mutiny at Fort Cummings." *New Mexico Historical Review,* 46 (1971): 337–50.

Nalty, Bernard C. "Reaction in the South, Action in the West." In *Strength for the Fight: A History of Black Americans in the Military,* 47–62, 364–66. New York: Free Press, 1986.

Nalty, Bernard C., and Morris J. MacGregor, eds. "Freedom and Jim Crow, 1865–1917." In *Blacks in the Military: Essential Documents,* 43–71. Wilmington, Del.: Scholarly Resources, 1981.

Nance, Carol Conley. "United States Army Scouts: The Southwestern Experience, 1866–1890." Master's thesis, North Texas State University, 1975.

Nankivell, John Henry. *History of the Twenty-fifth Regiment, United States Infantry, 1869–1926.* Denver: Smith-Brooks Printing, 1926. Reprint, Fort Collins, Colo.: Old Army Press, 1972.

Nash, Gerald D. *The American West in the Twentieth Century: A History of an Urban Oasis.* Albuquerque: University of New Mexico Press, 1977.

Nash, Horace Daniel. "Blacks on the Border: Columbus, New Mexico, 1916–1922." Master's thesis, New Mexico State University, 1988.

———. "Community Building on the Border: The Role of the 24th Infantry Band at Columbus, New Mexico, 1916–1922." *Fort Concho and the South Plains Journal* 22 (Summer 1990): 77–89.

———. "Town and Sword: Black Soldiers in Columbus, New Mexico in the Early Twentieth Century." Ph.D. diss., Mississippi State University, 1996.

Nichols, Roger, ed., *American Frontier and Western Issues: A Historiographical Review.* Westport, Conn.: Greenwood Press, 1986.

Nunn, W. Curtis. "Eighty-six Hours without Water on the Texas Plains." *Southwestern Historical Quarterly* 43 (January 1940): 356–64.

O'Connor, Richard. "Black Jack of the 10th." *American Heritage* 18 (February 1967): 14–17, 102–107.

Odintz, Mark. "Buffalo Soldiers." *Handbook of Texas Online.* http://www.tsha.utexas.edu/handbook.

Park, Phocion Samuel Jr. "The Twenty-fourth Infantry Regiment and the Houston Riot of 1917." Master's thesis, University of Houston, 1971.

Parker, James. *The Old Army: Memories.* Philadelphia: Dorrance, 1929.

Parkhill, Forbes. *Mister Barney Ford: A Portrait in Bistre.* Denver: Sage Books, 1963.

Perkins, Francis Beecher. "Two Years with a Colored Regiment: A Woman's Experience." *New England Magazine* (January 1898).

Perry, Alexander. "The Ninth United States Cavalry in the Sioux Campaign of 1890." *Journal of the United States Cavalry Association* 4 (March 1891): 36–40.

Peterson, Robert. *Only the Ball Was White.* New Jersey: Englewood Cliffs, 1970.

Pewewardy, Cornel. "Buffalo Soldiers Were Federal Hired Guns." *Indian Country Today* (June 30, 1997).

Phillips, Thomas D. "The Black Regulars." In *The West of the American People.* Edited by Allan G. Bogue, Thomas D. Phillips, and James E. Wright, 138–43. Itasca, Ill.: F. E. Peacock Publishers, 1970.

———. "The Black Regulars: Negro Soldiers in the United States Army, 1866–1891." Ph.D. diss., University of Wisconsin, 1970.

Pickens, William. "Death Detail: Trial and Execution of Thirteen Negro Soldiers at Fort Sam Houston, Texas, December, 1917." *World Tomorrow* 13 (April 1930): 162–65.

Pierce, Walter. "The Brownsville Raid: A Historiographical Assessment." In *Studies in Brownsville History.* Edited by Milo Kearney. Brownsville, Tex.: Pan American University, 1986.

Pitman, Ruth. "Allen Allensworth: Man of Ambition." *Crisis* 98 (February 1990).

Place, Marian T. *Rifles and War Bonnets: Negro Cavalry in the West.* New York: Ives Washburn, 1968.

Plante, Trevor K. "Researching African Americans in the U.S. Army, 1866–1890: Buffalo Soldiers and Black Infantrymen." *Prologue* 33.1 (2001): 56–61.

Porter, Kenneth W. "Negroes and Indians on the Texas Frontier, 1831–1876." *Journal of Negro History* 41 (July, 1956): 185–214; 41 (October 1956): 285–310.

———. "Negroes and Indians on the Texas Frontier, 1834–1874." *Southwestern Historical Quarterly* 53 (October 1949): 151–63.

———. "The Seminole [and Seminole-Negroes] in Mexico, 1850–1861." *Hispanic American Historical Review* 31 (1951): 1–36.

———. "The Seminole-Negro Indian Scouts, 1870–1881." *Southwestern Historical Quarterly* 55 (1952): 358–77.

———. "The Seminole Negro Indian Scouts, Texas, 1870–1914." In *The Black Seminoles: History of a Freedom-Seeking People.* Edited by Alcione M. Amos and Thomas P. Senter, 173–214. Gainesville, Fla.: University Press of Florida, 1996.

Porter, Kenneth W., and Edward S. Wallace. "Thunderbolt of the Frontier." *Westerners New York Posse Brand Book* 8 (1961): 73–75, 82–86.

Pospisil, Jo Ann. "Black Defenders in the American West, 1865–1890." *West Texas Historical Association Year Book* 76 (2000): 106–25.

Powell, Anthony L. *The Post Civil War Army and the Black Soldier, 1866–1898.* n.p.: privately printed, 1985.

Powell, Colin, and Joseph E. Persico. *My American Journey.* New York: Random House, 1995.

Prebble, John. *The Buffalo Soldiers.* New York: Harcourt, Brace, 1959.

Prentiss, A., ed., *The History of the Utah Volunteers in the Spanish-American War and in the Philippine Islands.* Salt Lake City: Tribune Job Printing, 1900.

Price, Byron. "Mutiny at San Pedro Springs." *By Valor and Arms* 1 (Spring 1975): 31–34.

Prucha, Francis P. *The Great Father: The United States Government and the American Indians.* Lincoln: University of Nebraska Press, 1984.

Quarles, Benjamin. *The Negro in the Civil War.* Boston: Little Brown, 1953.

Railsback, Thomas, and John P. Langellier. *The Drums Would Roll: A Pictorial History of U.S. Army Bands on the American Frontier, 1866–1900.* London: Arms and Armour Press, 1987.

Rampp, Lary C. "Negro Troop Activity in Indian Territory, 1863–1865." *Chronicles of Oklahoma* 47 (Spring 1969): 531–59.

Reddick, L. D. "The Negro Policy of the United States Army, 1775–1945." *Journal of Negro History* 34 (1949): 9–29.

Redkey, Edwin S. "Black Chaplains in the Union Army." *Civil War History* 33 (December 1987): 331–50.

———., ed. *A Grand Army of Black Men: Letters from African-American Soldiers in the Union Army, 1861–1865.* Cambridge: Cambridge University Press, 1992.

Reef, Catherine. *Buffalo Soldiers.* New York: Twenty-first Century Books, 1993.

Reeve, Frank D., ed., "Frederick E. Phelps: A Soldier's Memoirs." *New Mexico Historical Review* 25 (1950): 217.

Remington, Frederic. "A Scout with the Buffalo Soldiers." *Century Magazine* 37 (April 1889): 899–912.

———. "A Scout with the Buffalo Soldiers." *Pacific Historian* 12 (Spring 1968): 25–39.

———. "Vagabonding with the Tenth Horse." *Cosmopolitan* 22 (February 1897): 347–54.

Richter, William L. *The Army in Texas during Reconstruction, 1865–1870.* College Station: Texas A&M University Press, 1987.

Rickey, Don Jr. "An Indian Wars Combat Record." *By Valor and Arms* 2 (Fall 1975): 4–11.

Robinson, Charles M. III. *The Court-Martial of Lieutenant Henry Flipper.* El Paso: Texas Western Press, 1994.

Robinson, Michael C., and Frank N. Schubert. "David Fagen: An Afro-American Rebel in the Philippines, 1899–1901." *Pacific Historical Review* 44 (February 1975): 69–83.

Rodenbaugh, Theodore F. *The Tenth Regiment of Cavalry.* New York: Maynard, Merill, 1896.

Rowe, Mary Ellen. "The Early History of Fort George Wright: Black Infantrymen and Theodore Roosevelt in Spokane." *Pacific Northwest Quarterly* 80 (July 1989): 91–100.

Salter, Krewasky. "Sable Officers: African-American Military Officers, 1861–1918." Master's thesis, Florida State University, 1993.

Savage, W. Sherman. "Blacks in the Military." In *Blacks in the West*, 48–64. Westport: Greenwood Press, 1976.

———. "The Role of Negro Soldiers in Protecting the Indian Territory from Intruders." *Journal of Negro History* 36 (1951): 25–34.

Sayre, Harold Ray. *Warriors of Color*. Fort Davis, Tex.: privately printed, 1995.

Schoenberger, Dale T. "The Black Man in the American West." *Negro History Bulletin*, 32 (March 1969):7–11.

Schubert, Frank N. "Allen Allensworth." *Dictionary of American Negro Biography*, edited by Rayford W. Logan and Michael R. Winston, 13–14. New York: W. W. Norton, 1982.

———. "The Black Regular Army Regiments in Wyoming, 1885–1912." Master's thesis, University of Wyoming, 1970.

———. "Black Soldiers on the White Frontier: Some Factors Influencing Race Relations." *Phylon* 32 no. 4 (Winter 1971): 410–15.

———. *Black Valor: Buffalo Soldiers and the Medal of Honor, 1870–1898*. Wilmington, Del.: Scholarly Resources, 1997.

———. "Buffalo Soldiers." In *The Oxford Companion to American Military History*. New York: Oxford University Press, 2000.

———. "The Buffalo Soldiers: A Little History and a Little Mythology." http://www.captainbuffalo.com.

———. "Buffalo Soldiers at San Juan Hill." *Army History* (Summer 1998).

———. *Buffalo Soldiers, Braves, and the Brass: The Story of Fort Robinson, Nebraska*. Shippensburg: White Mane Publishing, 1993. Also published as *Outpost of the Sioux Wars*. Lincoln: University of Nebraska Press, 1995.

———. "Buffalo Soldiers: Myths and Realities." *Army History* (Spring 2001): 13–18.

———. "Buffalo Soldiers: The Stamp, the History, the Myth, and the Controversy." *American Philatelist* (June 2006): 544–49.

———. (eight black soldiers). "Edward L. Baker," "Horace W. Bivins," "Thomas C. Butler," "David Fagan," "George W. Ford," "George Jordan," "Rienzi B. Lemus," "Emanuel Stance." In *Dictionary of American Negro Biography*, edited by Rayford W. Logan and Michael R. Winston. New York: W. W. Norton, 1982.

———. "The Fort Robinson Y.M.C.A., 1902–1907: A Social Organization in a Black Regiment." *Nebraska History* 55 (Summer 1974): 165–79.

———. "George W. Prioleau." In *DANB*, edited by Rayford W. Logan and Michael R. Winston. New York: W. W. Norton, 1982.

———. "Gunfire at San Angela." *Wild West* (February 2004).

———. "Henry Vinton Plummer." In *DANB*, edited by Rayford W. Logan and Michael R. Winston, 498–99. New York: W. W. Norton, 1982.

———. *On the Trail of the Buffalo Soldier: Biographies of African-Americans in the U.S. Army, 1866–1917*. Wilmington, Del.: Scholarly Resources, 1994.

———. "The Seminole Negro Scouts." In *Black Valor: Buffalo Soldiers and the Medal of Honor, 1870–1898*, 27–40. Wilmington, Del.: Scholarly Resources, 1997.

———. "The Suggs Affray: The Black Cavalry in the Johnson County War." *Western Historical Quarterly* 4 (1973): 57–68.

———. "Ten Troopers: Buffalo Soldier Medal of Honor Men Who Served at Fort Robinson." *Nebraska History* 78.4 (1997): 151–57.

———. "Theophilus Gould Steward." In *DANB*, edited by Rayford W. Logan and Michael R. Winston, 570–71. New York: W. W. Norton, 1982.

———. "Troopers, Taverns, and Taxes: Fort Robinson, NE, and Its Municipal Parasite, 1886–1911." In *Soldiers and Civilians: The U.S. Army and the American People.* Edited by Garry D. Ryan and Timothy K. Nenninger, 91–103. Washington, D.C.: National Archives and Records Administration, 1987.

———. "The Violent World of Emanuel Stance, Fort Robinson, 1887." *Nebraska History* 55 (Summer 1974): 203–19.

———. *Voices of the Buffalo Soldier: Records, Reports, and Recollections of Military Life and Service in the West.* Albuquerque: University of New Mexico Press, 2003.

———. "The Wham Escort." *Arizona Territorial Justice Forum, April 4, 2003.* Tucson: Arizona Humanities Council, 2006.

———. "William Cathay/Cathay Williams." *Voices of the Buffalo Soldier,* 33–35. Albuquerque: University of New Mexico Press, 2003.

———. "William T. Anderson." In *Dictionary of American Negro Biography,* edited by Rayford W. Logan and Michael R. Winston, 15–16. New York: W. W. Norton, 1982.

Schubert, Frank N., and Irene Schubert. *On the Trail of the Buffalo Soldier: Biographies of African-Americans in the U. S. Army, 1866–1917, vol. II.* Wilmington, Delaware: Scholarly Resources, 2004.

Schubert, Frank N., and Michael C. Robinson. "David Fagen: An Afro-American Rebel in the Philippines, 1899–1901." *Pacific Historical Review* 44 (February 1975): 69–83.

Schuler, Edgar A. "The Houston Race Riot, 1917." *Journal of Negro History* 29 (July 1944): 300–338.

Scipio, L. Albert II. *Last of the Black Regulars: A History of the 24th Infantry Regiment (1869–1951).* Silver Spring, Md.: Roman Publications, 1983.

Scott, Edward Van Zile. *The Unwept: Black American Soldiers and the Spanish-American War.* Montgomery, Ala.: Black Belt, 1996.

Scott, Emmett J. *Scott's Official History of the American Negro in the World War.* 1919. Reprint, New York: Arno Press, 1969.

Seraile, William. "Fort Missoula, 1891–1898." *Voice of Dissent: Theophilus Gould Steward (1843–1924) and Black America.* Brooklyn: Carlson Publishing, 1991.

———. "Saving Souls on the Frontier: A Chaplain's Labor." *Montana, the Magazine of Western History* 42 (Winter 1992): 28–41.

———. "Theophilus G. Steward, Intellectual Chaplain, 25th U.S. Colored Infantry." *Nebraska History* 66 (Fall 1985): 272–93.

Shaffer, Donald. "'I do not suppose that Uncle Sam looks at the skin': African

Americans and the Civil War Pension System, 1865–1934." *Civil War History* 46 (June 2000): 132–47.

Sheffy, L. F., ed. "Letters and Reminiscences of Gen. Theodore A. Baldwin: Scouting after Indians on the Plains of Texas." *Panhandle Plains Historical Review* 11 (1938): 7–30.

Siler, Benjamin T. "The Brownsville, Texas Affray of August 13–14, 1906 and Subsequent Proceedings (A Historical Interpretation)." Master's thesis, North Carolina College of Durham, 1963.

Singletary, Otis A. *Negro Militia and Reconstruction.* Austin: University of Texas Press, 1957.

———. "The Texas Militia during Reconstruction." *Southwestern Historical Quarterly* 60 (1956): 23–35.

Sivad, Doug. *The Black Seminole Indians of Texas.* Boston: American Press, 1984.

Smith, C. Calvin. "The Houston Riot of 1917, Revisited." *Houston Review* 13 (1991): 84–102.

———. "On the Edge: The Houston Riot of 1917 Revisited." *Griot* 10 (Spring 1991): 3–12.

Smyth, Donald. "John J. Pershing at Fort Assiniboine." *Montana* 18 (January 1968): 19–23.

Solomon, Irvin D. "Blacks in the Military." *The Crisis* 94 (February 1987): 15–18, 20–24, 26.

Sommers, Richard J. "The Dutch Gap Affair: Military Atrocities and Rights of Negro Soldiers." *Civil War History* 21 (1975): 51–64.

Spicer, Edward H. *Cycles of Conquest: The Impact of Spain, Mexico, and the United States on the Indians of the Southwest, 1533–1960.* Tucson University of Arizona Press, 1961.

Spiller, Roger J. "Honoring the Buffalo Soldiers." *American Heritage* 43 (February–March 1992): 84–86.

Stallard, Patricia. *Glittering Misery: Dependents of the Indian Fighting Army.* Fort Collins, Col.: Old Army Press, 1978.

Steele, Matthew F. "The 'Color Line' in the Army." *North American Review* 183 (December 21, 1906): 1288.

Steward, Theophilus G. *The Colored Regulars in the United States Army.* New York: Arno Press, 1964.

———. "Two Years in Luzon." *Colored American Magazine* 4 (November 1901): 4–10.

Stiles, T. J., and Arthur Shilstone. "Buffalo Soldiers." *Smithsonian* 29.9 (1998): 82–86, 88, 90, 92, 94–95.

Stover, Earl F. "Black Chaplains." In *Up from Handymen: The United States Army Chaplaincy, 1865–1920,* 88–92, 98–99. Washington, D.C.: Department of the Army, 1977.

———. "Chaplain Henry V. Plummer: His Ministry and His Court Martial." *Nebraska History* 56 (Spring 1971): 20–50.

Strong, Eric Emmerson. "The Lost Treaty of the Black Seminoles." *West Texas Historical Association Year Book* 75 (1999): 120–30.

Sullivan, Jerry, ed. "Lieutenant Colonel W. R. Shafter's Pecos River Expedition of 1870." *West Texas Historical Association Year Book* 47 (1971): 146–52.

Swisher, C. Kevin. "Frontier Heroes [Seminole-Negro-Indian Scouts]." *Texas Highways* 39 (July 1992): 48–51.

Taylor, Quintard. "Blacks in the American West: An Overview." *Western Journal of Black Studies* 1 (March 1977): 7.

———. "Buffalo Soldiers in the West, 1866–1917." In *In Search of the Racial Frontier: African Americans in the American West, 1528–1990*, 164–91. New York: W. W. Norton, 1998.

———., ed. *The Colored Cadet at West Point: Autobiography of Lieutenant Henry Ossian Flipper, U.S.A.* Lincoln: University of Nebraska Press, 1998.

———. "Comrades of Color: Buffalo Soldiers in the West, 1866–1917." *Colorado Heritage* (Spring 1996): 3–27.

———. "From Esteban to Rodney King: Five Centuries of African American History in the West." *Montana: The Journal of Western History* 46 (Winter 1996): 9.

Temple, Frank M. "Colonel B. H. Grierson's Texas Commands." Master's thesis, Texas Tech University, 1956.

———. "Colonel B. H. Grierson's Victorio Campaign." *West Texas Historical Association Year Book* 35 (October 1959): 99–111.

———. "Discipline and Turmoil in the Tenth U.S. Cavalry. *West Texas Historical Association Year Book* 58 (1982): 103–18.

———. "The Tenth United States Cavalry in Texas." *Fort Concho Report* 17 (Winter 1985): 11–17.

Terrell, Mary Church. "A Sketch of Mingo Saunders." *Voice of the Negro* 4 (March 1907): 128–31.

Thiesen, Lee Scott, ed. "The Fight in Lincoln, N.M., 1878: The Testimony of Two Negro Participants." *Arizona and the West* 12 (Summer 1970): 173–98.

Thompson, Erwin N. "The Negro Regiments of the U.S. Army, 1866–1900." Master's thesis, University of California at Davis, 1966.

———. "The Negro Soldier and His Officers." In *The Black Military Experience in the American West.* Edited by John M. Carroll, 258–80. New York: Liveright, 1971.

———. "The Negro Soldiers on the Frontier: A Fort Davis Case Study." *Journal of the West* 7 (1968): 217–35.

———. "Private Bentley's Buzzard." In *The Black Military Experience in the American West.* Edited by John M. Carroll, 437–40. New York: Liveright, 1971.

Thornbrough, Emma Lou. "The Brownsville Episode and the Negro Vote." *Mississippi Valley Historical Review* 44 (December 1957): 469–93.

Thrapp, Dan L. *Victorio and the Mimbres Apaches.* Norman: University of Oklahoma Press, 1974.

Thybony, Scott. "Against All Odds, Black Seminoles Won Their Freedom." *Smithsonian* 22 (1991): 90–101.

Tiller, Veronica E. Velarde. *The Jicarilla Apache Tribe: A History.* Rev. ed. Lincoln: University of Nebraska Press, 1992.

Tinsley, James A. "The Brownsville Affray." Master's thesis, University of North Carolina, 1948.

———. "Roosevelt, Foraker, and the Brownsville Affray." *Journal of Negro History* 41 (January 1956): 43–65.

Troxel, Orlando C. "The Tenth Cavalry in Mexico." *Journal of the United States Cavalry Association* 18 (October 1917): 197–205.

Trudeau, Noah Andre. *Like Men of War: Black Troops in the Civil War, 1862–1865.* Boston: Little, Brown, 1998.

Tucker, Phillip Thomas. *Cathy Williams: From Slave to Buffalo Soldier.* Mechanicsburg, Penn.: Stackpole Books, 2002.

Turner, Charles. "Military Cycling." *The Outing Magazine* 17 (1891): 194.

Urwin, Gregory J. "'We Cannot Treat Negroes . . . as Prisoners of War': Racial Atrocities and Reprisals in Civil War Arkansas." *Civil War History* 42 (September 1996): 193–210.

Utley, Robert M. "The Buffalo Soldiers and Victorio." *New Mexico Magazine* 62 (March 1984): 47–50, 53–54.

———. *Frontier Regulars: The United States Army and the Indian, 1866–1891.* Lincoln: University of Nebraska Press, 1984.

———. "'Pecos Bill' on the Texas Frontier." *American West* 6 (January 1969): 4–13, 61–62.

Vandiver, Frank E. *Black Jack: The Life and Times of John J. Pershing.* 2 vols. College Station: Texas A&M University Press, 1977.

Vaughn, William P. "West Point and the First Negro Cadet." *Military Affairs* 35 (October 1971): 100–102.

Villard, Oscar G. "The Negro in the Regular Army." *Atlantic Monthly* 91 (June 1903): 721–30.

Waide, C. D. "When Psychology Failed: An Unbiased Fact—Story of the Houston Race Riot of 1917." *Houston Gargoyle* (May 15, 22, 29; June 5, 12, 1928).

Wallace, Andrew. "The Sabre Retires: Pershing's Cavalry Campaign in Mexico, 1916." *Smoke Signal* No. 9 (Spring 1964): 1–24.

Wallace, Edward S. "General John Lapham Bullis: The Thunderbolt of the Texas Frontier, I." *Southwestern Historical Quarterly* 54 (April 1951): 452–61; 55 (July 1951): 77–85.

———. "General John Lapham Bullis: Thunderbolt of the Texas Frontier, II." *Southwestern Historical Quarterly* 55 (1951): 77–85.

Warner, Ezra J. "A Black Man in the Long Gray Line." *American History Illustrated* 4 (January 1970): 30–38.

Weaver, John D. *The Brownsville Raid.* New York: W. W. Norton, 1970.

———. *The Senator and the Sharecropper's Son: Exoneration of the Brownsville Soldiers.* College Station: Texas A&M University Press, 1997.

Wesley, Charles H., and Patricia W. Romero. *Negro Americans in the Civil War: From Slavery to Citizenship.* New York: Publishers, 1968.

West, Jeffrey D. "Camp William Penn and the Black Soldier." *Pennsylvania History* 46.4 (1979): 335–46.

Wharfield, Col. H. B. "The Affair at Carrizal: Pershing's Punitive Expedition," *Montana* 18 (October 1968): 24–39.

———. *Tenth Cavalry and Border Fights.* El Cajon, Calif.: Privately printed, 1964.

———. *With Scouts and Cavalry at Fort Apache.* Edited by John Alexander Carroll. Tucson: Arizona Pioneers' Historical Society, 1965.

White, Richard. "Race Relations in the American West." *American Quarterly* 38 (1986): 394–416.

———. *The Roots of Dependency: Subsistence, Environment, and Social Change among the Choctaws, Pawnees, and Navajos.* Lincoln: University of Nebraska Press, 1983.

Whitney, Henry H. "The Adaption of the Bicycle to Military Uses." *Journal of the Military Service Institution* 17 (1895): 543–51.

Wickett, Murray R. *Contested Territory: Whites, Native Americans and African Americans in Oklahoma, 1865–1907.* Baton Rouge: Louisiana State University Press, 2000.

Willard, Tom. *Buffalo Soldiers.* New York: Tom Doherty Associates, 1996.

Williams, Charles H. *Negro Soldiers in World War I: The Human Side.* 1923, Reprint, New York: AMS Press, 1970.

Williams, Clayton W. "A Threatened Mutiny of Soldiers at Fort Stockton in 1873 Resulted in Penitentiary Sentences of Five to Fifteen Years." *West Texas Historical Association Year Book* 52 (1976): 78–83.

Williams, George Washington. *A History of Negro Troops in the War of the Rebellion, 1861–1865.* New York: Harper and Brothers, 1888.

Williams, Mary L. "Empire Building: Colonel Benjamin H. Grierson at Fort Davis, 1882–1885." *West Texas Historical Association Year Book* 61 (1985): 58–73.

———. "Fort Davis, Texas: Key Defense Post on the San Antonio–El Paso Road." *Password* 31 (Winter 1986): 205–10.

Wilson, Keith Philip. "White Officers in Black Units in the Civil War" Ph.D. diss., La Trobe University, 1985.

Wilson, Steve. "A Black Lieutenant in the Ranks." *American History Illustrated* 18 (December 1983): 31–39.

Woodhull, Frost. "The Seminole Indian Scouts on the Border." *Frontier Times* 15 (1937): 118–27.

Woolley, Bryan. "Freedom Fighters." *Dallas Life Magazine* (February 2, 1992): 8, 10–12, 15.

Wooster, Robert. *Fort Davis: Outpost on the Texas Frontier.* Austin: Texas State Historical Association, 1994.

———. *History of Fort Davis, Texas.* Santa Fe: National Park Service, 1990.

———. *The Military and United States Indian Policy, 1865–1903.* New Haven: Yale University Press, 1988.

———. *Soldiers, Sutlers, and Settlers: Garrison Life on the Texas Frontier.* College Station: Texas A&M University Press, 1987.

Wynne, Lewis N. "Brownsville: The Reaction of the Negro Press." *Phylon* 33 (Summer 1972): 153–60.

Young, Richard. "The Brownsville Affray." *American History Illustrated* 21 (October 1986): 10–17.

Zollo, Richard P. "General Francis P. Dodge and His Brave Black Soldiers [1879, Wyoming]." *Essex Institute Historical Collection* 122 (July 1986): 181–206.

Contributors

De Anne Blanton is a senior military archivist at the National Archives, specializing in nineteenth century army records. She is coauthor of *They Fought Like Demons: Women Soldiers in the Civil War.*

Thomas A. Britten is an assistant professor of history at the University of Texas at Brownsville; he is author of *A Brief History of the Seminole-Negro Indian Scouts.*

Thomas R. Buecker is curator at Fort Robinson Museum, Nebraska State Historical Society, Crawford, Nebraska. He is author of *Fort Robinson and the American Century, 1900–1948.*

Paul H. Carlson is a professor of history at Texas Tech University in Lubbock, Texas, and fellow of the Texas State Historical Association. He has written many articles and several books including *"Pecos Bill": A Military Biography of William R. Shafter* and *The Buffalo Soldier Tragedy of 1877.*

Garna L. Christian is a professor of history at the University of Houston–Downtown. He has written extensively on black military units in Texas and is author of *Black Soldiers in Jim Crow Texas, 1899–1917.*

Michael J. Clark is professor emeritus of ethnic studies at the University of Utah. Clark also taught at California State University, Hayward (for a time a colleague of Glasrud), and was the director of the Institute for the Study of Black Life and Culture at the University of Utah.

Bruce J. Dinges is director of the publication division of the Arizona Historical Society and editor of *The Journal of Arizona History.* He has written a number of articles on the buffalo soldiers and their officers.

William A. Dobak is on the staff at the National Archives; he is the author of *Fort Riley and Its Neighbors: Military Money and Economic Growth, 1853–1895* and coauthored *The Black Regulars, 1866–1898.*

Charles M. Dollar is on the staff of the National Archives and Records Administration. He authored *America, Changing Times.*

Marvin E. Fletcher is professor of history at Ohio University, Athens, Ohio. He is author of *The Black Soldier and Officer in the United States Army, 1891–1917* and *America's First Black General: Benjamin O. Davis, Sr.*

Bruce A. Glasrud is professor emeritus of history at California State University, East Bay, and retired dean, School of Arts and Sciences at Sul Ross State University. Among his publications are *African Americans in the West: A Bibliography* and *The African American West: A Century of Short Stories*. Glasrud currently resides in Seguin, Texas.

Alan K. Lamm is professor of history at Mount Olive College, Mount Olive, North Carolina. He published *Five Black Preachers in Army Blue, 1884–1901: The Buffalo Soldier Chaplains*.

James N. Leiker is an associate professor of history at Johnson County Community College, Overland Park, Kansas. He is author of *Racial Borders: Black Soldiers Along the Rio Grande*.

Douglas C. McChristian is retired from the National Park Service in 1996. The author of *The U.S. Army in the West: Uniforms, Weapons, and Equipment 1870–1880*, he continues writing. McChristian currently resides in Tucson.

Horace Daniel Nash earned his Ph.D. in history at Mississippi State University; his dissertation is entitled "Town and Sword: Black Soldiers in Columbus, New Mexico, in the Early Twentieth Century." He is a history professor at San Antonio College.

Frank N. Schubert retired as historian in the Joint History Office, Office of the Chairman, Joint Chiefs of Staff, Washington, D.C. He is the author of numerous articles and several books on the buffalo soldier including: *On the Trail of the Buffalo Soldier: Biographies of African Americans in the U.S. Army, 1866–1917* and *Black Valor: Buffalo Soldiers and Medal of Honor, 1870–1891*.

Michael N. Searles is an assistant professor of history at Augusta State University, Augusta, Georgia. He consults and presents nationally on the black West as "Cowboy Mike," and is a contributor to *Black Cowboys of Texas*.

C. Calvin Smith is Presidential Distinguished Professor of Heritage Studies at Arkansas State University. He has especially been interested in the Houston Riot of 1917.

Permissions

Glasrud, Bruce A. "Western Black Soldiers Since *The Buffalo Soldiers:* A Review of the Literature." *The Social Science Journal* 36 (1999): 251–70. Reprinted by permission of the author and courtesy Western Social Science Association. Revised and updated.

Dobak, William A. "Fort Riley's Black Soldiers and the Army's Changing Role in the West, 1867–1885." *Kansas History* 22 (1999): 214–27. Reprinted by permission of the author and courtesy Kansas State Historical Society.

Carlson, Paul H. "William R. Shafter, Black Troops, and the Opening of the Llano Estacado, 1870–1875." *Panhandle-Plains Historical Review* 47 (1974): 1–18. Reprinted by permission of the author and of the *Panhandle-Plains Historical Review.* Includes minimal word changes.

Lamm, Alan K. "Buffalo Soldier Chaplains of the Old West." *Journal of America's Military Past* 26.1 (1999): 25–40. Reprinted by permission of the author and courtesy Council of America's Military Past.

McChristian, Douglas C. "'Dress on the Colors, Boys!': Black Noncommissioned Officers in the Regular Army, 1866–1898." *Colorado Heritage* (Spring 1996): 38–44. Reprinted by permission of the author and courtesy Colorado State Historical Society.

Blanton, DeAnne. "Cathay Williams: Black Woman Soldier, 1866–1868." *Minerva: Quarterly Report of Women and the Military* 10 (1992): 1–12. Reprinted by permission of the author.

Buecker, Thomas R. "One Soldier's Service: Caleb Benson in the Ninth and Tenth Cavalry, 1875–1908." *Nebraska History* 74 (Summer 1993): 54–62. Reprinted by permission of the author and courtesy Nebraska State Historical Society.

Dinges, Bruce J. "The Court-Martial of Lieutenant Henry O. Flipper: An Example of Black-White Relationships in the Army." *American West* 9 (January 1972): 12–17, 59–61. Reprinted by permission of the author. Includes minimal word changes.

Britten, Thomas A. "The Seminole-Negro Indian Scouts in the Big Bend." *Journal of Big Bend Studies* 5 (1993): 67–77. Reprinted by permission of the author and courtesy SRSU Center for Big Bend Studies. Includes minimal word changes.

Leiker, James N. "Black Soldiers at Fort Hays, Kansas, 1867–1869: A Study in Civilian and Military Violence." *Great Plains Quarterly* 17 (Winter 1997): 3–17. Reprinted by permission of the author and the *Great Plains Quarterly*.

Schubert, Frank N. "Black Soldiers On the White Frontier: Some Factors Influencing Race Relations." *Phylon* 32 (1971): 410–15. Reprinted by permission of the author. Includes minimal word changes.

Christian, Garna L. "Rio Grande City: Prelude to the Brownsville Raid." *West Texas Historical Association Yearbook* 57 (1981): 118–32. Reprinted by permission of the West Texas Historical Association and the author. Includes minimal word changes.

Smith, C. Calvin. "The Houston Riot Revisited." *The Houston Review* 13 (1991): 84–102. Reprinted by permission of the author and *The Houston Review*.

Clark, Michael J. "Improbable Ambassadors: Black Soldiers at Fort Douglas, 1896–1899." *Utah Historical Quarterly* 46 (1978): 282–301. Reprinted by permission of the author and courtesy Utah State Historical Society.

Dollar, Charles M. "Putting the Army On Wheels: The Story of the Twenty-fifth Infantry Bicycle Corps." *Prologue* 17 (Spring 1985): 7–24. Reprinted by permission of the author.

Fletcher, Marvin E. "The Black Soldier-Athlete in the United State Army, 1890–1916." *Canadian Journal of History of Sport and Physical Education* 3 (December 1972): 16–26. Reprinted by permission of the author. Includes minimal word changes.

Nash, Horace Daniel. "Community Building on the Border: The Role of the 24th Infantry Band at Columbus, New Mexico, 1916–1922." *Fort Concho and the South Plains Journal* 22 (Summer 1990): 77–89. Reprinted by permission of the author and *Fort Concho and the South Plains Journal*.